Declare War!

Wayne Green

Printed in the United States of America.

1 2 3 4 5 6 7 8 9 10
First printing, August 1992

Published by
WGI
70 Route 202 North
Peterborough, NH 03458.

Disclaimer

While a few of the concepts I'm proposing are original, most aren't. I've done a lot of homework, looking for new approaches to our problems which have been tested and proven successful. Educators and bureaucrats may have trouble reading me because I'm used to writing for the general public and, while I can translate their writings into plain English, I'm unable to reverse the process.

I hope you'll stick with me as I try to explain my vision for our country — for the world. I'm convinced that it's possible for us to change our educational system and make it far more productive — allowing kids to learn much more in less time and have it cost far less than we're spending today — even including computers and other modern technological tools. I believe it's possible for us to cut the costs of government in half (or more) and end up with an infinitely more responsive system. I believe it's possible for us to enormously reduce crime and to almost completely eliminate poverty.

I hope you'll buy into my utopian vision and help make it happen. I don't underestimate the problems ahead. It means fighting organized crime, the government, the political parties, our educational establishment, and probably most of our liberal, scum-sucking media. Hey, this oughta be fun!

We Need To Declare War . . .
. . . And The Enemy Is Us!

It all started with a phone call from Governor Gregg's office. Would I be interested in being a member of an Economic Development Commission, which was being formed to help guide New Hampshire out of the recession? You bet!

After a couple of short leisurely Commission meetings, a month apart, meetings at which, with 32 members present, there was almost no opportunity to ask questions or offer ideas — meetings at which the political appointees to the Commission and who made up most of the Executive Committee, controlled the agenda, my frustration limits were exceeded and I resorted to writing.

As you read you'll see that I was not particularly successful in hiding my frustration. And as I wrote, I found myself saying the heck with the agenda and the politicians, here are our problems, here's why we have them, and here are some ideas on how to solve them. Once I got going on this track, there was no stopping.

To get New Hampshire going again I've proposed a number of initiatives. Many of these are quite applicable to any state. Beyond that I've looked for solutions to our long range problems, such as the mess our educational system is in. And since a good deal of the miseries we're suffering in New Hampshire originate in Washington, it was natural for me to tackle the federal government too.

The result is a report to the New Hampshire Economic Development Commission which proposes ideas for solving many national problems such as the deficit, the imbalance of payments, poverty, welfare, drugs, crime, crowded courts, overloaded prisons, the federal bureaucracy, government waste, the mess Congress is in, health care, state government costs, inner city riots, college tuitions, teacher pay, school dropouts, family values, and so on. My proposals, a few of which are original, but most discovered while researching for my report, will enable us to put America back into the number one spot in the world in education, technology, manufacturing, wealth, and even in honesty and efficiency in government — two characteristics which do not currently describe it.

Yes, the deficit can be wiped out in a few years! Yes, we can educate our children infinitely better and at lower cost. Yes, college educations can be made available tuition free, yet without any taxpayer support. Yes, we can virtually eliminate poverty in America — but not through any program we've seen proposed in the past. Yes, we can have far better health care at a fraction of the cost. Yes, we can eliminate most of our drug and crime problems, and in short order — but not the way we've been trying to do it. We have some new ideas — new tools to use — and we should use them.

The one basic problem we have in America — perhaps our worst problem — I don't have any instant fix for — and that's the sheep like willingness of almost everyone to ignore what's happening and refuse to personally do anything about it. The "I'm mad as hell and I'm not going to take it anymore" attitude was just a figment of fiction. Oh, we have a few people who get upset over some particular issue and demonstrate for or against it. But these are more often in support of religious beliefs — and I don't see any way to turn making our country strong and healthy for our children into a religion.

Our political parties, our unions and other organized groups are dedicated to fighting change. Yet, as our problems mount, we know we must change. And that all comes right down to you. You are the problem. You are our teachers who are not teaching — and who will fight to continue not teaching. You are the civil servants watching billions being wasted and fighting to keep it happening. You keep re-electing Congress, no matter how bad it gets. You are the only ones who can change the road our country is on. Only you can get your state legislatures and administrations to change your educational system — and without that fundamental change, the future of America is bleak.

You have to decide whether watching soaps, sitcoms and ball games is more important to you than upsetting your state government. Will you be happier with yourself if you close your eyes and ears to the mess and hypnotize yourself with home entertainment or if you start forming local groups to bring about change? To force change!

I hope, as you follow the evolution of my thinking, that you'll be excited enough to get others to read what I'm proposing — that you'll help start a second American revolution. The 21st Century is almost here, so let's break away from the 20th and get a fresh start. Let's put an end to government corruption, to the homeless, to drug rings, ghettos, and kids that can't read or write. Let's end our fear of crime.

There's a lot of media griping because so few people bother to vote. Vote for what? It's no wonder Perot built so much excitement. It suddenly looked as if we might have a real choice for a President for a change. It's been a long time since I was offered anything but the decision as to which candidate was the lesser of the evils. Well, I'm fed up, and this book is my answer. I'm not trying to con you that my solutions are the only solutions. If you've got some better ideas, I challenge you to put them forth. But please be able to back them up with facts and reason, not just convictions that you are right. Let's leave convictions to the convicts.

As I point out later, I'm not a politician. I'm not even remotely interested in running for anything. I'm an entrepreneur. I make my living by coming up with new ideas and solving problems. I enjoy that, I'm good at it, and reasonably successful. I didn't write my report to the Commission to make money — the proceeds, if any, will be used to help New Hampshire grow.

I'm sending a copy of this report to the entire Commission, but I haven't even the slightest hope that anything whatever will come of it. The Commission has been cleverly guided by the politician members. This has gradually weeded out many of the businessmen who were originally involved. The end result will, I'm convinced, be a bland mish-mash which will be an embarrassment to everyone involved.

Politicians do not think in capitalistic terms. They think in non-profit, bureaucratic terms. They think in terms of spending re-election, and not making changes. As you read you'll see my occasional exasperation with this mind-set.

The appearance, early on, was that the Commission was largely the doing of Senate President Dupont — who was also its chairman. His primary goal appeared to be a run for Governor. So, as I surmised after the first two meetings, a hidden agenda was driving us, not our stated purpose. We were being used and controlled.

I do not believe that the Commission's report will propose any changes in education which will be meaningful. I don't believe the whole tax situation will be tackled. I sure would love to be surprised.

The world was going down the tubes. They needed a scapegoat. They found Wayne.

000 Introduction

Chicken Little was right! The sky really is falling! I suppose we should've paid more attention when the 1986 Tax Reform Act torpedoed our largest industry: vacationing. It also put a stop to those nasty IRAs, which had been encouraging Americans to save money.

But perhaps I'm taking this Commission thing too seriously. Perhaps I'm supposed to be part of a window-dressing scheme aimed at helping some politicians, who are under pressure to *do* something, to just mark time until the recession cures itself enough to lower the heat.

I'd say the chances are about 80:20 that Washington will panic and do something that will cause even more trouble for us in the long run . . . which is what I expect most of the proposed federal fixes I've read about so far would do.

While many of the problems that have helped sink New Hampshire undoubtedly can be traced to Washington, there are some critical factors peculiar to our area that some of us saw coming and warned against several years ago. By the time you add our own special miseries to those affecting the rest of the country, it's understandable why New Hampshire has been the hardest hit of all states.

So, are we going to fritter around, hoping that time will solve our problems? Or are we going to actively fight back? As you can see from the lengthy document I've generated, I'm in favor of fighting.

My hope is that our New Hampshire recession looks so much like a depression that even the most timorous politicians will sense the urgency of our need and be open to not just accepting change, but champing at the bit to implement it.

We know we're in a serious fix. We also know that Washington is dithering about it, totally wrapped up in politics, fighting each other and posturing . . . as the country sinks.

We know many of the basic problems that have brought the recession about. We know that we've lost one industry after another to Japan. We know we've been borrowing money from other countries in order to overpay ourselves to do uncreative, poor quality work. The deficit is at $3.6 trillion, which means that just the interest payments are running $210 billion . . . never mind the principal.

We didn't even use the money to invest in better plants or worker skills. We borrowed it, as Senator Moynihan puts it, to throw a party. Now the party's over and it's time to clean up the mess.

Since New Hampshire is the hardest hit state, we have the most to gain from making changes . . . so let's start planning our revolution. Walt Kelly had it right when Pogo said, "We've found the enemy, and the enemy is us." Are you game to fight?

Like most big messes, there aren't any simple fixes. We're familiar with the enemy (us), so we already know where our campaigns will have to be aimed. We know our state and federal governments are a mess. We know our educational system is a mess. We know about our problems with welfare, the homeless, drugs, crime, the environment, nukes and so on.

I've got some suggestions for ways to fix many of our problems . . . and that's what this "report" is about. I'm not comfortable reading or writing in governmental or educational gobbledegook, so if one of those is your language, I hope you'll still be able to follow my thoughts.

Now let's start planning our war on New Hampshire poverty.

My recommendations for changes are many. I've resorted to putting them in writing, along with brief explanations of my reasoning, as a way of helping to solve the otherwise impossible task the Commission has undertaken. If I were to present all this material during the Commission meetings, I'd tie them up for days . . . providing there was no discussion or questions.

I presume that my interest is the same as many other Commission members. Thus, the prospect of 32 Commissioners all talking for hours about their recommendations is clearly impossible. I agree that it's far more difficult to put these ideas and their explanations into writing, but I see no other practical solution to the problem. I'm sure most of the other Commission members are limited in the time they have available for meetings. A trade show in Las Vegas made me miss the first January meeting. I was able to rearrange my flights from France (another trade show) to get back for the second January meeting.

Breaking the Commission into committees will force many of us to make choices we won't like . . . and which would, because of time constraints, tend to chill participation, keeping us from benefitting from some Commission member's expertise.

May I suggest that as much of the work of the Commission as possible be done in writing, with meetings reserved for brainstorming sessions and the resolution of conflicts. In this way it will be possible to break the Commission into any number of special interest committees, yet the committee members won't have to drive the length of the state to meet in person.

Communications can be facilitated by either Senator Dupont's office or the Intern group at UNH. The communications could be sped via fax, for those interested in fast turnaround.

There's another benefit to putting things into writing. I'm sure we're all familiar with the low level of retention of orally received data vs. reading retention. We remember much more of what we read . . . and we have the benefit of reading it at our own comfortable speed.

The matter of special interest committees was brought up by the Executive Committee and not resolved. This is understandable, there not being any practical way for the Commission to do this with face-to-face committee meetings.

This report has taken me several weeks to research and write. I've been happy to spend this time, since it seems like the only practical approach to our communicating. Parts of the report were written in New York City, Denver, Houston, Fresno, and San Francisco. Parts were written while in flight or in my van while being driven to business meetings. This is the legacy of the portable office and the laptop computer. This flexibility has allowed me to maintain my travel schedule, run my businesses, and communicate with the Commission members.

I've numbered the major divisions of my report to make it easier for you to respond. I'm also including an outline index to the report.

Warning: my report is not nearly done. Once I've received information from the interns or Senator Dupont on the work being done by our state agencies, reports from other economic development groups, etc., I'll be responding to these. Also, should any Commission members decide to respond to my report with arguments . . . reasonable or unreasonable . . . I'll try to address them. I'm also pursuing several other research leads which I think will interest you.

Apropos of my educational recommendations, I hope you taped "The Wrong Stuff," a program on WBZ-TV about education (Dec. 27th). I was greatly pleased that it supported so many of the recommendations I've made in this report.

Chapter I

001 Fellow Commissioners:

New Hampshire's financials are grim, indicating a need for immediate action if we're going to start turning things around. Considering the problem's urgency, I was a bit disappointed that nothing seemed to be planned as far as generating ideas in this area.

Of course we need, as a group, to creatively tackle both the immediate and the longer-range problems. But I suggest the immediate ones might warrant more urgent consideration.

002 The Mission Statement

Perhaps I suffer from a need to make things as simple and direct as possible. I realize this probably puts me completely out of step with many people in the public sector who are more comfortable with redundant statements.

I suggested we adopt "improving the quality of life in New Hampshire" as our mission statement (eight words). This goal implicitly includes a satisfaction with work, pay, education, health care, freedom from crime and drugs, entertainment, arts, infrastructure, etc.

If anyone can come up with an area which our Commission might improve, but which would not, as a result, improve the quality of life, I'm quite agreeable to tacking that onto the mission statement. Good luck. Lacking that, let's keep our statement simple and under the recommended 20-word limit.

003 The Commission

It was encouraging to see so many successful entrepreneurial businessmen appointed to the Commission. Entrepreneurs tend to be able to tackle problems creatively, often resorting to paradigm shifting when simple changes are obviously insufficient.

Entrepreneurs, in order to solve the wide variety of problems they face, tend to do their homework on a continuing basis. The average person listed in *Who's Who* reads 20 books a year . . . plus an enormous number of magazines.

Surveys show that most entrepreneurs find it necessary to read news and business publications such as *Newsweek, Time, U.S. News* and *Insight*, and business magazines such as *Business Week, Forbes, Fortune, Success,* and *Inc.* Then there are publications which go beyond immediate events and provide the background we need to understand how things are changing, such as *The New Yorker, The Public Interest, Foreign Affairs,* and *Reader's Digest.*

There are several science magazines which are minimal required reading for anyone concerned with our American technology industry problems, such as *Discover, Omni, Scientific American,* and *Popular Science.*

There are many specialized publications which are cogent in education, health care, communications, computers, and information technology.

Presuming that you've all done your homework and thus understand what's basically gone wrong with our educational, health care, and other systems, we hopefully can devote our time to working on proposed solutions instead of wasting time trying to educate members who haven't done their homework.

004 What's Gone Wrong

There are many factors which have impacted the American economy, resulting in the current recession. Much of our problems are due to the domino effect of a loss of manufacturing to foreign companies.

For instance, the less New Hampshire firms are able to sell outside of the state, the less money there will be in New Hampshire with which to build new homes, to spend on entertainment and travel, and even to buy food and clothing.

New Hampshire firms are in competition with those in other states and other countries. In general, higher technology products tend to have higher prices and thus result in higher profits. Thus, in the long run, the more technically educated our New Hampshire work force, the higher likelihood that we'll attract high-tech businesses to the state.

Changing our educational system, so we will be able to provide the work force we need to attract high-tech businesses, is obviously a solution to our long-term problems and is not something which will bring about an immediate increase in revenues from out of state. It's something we have to consider, but it shouldn't have first priority.

005 Big Vs. Small Business

Our job loss has primarily been from cutbacks by large corporations owned outside of New Hampshire. Indeed, entrepreneurs have been the main source for new jobs. Thus, in the long run, it may be worthwhile for the Commission to pay particular attention to ways for New Hampshire to provide the best business climate possible for small, entrepreneurial companies.

006 Technological Blindness

Much of New Hampshire's economic woes stem from the blindness of computer giants such as Wang, Digital Equipment, and Data General. These Massachusetts-based companies edged into New Hampshire when they found the Route 128 area running out of space and workers.

Students of computer technology have realized for almost ten years that mainframe computer firms (such as IBM) and minicomputer firms will inevitably be replaced by microcomputer-oriented firms. And since large minicomputer and defense electronics firms are our major employers, the recent downturn can be seen as a harbinger of even worse job losses to come.

Just as Digital Equipment bet their farm on a dying technology, New Hampshire has bet its "farm" on DEC and the other minicomputer firms. There were voices such as Will Zachman, who was the V.P. of the International Data Corporation and is now a columnist for *P.C. Week*, warning those who would listen about this paradigm shift and the disastrous business results likely to follow.

For those unfamiliar with the paradigm shift concept, it means viewing a system from a completely new frame of reference.

Thus it would seem that one responsibility for the Commission will be to draw upon our technical expertise and decide which technologies will be best for New Hampshire to bet on for the future. Then we'll have to plan to provide the educated work force these future technologies are likely to require.

And since small business is both a major source of new jobs and highly resistant to technological obsolescense, we should endeavor to build the friendliest climate possible for the incubation of new entrepreneurial businesses.

We can get into the details of this later on, once we've tackled our need for a fast turnaround to the present recession. I have in mind our encouraging things such as continuing education for entrepreneurs in marketing, advertising, promotion, importing, exporting, financing, public relations, communications, data processing, desktop publishing, personnel handling and development, etc.

We might discuss encouraging the development of a private data base to bring together workers and jobs . . . another to bring together venture capital sources and entrepreneurs . . . and perhaps another to help new firms with site selection.

007 What About Now!

I don't believe for a minute that I'm the only one on the Commission who has for some time been thinking creatively about our problems, so I'd like to see what ideas you've come up with.

Things are in such a serious mess right now that we don't have the luxury of starting with a ten-year development plan. We need to come up with some plans which can kick in immediately and start turning things around.

Yes, of course I have some ideas which I believe would be able to generate another billion in revenues within 18 months. But, having served on many committees and boards, I know how they work. While there are a few creative, positive people, most groups tend to concentrate on negatives. When ideas are suggested there is generally far more effort spent on shooting them down than on developing them. And this holds in spades for paradigm shifting concepts, where people have to make a major change in their entire frame of reference. It's natural and normal for most people to resist change. Indeed, many will fight it to the death of their business.

A billion dollars in added revenues would result in about 25,000 more jobs, which would ease the current recession. This would reduce the unemployment to less than half the current 44,000 level. It should also, if the growth is in the right industries, substantially increase state tax revenues. One plan I have in mind should increase state tax revenues by about $25 million. Being practical, how much would be reasonable for the state to invest to initiate a self-financing project which would generate at least 25,000 jobs and $25 million in additional tax revenues? Yes, I already know the answer . . . sorry, we don't have it in the budget. We won't spend $1 to earn $25 million.

Now where did I get those two numbers? Are they the usual grossly exaggerated figures which people bring in from left field to try and convince others of something?

First I checked the latest "Economic Conditions in New Hampshire" report (September 1991) and found that we have about 650,000 people employed in the state. Next I found the gross state product listed on page 19 of the "1990 State Development Plan." Dividing one into the other showed that we have been generating about $40,000 or so in revenues per worker . . . thus an additional billion in revenues should put about 25,000 more people to work . . . particularly if we add the revenues in people-intensive businesses rather than automated manufacturing.

008 Thinking Long Term

Our best bet for achieving short-term revenue gains will be to look creatively at some of our larger industries and generate ideas for quickly expanding them.

This brings up the question of what resources our Commission has available. How likely is it that our recommendations will be implemented? If some plans require financing, what are the probabilities that the state may invest in them? If some require changes in the laws, what then? How much weight do we have? Or will we find ourselves in the middle of political turf battles between the legislature, the governor, the state bureaucracy, plus, with any luck, the Republicans vs. the Democrats? Are we a task force or are we just another facade spinning our wheels? The first meeting of the Commission was not comforting in this respect.

No, I'm not referring to my defeat for the vice-chairmanship. I was quite relieved by that outcome. I accepted the Commission appointment because I thought I'd be able to help improve New Hampshire, not for the enormous prestige involved. I tend to avoid wallowing in my prestige.

Now, while we desperately need some short-term revenue enhancement, we should also start considering medium and long-range projects. For instance, the amazing changes going on in Europe, both East and West, present some exciting business opportunities which will have to be acted upon quickly or will be lost. Such extraordinary windows of opportunity are rare, so it would be a shame for New Hampshire to miss them.

In the long run, a technologically educated work force will help attract high-tech businesses. But how can we hope to buck not just the New Hampshire educational establishment, but that of the whole country? You do know one thing, if you've read any of the many reports on the subject, and that's that our educational system is the pits. We don't need to waste time arguing about ways to improve it. We need a complete paradigm shift.

When we get around to discussing ways to help our New Hampshire educational system produce a qualified, technically literate work force, I have some ideas. This is a field in which I've done a great deal of homework.

I believe it's possible for New Hampshire to prove to the country (and to the world, for that matter) that it's possible to produce a high-tech work force without having to spend any additional funds. Indeed, it may well be possible to substantially cut the state educational budget and still produce a better educated work force.

009 More Quality

At our initial meeting, concerns over health care were brought up as the first matter of importance. This is an area of great emotion and offers endless opportunities for demagoguery . . . possibly even more than education.

Our deteriorating infrastructure will be good for more lengthy discussions. We'll undoubtedly agree that "something must be done" about our roads, bridges, crime rate, drugs, water, waste disposal, etc. These are all legitimate subjects for us to tackle, but I suggest they're of less immediate importance in countering our current recession. Our goal of improving the quality of life in New Hampshire will certainly call for us to address infrastructure concerns.

We'll also want to understand other infrastructure concerns such as communication systems, power costs, and building codes. We'll want to know what the state might be able to do to encourage entrepreneurs to establish research and development companies working on new technologies in New Hampshire.

010 Communism and Socialism

With the worldwide failure of these two systems, it may be getting close to a time when it will at least be possible to consider reversing some American socialistic experiments . . . particularly those which have been the most spectacular failures. On the other hand, perhaps we've been so thoroughly inculcated with the socialist concept that it's too soon to even consider thinking about changes.

For instance, I've grown suspicious of government-run businesses. How many can you point to which are run efficiently? Every study of the post office shows that we'd get far better service at a fraction of the cost if we'd allow private industry to compete with it.

As an entrepreneur I tend to think in terms of making projects pay for themselves. If you read *Inc.* magazine you know that studies of successful entrepreneurs show that (a) none of 'em are driven by a need to make money and (b) few bothered to complete their college educations.

Entrepreneurs don't become successful unless they recognize that their businesses must make money, but they aren't money-driven. So I tend to think in entrepreneurial terms when it comes to providing government, educational, health care, and other services. Let's set them up as for-profit enterprises.

But what about people who are too poor to afford medical services or an education? I've got some good practical answers to just about every one of the almost endless arguments against capitalism. We don't have much of a homeless problem in New Hampshire, so we're probably not the best state to set up a beta site to show how this can be resolved on a for-profit basis. We don't even have a serious welfare problem . . . for which I have some ideas that, if we ever get around to tackling the problem, I think you'll like. Again, welfare can be solved, I'm convinced, by using a well-known successful model from another country, on a for-profit basis.

But what about the dramatically increasing costs of health care? What can we do to solve that seemingly intractable problem? Having served on the Monadnock Health Services board of directors, I'm intimately acquainted with all sides of this situation. I believe it will be possible to provide far better services at a much lower cost if we recommend some basic changes in the whole system. I'm talking about another paradigm shift.

011 Information Management

One short and several longer-range problems can be solved by encouraging some computer networks to be set up. For instance, we need a system to help our unemployed match their skills and goals to the available positions in their area . . . and to help our businesses find the workers they need at all levels quickly and inexpensively.

Between computers and recent telecommunications technology developments, the Information Age is coming to New Hampshire. A fast access to information will help our businesses build revenue sources both out of state and in foreign countries.

For instance, New Hampshire is in a good position to act as a distribution center for imports from Europe. We'll need to provide the best business climate possible to encourage this. If you watched the recent PBS series on Columbus you understand how Venice prospered by providing a liaison for goods going between Europe and Asia.

I mentioned the potential for a communications service to bring venture capitalists and entrepreneurs together, possibly with some guarantees by the state where New Hampshire would stand to benefit from the new businesses.

012 Modus Operandi

How can a commission made up of individuals from all over the state hope to tackle all of these problems in a timely manner? New Hampshire is in need of an immediate fix to stem the current recession. This will help restore housing values, encourage building, and benefit the entire revenue chain.

The urgency of our problems suggests to me that we don't really have the luxury of monthly meetings, which could easily drag on for years. Yet I don't see any practical way to fragment the Commission into committees either. There are only a couple members within easy driving distance of Hancock, so dividing the Commission into regional groups wouldn't be very helpful.

Splitting the Commission into committees sounds at first like a way to simplify our work. But since it seems our #1 priority should be to come up with creative plans for quickly improving our economy, along what lines could committees be formed?

013 Committees - Committees

Will we set up wetlands, roads and bridges, banking, tourism, waste disposal, and umpteen other committees and wait a year or two to see which bear fruit? What's our alternative?

Most of us can't spare much time from our businesses, particularly if we start feeling that it is being largely wasted. As it says on my Scrooge McDuck watch, "Time Is Money." This means that Commission meetings should be run efficiently . . . like an entrepreneurial business would, not on a non-profit government timetable.

Having served on the FCC's Long Range Planning Committee from its inception, I know that it's actually possible to make committees work efficiently.

014 Helping Entrepreneurs

Since in the last few years 82% of all jobs created in New Hampshire were in the small business sector, it would seem a worthwhile investment for the state to concentrate on encouraging entrepreneurs to start new businesses.

Let's be specific about this by considering some areas where the state might be able to support small business startups or growth. For instance, entrepreneurs need to be able to find venture capital to get started. I'd like to see the state encourage the starting of an entrepreneurial brokering service. By charging both the venture capitalists and entrepreneurs a fee for the service, it could be a for-profit venture. I worked up plans for this several years ago as a publishing project, but I've been too involved with revamping the music industry to pursue them.

Entrepreneurs, particularly those involved with high-tech startups, need a wide variety of supporting services such as accounting, legal, publishing, purchasing, advertising, photography, art, promotion, public relations, waste removal, financial, warehousing, etc. A supporting, incubating environment should be able to provide these needed services.

Is it better to leave the development of these services to luck or to plan ahead and encourage other entrepreneurs to start them in or near the business incubator areas?

Incubator areas? These, too, can be planned. Site surveys would show the areas which have economically available space and the supporting infrastructure entrepreneurs need. For instance, there's an 80,000-foot vacant manufacturing building in Antrim . . . plus a nearby available work force. There's even Marusen Hawthorne College just getting started in Antrim, with students who could be a resource for part-time workers. The college might be encouraged to offer supportive evening business courses.

New high-tech businesses result in a need for housing, restaurants, entertainment, motels, markets, and other such people-oriented businesses.

015 Business Education

Local schools and colleges can be encouraged to provide business-oriented evening courses. Employees will be wanting to learn about business, creative writing, speed reading, selling, telemarketing, accounting, marketing systems, desktop publishing, computers and data processing, communications, photography, public speaking, commercial art, advertising, public relations, business law, personnel management, graphic arts, psychology, purchasing, mail handling, heating/cooling, building maintenance, etc.

016 Consultants

Another valuable data base for entrepreneurs would be a listing of available consultants, both paid and free. For instance, I'd like to find someone to help me get financing for several proposed new publications. Should I turn to venture capitalists? To a bank (ha-ha)? To the SBA? Where can I find suitable consultants and how much will they cost?

017 Business Councils

Entrepreneurs need to be encouraged to share their problems/solutions with each other. The state could easily establish industry councils which would attract high-tech entrepreneurs. I'd be interested in meeting with compatriots in the publishing, computer, music, communications, and audio industries. Who, other than the state, could organize such councils? A small membership charge would more than cover the cost of organizing the councils and providing newsletters. Once this venture is profit-making it might be turned over to an entrepreneur, with the state getting a percentage of the revenues.

With this kind of thinking we might be able to turn New Hampshire into a for-profit state and start reducing property taxes.

The state might begin considering which services are wanted by the public and how to equitably charge for them. How much does it cost to provide our roads and highways? Can this cost be covered by the users via license fees and gas taxes?

Do we need to collect fines for traffic infractions? Instead of a $50 fine for speeding, could we levy a 10-day license suspension? This would cause far more aggravation than levying a fine for most people. For drunk drivers perhaps we could emasculate them instead of a fine. That should quickly end the problem. Litterers might have to put in a week at no pay in a New

Hampshire waste disposal facility. I sure get tired of picking up a seemingly endless supply of empty beer cans on my road.

We might encourage more schools to adopt local roads and keep them clean. How much would it cost to take fingerprints from empty beer cans and match them with the drinkers? Figure out the cost, then arrest them and charge them triple that. Make it another profit center. Three arrests and they get thrown out of the state. Well, it's not as severe as the drunk driving fine, but it would certainly improve the quality of life for all but the perps.

Please do not pass this to any newspapers, for sure as hell there'll be some humorless reporter stupid enough to take the above seriously.

018 Exporting

With the opening of the Eastern European countries to capitalism, there are going to be many opportunities to build new trading partners. We need to creatively explore which industries will best be able to take advantage of this window of opportunity and open this window toward New Hampshire.

We know that countries such as Czechoslovakia, Hungary, and Poland will be in serious need of high-tech products such as computers, software, and communications equipment. They will be needing to leap over a lost 50 years in technology, management, and marketing.

Having visited Poland and Czechoslovakia recently, I have established good contacts in communications and computers and may be able to help in developing bridges to most Eastern European countries.

019 Attracting Big Business

The potential Airbus Industries plant for Pease looks attractive, but it's more of a gamble than betting on small businesses. Big business has turned into international megacorporations, making it difficult to depend on. These corporations have been cutting their work forces, particularly the higher-paid blue collar workers and middle management, the two kinds of jobs we're most interested in preserving in New Hampshire.

Small businesses tend to be much more resistant to international pressures. They don't generally build new plants in India, The Philippines and Mexico to take advantage of lower wage labor.

New Hampshire does have to recognize that it is part of a world market and that its businesses must compete with lower wage foreign manufacturing. We can do this by stressing quality and customer service. Customers these days want new products, new services and variety. Small firms are better at meeting rapidly changing customer demands.

There are dangers in foreign ownership of New Hampshire businesses. It's nice to bring in outside investment capital, but with that comes risks. For instance, a compact disc manufacturing plant was built in Kennebunk, Maine, by local entrepreneurs a few years ago. Unfortunately, it was miserably managed and went broke. It was then bought for peanuts by a European company and new management installed. They then built some new, state-of-the-art equipment so they'd be able to handle the growing need for CD manufacturing. The new machines were so good the company shipped them to Europe, leaving their Maine facility unable to meet its manufacturing commitments.

We may be in a recession in America, but every CD plant in the country is running flat out and is backed up for months with orders. The Kennebunk plant is losing millions of dollars because they don't have the new machines they designed and built.

020 The Singapore Lesson

When Malaysia broke away from the British Empire in the 1960s it didn't want Singapore, which was a small island with no resources and a mainly-Chinese population living in terrible poverty. So Singapore formed its own country, went to the United Nations and asked for a task force to come and help.

The UN team looked over the resources and the markets within easy shipping distance. Then they went to the European investment market and got the money to build factories to make the needed products using the nearby resources. Within four years Singapore's 50% unemployment was down to about 5% and the poor had been moved to new high-rise apartment complexes, complete with movie theaters and other entertainment services.

With modern air transportation and satellite communications, Singapore today is in competition with the entire world . . . and doing very well. New Hampshire is in competition with Singapore, Hong Kong, Taipei, Seoul and all of both Eastern and Western Europe . . . as well as our other 49 states. That's today's world, and isolationists had better understand this fairly recent paradigm shift.

I'm in the music business. But I have to understand that this is a high-tech business today. The change to digital sound has essentially obsoleted 99% of the recording studios of the world, so I've just finished building a state-of-the-art studio which is capable of producing the sound today's technology demands. It's the quality concept again . . . the one Ed Demming sold to Japan 40 years ago and they demolished us with.

To produce quality compact discs today a studio has to go to extremes in design, in the silence of the heating and cooling system, in microphone technology, in digital signal processing, and in complete computer controlled digital recording systems.

The studio is attracting recording artists from all over the world. This week Marty Balin (Jefferson Starship) is recording. Next week it's Kukuruza, the Russian bluegrass group. Masanobu Ikemiya, the remarkable Japanese pianist, is scheduled to record some Gottschalk on our new Young Chang (Korean) grand piano.

The music business is just beginning to go global, thus presenting opportunities for entrepreneurs to export American music and import music from Europe and Asia. I'm planning to bring as much of this new world music trade to New Hampshire as possible. It's a new high-tech industry.

I'd like to see the Commission be alert for other new high-tech industries which could be attracted to New Hampshire. Then, using our many resources, put together the investment and entrepreneurs to make it happen. Why depend on chance? You can bet that other states (and countries, for that matter) aren't going to.

Yes, I have some ideas on ways for New Hampshire to be on top of new technologies and attract entrepreneurs to the state to help develop them. I prefer to discuss my ideas with positive thinkers rather than have to defend them against carpers. Almost anything can be done if you really want to. It's just a matter of going about it creatively . . . a frame of reference which is far too rarely encountered.

Look at what the little microcomputer has done to the seemingly impregnable computer industry! Even mighty IBM is beginning to disintegrate! And we here in New Hampshire know all too well how DEC, DG and Wang have been decimated by the microcomputer.

Centronics, in Hudson, NH, was the largest manufacturer of computer printers in the world just a few years ago. But the management refused to face the changes the microcomputer would inevitably bring. American inventors of lower-cost printing systems found Centronics uninterested, so they were forced to turn to Japan. Today, Japan dominates the printer market and they're making pancake turners in the old Centronics factory. New Hampshire lost a potential $10 billion industry. I saw this coming and tried to convince the Centronics management of the need to develop low-cost printers to work with microcomputers. They said it couldn't be done, and who knew better than they?

With the opening of Eastern Europe and the eventual opening of Russia, there's going to be an enormous need for new high-tech products and services. Are we in New Hampshire going to have the work force and the state organization to figure out ahead of time what's going to be needed and be there firstest with the mostest?

021 Improving Our Quality of Life

If we're going to improve the quality of life in New Hampshire, we're going to have to improve our people's education, their motivation and their productivity. Big order, but every little bit we're able to do it is money in the bank.

Not that New Hampshire is all that different from the rest of the country, so if we're able to improve our quality of life, perhaps our approach will be copied by other states. New England, and New Hampshire in particular, has often been a leader in change. We had the first aerial tramway in North America. We pioneered the lottery . . . things like that.

By the way, as a hysterical note, many members of our New Hampshire legislature fought against the tramway project vigorously, delaying it for several years. The main force behind the plan was Littleton's Jack Eames. The tramway recovered its cost in its first year of operation.

New Hampshire, despite far too much political timidity, has been outstandingly progressive. We've another opportunity to step out and show the country that one of the first states is still the most progressive. And by that I mean conservatively progressive, not liberally.

My personal bias is toward capitalism and for-profit ways of getting things done. I've visited far too many socialist countries to have any respect for the weaknesses of non-profit ventures. Adam Smith had it right way back when our country started.

We do have to have laws and police . . . to keep neighbor's dogs from pooping on our porches and morons from throwing beer cans out their car windows. We need to discourage murder and mayhem, and these services are going to have to be paid for collectively. But let's aim to use for-profit services wherever we can, allowing those who benefit from them to pay the piper.

Let's, as a group, look into what progress we may be able to spark toward improving our quality of life via better education, improved motivation and productivity.

Since these are national as well as New Hampshire problems, our solutions, if any, should be helpful to America as well as to our state.

022 Some Problems To Face

You're probably aware that America is in dire straits when it comes to patents. In 1986, 44% of the patents issued were to foreigners . . . mostly the Japanese. What they do is take a new technology which has been discovered in America and then so encircle our basic patents with their application patents that we no longer can use our own inventions.

We know that the American concentration on quarterly profits has drastically reduced our industrial R&D investment. Large companies are selling off divisions to stay in business instead of developing new products and new revenues.

The Japanese government coordinates "Japan, Inc." with its MITI. Our Defense Intelligence Agency was keeping tabs with foreign technology developments via its Project Socrates, but the Bush administration zeroed that out. John Sununu, where were you when we needed you?

Japan's R&D growth has been three times as great as ours . . . and that's all business R&D, not military!

Our federal government is enormous. Few of us appreciate how big it's gotten. For instance, according to the *New York Times*, the government owns one third of all land . . . 744 million acres. It occupies 2.6 billion square feet of office space, the equivalent of all the office space in the 10 largest cities in America, times four! It owns and operates 437,000 non-military vehicles. It provides 95 million subsidized meals a day. It issues 4.8 billion publications annually. It delivers medical care to 47 million people.

If anyone started trying to try and find out how much of a footprint the feds have just here in New Hamphsire, I'll bet the FBI would put a stop to that seditious nonsense.

Then there's our problems with innovation and quality. A 1988 MIT report showed it took American car industry suppliers three times longer to produce new dies, had 50% higher parts defects per car and one fourth as many innovative parts as Japanese suppliers.

Well, how about management? A recent *Forbes* article quoted Peter Drucker, "I have very little use for schools." He prefers apprenticeship and explains that management is a practice, not a science. Business schools need to be more like medical or law schools, where the students get their hands dirty.

It's easy to start fretting about the federal deficit and blame it for all kinds of miseries. It's easy, at least until you read what a few economists have to say - like Roberts (*Business Week* 7/30/90 p.10), "Economists of every political persuasion have searched exhaustively without success for evidence that the deficit is a significant problem." He quotes economist Hyman, "Inflation accelerated during the 1970s in part because taxes were increased. Inflation slowed during the 1980s in part because taxes were cut. Higher taxes in the 1990s will mean higher inflation and unemployment."

Obviously, many of our problems here in New Hampshire can be traced to Washington. There isn't much the Commission can do about that. How can we hope to counter the pressures to spend which drive Congress? There are an average of 2,500 phone calls a day from Capitol Hill to the Pentagon. And we know that 30% of the 22.4 billion in farm price supports went to 4% of the farmers. Congress has been stealing the Social Security tax money to try and make the budget look less a disaster.

We've seen what's happened in electronics. As a publisher in the electronics and communications fields for 40 years, I've watched America gradually lose its entire consumer electronic industry. Well, we didn't actually lose it, we *gave* it away.

I'm writing this on a Japanese computer; I review compact discs on Japanese hi-fi equipment; my ham radio equipment is Japanese. Even my Miata and Previa cars are Japanese.

Today we not only don't make consumer electronics equipment in America, we no longer make the parts. We don't make the machines to make the parts. We don't even make the machines to make the machines to make the parts. Imagine the problems we'd face if we ever decided as a basic American policy to rebuild our electronics industry!

It was the Japanese development of their consumer electronics industries — in TV, VCRs, CDs, hi-fi, cameras, cassettes, radios, computers, test equipment, radar, watches — which in a large part fueled their financial success, making them the wealthiest country in the world.

We know that we're heading into a high-tech world. We know that communications and computers are coming together and that the "information age" concept is much more than propaganda. It's real. Yet we're doing less and less to educate our children to not just cope with this electronic revolution, but to help them ride this wave of the future rather than forever paddling, trying to catch up.

One of the major factors holding back many firms today is the inability of their managers to personally cope with information systems. Now we're trying to make computers which can read handwriting or speech. Why? Because so few Americans have learned to type!

We've produced a generation of people being flooded with high-tech products which they are too uneducated to use. Granted that VCRs could easily be made simpler to program, is that any excuse for the millions of people who are too dumb or too lazy to learn to use them? More VCRs are flashing 12:00 than the right time because the owners can't even set the clock!

Telephones have gotten so complicated that we joke that employees have to be retrained after a lunch break. They're only complicated for people who don't understand them.

In the compact disc field we have a new technology, digital audio, which though simple to understand to anyone with a technical background, is beyond the grasp of almost everyone in the music business . . . and most of the people in the audio business. We see profoundly stupid articles such as the recent one in the *Wall Street Journal* claiming that CDs may have only a 10-year life. The reason for this claim? "Some people say," was the basis.

Having been in the CD business since it started, I know where this stupidity started. An early producer of laser video disks glued two together with the wrong glue and it destroyed the data stored on them. Journalists, ever alert to exaggerate bad news, jumped quickly to scare the public by writing that audio discs might also rot away.

Then we have experts such as David Denby, the movie critic for *New York* magazine, writing that CDs can be made to sound better by marking them with a green felt marker, rinsing them in ArmorAll, and other assorted voodoo.

That reminded me of when I found an old glass power pole insulator and brought it home to our farm in Bethlehem. A few days later we were struck by lightening. No argument on earth could convince my grandmother that the insulator hadn't attracted the lightning. As a high-tech person, I often find myself up against similar irrationalities . . . and wishing our school system was better.

We're proud of our high New Hampshire SAT scores, right? When I read about that I remember one evening when I was driving our babysitter, a senior in the Peterborough High School, home. I mentioned that I'd just talked with His Majesty King Hussein over my ham radio. She'd never heard of him. Hmmm. He's the king of Jordan. Never heard of Jordan either. Jordan is next to Israel. You're not going to believe this . . . she'd never heard of Israel!

I thought perhaps she was an anomaly, so I took some slides in to show the students what Jordan looked like. They enjoyed the show, but when I asked, only two of the 50 students had heard of Jordan before.

We are indeed fortunate that many of the more serious (and expensive) problems besetting many states are minimal here. We have a much smaller drug problem than Massachusetts . . . and therefore a smaller crime problem. We have a very small welfare problem . . . and no ghettos. Thus, we start out with a much higher quality of life. A recent report put N.H. as the best state in the country in which to live. That's fine . . . now let's see if we can't make it a lot better. I think, in view of the current recession, we agree that, good as it is, the quality of life here can definitely be improved.

Since I have some ideas for creative, money-saving ways to solve drug, crime, prison, welfare and homeless difficulties, I'm almost, but not quite, disappointed that New Hampshire doesn't have those as major problems. If absolutely forced, once we've successfully surmounted our New Hampshire problems, I'll share some of my concepts with anyone really interested.

Now, to recap briefly, it seems almost logical that as we improve our educational system, for both kids and adults, we'll all be able to make more money. This should, at the same time, improve productivity, since we'll be better able to make use of modern high-tech systems. By making education fun instead of drudgery, we might just improve motivation, too. It's worth a try, isn't it?

023 Education

I could go on for several pages listing the problems with our educational system. Presumably you've done some homework in this area and understand that the American educational system (which definitely includes New Hampshire) is the pits.

Well, if this Commission is going to do something significant toward improving the quality of life around here, we're going to have to make some substantial changes in education. In doing so, we will not only be doing a great big favor for New Hampshire, we'll be in a position to provide a model for the country.

We're actually in a rather good position to take on a project of this enormity. We have all sorts of pluses. We're a small state, so we have smaller bureaucracies to fight, both in our legislature and in the educational system. Since New Hampshire is not strongly unionized, we'll have an edge when it comes to trying to bring changes which are opposed by teacher unions. And one thing I think we can count on 100% is vigorous union opposition to virtually any proposed changes.

024 Making Money

I hope we can all agree that one's quality of life is generally improved when one is able to get work. There seems to be a general resistance to being out of work which leads me to see a connection. Indeed, there's so much grousing about unemployment, welfare and homelessness that I think we can rule these out as contributing positively toward a quality of life.

Once we agree that "making a living" is important, we're not far from agreeing that education is not just helpful in achieving this fairly basic goal. It is critical. Once I have your agreement on that step, it should be fairly clear that there's no way the Commission can avoid tackling the New Hampshire educational system.

Now, before you get your back up and are unable to read any further as your argumentative nature overrides reason, let me explain that I agree with you 100% that education shouldn't be geared entirely toward making money. I haven't made any such statements, or even suggested it, so let's go along with my reasoning and stop trying to pick nits right from the beginning.

I agree that an education should be broad and should include not only gearing our youngsters to the commercial world ahead, but also should open them to the excitement and enjoyment of the arts, to learning a wide range of skills, and even to an understanding of how to get along with others.

We should be opening youngsters to the fun of learning and get them excited about the many sciences, philosophies, religions, and histories of various peoples. There are so many things we want them to learn and skills we want them to develop that it's almost overwhelming to figure out how to pack all that into just 16 years. I think it can be done.

Not only am I convinced it can be done, I believe it can be done for less than we're spending today. And best of all, I believe we can make it so much fun to learn that we'll find ourselves having trouble keeping up with the kids, rather than having to be out there with a whip, forcing them to go to school and not drop out.

Costs? I believe we can cut college costs to near zero . . . and at the same time double or triple what's learned in the process. Reduce costs and improve productivity? Isn't that what they say we need to do to make America more competitive? Well, leave it to entrepreneurs to come up with something like that. Of course it'll never work. It's impossible, so there's no reason to even discuss it, right?

Here we are with college cost growth vying with health care costs and Wayne's smoking some obviously illegal substance and dreaming about not just cutting college costs, but almost eliminating them! Well, you might want to know that I've discussed the idea in depth with over a dozen college presidents and they all agreed it was a great idea. They also agreed that it called for such a paradigm shift that they'd never get their teachers to go for it. The students? Once they understood the benefits, sure. But the teachers (and their unions) would fight it to the death of the school. Lordy! My plan involves some unacceptable concepts such as teachers working 40 hours a week instead of five or 10. Obviously outrageous.

Is Wayne going to expect the Commission to take a leap of faith, accept an outrageous plan and gamble the fate of the state on its working? Not quite. As an entrepreneur I'm used to betting the farm on the validity of my ideas. But I also recognize that not everyone is an entrepreneur and that most people want to be sure something is going to work, no matter how good it looks, before they'll buy into it.

When a new technology comes along, there are a few pioneers who'll go for it immediately. I'm one of those. I'll bet I had the first home microwave in the state . . . one of the first video recorders (reel-to-reel) . . . the first microcomputer and so on. I'm always carrying around some new gadget to show off.

I not only bought one of the first compact disc players, I got so interested in CDs that I started a magazine to help this new technology grow. We're up to about 30% of American homes now sporting CD players. More significant, over 80% of the homes with hi-fi equipment now have CD players and LPs are now merely collectibles. We're already seeing them in antique shops.

Most entrepreneurs I know suffer from the same pioneering syndrome. I pull out a palm-sized CD player and they pull out a vest pocket computer. I don't tell 'em that I've got one too, but I found it wasn't as good as my old Radio Shack Model 100, which I bought the very first day it was introduced back in early 1983 . . . and am still using because nothing since then has been as handy for writing. My 100 has gone with me everywhere I've traveled for eight years. The freedom it's given me has made much of my traveling possible. It's my portable office . . . my typewriter, my calculator, my filing cabinet, my Rolodex, my memo pad. It even plugs into telephones almost anywhere and is my portable fax, my connection to data bases and electronic mail systems.

There are hundreds of laptop and notebook computers on the market now, but the first practical one, the Model 100, still beats 'em all for my uses. Oh, if I were restricted to just the accessories Radio Shack has available, I'd have retired it years ago. But entrepreneurs have added extra features which have kept it not just up-to-date, but ahead of the new computers for my applications.

If I were into large data bases or spread sheets instead of mainly writing, there are better computers. I prefer to let others do the big spread sheets and keep the data bases. I've got a small spread-sheet program which is fine for planning new projects and that's enough.

Getting back to education, I mentioned a sneaky scheme for modernizing our colleges. I'll go into that in more detail after we've considered what we may be able to do to improve our K-12 education. First things first. And yes, I have some creative ideas for changing K-12, too.

There's been a rising movement to increase our school year. While I agree that this is going to be necessary, I doubt that it will achieve much unless we make some other drastic changes first. Spending more time providing a lousy education doesn't make a lot of sense.

There's been increasing pressure to lengthen the school day. Knowing that most parents are working, I recognize some serious problems when I see school buses down my road delivering kids home at 2:30 in the afternoon. Seems to me I recall that only 6% of families still have the mother staying at home.

It was bound to happen. It got started during WWII when women had to replace men in so many companies. That was fairly rare before the war.

Then, after the war, women were used to working and wanted to continue. They liked making money. A two-worker family had much more money to invest in a better home, car and discretionary purchases.

It didn't take long for prices to rise to meet the available cash. People with houses to sell found that two-income familes could afford to pay substantially more. That gradually froze one-income families out of buying homes, thus encouraging mothers to go to work instead of bringing up children.

If we start having three-income families, home and car prices would quickly rise to take care of the combined income. Prices rise or fall to meet the demand for a product or service.

Where both parents are working, there's usually a need for some sort of child supervision between the time school lets out and the parents get home. Schools are excellent babysitters, but they'd be better if they supervised them for the full eight-hour day instead of five or six.

To some extent after-school sports or clubs can bridge the gap, but this isn't a dependable resource. It's something we might want to consider. When I went to K-12, I was on my own after school. I had plenty of friends to play with, so it wasn't a problem. Plus, I was fairly resourceful.

High school was better. They had over 120 different after-school clubs, so I was busy until after 5 every afternoon. I joined the camera club and had a great time using the darkroom to develop and print pictures. I joined the radio club and they encouraged me to get my amateur radio license and helped me build and test all kinds of electronic gadgets. The choral club met the second period every morning, allowing us to become a first-rate chorus. We performed in the school chapel and for radio broadcasts. The Savoyards practiced a couple of afternoons a week and we presented Gilbert and Sullivan operettas in the chapel.

It takes a large high school to support so many clubs. We had over 10,000 students, so that wasn't a problem.

025 What About Technology?

Before I go into any depth on teaching kids new skills, or the perhaps irrelevance of homework, let's discuss both the importance of teaching technology and the problems.

Unless you've been a hermit without a TV or radio, you know on some level that the world has turned high-tech. That's where the money is and that's where it's going to be for the forseeable future. Heck, even the arts have gone high-tech.

Few workers today don't have a computer around somewhere. Our VCRs are computerized. Our washing machines are computerized. Our microwaves, our clocks, our cars and so on. Are we going to allow our kids to be raised living in a world they don't understand? Just because setting VCRs is beyond our technical ability is no reason to bring up our children that way.

Just because we haven't a clue as to what's inside a radio or a TV is no reason for our kids not to understand how they work and be able to fix them. As a ham radio operator and having published ham radio magazines for over 40 years, I can assure you that surprisingly stupid people are able to understand how radios work. Indeed, we've had kids four years old get their ham licenses. We've had kids seven years old get the highest class license we have available.

Many kids, if encouraged, get so excited about electronics, computers and communications that they teach themselves. They buy magazines and books, go to club meetings, start building gadgets and have a ball. They have to be exposed to these things to get the virus, but once they do, they're usually changed for life.

Kids will learn because it's fun. So my sneaky idea is to help expose them to techno-hobbies and encourage them to learn more on their own. I'd love to see amateur radio, computer and electronic experimenter clubs in almost every school in New Hampshire.

Kid's minds have generally developed enough by the time they're ten years old to handle even the most complex technologies. Thus I propose that kids be taught the fundamentals of electronics starting in the 5th grade.

In learning technology they'll also learn the math that goes with it, thus making the math much more fun. Math is fun when you have actual applications for it. Abstract math can be a killer. I remember how much I hated trig. What a bore! Well, a lifetime later of never needing to use one single sine or cosine now makes me wonder at the value of grilling that stuff into our kids.

Have you ever actually needed solid geometry? How about calculus? How many simultaneous equations have needed solving in your life. I've tried careers in radio, television, electronic R&D, manufacturing, retailing, distribution, software development and publishing high-tech magazines, and found most of the math I hated so much has never been needed. Maybe we need to rethink some of our ideas on what's important to teach.

026 Education Solutions?

We have two points from which to work. First, we have a vague idea of what we want to accomplish, and second, we know what hasn't worked.

I'm sure that as a group we'll be able to argue endlessly on what we want to accomplish in education. Each of us undoubtedly has different ideas, some held firmly in place by either reason or emotion, and others open for discussion.

For instance, we're going to have to come to grips with our short school year (Japanese youngsters go to school 46 weeks a year, six days a week). And there'll be pressures to spend more money. Throwing money at problems has never worked, but that hasn't ever seemed to slow down proposing this approach. The fact is that the U.S. already spends more money per pupil than most other nations . . . yet American students have come in last in international math tests (*Forbes*, 10/14/91, p.43).

"There's nothing very mysterious about why our public schools are failures. When you select the poorest-quality students to be public school teachers, give them ironclad tenure, a captive audience, and pay them according to seniority rather than performance, why should the results be surprising?" (ibid). "Lengthening the school year is meaningless unless time spent in the classroom is better spent." (*US News*, 3/5/90 p.74).

In business we see the life cycles of products shortening and technical innovations becoming more rapid. Once we fall behind in our R&D, we'll never be able to catch up (*The New Yorker*, 9/9/91, p.39). R&D requires scientists, engineers and technicians. It means we need not the handful we have today, but hundreds of thousands more. R&D is the key to our success in technology — not just in the future, but right now.

Alas, we've allowed our educational system to fail us. We don't have the technologically trained work force we need. Worse, we don't even have a clue as to how to rebuild our engineering strength in the near future.

We know that only about 7% of our high school graduates are even capable of coping with the demands of engineering colleges. We know this is because we no longer teach the needed basics of math and science. We know that we don't have the teachers we'd need, even if we could start interesting youngsters in learning about math and science.

Naturally, what few efforts have been made in this arena have been backward. Instead of saying to ourselves that since we perceive a need for more engineers perhaps we should start interesting youngsters in technology, we've tried to get them interested in becoming engineers. It doesn't work that way.

If we want engineers we first have to get kids fascinated by technology. Once we have them hooked, we'll get our engineers. We've failed to make engineering look attractive. Worse, we've made a concentrated effort to shoo kids away from technology and engineering.

Can you recall one TV or movie sitcom or cop show where a youngster interested in technology hasn't been made to be a nerd? A dweeb? A techno-klutz? Now do you for one minute think that doesn't send an awesome message to our youngsters?

We know they're almost totally involved in responding to peer pressures. They buy their clothes and sneakers in order to get peer acceptance, not to keep warm or run faster. Their haircuts, the food they eat, their language, the whole works has to do with catering to (a) what the other kids think and (b) how horrified their parents will be.

Is there any way to make technology acceptable to youngsters, to get them not just neutral, but actively involved in it? Of course there is, but there's a problem here. If we're going to try and change human (I'm being generous here) nature, we're going to have to be smarter than the kids. Perhaps this is an insurmountable obstacle.

Let's say that, despite the vigorous efforts of neoconservatives to protect the status quo, we're able to mount a creditable effort to entice youngsters into high-tech arenas. Won't some disgruntled fink journalists rush to expose the plot and scuttle our efforts?

Undoubtedly, but here we have a decided advantage . . . you see, most kids can't read, and the few who have developed this unique skill don't bother to read. So most of 'em will go along happily tuned in to the chatter of their peers while we work our magic and gradually turn the herd in the direction we want.

Okay, call me a cynic, but have I really exaggerated all that much? I'd suggest that if you have kids, you talk to them and see what you can find . . . except that I recall seeing the statistic that the average American parent talks with his or her kids less than 15 minutes a week.

This situation, where the parents don't bother to teach ethics or religion to their children, and schools are prevented from doing the same, has been blamed for the continuing moral collapse of our society. Indeed, as a publisher, I'm well aware of the widespread pressures from parents to do all in their power to keep their children from coming to grips with the world in which they live.

Just a few days ago I got an angry letter from a reader of one of my radio magazines cancelling his subscription. We'd published a QSL card contest winner (these cards are sent by amateur operators to confirm their radio contacts) with a drawing of a beautiful woman in a snug-fitting, floor-length evening gown. This chap didn't want his grandson's mind polluted by seeing such pictures. Lord knows what will happen if the kid ever gets a look at a *Sports Illustrated* bathing suit issue!

Perhaps we can de-geek science for the kids if we go about it the right way. It's worth a try, isn't it? I think we can all agree that since our country needs more science-oriented workers, that we have to figure out how to accomplish this. And since New Hampshire is in a particularly desperate need for a technologically-trained work force if it's going to attract high-tech entrepreneurial businesses, perhaps it's worth our while to consider some ways of pioneering in this area.

Yes, of course I have some suggestions. But before you insist on me producing them so you can get to work demolishing 'em, I want to set some ground rules. For instance, I'm open to constructive criticism. The "it won't work" approach is a waste of time. That gets us into a Thomas/Hill confrontation . . . I didn't do it; yes, you did. It won't work; yes, it will.

To help avoid mixing politics in with our venture into education, with the Republicans over here, the Democrats over there, the unions in a third corner and the bureaucrats in the middle, I'd like to propose a whole new approach to solving our educational problems.

Sure, I have what I think is a gangbusters new approach to getting us the engineers and technicians we need. And I'm 100% certain that my approach will work, be fun to implement, and not increase educational costs one dollar. I'm also 100% certain that since it's a new approach and untested, there will be no end of reactionaries who will oppose even testing it to see if it'll work. Plus a long list of people who will perceive that this change in education will in some way negatively affect their lives. People are, in general, afraid of change and tend to resist it. They are able to come up with an endless number of rationalizations with which to convince themselves that they are right.

Having helped pioneer cellular telephones, single sideband radio, narrow band FM radio, slow-scan television, microcomputers and compact discs, I'm not a stranger to resistance to change.

027 Measuring The Results

The innovation in education which I'll be describing is only one of many which you'll be faced with evaluating. We know that we have to change because the present system stinks. We know we'll be faced with enormous resistance at every hint of change. So let's make it as difficult as possible for reactionaries to find supporting rationalizations which will suck in the unwary.

Mind you, it's very difficult to build a defense against polemics. One screaming extremist can hustle up pretty goo- sized crowds, no matter how ridiculous the proposition. Mass hysteria can knock the hell out of mass reason, as our liberal media know all too well.

So before I get up on my soap box and enthrall you with the righteousness of my cause, whipping you to a seething mob with a hanging rope for our educational establishment (which they may well deserve), I have one small proposal to make. This one is going to cost money, so I'm sure you'll hate it. Well, it actually won't cost a lot of money. Heck, it could even, once started, actually make money. I told you I'm in favor of getting our state to put as many of its services on a paying basis as we can so we'll be able to maintain our sneaky facade of having low taxes.

I'm not arrogant enough to try and convince you that my incredibly ingenious approach to getting our kids interested in technology . . . an approach which doesn't even call for our taking 10 years to train math and science teachers before it can be put to the test . . . is the only thing that will work. I haven't a moment's doubt that many of you have pet ideas for revamping our educational system. I also suspect that your interest in your ideas may keep you from paying much attention to mine. That's the way these things work. So I have a compromise to offer.

Presuming that you've done your homework and understand how our present educational system works . . . and what ideas are in vogue for changing it (meaning that you've been reading at least a few of the educational magazines and current books on the subject), you're in a position to make some positive contributions.

But one thing you know for sure, if you've done said homework, is that an awful lot of ideas for change have been suggested. Obviously, some of them are going to increase educational productivity and others are going to fail. So how can we sort the wheat from the chaff and not chaff ourselves into even worse trouble?

Oh yes, I'm well aware of the Bush American 2000 proposal. No, I don't think much of it. It smells strongly of pork . . . and not particularly fresh pork. It doesn't have that clean smell of Adam Smith and capitalism. It stinks of socialism and bureaucratic preservationism. How's that for doing a vague poop job on the 2000 project?

028 How To Pioneer Educational Productivity

If we think of education as a product and look for ways to improve the product the same way we might try and improve any other product, it begins to look easier to tackle and our problems more solvable.

In addition to knowing that our present product is the worst in the civilized world, we also know a few other things about it. We know that it isn't all bad. We know that we've allowed the buildup of a union/bureaucracy which has prevented change and has our legislature under tight control. And we know that despite the enormous pressures against change, that pioneers all over the world are experimenting with new educational approaches. Call these experimenters scientists, if you like. They're not working with test tubes or mice. They're working with the real thing . . . kids.

The one element we don't have is some way of gathering information on their experiments and publishing it. We don't have the normal scientific peer-review publishing system. And that's what I'm proposing New Hampshire establish.

It's been my experience that no new technology can get far without a supporting publication. A publication provides three invaluable benefits to an emerging technology . . . and that's what we have here, isn't it? We're working on an emerging new educational technology.

A dedicated publication first of all helps coordinate the experimenters in the field. It gives them the communications they need to help new ideas grow. Further, it provides a way for newcomers to the field to come up to speed and understand the new technology. Thirdly, and perhaps most important, a dedicated publication makes it possible for entrepreneurs to start providing products the experimenters need.

In the case of education there'll probably be a need for computers, software, film, video, projectors, slides, desktop publishing systems, CD-ROMs, CD-I systems, and so on. We don't yet know how much productivity our modern technology will provide, but we sure *need* to know.

Microcomputers got started in 1975 when the first practical microcomputer was put on the market by a small, almost bankrupt firm in Albuquerque. Sales that first year were under $5 million for the entire industry. But the appearance of the first dedicated microcomputer magazine, *Byte*, in September 1975 sparked the industry into a frenzy of growth. The industry grew by an average of 235% a year for the next seven years!

Byte was soon followed by *Microcomputing*, then *80-Micro*, the first magazine dedicated to one specific computer system, the Radio Shack TRS-80. This publication helped Radio Shack corner 40% of the market! Then came *InCider* for the Apple and soon Apple had another 40% of the market! There were perhaps 200 other computers, unsupported by publications, which shared the other 20% of the market. It's almost enough to make one think.

I believe an educational technology publication would help sort out the ideas which work from those which don't. It would help focus attention on educational research's importance. It would provide a nexus for the improvement of education, not just in America, but worldwide.

This isn't exactly a new idea for me, cooked up to help bootstrap New Hampshire out of its funk. I've been trying to interest Rensselaer Polytechnical Institute (Troy, NY) in the idea for several years. It seemed to me that RPI was an ideal center for such a publication . . . and that the need for it was desperate.

As a member of the Steering Committee, I've been pushing for the RPI School of Management to get into the publishing business. I did get the school to start a Center for Entrepreneurship of New Technological Ventures, which has worked out well. Indeed, the RPI Council, of which I'm a member, recommended that the school concentrate on promoting entrepreneurialism as an RPI specialty.

They did set up and fund a Center for Innovative Undergraduate Education (CIUE), but it got off the course I recommended and has been mostly involved with funding RPI research projects, instead of reporting on those in other schools which could increase educational productivity.

029 Time Binding

One basic difference between man and all other life is our time-binding ability. This is our ability to learn things and then pass them down to following generations. This concept, originally put forth by Alfred Korzibsky in his *Science and Sanity*, ties in with Santa Ana's warning about learning from history . . . or else.

In our case, while there are a wide variety of educational experiments going on all over the world, we haven't yet developed a central intelligence system to gather the results and make the ideas generally available. This is what our vaunted information society is supposed to be doing, right?

So I'm proposing that New Hampshire establish an information resource, not just for our own use, but as an international resource. Being close to the source, we here in New Hampshire will have the first and best opportunity to benefit from the information developed.

What I have in mind is a publication to help make new ideas and experiments in education more widely known. It would publish articles on experimental educational projects. It would review new educational products, helping the educational community know what tools and systems it has available.

Where new technologies or ideas have been tested and found helpful or even wanting, this information will help other educational pioneers in their search for ever more effective techniques and technologies. We need more productivity. If television can help, let's not fight it. Let's try it and see how we can best use it to increase productivity.

Educational productivity? Of course, like any other product, we want to be able to provide the most/best education at the least cost . . . in time and resources. This concept may be at odds with the normal union mind-set which often puts providing "jobs" far above efficiency. With our costs of education going out of control in America, we can't afford educational featherbedding.

I hope you read the short interview in *Time* (10/28/91) with the president of American Airlines, the chap who fired a dog as a cost-cutting measure. This is the kind of creative problem solving which needs to be applied to education.

030 Useful vs. Useless

There's a big controversy over the use of hand calculators in school. We know that they've forever changed our approach to math. They're even building calculators into wristwatches. We need to know more about how best to use electronic calculators in schools.

No doubt you've noticed the many low-cost scientific calculators. They look like fun — until you try to use one and find you've forgotten most of what you . . . er . . . "learned" in school. And worse, the instruction books that come with them are almost useless. Are our schools teaching youngsters how to use these new tools?

In college and in the Navy electronic schools I got to be a whiz with my log-log-duplex-decitrig slide rule. It was up in my attic for years until someone swiped it. You know, I've never needed it once since I got out of school!

If they had a handbook on using a scientific calculator — and if they had some practical examples of calculations which would help me in my work (which is unlikely), I'd enjoy learning how to use it. But first I want to know what good it's going to do me to take the time and spend the money.

The same goes for learning a foreign langauge. Never mind that I hated French in high school and it was the bane of my existance. Also never mind that what little French I did learn saved the lives of me and several companions 20 years later on an expedition. That was just a fluke. Another fluke was when my knowledge of Morse code saved my submarine from getting sunk during WWII. These foreign languages have come in handy for me.

Unless you start with youngsters two or three years old, learning a foreign language can be a dreadful experience. It's the endless vocabulary memorizing that does it. Worse, unless you continually refresh these memories they quickly fade and your time was wasted.

Indeed, several of my friends who moved here from foreign countries found that within a couple of years they were forgetting their mother language. On visits home they were having problems remembering the words they wanted. Heck, it's tough to maintain an English vocabulary. Most Americans get by with a surprisingly small vocabulary.

Our educational system is going to have to come to working terms with technology. It's going to have to make sure that kids know what scientific calculators can do and understand how to use them. We're soon going to have enormous data bases available in small hand-held CD-ROM readers. They're already being sold in Japan.

Sony has announced a new mini-disc (MD) technology which will allow a shirt-pocket recorder/player to give us 74 minutes of excellent quality sound. It'll soon be able to handle graphics and eventually video.

They're already able to put a complete encyclopedia on a 2" disc, so who knows what'll happen to text and reference books in the future? These discs allow an almost unlimited searching capability, dwarfing even the best of the old-type indexes.

An educational technology publication would help spread the word on new approaches to teaching. It would not just explain about the new tools we have available, but run articles by educators who have pioneered their use in classrooms.

031 Who Will Pay

New Hampshire may need an educational technology publication to help our state pioneer a revolution in education, but one thing we don't really need is another growing state-run bureaucracy.

As I've said, I'm in favor of having as many state projects as possible not just no-cost, but actually making a profit which can be used to help our non-profit projects require fewer taxes.

A publication normally makes about half of its income from its readers and the other half from its advertisers. Our educational technology publication — we might call it *New Educational Technology* (*NET*) — should be able to build a paying subscriber base within a year or two. It'll be of interest to educators all over the world. No, it'll be much more than of interest, it'll be absolutely required reading. It may irritate them to have to pay for information they need, but they'll pay. And, considering the value of the information to them, they'll pay rather well. Remember, just one useful new educational idea can make an enormous difference to schools.

We know there's a move to have schools become accountable. We're heading toward standardized national testing. This is going to have more and more educators looking for ways to improve their schools.

But do we really want advertising in our publication? You bet we do! And contrary to uninformed "concerned" people, many magazines do not cater to their advertisers. My former music magazine, *Music & Audio Reviews*, would never have grown the way it did, even defying the recession which hit publishers very hard, without the confidence of our readers in our reviews being unbiased.

Some of the larger record companies have had a difficult time adjusting to our even-handed review policy, but the economic might of readers who are spending $40 million a month buying CDs has forced them to stop trying to get favors.

Having started a number of publications, I'd estimate that getting *NET* up to where it would be self-sustaining (in the black) would probably take one to two years and require, at most, an investment of about $500,000. It should, in my experience, be able to repay the investment within five years and turn a nice profit from then on.

I won't go into all the details, but this is a road I've been over many times, so it's familiar. I know all of the pitfalls and could help a publication avoid missing any.

Since publishing and technology are my major fields, I hope it's no surprise that I tend to think in these terms when it comes to solving problems.

We're aiming, I hope, at building a work force which is so technically well-trained that it will attract high-tech entrepreneurial businesses to our state. If we build the field, they'll come.

And the more we can trade in information, the better off we'll be. Information is getting to be a major product, so we should be thinking in terms of gathering and selling information. Look at the publishing center which developed in the Peterborough area! If we start thinking in terms of dealing with information as a high-tech product, we can find a wide variety of publications we can nurture and build into a major New Hampshire industry base.

I like publishing as an industry. It has almost no lower-wage blue-collar workers. That's a plus these days when unskilled, semi-skilled and craft work is fast moving to lower-wage countries. It's a product with no resource and no sales limitations. My *73 Amateur Radio Today* gets articles submitted from all over the world and has subscribers in over 200 countries.

When I visited Brunei, a tiny northern Borneo country, I met one of my *80-Micro* and several *73* subscribers. On Guam I was given a big party by a combination of over 50 of my *80-Micro* and *73* subscribers.

Yes, of course I have in mind several publications which are needed and would be great for New Hampshire. For instance, I have in mind one which would, I believe, be capable of not only bringing badly needed cash into the state for the magazine, but would also be able to double our tourist industry within two or three years.

Beyond that, I have in mind a number of other new publications which are needed, would not duplicate any current publications, and which would be able to build our publishing industry strength.

032 Educational Basics

Before we can define what we consider a "good" education, we need to agree on our fundamental goals. I'd like to propose some.

In the long run, I hope you'll agree, the quality of life in New Hampshire will depend to a fair degree on the quality of life in America. The next step is to agree that America's economic climate will to some degree correlate with that quality of life. Thus, the more successful we are as a country in competition with other countries, the better we can expect our quality of life to be. It would seem prudent to do what we can, as a country, to be as competitive as possible economically.

I hope you'll also agree that the better educated and motivated our work force, the better our prospects should be for coping with world competition.

While it takes no great leap of faith to accept this concept, my next step may strain the contentious. I can hear the sputtering now . . . hey, money isn't everything, you know. Yes, I know. I agree, but I also suspect that most of you will agree that though it isn't everything, it sure beats whatever is in second place.

Look, I'm in the music business, so if I forget about cooking some art education into the mix, I'm goring my own ox.

Now, back to business, so to speak . . . er . . . write. Let's, for the sake of reduced argument, consider the number one goal of education as readying youngsters for success in the workplace. Let's argue later, if necessary, about the other goals.

Okay, we want to prepare our kids to cope with the world/U.S./New Hampshire economy of the next decade. We know it's going to be competitive and that the better educated are going to walk away with the winnings. We know that technology is going to make the future world far more competitive than it is even today.

Technology is lowering communications and transportation costs. This lowers the barrier of distance, putting our kids in closer direct economic competition with youngsters in Japan, Germany, and Mali.

I suggest that we not only have to revamp our educational system to meet the demands of goal #1, but we should look for any possible edges we have. Can we substitute some smarts for hard work? Of course we can, or I wouldn't have brought it up.

033 The Japanese Achilles Heel

Japanese youngsters go to school about half again as long as our kids, thus giving them an enormous apparent advantage over us. Well, while I'm going to eventually recommend that we too keep our kids in school around 48 weeks a year and even go for a six-day school week (like the Japanese), please hold off your objections until I've had a chance to make a case for a whole new approach to education . . . one where the kids actually enjoy learning and are having fun in school. I most certainly don't recommend extending the school week or year until some major changes have been made.

034 Cognitive vs. Rote Teaching

One enormous fundamental advantage I see for us to beat the Japanese lies in their dependence on memorization as a way of teaching. We know enough about how the mind works to recognize that rote learning is extremely inefficient. It's easy for teachers to require their students to memorize information and then regurgitate it at exam time. But supposedly our educational system is there to educate children, not just to provide economic security for teachers. One thing memorization doesn't do is teach.

Indeed, it's this almost total emphasis on rote memorization which has held back the Japanese in their efforts to become creative. It's also made it far more difficult for them to develop entrepreneurs. These are two powerful strengths we have.

While lazy teachers have depended on memorization exercises and homework to keep their own workload down, we have had a few smarter teachers who have recognized the critical importance of cognitive teaching. Teach the kids to understand things and where to get the details.

In college, instead of teaching us how much fun reading books could be, we had to memorize names, titles, dates and a brief synopsis of hundreds of books. Within hours of the final exam these totally unimportant details were evaporating from our minds. And, instead of having developed an appetite for reading, we'd developed an aversion.

The memorization of hundreds of calculus formulas, without even a hint as to their application in the real world, didn't help make that course enjoyable. The fact that, despite my pursuing several careers in business, I've never run across the slightest need for calculus . . . or even had to deal with simultaneous equations . . . has, I admit, colored my perspective.

I'm for helping kids understand how things work. There's a rush of excitement when a new concept is grasped. It makes learning fun! So I tend to push for cognitive education instead of memorization.

My college was very proud of the homework load it required. Having gone through this grinder, my perspective 50 years later is that at least 99% of it was worse than a waste of time. It was cruel and unusual punishment and should have resulted in legal suits against the college.

I was lucky in a way. We had a war while I was going to college. I was fat, dumb and miserable, hating almost every minute of college . . . and doing poorly as a result. So when the war came along I knew I'd be nominated for cannon fodder instead of a sheepskin. I joined the Navy in 1942. The details of how I came to join the Navy and what happened are interesting, but this paper is aimed at helping New Hampshire cope with a recession, rather than as a recitation of my adventures.

The good part was that the Navy, for some unexplainable reason, actually did things right. I went through their electronics school and it was superb. It took youngsters who didn't know a volt from an ohm and taught them how to fix any piece of electronic equipment the Navy had. It taught us how things worked so we could reason our way through problems.

No memorization at all! It was all cognitive education. They'd give us the talk and chalk explanation of how something worked. Fine, but we might eventually forget that. Next, we went into a lab where we were faced with fiendishly disabled equipment which we had to fix.

It's one thing to learn how a superheterodyne receiver circuit works in theory. It's another to face a radio with several faulty or even intermittant parts. Within nine months, the Navy turned out superb electronic technicians. Indeed, I learned more in the first three months of that school than I was taught in four years in college.

One would think that any intelligent person would learn from that experience. Alas, I was so completely brainwashed about the critical importance of college that it never even occurred to me to question the process, no matter how painful. When the war was over I dutifully went back to college and blew two more of the best years of my life, memorizing and forgetting facts and formulas at an amazing rate.

A recent article in *Inc.* magazine on highly successful entrepreneurs showed that only one of them had completed college. The rest were smart enough to drop out and stop wasting their time. I could have been smarter.

My goal isn't to get rid of college, it's to make it relevant. But memorization doesn't start in college. That starts right from the earliest days of grammar school. Yes, I suppose we have to have some memorization. But let's only include items which we will tend to be using on a daily basis for the rest of our lives.

It is helpful, for instance, to know the alphabet. It makes it easier to use filing systems. It's helpful to learn to spell, though the looming ubiquity of spell-checkers in word processors may reduce the importance of spelling as hand calculators have reduced the importance of memorizing the multiplication tables. There's always the question . . . what will you do when the battery goes dead?

Faced with the alternative of memorizing the spelling of 100,000 or so words, I'd tend to spend my time developing a battery backup system. To the extent that memorization is involved in building a vocabulary, I'm in favor of that. But a vocabulary unused is a vocabulary wasted because it'll blow away.

Yes, it's going to be a challenge for educators to reorient the system so it's aimed at teaching concepts instead of memorization. This is going to raise holy hob with somewhere between 99% and 100% of the teachers. In my 16 years of formal schooling (note I did not use the term "education") I had exactly two teachers who made their courses fun.

In retrospect, the fact that my college accounting professor committed suicide a couple years later wasn't very surprising. I suspect he was under enormous pressure from the college to stop all that nonsense and conform.

As an entrepreneur, when I find my company competing with international megacorporations or organized crime, I tend to think in terms of what I call guerrilla marketing. This means looking for weaknesses in the dragon's armor and attacking the weak spots. It's really dumb to attack an overwhelming force . . . or a dragon . . . straight on.

Well, the U.S. is in competition with Japan for world financial supremacy . . . and we've been losing badly. So why not look for their weaknesses and attack them? And one long-range weakness is their educational system. It has a fatal basic flaw which I doubt they'll be able to change. It's too ingrained.

Of course there's always the possibility that just as they imported Ed Demming and paid him to teach them how to compete with quality products, they might come after me and pay me to come over and reorganize their educational system. We know they are a pragmatic people or they wouldn't have been able to buy into the Demming philosophy and beat us into second place in the world with it.

So let's get the jump on Japan and start teaching concepts. This will give us a jump on most of Europe too, where rote teaching is still going strong.

There's one more bad aspect to rote teaching vs. conceptual. All too often it's quite possible to memorize things without giving them any thought. Thus we may memorize data, but then not use the memorized data for thinking.

As singers can tell you, it's easy to memorize foreign language songs and sing them, even though you have no idea of what the words mean. I learned a Spanish song in grammar school that for some reason I still remember. I haven't a clue as to what the words mean. And while singing in a church choir I learned a song in Latin. I still know the song.

I found the same thing happening with songs in English. Sometimes years later, to my surprise, I'd suddenly realize what the words meant. When I sing I don't have to consciously remember the words. They come automatically. Of course this makes it difficult for me to start in the middle of a song.

If we apply the same concept to rote "learning" we see that it's unlikely the memorized matter will be of much use for reasoning.

035 What About Homework?

If we're going to change our system and try to eliminate memorization, won't that also eliminate most homework? It shouldn't. I don't know about you, but I do far more homework now than I did during most of my school years . . . except for those dreadful memorization bouts for college.

My homework these days (and nights) consists mainly of reading books and magazines. In addition to business, scientific and news magazines, I also keep up with trade publications in my business fields. This means reading printing, publishing, circulation, graphics art, computer, music, amateur radio, communications, and so on. Plus I have some personal interests I follow such as skiing, scuba diving, sports cars, psychology, unusual phenomena, travel, astronomy, cosmology, and so on.

Like any other student I read with a highlighter in hand. I mark interesting pages with Post-It tabs for easy reference.

If we expect youngsters to learn about the world . . . to get concepts of history, politics, religions, math, language, and science, we're going to expect them to do a lot of homework. Their homework will be different from what you might at first expect.

While most of my homework involves reading books and magazines, I also spend a good deal of time watching TV. While some of this is obviously recreational, most of it is for education. I tape the science programs . . . most of them via PBS . . . and watch them at my convenience . . . usually while eating, as an efficiency measure.

I have high hopes for the future of video in teaching. Some of the programs are superb and show what can be done. They might be even better if PBS would make abbreviated study notes available to help us review the material and thus keep it fresh in mind.

Television? Sure! But what about computer-assisted teaching? I'm sure that'll eventually help. It has great potential, but so far there have been very few real success stories.

Educational computer applications got off to a terrible start. Apple, IBM and other computer firms pushed hard to get computers into the schools. Well, they got 'em there all okay, relieving school systems of millions of dollars. The down side was that (a) the teachers didn't know what to do with them, being untrained and (b) there was no useful software.

036 Teacher Fears

While kids love 'em, most adults tend to be afraid of computers and to resist learning to use them. And that includes teachers.

As a general rule, teachers tend to be wary of any new technologies. They tend to view them with a fear of being embarrassed in front of their students and losing their respect . . . and of possible job loss. Teacher groups have bragged about defeating the use of one technology after another . . . film, audio cassettes, video, and now computers.

But even in the few known instances where computers have been accepted by teachers the results have been disappointing. Computers are useless without software . . . so where's all the promised software?

I can tell you from personal experience where the software went. Back in 1977, when the first practical microcomputers were put on the market, I formed a software company called Instant Software.

Up until that time computer software had always been custom-written for computers and this was very expensive. I knew that with low-cost computers we'd need low-cost software. Instead of custom producing programs, we'd write software which had good general applications, mass produce it and sell it through computer stores. This was a completely new idea at the time.

Since I was the major publisher in the microcomputer field I was able to draw upon my readers for computer programs which might sell to the general public. I hired a bunch of programmers and set up a lab with 30 work stations to test submitted programs, perfect them and write the documentation.

We produced software for playing games, for business applications and some educational subjects. We had over 250 software programs selling in computer stores all over America and Europe. One of our educational programs won first prize as the best ever produced.

When we looked at the sales figures we were amazed. Our game and business software was selling very well, but hardly any educational software was selling. We wondered why, so we investigated our sales and found that we'd been selling one program to each school and they'd been copying it for the students to use.

We tried for another year to see if things would improve. Sales got worse. Now we found that we were selling one program to each school district and they were sending copies to each of their schools. Were these $195 programs? No, they retailed for $7.95.

I did the only practical thing I could, I stopped trying to sell educational software and pulled our programs off the market. I talked with the other major software companies and found their experiences and response had been exactly the same as mine.

How many textbooks would be published if each school bought only one copy? Or each school district? No software company with any sense is ever going to bother investing in educational software until this changes.

Technology is moving rapidly, so my question about the textbook is relevant. With today's page readers it's practical to scan the pages of a book into a computer and then let it print out the book, with the cost being that of the paper alone. This should be able to save schools millions of dollars in book costs.

Yes, this'll eventually stop textbook publishers from investing in new books, but I doubt this will stop one single school from running off royalty-free copies.

Perhaps we'll see publishers suing scanner manufacturers for their losses and demanding that scanners be electronically prevented from scanning their books. This was the reaction of the music industry when digital audio tape recorders were starting to be sold.

I've talked with teachers about this and their explanation is that since schools are non-profit, they should be permitted to steal software and copy books all they want. Book publishers have been suffering from the "mimeograph syndrome" for years.

Until some solution to the theft problem is found it is unlikely that any very useful educational software will be developed. Alas, we just haven't been able to find programmers willing to work for what schools are willing to pay: nothing.

With computer scanner prices dropping fast, it won't be long until either the textbook companies go under or some way to force teachers not to steal is devised.

If you're interested in keeping up with what little development is being done in this field I recommend you subscribe to *T.H.E. Journal*, That's *Technical Horizons in Education.* It's rather depressing to see how little has been done with such an enormously powerful tool.

037 The Parents?

Many American parents get bent out of shape when they find that Asian kids are outperforming theirs. The first reaction is to want to get rid of those damned Asian kids who are showing theirs up.

Studies show that it isn't IQ that's making the difference, it's motivation. That's the same thing employers are finding in such short supply in today's work force. Asian kids excel because their parents are pushing them. The Asian parents care and their kids know it.

American parents generally tend to ignore their kids. If their kids don't make it in school, instead of helping their kids do better, they push the teachers to pass them anyway.

Be reasonable about it. Most parents today have to work a full day. When they get home they want to take it easy and watch TV, not try to help junior with trig formulas. Who remembers trig anyway? The capital of Sabah? Who cares? One of those African countries, right?

It's going to take a good deal of selling to get parents to take an interest in their children. We've got to figure some way where they'll get some perceivable benefit from it. That works far better than trying to shame them into it.

We'll do better if we can get parents involved with their kids. Sadly, it's more normal to ignore them and then be astounded when they get into trouble or kill themselves by accident. One beer-filled teenager killed himself almost in front of my house. Darned near killed the guy coming the other way, too. There's this little hump in the road and he was seeing how far he could loft his car.

So our kids drink. They try drugs. They get pregnant. They cruise. They "go bad." And one more thing, they are next to useless as workers.

The number of unskilled jobs has dwindled. The number of high-paying unskilled jobs is way down and sinking fast.

We're very fortunate in New Hampshire not to have inner-city and racial problems. This has tended to help our kids avoid serious drug and crime involvement. It has not kept them from drinking beer or killing themselves driving. It hasn't kept them from wasting their time cruising or hanging out in shopping malls.

Can we blame parents for not pushing their kids to spend more time on school work when they are well aware of how bad the schools are?

Yes, I have an idea for a way out of this Catch-22 situation. We need a way to get parents interested in talking with their kids — a way to get them to want to help their kids be better able to deal with the problems of careers and family.

If you were charged with coming up with some way to get parents to start communicating with their children, what would you suggest? My approach is to look at this as another product we want to market. What benefits can we offer? What resistances are there that we have to overcome?

Once we get into it there are plenty of benefits. If kids can be changed from the monsters they are now into cooperative, enthusiastic, active, anxious-to-learn people, they'll be a whole lot easier to live with and you'll be able to be much prouder of them. If they do good things it'll help your esteem.

I'm reminded of dogs. When I visit some people who have dogs they jump up on me and are a real nuisance. They beg for scraps at the table. They bark. They chew things. Some even aren't well housetrained!

Then, when I go to Europe, I find many restaurants permit customers to bring in their dogs. The dogs sit under their chairs and never cause any trouble. What's going on here? It's a simple matter of training.

There are plenty of inexpensive dog training books available, it's just that few Americans seem to have enough interest in their dogs to spend the few hours it takes to train them. Dogs love to learn and are easily trained when it's done right. It gives them a sense of belonging, of confidence, and a way to show love to their master.

If you've read any dog books you know that the most practical training method involves using love and patience, not punishment and reprimands, to get the dog to want to do what you want it to do. You just have to be a little smarter than the dog. Perhaps that's too much of a requirement for most people.

Oddly enough, many of the same techniques used to train dogs and other animals will work just fine on your kids. You can argue with me after you've done your homework and read some animal training books.

Since I think we can make a good enough case for parents to start training their children — can come up with enough benefits to sell the product — the next question is what kind of training instructions are we going to provide. It's got to be good. There's no use trying to sell a shoddy product. It's got to be easy to use and work 100% of the time.

038 How About Video?

Since so few people seem to be into reading these days, I'd suggest making the information available on videotape. That way even high school drop-out parents will be able to train their kids.

Never one to sell one product when I can sell five, I'd start my series out with parenting 10-year-olds. Then I'd have one for 12-year-olds, and in two-year jumps up to around 22. By then it's probably time to change the lock on your front door.

Ten-year-old kids have different problems than 12-year-olds, so in addition to showing parents how to get into communications with their kids, we can also give them information which will be of particular help for specific age groups.

We should try to cover as much as possible — like how to handle peer pressures, how to deal with teachers and schools, how to pick sports to pursue, how to learn some skills, how to get into hobbies, how to behave when you're with your parents, and things like that.

Heck, I'll bet I could sell hundreds of thousands of Parenting 10-Year-Olds tapes. I could probably even sell an Advanced Parenting series for each age group.

The tapes would be down-to-earth and not preachy. Parents need help in dealing with their kids. They need help in trying to honestly discuss sensitive topics like sex, religion, politics, their haircuts and so on.

Is making tapes like this available something New Hampshire should get involved in? Well, as I've mentioned, I'm not in favor of the state going into private business. I think it's important for states to look for problems which private industry might be able to solve — and then offer to either provide venture capital for the needed business to get started or to help put an entrepreneur together with a venture capital source — perhaps with a limited guarantee, if the venture is perceived as benefitting the state.

Only when our entire educational system is back in private hands will it be possible for capitalist market forces to act to improve our system. The providers of lousy education would be forced out of business. Prices would tend to be kept down by competition.

Hopefully you've read articles and books on the subject, so I won't have to cover all of the arguments for and against the privatization of our educational system. Having read extensively on the subject, I've turned into a privatization fan.

People who argue that this might hurt the poor haven't done their homework. Question: Has free public education increased or decreased literacy in America? If you've read much you know not only the answer, but the amazing percentages involved. You also will know that most of our educational budget in this country never reaches the kids — it's absorbed by an ever-growing socialist-oriented bureaucratic administrative elite.

039 Education In Perspective

What we should face when we start messing with our state educational system is that we really have to help educate our people from birth to grave.

We know that the better prepared children are when they enter school, the faster they will learn. We know that with most families having two working parents, we're going to have to help provide day care for young children. When you put those two together, you have a child's education getting started right from the first few weeks after birth.

If we want to help New Hampshire provide a good quality of life we've got to help develop our educational system so it will take hold with the beginning of day care and continue through K-12, college, and then adult education.

Perhaps, in a final circle, we can combine some elements of day care with care for the elderly, letting them care for and help teach our babies. This has been working well in many areas and seems to provide mutual benefits — plus help keep costs down.

040 What To Teach

In addition to science and math, which will be necessary for our high-tech work force, we also may consider it worthwhile to see that more mundane subjects are covered — like information which is important for everyday living. A Maine educational newsletter put it this way, "Did you know that after more than 11,000 hours of education most high school graduates cannot change the oil in a car engine, fix a leaky faucet, replace a blown fuse, or repair a broken lawn mower? Do you realize that most high school graduates do not know how to fill out a tax return, apply for a mortgage, manage a checkbook, or register to vote? Imagine, after more than 11,000 hours of classroom 'learning,' most high school graduates do not know where pencils come from, or how furniture is made. They do not know why the lights go on in a room when a switch is thrown. They have never seen the insides of a radio or TV set and could not repair any of the electronic equipment or simple appliances that they use every day.

"Did you know that most high school graduates have no information about how to choose a compatible mate, a choice that represents the single most important decision in life? Most high school graduates don't know how to choose a competent physician or dentist. They don't know anything about childbirth or pregnancy. After 11,000 hours of education, very few high school graduates know how to care for an infant or raise a child. They do not know how to tend a sick family member or care for an aging parent."

I wish they were exaggerating.

I'd add to that. They also don't know how or what's best to eat, or how to cook a meal. Heck, in college when my fraternity's cook quit on Thanksgiving morning, I took over and cooked the whole turkey dinner for 30 people. We had a great dinner and it was fun! Well, I did call my dad to find out what seasonings he put in his dressing. It was Bells.

The newsletter makes a good point. I don't think our Commission needs to try and list every aspect of the education we'd recommend. But we can sure come up with some rough guidelines and I'd suggest the above areas be included.

Are classes still being taken to visit manufacturing plants? I always enjoyed that as a kid. I remember visiting the Daily News plant and seeing how a large newspaper was done, from beginning to end. And we visited a car assembly plant, a rail forging mill, a radio station and so on.

Even videos showing how factories work would help kids get some perspective on 'em. I think they'd enjoy seeing some of the modern electronic plants in Asia, where virtually everything is automated. They should see the Japanese electronic research labs with hundreds of engineers and technicians hard at work. They should see how compact discs and integrated circuit chips are made, from beginning to end. This will help them come to grips with the high tech world they're going to be part of.

041 How Bad Is It?

It's awful. *National Geographic* found that 14% of American adults couldn't find the U.S. on a world map. 56% don't have any idea of our population. 25% couldn't find Central America on a world map. Even the Mexicans beat us in geography!

Omni pointed out that among young adults less than 40% can understand a *New York Times* article or figure out their change when paying for lunch! Only 20% of high school juniors could fill out a job application for summer work. Less than 30% of high school seniors can place the Civil War within 50 years. The top 5% of our 12th graders came in last of 11 competing nations in standardized math tests. These are our politicians, businessmen and scientists of the 21st century.

Even today, engineers find half of their professional knowledge obsolete within five years. We've got to make sure our youngsters are on a life learning track.

As an engineer used to designing and building circuits with vacuum tubes, I had to start all over when transistors replaced them in the 1960s. Then came digital electronics and computers, so I had to start over again and learn a whole new technology in the 1970s. Then came digital audio in the 1980s, sending me back to my books again. Now it's quantum electronics and chaos theory applications which have me busy learning.

With new technologies developing at an ever faster clip, the importance of continuing one's technical education is going to be even more important. Can we afford to leave this to luck or should we recognize this fact of modern life and make sure New Hampshire does all it can to provide what's needed to keep our state on top?

As we need ever more high-tech courses we're going to have to recognize the value of known experts and make it possible for them to come in and help teach. The exclusion of people with specialized experience from teaching because they haven't graduated from a teacher's college needs to be ended.

In addition to making it possible for experts to be brought in to help teach, we need to examine our New Hampshire teaching institutions and make some major changes in their curricula. Instead of dictating how they should teach our teachers, perhaps we can give them an outline of what we expect their teachers should be able to teach and let them work out the details.

044 Accountability

It's interesting that while the costs of public school education have risen from $1,000 per student in 1951 (in constant dollars) to $5,000 today, SAT scores have dropped 10%. So much for spending more on "education" (*Forbes* 5/14/90 p82). "SAT scores, whatever their weaknesses, do have one indisputable virtue: They are the single best predictor of the college grades the test-takers will eventually achieve.

"Spending per pupil after adjusting for inflation has roughly quintupled since 1946 . . . which means that productivity has apparently fallen by 80%, even assuming the output quality is constant."

And one more little quote from the *Forbes* article, " . . . graduate degrees have no demonstrable relationship to better teaching." Golly, that almost is enough to make a reasonable person question what's going on.

The above data suggests that a major reform of our educational system here in New Hampshire could cut our school costs by 50-80% and we could still end up with a far better product.

New York City spends over $6,000 per high school student. Of that, one half is spent by the central bureaucracy. Less than one-third reaches the classroom to pay for teachers and other costs (*Forbes* 6/25/90 p.52). "In the state of New York there are more administrators than there are in all of the European Community, and the E.C. has 12 countries and 320 million people" (*Time*).

A science survey showed that only 73% of Americans know that the earth goes around the sun; 45% knew that it does so once a year; 43% knew that electrons are smaller than atoms (*US News* 11/4/88 p.60).

"The most recent international mathematics study reported that *average* Japanese students exhibited higher levels of achievement than the top 5% of American students enrolled in college preparatory mathematics courses." (*Society for Applied Learning Technology Newsletter,* Summer '88). It goes on to say, "Despite the fact that demonstrations of technology-based learning systems produce significant positive change, there is yet to be the recognition that the present methods are inadequate, are not working, and show little promise of making the positive changes that technology-based learning has shown to accomplish."

How do American kids compare with the Japanese in the way they spend their time? "During elementary school, Japanese kids spend 52% more hours in the classroom than American children. In high school the gap widened to about 60%. The homework comparison is even more lopsided. In primary school, Japanese youngsters spend 8.3 hours a week studying, while American kids spend just 1.8 hours. In junior high school, the gap grows to 16.2 hours vs. 3.2 hours. And in high school, it is 19 hours vs. 3.8. In addition, Japanese kids spend two to three times as many hours reading as American kids." (*Business Week* 7/22/91 p.12).

043 Okay, It's Bad

With the situation a national problem, what can New Hampshire do to at least start turning it around in our state? I believe there are three major initiatives we can implement which could serve as an example of what can be done. They would also help give New Hampshire a clear advantage over other states in building a high-tech work force.

One is the founding of a publication to provide communications for educators anywhere in the world who are interested in improving educational productivity.

The second would be to establish a for-profit research institute to study the impact of our current educational process through surveys of graduates and their employers.

The third would be the introduction of an eight-year course in the fundamentals of electronics, communications and computers for grades 5-12. This would be taught by a combination of a weekly magazine and what is called peer-teaching.

I'll go into these last two concepts in some depth, hoping to at least counter a fair number of the horrified objections which could be raised by people who haven't much background in science or new teaching technologies.

My three basic proposals all have two common threads — they are relatively inexpensive to initiate and they should be profit-making enough to more than pay back the startup investment. I can't help it, that's my entrepreneurial approach and I apologize for any stress this causes dedicated true-believing socialists.

044 Teaching Skills

In addition to teaching our children what they need to know to make a good living, introducing them to the arts, teaching them how to get along in society, and so on, isn't it a good idea to include some skills they may find useful . . . in addition to basic skills such as reading and writing. Even these can be expanded to speed reading, business correspondence writing, report writing, and public speaking.

Other skills? How about teaching the fundamentals of skiing, roller and ice skating, driving, dancing, cycling, running, horseback riding, sailing, playing an instrument or two, swimming, scuba, typing, drawing, fencing, and bowling? These fun skills are worth having, so why not include 'em at least as options in the curriculum? How about metal working, woodworking, printing, and typesetting?

Some of these skills call for fairly heavy equipment expenditures. We can't very well teach woodworking without shop equipment, so how can we possibly hope to be able to afford to equip a hundred or more schools with what's needed to teach carpentry, metalworking, electronics, chemistry, computer use, basic plumbing, etc?

Faced with the obviously impossible, should we give up and settle for less? Or should we look for creative answers? Like perhaps workshops on wheels which can be moved from school to school, bringing the equipment to the students instead of the other way around?

I enjoyed learning how to use wood and metalworking equipment in school. I enjoyed using a forge to make a length of chain and building a small radio in the electronic lab.

They taught us to read music in the second grade. I wonder if they do that in any New Hampshire schools? And they brought in a record player and taught us to recognize a wide variety of classical music in grammar school.

I'd like to make sure that every youngster in New Hampshire is at least exposed to a hundred or so kinds of music. If we leave it to their parents, as we have so far, apparently all they'll hear is rock and rap. That's terrible! I'd like to make sure that they at least have an opportunity to hear some other kinds of music . . . and hear it under good conditions.

I'm about to try and educate the general public along this line by setting up "Rock Free Zones" in record stores. Here they'll find all kinds of music . . . except rock. There'll be ragtime, old time piano, country fiddling, square dances, cajun, zydeco, polkas, accordion, French Canadian, bluegrass, Russian bluegrass, German folk, marches, classical music of all genres, theater organ, show tunes, movie music, dixieland, jazz of all kinds, blues, big band, carousel band organ, circus band, calliope, calypso, Antilles, Caribe, Chinese, creole, choral and so on.

I hope some day to make special compact discs for schools so kids can hear what they've been missing by tuning in exclusively to the Top-40 stations. I'd like to organize some reasonably priced hi-fi systems on wheels which can be moved in a small van, making it so several schools could have the benefit of each system once a week for an hour. It might be possible to schedule the music hour into up to four schools a day, thus making one equipment investment serve up to 20 schools. One teacher/driver, with the help of students to roll the equipment, could handle the whole works.

Yes, I might eventually make some money from such a project, but if I do, I'll do the same as I have always done when I've made money . . . I'll reinvest it in still another project which I believe has long-range benefits for society.

045 Vocational Education

Since I've made few bones about my feelings about colleges as they are now being run, what alternatives are there? I suppose it's impractical to expect everyone to be an entrepreneur, so I shouldn't try to get all our youngsters educated for entrepreneurship.

I'm not going to instantly change our college system, no matter how rotten it is. But if we make more youngsters aware of how little they are going to gain from college we might be able to encourage enough of them to pursue other alternatives so that colleges will be forced to change or go out of business.

Indeed, it wouldn't take much of a drop in college-bound students to kill off hundreds of colleges. Colleges are hurting. The baby bust is here and those piles of applications are a memory. Colleges have to advertise and promote to fill their classes. And it's only going to get worse.

Until we start seeing some re-invented colleges which are geared to providing the education youngsters actually need to cope with our high-tech world, I'd recommend youngsters consider apprenticeship as an alternative.

I'd hire someone who walked in and wanted to learn everything in the world about magazine circulation in a minute. I might not even check to see if they could read or write. Ditto anyone who asked to learn advertising sales.

I desperately need people who can write, copy edit, proofread, telemarket, and so on. When I hire someone to work in the mail room, it's with the understanding that if they're still there in six months, they'll be fired to make room for someone who wants to use the opportunity to learn about publishing, marketing, mail order, and so on. The last thing I need is to have people working for me who are content to do one particular job for life.

That brings me to vocational education, which is a great concept. We need apprentice carpenters, plumbers, printers, electronic technicians, heating experts, air conditioning experts, car repairers, and so on. I would like to encourage voc-ed schools to add courses in entrepreneurial fundamentals so their students will at least have an opportunity to do better than be a plumber's helper for the next 10 years. We should also teach them how to run their own businesses . . . things like accounting, salesmanship, speaking, writing, desktop publishing, purchasing, etc.

Alas, most of these people will not be contributing directly to the income New Hampshire firms derive from other states and countries. But at least our supporting businesses will be run more efficiently and with better quality control.

046 A Technical Institute?

If it's possible to implement my plan to teach technology to grades 5-12, which should result in our generating two or three thousand engineering oriented high school graduates a year within five to 10 years, we're going to lose them to out-of-state technical schools unless we build one in New Hampshire for them.

Several years ago I was considering starting just such a college, but it just wasn't the right time. I found I would be facing almost insurmountable odds in finding teachers who would teach the way I wanted. I found the college accreditation system would be even more impossible to challenge.

I found a great spot for the college on the north side of Manchester, where it would be close enough to Manchester, Concord and Nashua to service not only youngsters, but also to run evening classes for business people interested in developing their marketing and other business skills.

If New Hampshire were to back the building of a state-of-the-art polytechnical institute based on my concepts it would (a) offer free tuition to all students, (b) make a profit and thus recover its building and start-up cost, (c) would revolutionize American education, (d) would turn out engineers in three years instead of four, (e) would be worldclass in research, (f) would attract the best in teachers, (g) would help New Hampshire attract high-tech entrepreneurial businesses, (h) would attract highly motivated students from all over the world.

Further, by including a heavy schedule of entrepreneurial subjects, the graduates would be equipped not only technically, but also would be well grounded in business, making them ideal employees for New Hampshire high-tech businesses.

The school would be open evenings and weekends for local business people interested in building their entrepreneurial skills.

The school could not only develop these business courses for local consumption, but could then put them on videotape and sell them to people in every country in the world, dubbed into the local language. Business information is desperately needed today to help Eastern European countries convert from socialism to capitalism . . . plus their eventual need in the USSR and even China . . . plus a hundred or so third world countries. There is a multi-billion-dollar market for first-rate educational videos.

The technology will be here soon allowing educational videos to be interactive with students. 3-D, even holographics are coming. Such videos, backed by the power of peer teaching, with perhaps direct satellite access to live experts once a week, are the way things are heading.

These things aren't far in the future. You should see the state-of-the-art recording studio in my barn. And then there's the video editing and desktop publishing system my wife has in our dining room, which it fills. She's in the video production and marketing business, with over 120 how-to-dance videos (so far) being marketed worldwide.

Later in this possibly endless report you'll find details on the business courses I recommend be taught. If your reaction is normal, you'll want to sign up for a dozen or so right away.

Chapter II

047 Commission Resources

Not being a big fan of re-inventing the wheel, I suggest we (the Commission) draw upon every resource we can in our pursuit of a quality set of recommendations to the legislature and the executive for ways to improve the quality of life in New Hampshire.

For instance, in looking through what information I've gotten so far I see that there are a number of state groups which may well have done some research which would benefit us. We may be able to get reports on their research and even on any possible recommendations which they may have made based upon that research. We would be delinquent if we passed up investigative work which has already been done.

Here's a list of the state groups which seem likely to be able to help us with input on their research and recommendations. We need to know in which areas of our economy there have been changes, so historical data from many of these groups should be valuable.

NH Job Training Council, Inc.
NH Small Business Development Center
Office of State Planning
Venture Capital Network, Inc.
NH Dept. of Employment Security
NH Dept. of Environmental Services
NH Port Authority
NH Dept. of Postsecondary Technical Education
NH Industrial Development Authority
NH Dept. of Labor
NH Dept. of Transportation
State Occupational Information Coordinating Committee
Governor's Energy Office
Governor's Educational Task Force
Job Training Council
NH International Trade Association
Small Business Development Center

I'm sure there are many more which I haven't discovered and would appreciate your helping me make the above list more complete.

Of course, the above array of departments, councils and so forth make me wonder who's in charge of which, how many people are involved in each, what the mission is of each entity, how much they are costing, who's paying the bill and how we can find out what costs are being charged to what?

This also brings up, in my mind, what duplication we may be inadvertantly considering with similar groups in other states . . . and how we can go about getting copies of their data, reports and recommendations.

For instance, in *Forbes* (9/16/91 p.124) the Massachusetts Pioneer Institute for Public Policy Research has done some valuable studies. There's the Hartford-based Yankee Institute for Public Policy Studies, Pennsylvania's Commonwealth Foundation for Public Policy Alternatives, the Washington Institute for Policy Studies, the Mackinac Center for Public Policy and so on. How can we get inputs from these and other such resources?

As we get into educational reform recommendations, we'll want to get as much input as we can from think tank groups in this field such as the National Assn. for Industry-Education Cooperation (NAIEC).

Despite all of the reading I've done on education; despite my visiting endless colleges and talking with college presidents; despite my keeping up with the major educational publications, I realize that there's still an enormous amount of homework to be done if I'm to have a good grasp of the history, the problems and the potential solutions to our educational disaster.

Governor Gregg made it clear in his talk to the Manchester Chamber that we're going to be facing incredible obstacles from well-heeled unions when we start to make recommendations involving either the state bureaucracy or education. We'll be up against massive lobbying power in Concord. However, if we're careful and have the strength of logic and reason on our side, and if we go about backing up our recommendations with a good marketing plan, we have a good chance at success.

Since we know that the present educational system isn't working, the pressures against change are working from a weak position. Keeping in mind that when politics (money) is involved, reason can get seriously twisted and mangled by clever media manipulators.

Perhaps, knowing how the media work and their penchant for emphasizing bad news and tending to go for headlines, we might consider a preemptive move. For instance, could we include investigative reporters from several of the larger New Hampshire news organizations as ex-officio (whatever that means) members of the Commission? By their being part of the Commission, they would be able to help keep the public aware of our progress. They would be in a position to counter dishonest or distorting attacks from threatened organized power groups and help the media be even-handed in its reporting.

The downside of making our workings open to the media is that it might tend to frustrate any ideas we might have of organizing a coup and taking over the state government. Other than that, the more distribution the information we develop gets, the better. We're trying to find out what's wrong, what's right, repair the wrongs as best we can and reward those doing right. Are we going to be doing anything we should keep secret?

048 An Action Plan

Presuming that all of us will be wanting to get as much information as possible, how can we go about (a) getting it and (b) distributing it?

And what about our exchange of ideas? I've taken the initiative of putting my ideas into writing, dumping 'em into a Macintosh desktop publishing system, printing 'em out, photocopying the results and mailing them to the Commission members. I doubt if all of you are as geared up for the information age as I am.

We need to get input from every Commissioner so we can take advantage of the wide variety of experience and skills which have been tapped. Here we are several weeks into the Commission's operations and communications have so far been minimal.

I have gotten a couple faxes about the proposed mission statements. This was the first that I became aware that an executive committee had been elected by our Commission. No doubt I was dozing off during our first meeting when this election happened. All I remember clearly was my intense relief when someone else was elected as the vice chairman of the group. I'm trying to run a fair-sized publishing, recording, mail order, music distribution, importing, exporting, etc., company, so my time is limited.

So how are we going to be able to work as a group? What communications system do you propose so we can share data and ideas? Will we have a central office and a staff to get the data we need? What about a budget for all this? If I want to know what a Michigan think tank has found out which might well save us a lot of time, do I have to find their address and get in touch with them myself? Then how do I share the information with you?

We're coming on to our second meeting and I've no hint as yet as to how we're going to be able to work as a group when we are so geographically separated. Will we have 33 Commissioners faxing each other day and night? And what about Commissioners who don't have fax machines at hand? I have three at the office and one at my home office. Plus I'm on Prodigy, MCI, Compuserve and even have my own bulletin board system. How about you?

Perhaps we can address this concern of mine at the next meeting.

049 Whistle Blowing

Are there any members of the Commission who disagree that lowering taxes will tend to improve New Hampshire's quality of life? I hope you'll further agree that one very good way to make it possible to lower taxes is to cut state spending. Another is to tap the federal government for every penny we can get. That's presumably one of the more significant goals of our senators and congressmen in Washington.

Governor Gregg was quite clear in his Chamber address this year that he is opposed to a broad-based tax. I hope you've read his talk. He points out that New Hampshire already has the lowest tax burden on its people as a percentage of income in the country with a total tax of less than 10%.

He goes on to point out that you can't manage government from the spending side of the ledger. "If you turn revenues over the the legislative body, whether at the local level, the county level, the state level or especially the federal level, it will be spent . . . unless you can contract revenue sources, you will never contract or control the rate of growth of government." Bravo Guv!

As we sort through what the state is doing, has done and plans to do, I suspect we'll find some areas where we will recommend that more money be spent. These will probably be popular with our legislators. We'll also be likely to find some areas where we believe economies can be observed. I doubt these will be popular with anyone. Indeed, I expect we'll be faced with a good deal of obfuscation when we get into these areas.

There are a couple of possible approaches to tackling this problem. Let's first look at finding areas of fairly obvious waste. As parsimonious as we are up here in New Hampshire, you know as well as I that we're going to be able to uncover some really upsetting waste. It's a given with any bureaucracy, private or public.

One more thing we know . . . where there's wasted money there are some people who know it's happening. We also know that we martyr the hell out of anyone who dares blow the whistle. We fire them. We blackball them. We even kill them. They are hated and scourged. We call them rats or finks.

Even so, when the waste gets really bad there are some public-spirited people who are willing to brave the consequences. They complain first to their supervisors. Nothing, of course happens other than a warning to shut up. It isn't until we see a segment on "60 Minutes" that the fat finally hits the fire. Then, extremely reluctantly, something occasionally gets done to fix the problem.

Did you see the recent segment about how the Rural Electrification Authority (REA) is giving about $600 million in low interest loans to huge corporations? No amount of whistle blowing has managed to counter the lobbyist pressures which control Congress. Even the REA president hasn't been able to stop the give-away.

Things might be a little easier to tackle on a state level, if we're really seriously interested in cutting waste. Of course, with fairly heavy legislative representation on the Commission, perhaps I'm getting myself into deep trouble by even bringing this up. Is the fox minding the chicken house? Have we a conflict of interest? I hope not.

Let's look at the thing creatively. We know we have waste in our state government. We know also that we'd like to cut as much of that as we can. At least I hope that's what we want. Yes, it might mean putting an uncle or cousin out of work. Ouch!

We also agree, I hope, that we may be able to find some state employees who are well aware of the waste and are not happy about it . . . but may be justifiably afraid to say anything. How can we make it safe for whistle-blowers? How can we protect them from the normal vicious bureaucratic backlash?

One way might be for a third party, pledged to total secrecy, to get the information and pass it along to us. We can't ask for it directly as long as we have legislators as members of our group. Is this a group that the governor might be able to set up? Since he's committed to cutting expenses, as far as I know, a committee reporting to our Commission and the governor might be able to insulate whistle-blowers from retribution.

Or we might set up a Commission sub-group which would be made up of non-government members.

050 A Second Approach

Another way to cut state expenses would be to set up a system which would make it worthwhile for the state employees involved to effect economies. For instance, we know that there's often a rush to spend everything in a department budget before the end of the fiscal year. The employees know that if it isn't all spent they'll have a hard time getting even more next year. I believe there was a department in a western state once which did not request a higher budget for the next year.

Suppose we set up a system where the employees of a department would be able to split what was left over unspent at the end of the year? The hand of Adam Smith would smite them and temporary greed would overcome any long-range charitable motives. They'd save every nickel they could and make the year-end jackpot as big as possible, and to hell with next year. That's the way capitalism works.

No, we wouldn't save any money the first year, but we'd see a downward spiral of state expenses thereafter. Supervisors would weigh the prestige of having three assistants against splitting one of their salaries at the end of the year. Prestige or cash? We'd see some nervous breakdowns over those decisions. I think cash will win every time.

Presuming that you've read Parkinson's books on bureaucracies, wherein his rule number one is that the work will expand to fill the time available to do it. The opposite should hold just as well . . . work will contract as the time available to do it is reduced.

Parkinson showed that in one bureaucracy after another the tendency was to expand, even when the overall amount of work was lessening. I'd like to see our state government get boiled down to the minimum of departments and staff. Of course I'd like to see the same process in Washington, but that's going to be much more than 50 times as difficult to tackle.

But, you object, how can we know when we're understaffed and doing too little? That's easy, let's ask the customers. Let's ask our people what they think of our state employees and departments. When we find the quality, let's reward it. When we get complaints, let's make changes. Let's run our state government just like we would a business, trying to provide a quality service. Just as quality pays for itself in business, I believe quality will pay for itself in government . . . state or federal.

Yes, I know, as Aesop taught, you can't please everybody. But we can be sensitive to quality problems and consider correcting them when it is practical. Last night I was shopping in Sun Foods in Keene and I had a gripe. They've recently redone their store and since then several of the things that I've gone there to buy for years were no longer available. I mentioned this to the checkout woman. She said that wasn't her department, that I should talk with Customer's Service. I went there and explained my problem to the woman behind the service counter. She gave me a form and said I would have to fill it out, that it wasn't her job to listen to customer complaints.

I only spend about $60 a week at Sun Foods, so I doubt they'll miss my $3,000 a year . . . and I'm probably the only person in New Hampshire who would be upset enough over a little thing like that to shop elsewhere. Yet, what they're doing goes against the way the world is going. Business has been finding that it has to provide the products and services people want, when they want them. This is beginning to be difficult for megacorporations. They can't react fast enough to market changes and new technologies. I hope you haven't missed the Tom Peters PBS shows on this subject.

This is another reason for New Hampshire to make our business climate as cooperative as possible for smaller businesses. But even our state bureaucracy is going to have to bow to this change in consumer pressures and be more responsive in giving us what we want, when we want it, and at the price we want to pay.

We want the police to help when we need help and not to harass us at other times. We want to have as much freedom as we can, recognizing that this is not a license to upset others. We don't mind paying our fair share of expenses, but we do object to being taken advantage of.

If we had some sort of a state Quality Control department where anyone could bring complaints and suggestions, we might be able to start making state services more cost effective. I'd be surprised if we might not be able to eventually cut state expenses to a fraction of what we're spending today. What an example we'd provide for the rest of the country . . . and even for other countries. This is, I believe, all within our grasp as a commission, if we have the courage to tackle it. This small group is in a position to make a profound change in the world. It wouldn't be the first time that the world was changed by some gutsy people in New England.

051 More Help For Entrepreneurs

In the short run, say in two to three years, I believe we can increase New Hampshire's revenues best by concentrating on building up our tourist industry. In the long run, say in 10 years, we're going to have to provide business with an educated, motivated high-tech work force. That leaves the medium run to be covered, so let's consider what we can do to improve our business climate so as to have a strong impact in perhaps three to five years.

I hope you'll agree with me that our best bet for New Hampshire's long-range strength lies in building up currently active small businesses, attracting new ones, and helping new businesses to get started. I can think of at least a couple of things we could do which should help improve New Hampshire's small business climate. I'm sure the other Commission members will have many more excellent ideas for us to consider.

I'm not sure how good a system we have in place right now for putting jobs together with people, but we should take maximum advantage of computers to offer a statewide service for both people and employers. Can I call now and get a list of people looking for work who are experienced in working with Macintosh desktop publishing systems? Or perhaps I'm looking for an assistant, what we used to call a Gal Friday. Now, I suppose it's a Person Friday. But with a computer system that can search only by job title and not skills, I'm not going to get much help.

Another way we can help small businesses to prosper is to implement adult education courses designed specifically to help them cope with their needs.

While I've included these adult courses in my proposal for a New Hampshire Polytechnic Institute, which I believe will be needed to cope with a flood of high-tech oriented high school graduates, we could keep our local schools busy evenings with them, thus providing a boost for entrepreneurs almost immediately.

053 · Entrepreneurial Education

Here are some courses I would have found of enormous value if they'd been available when I was frittering away my school years with junk like Strength of Materials, Mechanics (bridge design), Economics, Advanced Calculus and so on.

Speaking. This is a critically important skill for entrepreneurs. We have to be comfortable and persuasive addressing trade, engineering and public groups. We have to be able to do radio and TV interviews, and chair symposiums. Being able to speak well also helps in committee and corporate board meetings.

Writing. Having evaluated and edited thousands of articles submitted to my magazines over the last 40 years, I assure you that the ability to write clearly and simply is rare.

Speed Reading. To keep up with today's world you have to be able to speed read. With political events and technologies moving rapidly, we need to read a couple books a month, plus a stack of magazines.

Personnel Management. How do you convince people to do what you want them to and like it? This skill does not come naturally, it has to be learned. It's a very necessary skill because without it a company can flounder. Few committee-managed companies last long. It takes the driving passion of an entrepreneur to keep small companies strong while technology and public demands constantly change. I've watched many large companies lose billions through bad management. I've watched thousands of smaller ones fail.

Quality Control. Shades of Ed Demming, who convinced the Japanese that quality could turn their weak economy around. He tried to sell quality to American business, but we wanted no part of it. "Americans will always buy American cars, no matter how we make them." Sure. But we're in competition with the whole world now, so we have to understand that quality control is no longer just in manufacturing, it's also critically important in research, design, customer service, advertising, promotion, supplier dealings and so on. Youngsters need to understand the concept that "quality is free." The costs of providing quality will always more than repay themselves.

Statistical Analysis. Modern scientific calculators can help us sort through a maze of statistics, once we know how to use them. For instance, about the only way to accurately determine the best retail price for a product is to test it statistically. How many people know how to handle that?

Advertising. Businesses waste tons of money because they have no one with an education in advertising around. One of the best business moves I ever made was taking a night course at the New York Advertising Institute. I've run into a few ad agencies that know what they're doing, but most are shams and make up for their ignorance with outrageous prices.

Promotion. I got so fed up with trying to deal with inept PR firms that in frustration I put together a $99 video explaining the inside secrets on how to generate an extra million dollars in sales just with PR. Small businesses should learn how to use new product releases and reviews to increase their visibility. If their prospective customers are unaware of their company and their products, they sure aren't going to sell. Advertising, when done right, works fine, but well done PR can save a fortune.

Business Planning. Entrepreneurs need to know how to put together business plans. They need them to attract venture capital and as guides for running their businesses. They need to know how to build action, cash-flow, P&L, and net worth plans.

Accounting. With hundreds of computer accounting programs, which are going to be best suited for your business? You don't want to have to contort your business to make it work with the wrong accounting program. Worse, complex businesses may call for several accounting systems. You may need one to generate IRS reports, and another to manage cash flow.

Desktop Publishing. Entrepreneurs need to know about the latest systems. They need desktop publishing for newsletters, catalogs, advertising, spec sheets, instructions, booklets, or perhaps to present a report such as this. My wife uses a Macintosh system to design her video boxes, produce catalogs, a newsletter and so on. My own firm is in the process of replacing a $500,000 typesetting system with Macintoshes costing less than one-tenth that. We use 'em to produce over a dozen publications, plus liner notes for CDs and a variety of catalogs.

Financing. Enterpreneurs need to know where and how to get money for startups and growth. Banks? Venture capital firms? How about going public? ESOPs? Limited partnerships?

Selling. Selling is not a natural talent, it has to be learned. It's a marvelous skill and no entrepreneur should be without it. Nor should any salesperson. Once you know how to sell, you'll never go hungry.

Direct Mail. Entrepreneurs need to learn how to design and write direct mail packages. They need to find out what has worked for others and what hasn't. Billions of dollars have been spent on direct mail research, yet most entrepreneurs dive into this business blind . . . and waste enormous amounts of money.

Numerical Control. Most manufacturing these days is automated and that means computer control of machines. This is a specialized business, but it still needs to be learned.

New Product Introduction. This calls for a combination of advertising, PR, new products releases, catalog sheets, packaging, pricing decisions, distribution alternatives, and so on. I'm planning on changing the music industry with an entirely new distribution system.

Packaging. How would you go about getting a special box made for your product? How about a molded box? Or a foam-lined shipping container? What works best in advertising on the package?

That's just a few courses which would help small businesses operate more efficiently. I'd also recommend courses in graphic arts, product photography, purchasing, ergonomics, building and site selection, production planning, office planning, dressing for success, print buying, bill collecting, taxes, business law, word processing systems, communications systems . . . including paging, fax, bulletin boards, intercoms, data services, etc.

Entrepreneurs need to be able to learn about computers, data base management, inventory handling, and payroll systems. They need education in office equipment buying and leasing. What are the best copiers, telephone switches, microfilm systems?

If New Hampshire can organize adult educational courses such as these, we'll start attracting new businesses from all over the country. Just think of the promotional piece the state could send out to entrepreneurs promoting New Hampshire as the entrepreneur's paradise!

New Hampshire businesses, by being able to operate more efficiently, would soon be big winners. Wasting less money on poor ads, PR, packaging, inefficient distribution and so on will enrich us all and contribute positively to our New Hampshire quality of life.

And since every one of these educational courses will make money for the school offering it, there's no expense to the state. Everybody wins.

If the courses are good, businesses will be sending their people in for them, paying their way. I'll bet a good course in how to sell would be sold out in an hour.

Where can we get the expert teachers we'll need? I suggest we call on local entrepreneurs. I love to teach and have lectured at colleges all around the country and on every continent. You'll find plenty of volunteers who will be delighted to teach the things they've learned.

The courses I've outlined are the same ones business schools should be teaching, but aren't. If you've been reading your business magazines you know that business schools have been losing their charm because they aren't teaching the right things. This opens an opportunity for New Hampshire to become the business school capital of the country. We could have businesses sending in customers from all over the country.

We could organize two-week intensive management packages, charge $2,995 or so (plus room), and get it. We'd work 'em night and day, seven days a week, giving them more than their money's worth. Oops, there's my entrepreneurial spirit showing again.

053 Doubling Tourism

Since we're in need of a fast fix for our recession, the most practical approach for generating more revenues for the state seems to me to try and expand what is already our largest industry: tourism. Since this is an entrepreneurial industry, we'll quickly generate more jobs this way too.

The first step is to creatively approach the problem. What changes can we make in what we've been doing to increase tourism? Being in the information business, I oddly enough tend to think in terms of information.

When you want to sell a product your first move is to put yourself in the position of your customer and ask what would sell me? Okay, what would convince me to spend some vacation time in New Hampshire? Having done that many times, I didn't have any problem coming up with some ideas.

Now, with all due lack of respect to the brains that generated our license plate mottos, "Scenic New Hampshire" and "Photoscenic New Hampshire, " I think we can do a bunch better than that. Sure, I enjoy scenery and love to take pictures, but that's not likely to get me to drive from New York City to New Hampshire.

What have we got that's even better than scenery to sell? We've got *fun* to sell, so let's get started selling it.

When it came time to bid on producing a new New Hampshire tourist guide I bid on the job, suggesting a whole new approach to selling the state. I wanted to put out a guide to what there is to do in New Hampshire, not another boring scenic guide to the various regions, as in the past. The tourism department bought scenery again. Playing it safe, no doubt.

Like most people, I enjoy doing things, so I knew what I wanted in a guide for myself. I wanted to know what there is to do, where I can do it, how much it costs, and so on.

Take water sports, for example. We have canoe rentals where you can paddle down a river all day, stopping off for a swim and picnic lunch. At the end you and your canoe are picked up and driven back to the starting point. It makes a wonderful day's vacation.

We have tubing rentals, kayaks, water slides, wind surfing, and white water rafting. How about a guide for visiting fishing fans? And one to New Hampshire swimming holes and beaches?

How about winter when we have downhill and cross country skiing, snowmobile trails, winter mountain climbing, ice racing, ice fishing, and snowshoeing? We may even have ice boat racing, for all I know. I'd sure love to try it.

Then there's the air, with flying lessons, gliding, para-gliding, ultra-lights, ballooning, hang-gliding, and sky diving. We have things like these going on all over the state.

Where and when are the antique fairs, flea markets, and collections? We have county fairs, antique shows, mineral shows, crafts fairs, and much more.

Then there are our musical and theater events. If people in nearby Massachusetts and Vermont had a way of knowing that the famous Russian bluegrass group Kukuruza was playing at The Folkway in Peterborough, the place would have been packed solid. A few days later they were performing at the Grand Ol' Opry. We have name stars performing around New Hampshire. If we had some way to get the word out we'd have long lines of fans driving up and down to hear them.

If they can run successful music festivals in Aspen, we sure can run some whoppers in New Hampshire. There was a ragtime music festival in Maine in late October, with world-famous ragtime performers doing shows in Madison, Camden, Bangor and Bar Harbor, to packed houses. We should have brought them into Manchester, Nashua and Keene at least.

We have an incredible number of fun things to do in New Hampshire. What we don't have is a good way to attract people to the state to enjoy the fun. We need to get information about our activities to everyone in New England and points south and west.

I have in mind two solutions to the problem. Both would require initial funding, but would eventually not only repay the funding, but would turn profits. I don't know any way to set up a new business without some up-front costs.

054 New Hampshire ToDo

Being a publisher, for some odd reason I tend to think in terms of publications when there are things which need promoting. The idea I'm about to suggest is not a new one for me. I almost started a *Boston ToDo* magazine. I'd hired an editor, writers, an ad sales staff, and rented sales offices in Winchester when the gasoline shortage brought pleasure travel to a halt. Oops!

A year later I got involved in starting a series of computer magazines and never had time for my ToDo idea. Then I got involved in the music industry, but even so, starting ToDo publications has always been not far from the front burner.

Since it would obviously be not just an enormous conflict of interest if I were to suggest me starting a *New Hampshire ToDo* publication, but would probably get me drummed off the Commission, I'm not even going to hint at such a move. Wild horses wouldn't change my decision on this.

Being into doing things, the idea of a publication devoted to encouraging people to get out and have fun is exciting. I love to swim, ski, scuba dive, fly, and drive around. The N.H. Miata Club recently climbed Mt. Washington and now is planning a rally. I've got a carton of rally trophies up in the attic somewhere. And one of my editors wants me to go in with him on a couple of ultra-light planes. I've got plenty of room in my back pasture for a landing strip.

Between ads for activities, hotels, restaurants and stores catering to clothes for activities, a publication should be able to get into the black in short order. Building circulation throughout New England and New York might take a little while.

But you know as well as I that if we organize music festivals, winter festivals, fly-ins, car rallies, and so on, we'll pull 'em in from a thousand miles around.

Lacking a *New Hampshire ToDo* publication, which I think could easily double tourism in a couple of years, I have another approach which should help boost the industry.

055 Mini-Vacations

I suggest we start promoting New Hampshire for four-day weekend mini-vacations. Let's get 'em up here Thursday night and send 'em back Monday night. To make it stick we can organize four-day festivals for different interests.

Now, to help visitors find out what is doing where, I suggest we set up computerized kiosks in our state liquor stores. These would have the lastest information on what's doing and make it possible to not only reserve tickets, but also to get guaranteed accommodations. Many foreign cities offer a similar service. It's free to the visitors because the cities get a commission from the hotels. The same system would work here with the commissions paying for the whole system and its operation.

Upon entering New Hampshire I'd stop at a liquor store near the border and find out what special events are on around the state. I could find out where I could go horseback riding and even reserve a horse. I could find out what restaurants are having special feasts, like an Indonesian rijstafel in Derry.

I'd prepay to make sure I had a room, get a receipt, and the computer would pass along my reservation to the hotel, restaurant, theater, etc.

056 Video Too?

With multimedia coming on strong, sales kiosks will eventually have to include not just words and still pictures, but full color videos. As a visitor, wouldn't you like to see a short video showing you a hotel you're thinking of visiting? Or, a little less costly, and easily stored on compact discs, is combined still pictures and text (CD-ROM). It's possible to store an enormous amount of data on these discs, on 8mm videotapes and on 4mm DAT tapes.

I'm familiar with the technology because I've released a CD-ROM which lists over 45,000 compact discs, complete with 30-second digital sound samples and full-color pictures of the CD covers for many of the CDs. It also contains every review published in my magazine since it started . . . thousands of them. It's amazing how much information can be stored on these CD-ROMs.

I'd like to be able to stop off at a state liquor store/information center and see videos of hotels and other entertainments. Do I want to visit Mystery Hill? Do I want to take kids to the Friendly Farm in Dublin? I'd type in my interests and the system would tell me where to go to have fun.

They'd get me out skiing much more often if I could see a video showing me yesterday's snow conditions at some ski areas. They don't seem to be able to prevent themselves from lying when I telephone to find out conditions. Tough to do? Not with videotape. The ski areas could make tapes in the afternoon, send them by radio to a communications center atop Mt. Washington, where they would be relayed to the information centers during the night. The computer-integrated video system would then find the mountain I'm interested in and let me see for myself how snow conditions were the day before.

If we're going to gear New Hampshire to bring in tourists in larger numbers, we've got to help thousands of small businesses with their marketing. This is a project the state could start, incubate, make profitable and then either sell or take public, with the state retaining an equity in the project and getting a percentage of the action.

We've got plenty of room in our state to develop tourism. I'd like to see some state-coordinated efforts at developing vacation centers. Can we learn from Aspen, Vail and other successful areas and encourage similar vacation towns to be developed in New Hampshire?

A group of my friends from around Boston join me in Aspen every year because we enjoy the restaurants, the shopping and the skiing. There isn't anything comparable in New Hampshire, so we go to the expense and difficulty of going to Aspen.

With some guidance and encouragement from the state we might be able to do more with Lincoln, Franconia and North Conway, making them even bigger winter sports and summer music centers.

With the nearby Eastern Megalopolis to draw from, we're within driving distance of tens of millions of people. All we have to do is (a) provide enough fun to get them to come here and (b) let them know what we have for them.

We might even vie with Atlantic City, attracting bus loads of skiers from Boston, New York, Providence, Hartford and other cities. We could organize tours which would include a Cog Railway trip up Mt. Washington, Lost River, The Flume, shopping in North Conway, and a Canon Mountain Tramway ride. That would fit into a four day mini-vacation just fine. We could even include one of my tapes on "How To Speak N'Hamsha" as part of the package. I can see the TV commercials for the tour now, with Fritz Wetherbee showing off a Cog Railway engine, going through the Lemon Squeezer at Lost River, and maybe taking a dive into the Old Man's Foot Basin. Brrr, that water is cold! I used to swim there before they fenced it all off. Now that's what I call a brisk swim, even in the middle of summer.

Of course, if all we've been appointed to do as a Commission is come up with a Bandaid because our state's economy got burned by the minicomputer disaster and there is no real interest in longer-range-planning, then I'm going to be disappointed. The current recession provides us with an opportunity that is a shame to pass up.

As the weeks go by, we'll see whether we're just a front to give some hidden agendas legitimacy or whether our counsel has honestly been solicited.

057 Mini-Malls

They're trying to teach creativity in some schools and they're not having a lot of success. Well, it's an elusive skill, and we don't do well at teaching skills, so it's no wonder we have so few truly creative people.

Our NEA members all have certificates saying they're qualified to teach. In my K-16 experience, those certificates are pitiful frauds and so are our teacher's colleges. Teaching is another skill which we haven't successfully learned to teach. Perhaps they're using the rote memory system here too.

Getting back to creativity . . . and my apologies for taking another swipe at our rotten educational system . . . but I doubt I'll ever get over my anger at being stunted by a system which was lousy when I was tortured by it 50 years ago and has obviously gotten substantially worse since then.

Does the slave who has been whipped and tied in chains for years and then has the gall to complain deserve to be punished for speaking up 50 years later? Yes, slavery still exists in America. After a couple hundred years of adult slavery we managed to stop that. But remember, it took one hell of a war before the southern half of our country could be "convinced." So we emancipated the adult slaves. It's almost amusing that at about the same time we instituted compulsory education, enslaving our children.

Yes, we did it for their own good. How many times have we tortured people for "their own good?" Great excuse. For some unexplainable reason . . . perhaps a defective genetic problem . . . I was conscious of this enslavery from as far back as I can remember. They're *making* me go to school.

I was a difficult kid. I didn't do things "because everybody did." I didn't cave in to peer pressure. Heck, I still don't. But I believe that most people work better when allowed freedom than they do as slaves . . . than they do when forced, whether they like it or not, to do things.

This lousy attitude caused me considerable grief with my parents and teachers. When I'd be told to do something, I'd want to know why. Yes, under the threat of punishment, I could be forced to comply, but not without anger.

I try to run my business that way. I try to have as few "managers" as possible because managers tend to *tell* people to do things instead of *asking* them. There's a world of difference. I'll do almost anything people ask, but I'll be damned if they're going to tell me what to do.

Oh yes, creativity and trying to teach skills. Speaking French is a skill. I took French in high school for four years and a summer and never learned to speak it. They tried to teach this skill by making me memorize a vocabulary and grammatical rules. Four years of frustration and growing anger for me.

I remember sitting down to memorize a hundred vocabulary words for my nightly homework assignment. In minutes I'd fall asleep at my desk. My folks tried a tutor, but even he couldn't keep me awake. The result was that I flunked French two terms in a row and was forbidden by my school to take it again.

Alas, one of the requirements for most colleges was a foreign language. There not being anyone like me to explain that going to college was just one more peer-pressure and societal con job, I had to change high schools.

I went from a public high school that was in many respects a lot of fun to a private high school. Erasmus Hall, in Brooklyn, had over 10,000 students. And it had a wealth of after-school activities and clubs. I loved these. The classes, with the exception of art, were a drag. Most were large, with 30-50 students, and the teachers bored stiff with their work.

So I changed to McBurney School, a small private high school sharing space in the West Side YMCA on West 63rd Street, just off Central Park. It was an hour and a quarter commute by subway (most of it standing up), plus a walk across the park.

Somehow they got me by and I managed to accrue the required three years of French.

Cut to thirty years later and the availability of an evening adult French course at Conval High School in Peterborough. Maybe by now they've improved language teaching, I thought, so I signed up. It would be fun to learn to speak French. I get to France every now and then and have visited several other French-speaking countries such as Haiti, New Caledonia, Tahiti and Quebec.

When I got back home after the first French class I sat down with a long vocabulary list they gave me to memorize and fell instantly to sleep. So much for learning French.

Am I going to ever get around to creativity? Yes, but first I had to dump my years of frustration and anger on you in hopes that this might help encourage the Commission to tackle the worst part of our educational system. We have an opportunity here in our small, remote state, to make a change. This Commission could instigate this change. I'm just afraid that timidity will reign . . . and we'll succumb to a "we've got to run our businesses, so let's get this Commission thing over with" approach.

Restructuring New Hampshire to be the number one state in America in education, in high-tech and quality of life isn't going to happen in a year. One report from our Commission isn't going to do it. Remember, we have no power other than to advise. Well, that really isn't true. The fact is that if we decide we want it, we have a good deal of power. We may find ourselves being vigorously fought by the legislature, by unions and even by the executive, but we can still prevail, if we have the guts.

I believe we can teach skills in our schools, it's just that they can't be taught using the old methods. Rote memory and quizzes won't cut it. Most skills have to be learned by doing. Years of lectures and demonstrations won't teach you to ride a bike or roller skate. You have to do it. Oh, chalk and talk can be helpful, but that isn't the way skills are learned.

You can't learn to speak to large groups by reading or listening to lectures. You have to do it. Well, creativity is the same. It's a skill and you have to do it. I've been doing it all my life, so I'm good at it. And that brings me, at long last, to mini-malls.

058 The Process

It went like this. I was talking with Jim Kendrick, my general factotum, and I mentioned how Connecticut had eliminated the tolls on their throughway by allowing McDonald's to build their restaurants in the plazas. That's a great way to pay for a highway.

Then Jim asked if it wasn't a little unfair to give one company an exclusive franchise like that? I said, what do you suggest, an endless shopping strip like 101A? Having recently visited the outlet stores in Kittery and Freeport and seeing the crowds they drew, the next jump was easy. How about expanding throughway plazas to mini-malls?

I've noticed some food boutiques in New York where a large restaurant has been broken into mini-restaurants, something like we see in malls, only even smaller. Next to the Empire Hotel on Broadway, just off 63rd (down the block from where my old high school was) is just such a place. It's like Burger King, Pizza-Hut, Chi-Chi, Subway and Steve's boutiques, all in one place.

Suppose we put in rest plazas on our interstates with mini-malls? We could open them to both food and outlet boutiques such as Dansk, Mikasa, TJ Maxx, and so on. The state would get a piece of the action, perhaps 5% off the top for the choice location.

This would give us money to repair and develop our highway infrastructure. It would also help attract tourists because it would make driving our parkways more fun. It could even help bring more business to the areas around the plazas. How about an area in the mini-mall where local businesses could advertise? There might even be some small kiosks with displays from local businesses.

If the mini-malls are located at interstate exits, that would make it even easier to get visitors to patronize nearby shops.

Well, you see how these ideas come into being and then expand almost endlessly. Our mini-malls would make driving in New Hampshire more fun. They would provide a source of revenue to pay for our infrastructure. They'd also help build local revenues.

Each mini-mall could be different, with some having boutiques with toys for kids, others with toys for adults. There'd be scrimshaw, gifts, records (CDs), health foods, snacks, books, magazines, local crafts, etc.

Since most cars have audio cassette players, someone ought to incubate a cassette exchange business. This would go gangbusters. What kinds of cassettes? History, old radio shows, music programs, comedy . . . similar to the programs on airplanes.

My wife bought some cassettes from Knowledge Products which explained in a very interesting way the history of Ireland and the Middle-East. I'd go for those two-cassette programs for $2 anytime!

There are hundreds of books now on cassettes, there just isn't any way to rent them . . . and I'm too cheap to buy most of them. I do have in mind a project for my new recording studios of reading all of the Oz books onto tape. I loved them when I was a kid and read them all over and over. So I had in mind that if they were available on tape it would be something which might keep kids quiet in the back seat during a trip, listening on their own Walkman.

I'm also going to read all of the Ernest Thompson Seton books onto tape for kids. These are the best nature stories I've ever read . . . too bad if you missed them during your childhood.

Kids need to be read to. It's important. "The biggest predictor of scholastic success is the time parents spend reading to their children." (*Fortune* 11/18/91 p.204). Mothers, who spend less than an hour and a half a day on child care (ibid) don't or won't take the time to read to their children . . . so I'll do it via cassettes. Fathers spend less than a half an hour a day with their kids.

My mother read to me during lunch every day and that helped get me interested in reading. "These days children spend more time in front of the television set than in school" (ibid).

"The higher a person's reading skills, the higher his professional achievement. Many media compete with print; none can replace it. No other information technology packs the data into as few widely comprehensible symbols as the written word. None is so portable or so suited to self-packing by users" (ibid).

Yet roughly half of American adults never read books or magazines. Leonard Riggio, CEO of Barnes & Nobel, says half the books his customers buy go unread.

If we're going to offer a motivated, educated work force here in New Hampshire, we've got to encourage our kids to read. I think cassettes of people reading books will help. I'm going to try.

For adults I'll be reading the Kai Lung books by Ernest Bramah. They're not well known, but they are examples of superb writing. You'll love 'em, I guarantee. If these cassettes don't get adults interested in reading, I give up.

We want to make visiting New Hampshire so much fun that we bring people up here from all over the East Coast several times a year. We want to make it easy for them to find out how to rent a cottage on Diamond Pond, a boat on Martin Meadow Pond, and to know about fishing the Connecticut Lakes. We want to get thousands of nature lovers up here to climb all of our mountains over 4,000 feet. Maybe we could offer a special Topping New Hampshire (TNH) passport and have a plaque atop each of the mountains to be photographed beside when they get there? They'd paste in the pictures and get a special award certificate signed by the Governor when they conquor them all. *New Hampshire ToDo* magazine could publish a running score of the TNH participants activities.

How about a Ski New Hampshire passport, with a place for each ski area to punch in the skier? People love contests like that. I've skied nine areas, but I'd hit 'em all if someone came up with an award certificate.

See how the ideas develop? Let's see, what else can we do to bring visitors to New Hampshire? Well, I mentioned music festivals, but I didn't go into 'em in any depth.

I know the ragtime group which performed in Maine would love to tour New Hampshire next spring. They're superb, even if they are personal friends. I don't have the time to organize a New Hampshire Booking Agency, but we sure need one. If one can be organized I'll keep it busy with artists. Being in the music business, I'm getting to know a wide variety of performers . . . and they all know each other.

Joe Walsh of the Eagles is planning to come up here to record some of his rags. He put me in touch with Randy Newman and Leon Redbone. Marty Balin (Jefferson Airplane) just finished a recording at my new studios and he knows dozens of rock artists. I'm not a rock fan, but it hasn't escaped me that a lot of people love rock.

With a New Hampshire Booking Agency we could have music festivals going all around the state almost all year around. In between we could book artists into restaurants, theaters and schools. In my area we have artists performing at the Rynborn in Antrim, The Folkway in Peterborough, Del Rossi's in Dublin, and so on. We can keep music lovers not only coming to New Hampshire, we can have them driving all over the state.

The more we can book artists into schools the better. The Maine ragtime group performed free in several schools and the kids went crazy over ragtime.

Those are just a few of my ideas. By now you're probably straining at the bit with a bunch of your own that mine sparked. I think we can keep New Hampshire busy with creative growth plans for years to come.

We can also make a big deal out of sports such as lawn bowling, orienteering, croquet, marksmanship, horse shows, etc., and promote championships. These activities make good television, and that's great free advertising for New Hampshire.

059 A High-Tech Generation

Let's look ahead 10 years . . . 2002 . . . our next palindromic year. We know that if New Hampshire is going to have a high-tech oriented work force available by then that we've got to make some massive changes in our educational system now.

We also know, unless we've truly hermitted ourselves, that the people who are going to be making the money are going to be working with their minds, not their hands. Modern communications and transportation will have, even more than today, destroyed both national and geographic borders when it comes to competition.

This means that for every educational level there will be competition which will force wages down. It means that the rich will get richer and the poor, poorer . . . not a new concept. It means that third-world countries that don't figure this out and start educating their people are going to be at the bottom of the world's economic food chain.

The top people in the chain will be the best educated . . . and not just the best educated in general, but those best educated to cope with technology.

I see it in a microcosm in my own work, and so do you. In publishing we're headed down the same path as the computer industry is going and this is destroying old companies which have not adapted to the new technology.

I mentioned earlier what is happening to the computer giants and how they are in the process of being destroyed by a new technology which they refused to face. IBM is a goner in the long run. The whole premise of the company was based on a technological infrastructure which is being destroyed by the microcomputer.

By miniaturizing computers and putting them onto smaller and smaller integrated circuit chips, the cost of computing has been coming down, month by month. It was this miniaturization and the lower costs it brought which made the minicomputer possible in the 1960s. Entrepreneurs jumped in and challenged the mainframe computer firms such as Honeywell, General Electric and RCA. And they killed them. Data General, DEC, Wang, Prime and Centronics grew into giants.

But these giants were blinded by their success and suffered the same arrogance that killed the mainframers and is presently eroding IBM. They ignored the inevitable technology changes. They ignored the history which created their opportunity and which will, if ignored, destroy them.

Chips got more complex and smaller at the same time, lowering the cost of computer power. IBM recognized this and did its best to slow its disintegration by getting into the microcomputer market just as soon as the courts and a consent decree would let them. They've done well in micros, but that has only delayed doom for them, not averted it.

In the publishing field our type used to be set on large, expensive and difficult-to-use Linotype machines. These were so complicated and costly that only printers could afford them.

Technology in the form of the IBM Composer, a lower cost system using magnetic tape and automated IBM typewriters not only killed off the old hot type machines, it made it affordable for publishers to set their own type. By the 1970s publishers were using low-cost photo-typesetting systems by Compugraphic and Varityper.

These were so inexpensive that a friend of mine who writes books had a Compugraphic system in a closet in her New York apartment. She not only wrote books, she set the type, did the illustrations and ended up with the film ready for offset printing.

By the 1980s microcomputers were taking over typesetting. They were able to set whole pages of type, not just columns which had to be pasted together and photographed. Illustrations could be scanned into the computer and mixed with the type. The output of this system was still a photographic system, often one made by Compugraphic.

One of the early success stories in this field was Bedford Computer in Bedford, NH. Alas, the company was run by an engineer and not an entrepreneur so, despite its technological leadership and the lower costs it provided, the firm went bankrupt. It eventually survived, but the technological momentum was lost.

When the Macintosh computer was introduced in 1984, I was there for the big party. It was a new kind of computer and had potential, but no one knew just what to do with it. By the late 1980s the Mac was beginning to stand out as a desktop publishing machine. The microcomputer world split into the IBM-PC and the Mac camps, with the PC going for business applications and the Mac for artistic.

The Mac has been getting better and better for publishers as software from third party firms has supported its development. Today, just as minicomputers were able to beat the Goliath mainframes by providing the same computing power at a tenth the cost, and microcomputers are doing in the minis at a tenth of their cost, we're seeing desktop publishing wiping out older composing systems at a tenth of their cost.

My Bedford system cost about $500,000 when I bought it in 1984. Now I'm replacing it with a $50,000 Mac system which will not only do more and do it faster, but does it better and takes less time to learn to use. It's so inexpensive that my wife has one in our dining room for her small video production business.

I went into some details on this because I've been so close to these technologies. But we've been seeing similar changes in telephones, calculators, consumer electronics, and business electronics.

If New Hampshire . . . and America, for that matter . . . is going to be near the top of the economic chain in the next century, it's going to be because we've generated an educated work force which will be able to work with minds instead of hands. It's going to take minds that are familiar and comfortable with technology.

Our educational system is not producing this kind of worker right now. In fact it has no hope, in its present incarnation, of doing so. We either have to make some big changes in the system we've allowed to dominate our whole society or we're going to go the way of other lost civilizations.

But how can we change this monster? It's protected by a union that is so powerful that it's almost unchallengable . . . not just in Washington, but even in the 50 statehouses around our country. Our educational system has been costing more and more and producing less and less ever since we socialized it 150 years ago.

060 A Daring New Approach

Yes, of course I have a plan for a way out of our educational dilemma. It's a way to almost immediately get our kids interested in high-tech and to start learning about it. It's a way to do it without taking 10 to 20 years to teach a whole new generation of science and math teachers before we can start working on students.

It's a way which will cost little to implement and which will quickly become a profit center rather than another sinkhole for public funds. This involves a whole new concept in education . . . making learning fun! It involves getting away from memorization and into teaching conceptual thinking.

How can we do all this right here in New Hampshire? And how can we do it without spending a billion dollars? How can we do it without having to educate a new generation of teachers first?

I know this is going to come as a terrific suprise, but publishing has something to do with what I'm going to suggest. It actually has a whole lot to do with it. You see, I've been publishing amateur radio magazines for 40 years now, so I've developed the hang of how to explain complicated technical matters to kids in a form they enjoy.

My magazines have helped amateurs pioneer one new communications technology after another. We were in there first with narrow band FM, which is about all that's used for VHF communications these days. Then came single-sideband-supressed-carrier, which now dominates high frequency communications. And yes, I can explain how these work in terms a ten year old kid can understand.

These days amateurs have combined computers with radio and are zipping messages around the world at up to 8,000 words a minute. Kids are doing it because my magazines have explained how, in simple terms, to build and use the equipment needed.

If we're going to teach youngsters about technologies we're going to have to make it simple and make it fun. We're going to have to get them personally involved. The young readers of my ham radio magazines read them because they are personally involved. It's fun for them. They're no more cowed by communications technology than other kids are by computers. Remember, it was kids who pioneered microcomputers, not old men. Micros started out as a hobby. I know because I started the first magazines and helped get the kids hooked.

061 Peer Teaching

Okay, we want to teach kids about technology, science and math, but we don't have the teachers to do it. We can't even get them for years. And even if we tried to get them by using our present teacher's college system, they wouldn't be worth any more to our kids than the present graduates of this miserable system.

So let's consider letting the kids teach each other. Am I suggesting we do this without teachers? None? You bet. And I know it can be done.

If you're doing your homework you're taping "60 Minutes" every Sunday and fast forwarding through it, sidestepping the juicy scandals, looking for some positive news. That cuts down your viewing time to a few minutes a week. Of course, if you just can't avoid scandal and soap, and only skip the commercials, you'll spend around 40 minutes a week. Even at that it's often worth it.

A couple years back they had a segment on a medical college where peer teaching was being tested. Yep, youngsters teaching each other to be doctors! The worst part of it was that it worked. They found that the students progressed about three times as fast as with regular classes and learned about twice as much. As I say, it's almost enough to make a person think.

It was this and other kinds of experimental teaching systems which got me to try and get RPI to institute (pardon) a Center for the Investigation of Undergraduate Education (CIUE). They liked the idea and did institute it. Boy, did they institute it, as I mentioned earlier. They instituted it into something not even remotely like the original concept. This is why I recommended that New Hampshire might set up a CIUE and do it right . . . as a for-profit enterprise.

062 A Magazine?

Here's my idea. Every youngster in New Hampshire schools, from grades 5-12 would get a weekly magazine which would teach them the basics of electronics, communications and computers.

Why not textbooks? Three major reasons. (1) These fields are moving so fast any textbook would be two to five years out of date before it could reach the classroom. (2) When have you ever read an entertaining text book? (3) Textbooks are expensive and we want to keep educational costs down. (4 . . . a bonus point) Textbooks eliminate any interactive element. A weekly magazine can provide fast feedback between students with letters-to-the-editor and weekly columnists talking about special interests.

How about a magazine which covers the technical matters of the week for the three basic subjects . . . plus it would have columns encouraging the youngsters to form amateur radio, computer, electronic experimenter, astronomy, science fair and other technology oriented clubs? If we can get the kids interested in learning by involving them in high-tech hobbies, we won't be able to stop them.

A few years ago, when I had a computer lab for developing mass-produced software, some local youngsters asked if they could come in and use our computers after school, at night and on weekends. Sure. Well, my programmers and techs said these kids were amazing, They didn't just ask questions, they were like industrial vacuum cleaners when it came to learning.

They came in, bringing sleeping bags so when they got too tired they could crash for a few hours and then have at the computers some more. Around the country we were reading stories about kids breaking into schools, not to trash them, but to use the computers at night. You almost can't stop them, once they find out how much fun learning can be.

Can we, through a weekly ham radio column, get kids into amateur radio? You bet we can! We'll tell 'em how to go on hidden transmitter hunts . . . how to be able to talk with people in over 200 countries . . . how to pass messages over the radio at high speeds . . . we'll tell 'em about our contests, our array of amateur radio satellites, about going on expeditions to rare spots just to set up a ham station for a few days, and so on.

We'll get 'em into computer clubs too so they can connect with any school in New Hampshire . . . or, working with the ham club, connect with kids around the world. You sure learn geography fast when you've made friends with people in a hundred or so countries. Hams will tell you the name and location of any country in the world . . . and who they know there.

I'm planning on a trip to the former USSR next spring to put some of the rarer Soviet Republics on the air. Can you spot Sabah, Lesotho, and Sarawak on a map of the world? I've been to them and operated my ham station. Any ham will tell you right where they are.

063 Teachers Can Learn

The basic concept is simple. The students get their weekly tech magazine on Friday. They read it over the weekend and come in Monday ready for a week of bull sessions about the material they've read. The "teacher" will be there mostly to resolve conflicts and will be learning right along with the kids.

The kids, by arguing and forming groups to look into special matters and report to the class, will teach themselves. If they find they need some outside help we'll have resources for them such as books, other magazines, and volunteers from local amateur radio clubs, computer groups, and so on.

Having published high-tech magazines and books for hobbyists for four decades, I've kinda got the hang of it. My license study guides have been so simple that even a four-year-old was able to get an amateur radio license . . . and seven-year-old kids have been able to get the highest of the five license grades, Extra Class. It's a question of having writers who can (a) make it simple and (b) make it fun. There aren't many who can do that, but there are some.

064 An Electronics Encyclopedia

In addition to weekly lessons in the fundamentals of electronics, communications and computers, once a month we'll have a special added section devoted to explaining one particular kind of electronic equipment.

For instance, we might have a section which explains how all the different kinds of printers work, such as dot matrix, type wheel, thermal, ink jet, and laser printers. Another might explain how fiber optics work. By the end of the eight-year course the students would have at least an 80-volume encyclopedia on electronic equipment, complete with updates as new technologies evolve.

In between these major sections we would run reference material such as lists of all coaxial cables and their characteristics, connectors and how to use them, lists of ICs, educational software, etc.

We'd also ask student groups to evaluate and review educationally oriented software. We certainly would encourage student groups to write software and share it.

065 What About Labs?

Once there's a market for simple experiments we'll find hundreds of entrepreneurs offering kits for kids to buy and play with. It doesn't cost much for parts to build simple test meters, small motors and generators and so on. You just have to look in an Edmunds Scientific catalog to see how reasonable these things are. You *do* get their catalog, right?

Eventually we'll want to make more elaborate equipment available to help the kids learn. Here's where we can put together labs on wheels which can be shared by many schools. They can be built into mobile-home-type trailers, on flatbed or other kinds of truck trailers. We can even get older kids to help build them on old trailer platforms and they'll love it.

We want labs to help kids learn about radios, television, computers, and so on. It's probably cheaper to bring the labs to the kids than the kids to the labs. But since most kids these days have computers at home and we'll soon have many kids with their own ham radio stations, a shortage of labs isn't going to slow things down much.

By the way, much of the equipment for our labs can be gotten for free. We really don't need state-of-the-art stuff at first, so let's offer some tax advantages to companies who pass along their older equipment for the kids. There's one chap already doing this in New Hampshire and he's had volunteers gathering old oscilloscopes, refurbishing them and then donating them to schools. The sorry fact is that hundreds of millions of dollars in old test equipment is thrown out every year – test equipment which would be of great value to help kids learn.

The kids would learn even more if they were involved with the gathering, refurbishing and distribution of the equipment. For that matter, the kids could set up electronic repair shops in their schools and go into business repairing VCRs, radio, TV, hi-fi, and even computers. By operating these services for a profit they could buy even better and newer service equipment.

It wasn't that long ago that Apple was giving thousands of computers to schools. Many private businesses also donated computers to schools. I donated complete computer labs to the schools in Peterborough and Jaffrey. We can encourage largess like this.

Others more acquainted with getting federal grants will know how to put a hand in that bottomless pocket. I know there's an almost endless supply of money sitting in Washington, just waiting for the enterprising to shake the tree. Just before Bill Bennett got pushed out as the Secretary of Education, I visited him and explained my idea for teaching technology to kids. He loved the idea and sent me a long list of available grants which could be tapped. There are hundreds of millions sitting down there waiting for us to put our name on the check.

066 Who Will Pay?

As I've made clear, I hope, I'm not in favor of getting New Hampshire to spend more money on anything, including education. I'm not at all opposed to our putting up some venture capital to get for-profit ventures going which will eventually cut state costs. Nor am I opposed to getting every dollar we can from Washington. If we don't, Senator Bentsen will send it to Texas. Let's get New Hampshire working right first and then we can consider trying to fix that godawful mess in Washington.

We're small. We're aggressive. We're progressive . . . in a conservative way . . . so let's show 'em what can be done.

So how can we provide around 100,000 students with a weekly magazine without having to charge them for it? We can do it the same way I'm able to send *Music Retailing* twice a month to around 9,000 record stores at no charge . . . I sell advertising.

Oh lord! Advertising? Expose our kids to advertising? Horrors. Sure, I know how much trouble Whittle got in when he sold ads to pay for educational TV for classrooms. My answer is "baloney." Look, we're all exposed to around 1,800 commercial messages a day. We get 'em on TV, the radio, newspapers, magazines, billboards, matchbook covers, posters, store windows, taxi tops . . . advertising is everywhere.

If I were going to start an educational magazine my first stop would be to Coca Cola to see how much they wanted to invest. Yes, I know, parents don't want their kids to even suspect Coca Cola exists. But would they be willing to spend $80 a year for a weekly magazine just so their kids wouldn't be exposed to Coke ads? And McDonalds?

No, no beer, no cigarette ads. I've never run any of these in any of my magazines in all these years and never will. But I don't have any problem with ads from enterpreneurs selling high-tech parts kits or with Sears, The Gap and so on. I might even okay ads for some of those foolish high-tech sneakers kids force each other to waste their money on . . . but have never even learned how to tie their laces.

Instead of techies being the nerds and dweebs, let's turn those pejoratives on the smokers, the beer drinkers and other such low-lifes.

By keeping printing and production costs modest through using a tabloid format and a good grade of newsprint paper, we can keep the advertising rates down to where entrepreneurs will be able to get new businesses started to cater to this particular market. High ad rates tend to freeze out entrepreneurs and tilt the market toward large firms.

I've always avoided letting my publications build too large a circulation for this very reason. I prefer to spin off second and third publications in order to keep the ad rates affordable, and this usually means keeping circulations under 150,000.

In this case we want to make it easy for entrepreneurs to offer young hobbyists all kinds of kits and gadgets . . . inexpensive optics and telescopes, etc.

We can keep costs low by starting out providing grades 5-12 the same material the first year. They're all beginners. The next year everyone but grade 5 would get new material. Grade 5 would get essentially the same material as the previous year except for some updates and re-writes where youngsters the previous year had some trouble understanding things.

In the third year grades 7-12 would get new material, and so on. Grade 5 would get another reprint of the first year's material . . . again updated and improved.

In this way one editorial staff could write eight years of the ongoing weekly "textbook" one year at a time. I'd have a second editorial staff working just on the special sections and reference materials.

By the time students graduate from high school they'll have a 320 volume textbook, reference manual and encyclopedia. And by then, I suspect we'll be able to put the whole works on either a CD-ROM, complete with almost infinite search capabilities, or on some sort of fast-scan magnetic tape such as DAT.

Monthly and yearly in-depth indexes will help make the material more user-friendly.

067 Delivering It

Duck soup. If we have it printed in New Hampshire, which we certainly should, we can deliver copies every Friday to every school in the state via trucks. The students can then see that they are delivered to themselves. Trucks from Concord or Manchester could reach every part of the state in two or three hours, keeping distribution costs to a minimum.

And that's it . . . the editorial, columns, letters, advertising, production, printing, distribution. Of course, it helps to have done this before a few times.

068 That Free Polytechnic College

As I've mentioned, if we're able to generate thousands of enthusiastic high-tech oriented kids, many are going to want to go on to college. Others will peel off as technicians and entrepreneurs and not want to waste their time at college. But if we can start a college such as I've outlined where students would find their time used productively to learn, and they could do it in three years instead of four, and tuition would be free, we might need to handle quite a crowd. I think we'd be foolish to force all those kids to go out of state, don't you agree?

Free? Sure, no problem. Not only can we cover the normal tuition costs, we can, at the same time, make it so the students will graduate with far more experience and skills than any other schools can provide.

The secret is simple, instead of our students working full-time in class we split their days into five hours working with associated high-tech businesses which are located in a nearby high-tech park . . . and five hours in class. Good lord, am I suggesting a 10-hour work day for kids? You bet I am. And it's even worse than that. In addition to working 10 hours a day, I'm suggesting we make it six days a week. Let me know when you recover from that.

That'll make it so our students are working for cooperative for-profit businesses 30 hours a week. If we get the firms to pay them $7 an hour, which is peanuts for dedicated, intelligent, enthusiastic help, that'll generate $210 a week toward tuition. If we do that 50 weeks of the year, they'll earn $10,500. We can organize a first-rate college which will make a profit at that rate. We might even be able to contribute toward the room and board for the students!

By rotating the students around the jobs in the participating high-tech firms, they'd get a wide variety of experience. They could work on production, testing, quality control, customer service, accounting, purchasing, sales, marketing and so on. They'll probably learn more at work than they will in class. Far more. But the combo will give us killer graduates.

With one set of students working mornings and the other half working afternoons, the firms would have two students for each position. The firms would be able to work 10 hours a day, six days a week, so they'd tend to outdo competitors with staffs working a more leisurely 35-40 hours a week.

Splitting the students into two groups would permit the school to operate with half as many classrooms and labs as would normally be needed. Plus, if we build the school near Manchester, we'll be able to use the classrooms for adult classes for a third shift.

By getting the students involved with entrepreneurialism we can encourage them to incubate new businesses as part of their education. RPI has been doing this very successfully.

They could both learn and make money by providing electronic and computer servicing, as I suggested earlier. They could write and service custom software for business customers. They could get into the desktop publishing business and provide publications supporting new and emerging technologies.

I've seen many potential new technologies flounder and die for the lack of a dedicated publication. Have you ever read about Ovshinski and his ovonics? These are amorphous semicondustors. No? Well, it was a technology which had enormous potential, but had no publication support. Too bad.

The students could learn about new technologies, make money doing it, and provide an enormously valuable service by providing support publications. These would help not only New Hampshire become a center for technological information, but would help America regain its world leadership in technology.

Publications like that would tend to attract entrepreneurs with products and services in these new technologies, providing good jobs and generating high revenues in New Hampshire. We could have a quality of life which would lead the country even more than we do now. We might have to fight off people wanting to move here.

I see New Hampshire as being a great place to develop these ideas.

Once we've proven them, they'll be implemented in other states and in other countries. In the longer run I'd like to see us export our educational system, particularly to third-world countries. I already have good contacts in many of these countries, so exporting would be easy. And they're going to need it, if they're to survive.

069 Will It Work?

Can we really get kids interested in tchnology just by exposing them to amateur radio, computer, science fair and electronic experimenter clubs? You bet we can and I've already proven it. I think you'll find it an interesting story.

After a trip around the world in 1959, where I visited and talked with amateurs in 18 countries, and another in 1966, where I visited amateurs in 22 countries, a concept evolved as I talked with them.

I wrote about this in my editorials at the time, but my first chance to use it came in 1970 when His Majesty King Hussein got a ham radio set from his wife for Christmas. I heard about it and sent him a cable, offering to come over and help him learn how to use it. Gutsy, eh? To my amazement he cabled back for me to come on over.

I jumped on a flight to London, then on to Beirut, and a shuttle flight on Alia, the Royal Jordanian Airline, to Amman. The Jordanian sitting beside me on the plane looked out the window and exclaimed that His Majesty was there waiting to meet the plane. Wow! I swelled with pride, but didn't say anything. Then the chap went on to explain that he was there to meet his daughter, who was on the flight with us. I was glad I hadn't said anything.

As I got off the plane I was met by a chap who said His Majesty was expecting me and would see me the next morning. He whisked me past immigration and into a waiting Mercedes. I would be a guest of His Majesty in the Jordan Intercontinental Hotel.

The next morning a Mercedes and driver were waiting and drove me a few miles out of Amman to the summer palace, where His Majesty was waiting for me. He showed me around and then we got down to talking about amateur radio, which fascinated him.

Over the next two weeks I operated his station in the summer palace, giving the amateur world their first contact with the country of Jordan in nearly 20 years. The pressures were enormous, with thousands of amateurs almost ready to kill to make the contact and get it confirmed via a postcard.

I knew this part of it wouldn't be any fun for His Majesty, so I wanted to make it possible for him to be able to get on the air without being driven to distraction by country hunting hams . . . who only wanted a very brief contact, and had little interest in actually talking.

So I operated at a fast pace day after day for two weeks, making thousands of contacts. In the afternoon His Majesty would come back from his office at his palace in Amman and we'd talk. I found him most interesting to talk with and surprisingly open-minded about trying to work out some way to deal with Israel.

Mind you this was 1970, just weeks before the civil war in Jordan, when the Palestinians tried to kill him and take over the country. The Palestinians were also very upset over America. They'd burned the American library the day before I arrived and attacked the American embassy.

I talked with several of the government leaders, including the Minister of Communications, to try and find out more about the situation. Frankly, before going over I knew very little about Jordan or His Majesty. I knew about the Palestinian situation and the wars in general, but hadn't read in depth about it.

It didn't take long for me to find that Jordan was a primitive country in many respects, so I talked with His Majesty about gearing Jordan to compete with the world. I explained about the importance of electronics and communications and that unless his people could be educated in technology, his country would be left further and further behind.

He asked what I suggested be done. I explained that I felt the best approach was to set up amateur radio clubs and stations in the schools and youth clubs and encourage his youngsters to learn about electronics because it was fun and they wanted to.

I explained that I'd talked with his people and found that they didn't even teach the very fundamentals of electricity in Jordanian schools. This was costing his country enormous amounts of money because they had to bring in foreign technicians and engineers for even the simplest of things . . . like installing telephones. And this meant paying $500 to $1,000 a day for technicians from Germany and Sweden.

I pointed out that electronics and communications were the future and that Jordan would have to pay a high price if it didn't have Jordanian technicians and engineers to install, operate and repair telephones, radio, television and so on.

His Majesty considered this and asked me to explain this to his government. The next day I went to the palace in Amman and was introduced to his government. They were all sitting around a large table, waiting.

I explained the problem and my proposed solution, pointing out that mine would be a very inexpensive solution to a very expensive problem. It didn't hurt at the end when His Majesty, at the back of the room, said, "And it shall be so."

I promised to write a set of rules and regulations for Jordan which would be tailor-made for their situation. This would outline the license classes, the content of the exams for each grade and so on.

When I got home I prepared the rules and regulations for them, had them printed and sent them a stack to get started. Soon after I was called by the CIA and asked what equipment I recommended they send over for the school stations. It seems that His Majesty had a little account with the CIA for things like that.

Within a few days of my leaving, Jordan was involved in a civil war. On the evening news I saw the hotel where I'd stayed being shelled.

Three years later, in 1973, I was on the air swapping some photographs of New Hampshire with a chap in Athens via slow-scan television when a voice broke in. It was His Majesty. He said he was going to be in Washington in a few days visiting and would like to see me. Hey, no problem!

I met him at Blair House, where His Majesty (called HM by his associates) thanked me for coming to Jordan and gave me two first class tickets to Amman, "So I could come back to see what I'd done."

When I arrived I was met by Hisham Ansari, the chap he'd chosen to teach electronics to the radio clubs. I'd recommended that he have someone go around and give classes . . . and Hisham was the one.

I was again put up at the Jordan Intercontinental, which had been completely repaired after the civil war. Hisham drove me from one end of Jordan to the other, visiting every city. In each city I met with the members of the radio clubs . . . and there were both boys' and girls' radio clubs. I met over two hundred enthusiastic new ham operators. They were having a great time.

That so much had been accomplished in such a short time was amazing. That this had been done while a civil war was going on was even more amazing. Most countries would be fearful of all radio communications during a war, not encouraging them.

So I got to see the mineral baths of Irbid, up near the Golan Heights, the ruined medieval fortress at Karnak, the 2000-year old mosaic floors of churches discovered in Madaba, the long lost ancient city of Petra, and I even got to swim in the Red Sea at Aqaba.

Further, as a result of this flood of young technicians, they were putting in the first electronics factory. Not bad for just three years.

This trip I brought over a complete automatic relay station (repeater) and a suitcase full of hand transceivers. I set the repeater up on a hilltop where it enabled anyone within miles to talk with anyone else. As I departed from the Amman airport I was talking with HM over the repeater.

He had his amateur station set up in the downtown palace, his summer palace having been turned over to his now divorced second wife. I made a few slow-scan TV contacts from it, just to keep my hand in. I had the pleasure of meeting his new wife, Alia, who was later killed in a helicopter crash while on a visit to a school.

Ten years later, when I stopped off to visit His Majesty on my way back from a tour of four Asian electronic shows, a special meeting of the Royal Jordanian Amateur Radio Society was held in my honor. Prince Raad introduced me as having had more of an influence on Jordan than anyone other than the king himself. Now I'd like to do the same for New Hampshire . . . and for America.

My idea worked in Jordan and it'll work here . . . if we'll give it a chance.

From the end of WWII in 1945 until 1963, a period of 18 years, amateur radio grew at 11% per year in America . . . and 80% of the newcomers were kids. 50% were either 14 or 15 when first licensed. These kids came into the hobby via over 5,000 high school radio clubs. It was knowing this that convinced me that all Jordan would have to do is expose their youngsters to the hobby and they'd love it.

Further, surveys here showed that 80% of our new hams were going on to high-tech careers. Amateur radio was a major factor in the strength of America's dominance of the world's electronic industries. It was our primary source of electronic engineers.

Then, in 1963, our national amateur radio society (the ARRL), in an effort to boost their membership, petitioned the FCC to change the rules. They did this, not considering the possible impact it might have in the long run. This triggered the virtual disintegration of the hobby. By 1964 sales of ham equipment were down 85% and most ham radio dealers were forced to close. Almost every manufacturer of ham equipment went out of business within two years. Famous names such as Hallicrafters, Hammarlund, National Radio and so on were gone. The worst part was that only about 200 school radio clubs survived. The infrastructure which brought us new hams was gone.

I'd just started *73* in 1960 and by 1963 had 850 ham radio stores selling it. By 1965 there were only 150 stores left. At the same time as we stopped growing, Japan instituted a no-code ham license which triggered incredible growth. Soon there were radio clubs in every school in Japan and while we were stagnant, they grew from about 18,000 licensees to over two million. We have about 400,000 licensed in America today. With our ham industry destroyed the Japanese had no problem taking over. Today 97% of the amateur radio sets sold here are Japanese.

These Japanese hams are going on to become engineers and scientists.

When I visit their research laboratories I am greeted by Japanese hams at every turn. Their best and brightest go into consumer electronic R&D. What few engineers we have are sucked into Military R&D, since that pays the most.

Recently our rules were eased a little for newcomers and we've finally started growing again, but at around 2%, and with almost no youngsters coming into our ranks. I feel that this is one of the main reasons our country is graduating even fewer engineers now than we did 25 years ago, despite the virtual explosion in electronic technology. I'm hoping that New Hampshire will be able to get youngsters interested in high-tech hobbies and show the way for our country to again produce technicians, engineers and scientists.

From where I sit it looks to me as if the future of not just New Hampshire, but America, is in your hands. How about it?

Chapter III

070 It's A Start

I was surprised at how many pages it's taken to cover just the major items I had in mind to bring up with the Commission. But I felt it was better to put it all in writing than to take the time at a meeting to try and work in abbreviated versions of my ideas and concerns.

I've offered a whole bunch of ideas. Some for the short run . . . some the medium . . . some for the long run. From this perspective perhaps you can understand why I pushed for a simple mission statement.

The idea that the Commission is going to be able to produce one master plan and present it doesn't make any sense, so I didn't want to see us get painted into a corner on that aspect. Running a business is an ongoing process, and it's this process which has resulted in New Hampshire being in the recession it's in right now . . . and facing a much worse one as our computer and defense industries wither away and our work force becomes less and less relevant in today's high-tech world.

Are we as a group to take a picture of the situation, size it up, and come up with a plan for solving only those problems we have right now? Is that it? Or are we going to be able to propose plans for helping New Hampshire to improve our quality of life . . . and then follow through with further plans as we see the results of our initial plans?

I like the idea of a relatively non-political group made up of business people and members from the legislature and executive as a sort of ongoing think tank guidance group to help New Hampshire compete with the other states . . . and the world.

Several of the ideas I've proposed are ones that I'm in a particularly unique position to implement. I agree that's a conflict of interest . . . at least to some degree. It doesn't seem that way to me because I know that I've got a full plate right now just with the companies I'm running. I don't need the aggravation of publishing an educational magazine or of publishing a *ToDo* tourist publication. But if they'll help New Hampshire . . . and perhaps the world . . . I'm willing to take on the responsibility.

Some of these projects might conceivably make a good profit. My past reaction to that has been to use any profits to start still more projects which I think will benefit the world. Like almost all true entrepreneurs, I've never been interested in making money. I know I have to not lose it, so I always aim to make modest profits, which I put right back into growth.

If the Commissioners are at all uneasy about my conflict of interest, no problem. Just ignore my ideas and come up with some of your own. I don't have any corner on ideas, and I assume most of you were chosen for the Commission because you are known creative problem solvers.

I'd like to see *New Hampshire ToDo* pack the state with families up here having fun. Then I'd like to do a similar publication for Boston, one for New York, Chicago, Atlanta, Munich, Berlin and so on.

I'd like to see my grades 5-12 electronics, communications and computer fundamentals publication (ECCF) spread to 50 states and then to a hundred countries. Jordan and India are already aware of the idea and anxious for me to start publishing the series.

If you have any questions about my information sources or my ideas, please write. I'm not a telephone person, so I'd prefer writing. Oh, I like to talk, but I hate telephone tag. I really hate it.

If you have any resources I may have missed, I'd appreciate being copied. In the meanwhile, I'm going to try and find out what that long list of state departments has been doing and what information they have available.

Be glad you're not a subscriber to my magazines. My *73* editorials go on for pages every month. I don't know of any other magazine that does that . . . and I've been doing it for over 30 years in that one.

The college? No, I'm not interested in starting one myself, but an advisory position would be okay. I almost started one eight years ago, but thought better of it. That was a good decision. But we are either going to need one or New Hampshire is going to be in bad shape in 10 years. Your choice.

One more caveat. I really don't want to hear that you enjoyed my offering, but didn't agree with all of it. Of course you won't. But if you find some areas where you disagree, please do me the courtesy of letting me know why you disagree. Perhaps you have some information or experience that I don't. Of course, if your disagreement is emotional and not based on facts, there's nothing we can do about that. Where emotions rule, reason flies out the window. But I do suggest that those ruled by emotion aren't going to be of much use to our work.

I hope we'll be able to communicate without hidden agendas clouding issues. I much prefer not to be forced to be sneaky, conniving and manipulative. I can, if I have to, but I don't have any respect for people who do business like that . . . and I hope you don't either.

071 Business Taxes

As I was reading "*A Business Plan For New Hampshire's Economic Future,*" put out by the Business & Industry Association of New Hampshire, I came across this statement: "The business community acknowledges and accepts its role in funding a large percentage of government programs and services in New Hampshire." Whoa, there Nelly, I think there's a goat in here with us sheep!

Let's look at this from a capitalistic viewpoint and see how it plays. I hope you agree that our New Hampshire businesses are in competition with those in other states . . . and other countries. Thus it's not much of an intellectual leap to understand the basic concept that the more we tax New Hampshire businesses, the less competitive they're going to be . . . and thus less successful.

When we have state taxes which make it cost us more to sell compact discs than it costs in Maine, we're going to have to get by on a smaller profit or sell fewer. We can't raise prices just because it costs us more, so we'll have to sacrifice profitability if we're going to stay in business.

The less profit we can make as a result of state taxes, the lower salaries we'll be able to pay our people. This isn't much different from taxing them individually. It's just putting business in charge of collecting an income tax, but not calling it that. Smoke and mirrors. And remember, for every extra dollar in taxes businesses have to pay, they will have to generate at least $10 in extra revenues just to break even . . . and that's if they're making a 10% net profit, which is pretty good these days.

I understand that our present business tax has brought in about half what was projected. Does that mean that the tax will be doubled to make up for the shortfall? That's the way with taxes, once you start them. More taxes will mean even less profitability . . . and that will mean more unemployment and lower salaries. Talk about a regressive tax!

If the state provides services which are just for businesses, I can see how that could honestly be charged to the business getting the services. But I'd like to see a list of the state offices which are providing these specific services and how much they're costing. Next, I'd like to have business people have some say in whether they really need those services enough to pay for them and become less competitive. I don't like the idea of being forced to pay for something I don't want or need . . . something which reduces the profitability of my company.

That brings up a question. How can the Commission find out what state departments are dedicated to helping business? How can we find out what we're paying for now? Once we know this, we can decide if we think these services are increasing our profitability enough to warrant continuing them.

If business is being asked to pay for general public services in lieu of a broad-based tax, we want to know this.

And I'd like to know which New Hampshire businessmen were responsible for the Business & Industry Association coming out in favor of business taxes. Let's name some names and not hide behind BIA anonymity.

Everything starts with manufacturing and marketing. When these are healthy we'll have the money for services, to buy cars, homes, and even to pay for government. But without industries bringing money into New Hampshire from out of the state and out of the country, we're going to run down fast.

New Hampshire went sour when its major industries didn't keep up with technology . . . or bet too much on defense gigabucks. Once the money stopped coming in, everything else stopped . . . clothing, homes, cars, advertising, travel, entertainment, etc.

Thus, the last group we want to tax in the state are those businesses which are attracting revenues from outside New Hampshire. If you want to support state services which may or may not be needed, let's tax our service businesses and hasten the downward spiral of their failure in order to pay for them. This will tend to encourage more businesses that bring revenues into the state to start and choke off those which merely recirculate revenues within the state.

I've already proposed a plan for cutting our state government services to the minimum we agree we actually need. This plan should eventually have the state running lean, setting an example for the other 49. By cutting taxes we'll be able to make our businesses more competitive, giving New Hampshire an edge.

072 Prison Reform

How much of an expense are our New Hampshire prisons? Probably not a major expense, yet it certainly might reduce our taxes a bit if we could cut our prison costs.

We're fortunate in not having major crime and drug problems like states with larger cities. Not that we're without them; it's just that they're relatively minor.

With it costing at least $20,000 a year to keep a criminal in prison . . . and that's just the direct costs . . . we might want to consider some alternatives. In addition to having to tax ourselves $20,000 to lock each criminal up, we also lose some $4,400 in revenues the person would earn for the state if not incarcerated. We're losing out both ways.

First, let's see if we can come up with any ways of cutting the cost of maintaining prisoners. How can we cut that $20,000? I'm sure you've got a bunch of ideas.

One thing we do know: When the government runs a business it isn't going to be run well. It's going to cost too much and do too little. Worse, it all too often doesn't attract top quality workers.

A few years ago I got to thinking about this problem and came up with the idea of America setting aside a remote island somewhere which could be made into a penal colony and run by the prisoners. It wouldn't have to be like Devil's Island in French Guiana. I thought about all of the American-owned islands and decided that Guam might make a good spot. It's isolated enough to keep anyone from swimming away. And it's in a warm climate. Nice place, really. Of course, I expected the Guamanians not to be all that enthralled by the idea.

Cut to a few years later when I stopped by to visit Guam for a few days. About 50 radio amateurs and computer hackers got together and threw a big dinner to welcome me. My stay at the Guam Hilton was a far cry from Camp Dealey, the quonset hut submarine rest camp of 1945.

During my talk to the group I cautiously mentioned my idea. They surprised me by thinking it was a great plan. It would give Guam something of value to contribute. There aren't any major industries or crops grown, so Guam just kind of gets by, mostly catering to short visits from Japanese tourists who fly down so they can buy beef to take back to Japan. The Japanese beef market is extremely controlled and you wouldn't believe the prices.

The idea of being sent 10,000 miles away and having to fend for themselves on a remote Pacific island, with other prisoners as neighbors, might be unattractive enough to help deter crime. They sure wouldn't be getting many visits from family or friends.

The only expense to New Hampshire for that would be to ship the prisoner to Guam. From there on the prisoner would have to find work and make a living, causing us no more expense.

Perhaps 10,000 miles seems too far. Well, we have a number of somewhat closer African countries which might want to bid to take care of our prisoners for us. We could even get an agreement that if any escapees make it back here, there would be a tidy forfeiture on their part.

It would cost far less to keep prisoners in Chad or Burkina-Faso than here in New Hampshire. I'll bet they'd bid under $2,000 a year for the privilege of taking care of our human refuse. This, too, might tend to discourage criminals from opting for prison.

The best part is that by pioneering a creative solution to prison costs New Hampshire might encourage other states to follow suit.

Yes, I've considered that a prison run for-profit in Burkina-Faso might not be a model of comfort. It'd probably be hot, dirty and miserable. It might be out in the middle of the desert, making escape all the more difficult. We might want to have an ombudsman there to keep an eye on things for us and let us know if the prison isn't living up to its contract.

073 How About Drugs

Other than a few hundred or so New Hampshire residents growing marijuana, I'm not aware of a significant drug problem in New Hampshire. Yes, now and then there's a drug bust, so we're not by any means immune. But I don't see TV news reports of crack houses in Nashua.

My approach to solving America's drug problem is an anathema to many people. I favor legalizing drugs . . . sort of. I'm not talking about encouraging the cigarette companies to sell pot over the counter in our supermarkets. I may be naive, but I'm not stupid.

We know one thing for sure by now: There's no way to keep drugs from being smuggled into the country. We've tried everything except shooting down incoming drug planes. It is going to keep coming in and it's going to come in in whatever quantities can be sold here. Why? Simple—because it's so incredibly profitable. You can't stop capitalism, not even with the military.

The sooner we recognize that interdiction isn't going to work and start considering alternatives, the sooner we'll be able to stem the drug traffic and cut down on our growing prison population.

Suppose we were to not just flat out legalize drugs, but were to kind of partially legalize them? What I have in mind is having all drugs available, sold inexpensively through state-run drug stores. It'd be very similar to our present state-run liquor stores.

The state would buy the drugs from authorized American suppliers, thus helping to put a few foreign countries out of the business. They'd be sold through our drug stores at a profit, but at a price which would eliminate the huge drug profits now being realized.

Part of the profits would be used to cut other state expenses. Part would be put into a continuing advertising and promotional campaign aimed at educating kids to be too smart to get hooked on drugs. One more thing: I would prohibit any and all advertising for drugs.

Even worse, if I had my way, I'd put all alcoholic beverages, including beer, into the state stores and stop their sale via convenience stores, grocery stores, supermarkets, and so on. That might help stop the beer cans on my farm road. It might even help make it a little more difficult for our teenagers to kill each other and us by driving drunk.

There's more. I'd move all tobacco products to these stores, too. And, like drugs and alcohol, I'd make their advertising in New Hampshire illegal. Yes, that would raise hell with Marlboro ads in magazines. Tough. And what about beer ads on TV? Fine, but not on N.H. TV stations.

Not even wine ads? Nope.

What are we going to do, stop magazines with illegal ads from being sold on New Hampshire newsstands? Why not? All it would take is a fine of a dollar for each displayed magazine that has tobacco or alcohol ads in it, and our newsstands would be wiped clean of that garbage. If a couple more states followed suit, the magazines would be forced to turn to other revenue sources and our kids wouldn't be under constant ad pressures to drink and smoke. Our kids might even buy the idea that these aren't exactly smart things to do.

How did I get to this kind of Calvinistic frame of mind? Being almost 70, I've watched most of my friends who smoked die long and painful deaths. I watched my father suffer through years of emphysema, having to have an oxygen bottle with him everywhere he went. I've heard months of screams of pain as neighbors slowly died of lung cancer.

Drinking? Mostly I'd like to stop drunken driving. I don't mind if people are dumb enough to think it's smart to get drunk. Getting drunk was part of going ashore when I was in the navy. If we sell all alcoholic beverages through our state-operated drug stores, it'll be more difficult for teens to get beer. And stopping advertising will eventually make it less attractive for kids to drink.

The revenues from alcohol and tobacco products — sin taxes — could go a long way toward reducing our state tax burden.

If my ideas are too revolutionary for you, how about some of yours? Most of you are businessmen and used to thinking in positive terms, so I expect that instead of telling me all the reasons why my ideas won't work, you'll come up with some better ones.

074 The Peterborough Debacle

The lack of entrepreneurial direction for the major Peterborough publications in recent years has resulted in them losing ground and cutting staffs. Many very promising publications have gone out of business. This loss has had a serious effect on the town.

The seeds of the loss started several years earlier when a small group of men got control of the planning board and used it to force new businesses to buy property from their group at inflated prices.

I moved to Peterborough in 1962, bringing with me a small amateur radio magazine I'd started publishing two years before. When the first microcomputer was put on the market in January 1975, I knew this could turn into a huge industry. That's when I started creating magazines to help this new industry grow. And grow it did, bringing over $100 million yearly into the Peterborough area from out of state.

By 1982 I'd filled just about every available building in town. When the motel failed I bought it and used it to develop special software for microcomputers. I had a book publishing business in North Peterborough, a shipping department in West Peterborough, and magazine production all through a 40-room house on Pine Street. Plus it also filled The Willows, the old inn next door.

With the invention of the compact disc, I knew a magazine would be needed to help this new technology grow. I tried to buy the old Goyette Museum on Elm Street, but the town refused to let me use it. Not enough parking, they said. I bought the only remaining business building in town, 202 North. That gave me barely enough room to get started, but I needed a lot more space.

I'd opened a string of computer software stores and needed space for a headquarters to manage them. I had a large warehouse in Manchester for my distribution company, which supplied the stores.

I approached the town with a proposal to buy some of the disintegrating old houses in the downtown area. They were being rented to semi-skilled workers and were in terrible condition. I was willing to buy them, recondition them into attractive houses, and use them for offices until I could build a new headquarters. The town said no; those hovels are still there.

So I bought an old factory in nearby Hancock and rebuilt it entirely. We insulated the walls, put on a new roof, put in lighting, heating, and so on. I sold my old computer magazines to a megapublisher and moved out of Peterborough.

So today Peterborough is on hard times and my businesses in Hancock are growing almost too fast to keep up with. I'm going to need more space soon. I don't know whether Hancock will force me to move again, or let me follow through and expand. There often seems to be a death-wish guiding some towns.

Indeed, I was interested in helping a hotel and golf course complex in Francestown expand, but when I found that the town was opposing it, I pulled out. It had the potential for being a major attraction for New England businesses to use for retreats and conferences and could have considerably helped the tax situation for the town and brought revenues into the state.

075 A Proposal

Okay, those are some of the negatives I've run into personally. I'm sure almost every businessman in New Hampshire can match or trump me with even worse cases. So what can the state do about this? Towns certainly don't want the state taking over their local planning functions.

Well, could we establish a group similar to the Economic Development Commission, which could be asked to mediate between towns and aggrieved businessmen? A combination of legislators and businessmen might be able to look into these situations and make recommendations.

The Peterborough Planning Board, it seemed to me, was driven more by a desire to sell me an inflated piece of property than by any interest in allowing my business to grow.

Organizing a solution to this problem seems to me to be well within the purview of our Commission. If we could establish a Planning Referee Committee to help resolve such conflicts, this might help New Hampshire businesses to grow. The PRC wouldn't need to have any state-given authority to override local planning boards. I believe that the force of their decisions would, in most cases, cause planning boards to reconsider. That, the attendant publicity, and the real possibility of a lawsuit based on the decision, would carry considerable weight.

I respect the interests of our citizens in protecting themselves against imagined problems, but sometimes they tend to be painfully shortsighted. I even had difficulty getting permission to buy the old Hancock factory building because one man was afraid the additional traffic my business might cause on Forest Road would inconvenience him.

076 Big City Alternatives

While in many parts of the world people are moving from rural areas to the cities, in America the trend is in the other direction. People are getting fed up with the urban rat race. They hate the traffic. They are growing to dislike being mugged. They are even beginning to be uncomfortable with having their homes broken into and robbed.

If you visit New York City and see someone smiling you know he's either (a) crazy or (b) about to try and con you. I figured this out 30 years ago and moved to Peterborough. Now I visit the city as seldom as I can . . . and feel nervous when I'm there.

Oh, I miss a few Broadway shows, but I get down there often enough to see most of 'em . . . and the rest when they come to Boston.

With the lowest taxes in the country, plus being the most livable state, it wouldn't take much promotion to attract entrepreneurial businesses to New Hampshire . . . particularly when we're able to provide an educated work force.

With business leaving the cities and settling in suburban and rural areas, we're going to want to make it even more attractive to settle in rural New Hampshire. How do we do that? Well, I've suggested the state might give a hand where town fathers are making things difficult. But we can do more than that.

Our quality of life depends on our providing things to do. We should provide more sports and cultural opportunities. For instance, when I was skiing in Winter Park (CO) they had some inner tubes to rent for sliding down a hillside. The place was lit up and packed with people having a ball. Some groups would hold hands and slide down a dozen at a time.

At the bottom they'd bring their tubes to a ground-level rope tow, lie on them, and be pulled back to the top. We're not talking about an expensive amusement to set up and run. I haven't seen anything like this in New Hampshire, so we might offer to set up a few operators in business with state-backed loans.

That's just one simple sport. We have a few rivers that might be fun to tube down in summer too.

In the arts we already are doing pretty well, with crafts shows, art exhibits, and little theater performances from Peterborough to Whitefield. There are many musical performances too, but not nearly as many as I think we could support.

I'm going to try and do something about this myself, but I can't do the whole thing. I'm advertising for a booking agent for my staff. This person will start out by trying to book ragtime concerts into Keene, Nashua, Manchester, Concord, Portsmouth, and Hanover. Some of the performers might be booked into The Folkway, Del Rossi's, Rynborn and other restaurants around the state, plus as many schools as we can organize for free concerts.

I've got a marvelous ragtime group that would love to make the rounds next spring. I know 'em all and they are first rate. In fact, one of them is recording in my studios as I'm writing this.

If we can put a concert series together and at least not lose money, then we'll see what we can do with a bluegrass series. We might try a Dixieland or jazz series. We may be able to provide better concerts up here in New Hampshire than they get in most cities. More varied anyway.

077 A Music Industry Center?

With the opening of Eastern Europe to capitalism, there's an opportunity to start importing and exporting music on a scale never seen before. Will this new industry go to New York, or can we get a jump on it and make New Hampshire the international music center?

In the past the music industry has been dominated by six international, mostly foreign-owned, megacorporations. They made sure that very little music was shipped internationally. Their contracts with artists prohibited it. Record stores that tried to import this music were prevented by Customs agents.

Now, with entrepreneurial independent record companies springing up by the thousands in America and Europe, it's a new ball game. Since no one has organized this new business yet, we have an opportunity to make New Hampshire the center. I'm working as fast as I can in this direction, but I'm limited by an inability to find the work force I need . . . and by a shortage of investment capital.

078 Eastern Europe

My recent visits to Russia, the Ukraine, Poland and Czechoslovakia convinced me that there is a wealth of marvelous music available from these countries. In fact, since about the only really first-class product they have available for immediate export is their music . . . and since their artists may no longer be state-supported . . . we could help their economies substantially by importing and distributing their music.

We can import the music on digital tape, manufacture the CDs here, and distribute them all over the world. Since the highest profits tend to be in manufacturing and marketing, we as well as the Eastern European musicians would benefit.

079 Build Our Small Towns

Instead of trying to attract new businesses to our cities, we should promote our most important benefit: small town life. In the 18th and 19th centuries, our towns tended to center around one or two large businesses. These brought in the needed revenues from outside the area. This isn't a bad idea.

For instance, I mentioned an empty factory building in Antrim. For over a hundred years they made tableware there. That industry has moved to lower-wage countries now and Chicago Cutlery, the most recent occupant, is a goner.

My idea is to set up a state department to inventory such facilities and try to match businesses interested in coming to New Hampshire with the available space. The Antrim factory, with over 80,000 feet, could house a number of small entrepreneurial businesses. My special interest in publishing inclines me to think in terms of a publishing complex which might house 10 or more small magazine companies. They'd share common services such as accounting, legal, circulation management, typesetting, graphics art, film prep, and so on. This is the way my own publishing business is set up and the system works well.

But these old factory buildings can be adapted to almost any kind of business. In Peterborough, in addition to the publishing businesses, there are several substantial mail order businesses such as Brookstone and New England Business Service.

A small state office could inventory and promote available facilities, getting a small piece of the action on sales or rentals to cover the expenses involved. Again, I prefer to put state government services on a for-profit basis. This will tend to limit their revenues and thus limit their expansion, just like in the private sector.

At present it's a matter of persistence and luck as to whether a business interested in locating in New Hampshire finds the place they need. I remember when I was looking for somewhere to build a new college. It wasn't easy. I spread the news as best I could and was shown a few potential areas, but none were right.

I remember getting a call from Governor Sununu suggesting I take a look at a property up in Enfield. I thanked him and mentioned I'd been out that morning with Sam Tamposi looking at some property. He said, "Oh, that 185 acres over near Durham?" Talk about being on top of the things!

080 Communicating With Our Towns

Having been the president of the Peterborough Chamber of Commerce, I know personally how much of a need there is for some sort of communications between the towns and the state. I'm talking about two-way communications, where towns would have a means of presenting their problems, both to the state and to each other. And a means for state departments to both respond and to help the towns know what's going on in Concord.

Our selectmen need to know. Our chambers of commerce need to know. Our legislators need to know. Even our state employees need to know. So how can we go about establishing the communications we need to pull our state together and to make it so we're all helping each other instead of arguing?

Here we are, well into the communications and information age, and we're still almost as isolated from each other as New Hampshire people were a hundred years ago. Is there a way for technology to help us start working together?

There are two absolutely inevitable concomitants when two groups which have to interact are in separate locations. Mark this down as Green's First Law of Communications Folly. Since communications between the two groups are limited by costs or time, the junior of the groups will tend to read far more into what communications they do get from the senior group. This quickly develops into full-fledged paranoia.

The senior group, also limited in the communications it gets from the junior group, assumes that the latter really must not be doing much. Time soon escalates this impression to the point where the junior group should be done away with.

Well, says the senior group, we have to make decisions the best we can. We certainly can't spend the time to explain every little detail that goes into our decisions. And so it goes.

With that concept in mind, we've got to make it as easy as possible for groups to communicate. Senior groups need to get as much information as they can to help them make decisions. Junior groups need to know as much as possible about why the senior groups are making these ridiculous decisions . . . and what they can do about it.

Of course we can find ourselves heading into a Japanese consensus situation, where decisions become almost impossible. Aesop observed a couple of millenia ago that when you try to please everybody you end up pleasing nobody. So let's aim for a middle ground where we have far better communications than we have now, but not enough to please everyone.

Speed is an important part of communications. While our telephone system seems to be getting worse and worse to use, with telephone-tag defeating three out of four calls, we at least have facsimile now and that gets through. I'd say that at least 5% of my communications have moved from the telephone to fax so far. And with my reluctance to return calls, this is bound to grow. Oh, I feel a little guilty about the stack of pink "While You Were Out" messages . . . but not guilty enough to pick up the phone.

The best solution I see for the present is the newsletter. This has been enormously simplified in the last year or two by Macintosh desktop publishing systems. With such a system, fed by information from town groups via floppy disks or even a BBS system, our communications within the state won't be perfect, by any means, but they'll be enormously ahead of what we have now. It'll be a good start.

I'm able to turn out *Music Retailing*, which is sent free twice a month to about 9,000 record stores around the country, using just such a Macintosh system. It takes a staff of only two editor/writers and an associate publisher to handle a 24-page publication. I also have two ad salesmen who sell by phone and bring in enough advertising to make the publication profitable.

With copies of a state newsletter going to our 250 towns, each with three selectmen, plus over 500 legislators, we'll need to print and mail around 2,000 copies. I'd estimate the whole project, including the staff, might cost about $100,000 a year. If we want to pay for this with advertising, we'd add another $50,000 for two ad salespersons.

But who would want to advertise in such a publication? This isn't exactly the best medium for Coca-Cola or McDonald's. Well, how about lobbyists who are trying to influence legislation? Wouldn't they want to get their messages to this particular group? At $1,250 a page we'd need to sell 10 pages of ads per month to put the project into the black. One salesman could probably do that.

There are a lot of firms that would like to sell things to the state and town governments . . . and even more that want to influence legislation. Imagine how much the power lobby would be willing to spend to try and stop New Hampshire from passing a law against their power transmission lines being anywhere near where people or animals are living.

And how much would the beer companies spend to try and keep beer from being sold only through state liquor/drug stores? This could turn out to be a major profit center for the state.

081 Health Care

This is a nasty subject to tackle. Very emotional. It's tied up with unresolvables such as euthanasia, abortion and other no-no topics. Well, I have my opinions on those matters, but I'm more of a pragmatist than a romantic, so I'm sure few will agree with me.

In considering health care, it's helpful to take a look at systems which have been tried in other countries. I found a great model for solving the welfare problem via this approach. But we're in trouble on health. I haven't been able to find a government-run health care system that seems to work well anywhere.

We're fortunate here in New Hampshire in that we have so few truly poor people, so few homeless, and even so few on welfare compared to most states. Thus we don't have a huge number of people who are too poor to afford at least basic health care.

When it comes to catastrophic problems, almost anyone except the very wealthy are in trouble. But then we start approaching the question of how much a life is worth. How much are we willing to invest as a group to keep alive a crack baby that has an estimated maximum possible life of 10 years? Will we happily spend one dollar per person for each such case? Supposing that there are a thousand in New Hampshire, are we willing to ante up $1,000 each a year to help these poor tykes? I think some of us are going to look for an exit.

If Willie Horton, in the passion of the moment, forgets his condom when he rapes a fellow prisoner and gets AIDS, are we willing to spend whatever it takes to keep him alive in prison as long as possible?

How about keeping Alzheimer's victims alive far after they are not much more than veggies? We manage to keep many alive for years, feeding one end and cleaning the other. Many have to be strapped to a chair or bed 24 hours a day to keep them from wandering away or bothering others. I'll tell you this, if I ever see any signs of Alzheimer's in myself, I'll buy *Final Exit* in a hurry.

I visited a person who used to be my mother, who eventually died of Alzheimer's, several times a week in a nursing home for years, so I'm not unfamiliar with this aspect of "health" care. She lived several years beyond what was even remotely merciful.

We've read about how our medical system keeps brain-dead people alive for years. Yes, one in 10,000 suddenly wakes up. I'll bet against those odds anytime. We make it very difficult for doctors or families to pull the plug . . . and we run up completely unneccessary astronomical costs. That's all emotional stuff.

One of our problems is that we tend to put too much trust in doctors . . . and far too few deserve it. One of the reasons chiropractors do well is that so few doctors are trained in osteopathy. Medicine is a trendy practice. Doctors tend to be far more worried about peer censure than their patients' well being.

Our health system is a misnomer. It's a lie. We don't have a health care system at all . . . what we have is sickness care. How many times have you gone to a doctor in perfect health? You go when something finally gets so bad you have to go. That's not health, that's sickness.

Well, doctors are trained to handle sickness, not health. They are not even remotely trained in health care. If they were, we'd get sick a lot less.

I remember when I got bursitis and my shoulder was hurting. I went to my friendly family doctor who gave me a shot of B-12 in the shoulder. That fixed it in a couple days just fine. So I asked him if I might not be able to prevent another attack by taking some B-12 on a regular basis. He had no idea, but thought perhaps not.

Doctors for years pooh-poohed vitamins. You don't need 'em, they said. You get all you need in a regular diet.

So here we are, eating things which are gradually causing us to die of "natural causes." Often, well advertised things. Doctors aren't taught what happens when the endocrine system is unbalanced by too much sugar and the calcium/phosphorus ratio is swung too far. They aren't taught the connection between this and a whole rash of disabling problems such as arthritis.

Doctors for years refused to believe that the mind had any connection with sickness. Now it's generally accepted that *every* sickness has a psychological component. Yet even today there isn't a doctor in the country I've heard of who treats the underlying trigger of an illness along with the symptoms it has caused.

If this meant that every doctor would have to become a psychiatrist as well as a physician, there might be some reason to withhold 50-90% of the treatment sick people should be getting . . . the treatment of the psychological component of their illness.

But the fact is that this process can be almost totally automated and used in any doctor's office. Finding the emotional component of an illness is not a complicated process. It's so simple even a relatively inexpensive microcomputer can do it.

But if the underlying cause of an illness is so easily found (and easily resolved too), in many cases eliminating the resulting illness with no further treatment being necessary, why isn't this being done? Simple . . . it's not taught in medical school and other doctors would get pretty upset if you did it.

A copy of *Wellness Today* came in the mail a couple of days ago. It says, "No drug can cut your chances of having arthritis or diabetes . . . no hospital can protect you against heart attack or cancer . . . no doctor can shield you from strokes or premature aging . . . but *you* can."

In the 1950s, doctors were doing commercials for cigarettes. In the 1970s they sneered at nutrition. The AMA said that any doctor who prescribed vitamins was a quack.

Doctors make their money when we get sick, not when we stay healthy. They have a powerful vested interest in our getting sick. One thing we know about capitalism . . . we might call it the dark side . . . is that Adam Smith's invisible hand on the market controls the overall path of civilization. Few people, including doctors, are so selfless that they'll work against their own best interests.

So how can we cope with the situation and start bringing this whole thing out of the dark ages? I suspect this is far beyond the scope of our Commission. It's beyond even New Hampshire to change quickly. But we can at least recognize what's going on and try to make some small inroads toward solutions.

As you know by now, I tend to think in terms of information as helping to solve problems. But what can you do when so much of the information available isn't dependable? I read *In Health* and *Longevity*, and while I find them interesting, I don't trust 'em completely. Nor do I trust *Prevention*.

But on the other hand, I trust the AMA even less. And having worked in the psychiatric field, I know what a bunch of baloney most shrinks are selling. Yes, there are some honest ones. There are some honest lawyers too, so it's not necessarily a contradiction of terms.

A magazine that I have in my long queue of needed publications would help sick people get better. It would publish reports in lay terms on the latest research results on the more intractible diseases. It would not tout rose hips as a solution for everything from chronic constipation to myopia.

For instance, people suffering from psoraisis are very interested in what's being found out about their disease. Right now there's no central information source for people with chronic problems.

Where can you turn for dependable information on things like the potential dangers of electric fields? Anyone who reads has been reading about the possible perils of power lines and electric blankets. Is this another media hype or the real thing?

We're supposed to be an information society, but we're awash in information which we don't know enough about to evaluate. Most of us don't have any good way to tell the good from the bad from the who knows. Perhaps this is one of the earlier problems we need to start solving.

082 Rampant Socialism

We know we need government. We need help in making and maintaining laws. But government tends to operate faithfully on Parkinson's Laws and expand without limit. We find ourselves paying a dollar which is intended to help someone else, but only 20 cents of it manages to get through the system . . . if we're lucky. And that's the way it is with most of what we kindly call transfer payments.

When we give a dollar to help the poor, they may get 20 cents of it. When we pay a dollar for public education we find about 20 cents trickling through the system to the classroom. The rest stays with the federal and state government agencies and our school administrators. Well, we're not doing any better with our socialized health programs.

It's even worse. In addition to the big bite taken as our health money goes through the government colon, we then find it heading into a very fine hospital administration bureaucracy. And the more money we put into these systems, the more becomes absorbed, with little benefit to the end customer. It's kinda like the roaring Colorado River, which is gradually used up and ends as a swamp down in Mexico.

A chap I knew well . . . a doctor, actually . . . got busy and set up Medicare centers around California. He took the system for millions. He's in prison now, but not for scamming Medicare. He made the mistake of paying someone, who was not outstanding at keeping confidentialities, to kill his wife.

The more we force business to pay for medical costs, the less competitive our businesses are going to be in the world market. Legislators seem to turn first to the people for taxes . . . then when the taxpayers get ready to revolt if it gets worse, they tax businesses and take the money before the employees can be paid.

Like government spending, the only way medical spending can be controlled is by limiting revenues. I suggest we concentrate our creative efforts in this arena.

083 Magnetic Dangers

I briefly mentioned the current (pardon) media controversy over the potential danger of electromagnetic fields. Having been involved in electronics for a lifetime, I found this of more than a passing interest.

I read the first material on this in an article in *The New Yorker* a couple years ago. It was by Paul Brodeur, the chap who'd blown the whistle on asbestos. He wrote a convincing article.

This was later expanded and published as a book. The power companies, with the potential for billions in lawsuits from families who'd lost members, bought the best scientists they could find to obfuscate.

One of the leading researchers in the field, Dr. Ross Adey, has since become a good friend of mine. He is a ham radio operator and a reader of my *73 Amateur Radio Today* magazine. He's sent me copies of the scientific literature so I could read firsthand about the depth of the experiments which have been conducted. It's a foot-high pile of scientific reports and they all unequivocally support the dangers of electric fields.

After reading a few of these, I bought a Gaussmeter to check the field strengths around my home and office. I quickly packed my electric blanket off to the attic. I was getting readings over 150 times those which have been shown to seriously affect the ability of our cells to perform.

A couple of months ago I got a call from a *73* reader who'd read my editorial about magnetics (EMF). It seems Duquesne Power was planning on running a high tension line near his home and he was concerned. He asked if I could help, so I posted on our telephone bulletin board (BBS) a long list of peer-reviewed papers showing the scientific results of EMF tests. He called and retrieved my list with his computer. Next he got copies of the papers from a medical library. Thus, when the power company claimed there was no scientific evidence that magnetic fields are dangerous to people, he was armed with a stack of solid proof. He not only defeated the power company in court, but the Pennsylvania legislature is now considering a bill prohibiting power lines to be run near residences.

I'd like to see the Commission recommend that the New Hampshire legislature enact a similar law. Further, I'd like to see an effort to get the word out about the danger created by electric blankets and the electrical heating in water beds.

The other danger concerns pole transformers located near homes. It was these which started the suspicion that power might be harmful. A researcher in Denver was checking to see if she could find a pattern to childhood leukemia cases. The one common factor turned out to be pole transformers near the affected homes. From there researchers started trying to find why this was happening and what level of magnetic fields might be causing the problem. They've duplicated the cell mutations in laboratories, with the only major surprise being how weak the magnetic fields could be and still affect cell growth and communication.

There's abundant evidence that the magnetic radiation from some computers can also cause problems such as miscarriages and deformed fetuses. People should be warned not to sit too close to TV sets and to sit off to the side of video monitors.

084 Cutting Health Costs

Having served on the board of directors of the Monadnock Health Foundation, the parent organization running the Monadnock Community

Hospital and several clinics in the surrounding towns, I'm painfully familiar with the escalation of health costs. The $239 billion American hospital industry is sick and needs help.

As medical treatment gets more and more high-tech, the costs zoom. Technology is expensive . . . which is why it's such a good business for New Hampshire to cultivate. Medical technology is particularly expensive because people tend to suddenly become much less concerned with costs when they or a loved one get sick. "Do whatever you can, no matter what it costs." That's music to some ears.

No, we don't want to stop developing ever better technology. But perhaps we can at least try to eliminate duplication and waste. Instead of having a million dollar neucleo-magnetic resonating imaging system in many hospitals, couldn't we just move the patients to the nearest NMRI unit and save a few million?

Hospitals and clinics might organize so they can share not-too-frequently used expensive equipment.

085 Health System Research

Just as we need a research project, complete with a publication, to evaluate new educational technologies and pioneering efforts, I believe a similar effort to study and report on health care pioneering efforts could help save enormous amounts of money . . . and could put New Hampshire in a very advantageous position in the field.

If we set up a special group to investigate health care productivity it could provide reports on innovative ideas which have proven effective. I've come across quite a few just from reading various health publications and even the *Reader's Digest*. It would stimulate progress if we had a team researching the subject and publishing the results. The publications would pay for the research.

For instance, one new approach I've read about is to provide mobile micro-hospital vans which can visit patients at home. These units can also be helpful for visiting nursing homes and child care centers. These vans carry far more diagnostic equipment than the normal ambulance.

I was reading recently in *The Wall Street Journal* that heart attack victims, if not revived immediately, are goners. By the time an ambulance is able to get them to a hospital, even the most drastic procedures are almost always a waste of money.

The idea is to promote productivity . . . to provide the best possible health care at the lowest cost. Thus, the more we can find out about new approaches which have been tried . . . anywhere in the world . . . the more data we'll have to help us make our New Hampshire sickness care the best . . . and at the lowest cost.

We're going to have to come to grips with some difficult situations. Religious groups will be putting on pressures, making pragmatic care decisions almost impossible. It'll get us mired in questions of long-term care, euthanasia, and so on. I'm no stranger to these problems and have developed my own philosophies to deal with them.

Since I'm not going to run for any office or try to win any prizes or medals, I'm warning you that I probably will not come across as a deeply caring person. I believe in the basic Darwin theory of the survival of the fittest and that when we screw around with this concept we do no favors for the world or mankind.

By the way, there are some strong reasons (other than religious) not to buy Darwin's theories wholesale, but I do agree that life seems designed to strive for survival. I find the theories of Fred Hoyle (the noted astronomer) on the sudden appearance of completely new species most intriguing.

By implementing new sickness care approaches, increasing both research and education on health maintenance, and ruthlessly pruning back our ever-growing administrative groups, I believe we'll be able to provide better health, longer, happier lives and at the same time substantially reduce our current health costs.

086 What To Do About Government

There seems to be a consensus that our federal government is a mess. In just a few years it's taken us from being the leading financial country in the world to the largest debtor. It's been unable to cope with drugs, crime, education, our decaying infrastruture, medical costs, the banking mess, the loss of our consumer electronics industry, the decimation of our automobile industry, and so on.

Government is a mix of the executive, legislative, judiciary and, most of all, government employees. The employees include not only hordes of government workers in Washington, but also our postal and military employees, plus who knows how many federal employees deployed in our states?

We've had a number of presidents running for office with promises to cut back this massive bureaucracy. All have failed.

One of our problems may stem from a basic incompatibility between capitalism and democracy. We're seeing this incompatibility increasingly warping the democratic process as our communications systems improve.

The egalitarian concept of everybody pitching in to elect representatives to handle matters of our common good is attractive. It seemingly affords us a way to replace our leaders when they disappoint us.

It's a great idea in theory, but we haven't figured out a way to make it work. As soon as we elect leaders they immediately set about controlling the information system which, in turn, controls who gets elected. Our information system, being capitalistic in nature, bends when pressured by money.

So we tend to end up with leaders who have been put into place by money and who are kept there by money. Our leaders are ever alert to the spigot which turns this money supply on or off, making sure that it's as on as possible.

There have been some solutions proposed to this problem, but oddly enough these haven't yet been endorsed by many of our elected leaders. Concepts such as limiting campaign spending, eliminating PAC donations, and so on have not flourished.

The first step toward getting out of the mess we've made is to recognize that we've made a mess. The next is to consider creative solutions to the problem. Term limitation is attractive. Ending paid political advertising is another. How about mandatory lie detector tests during each political speech, interview or debate? I can hear the buzzer now!

Like you, I'm being solicited for political donations almost daily. Having been a Republican ever since the party started, my growing disenchantment with Bush has been difficult to adjust to. I don't identify with the liberals — my belief in the capitalistic system is too strong. As I've mentioned, I haven't seen socialism work anywhere, nor does the concept even seem viable. I know that when not driven by necessity, I can be as lazy and unproductive as anyone. It's very pleasant to get unemployment checks and take it easy.

Having visited the USSR and seen firsthand what this does to a people — where no one seems to be working willingly, or to care even remotely about what they're doing — it's almost enough to make a person rethink the socialist concept. We may have people who hate commercialism, but it sure does work. Show me a non-profit business which is providing a quality product or service.

Thus, the more we can inject capitalism into government, the better chance we'll have of it working to our benefit. The more we make it a socialist system, the worse it's going to be. We all know that if we eliminated the post office monopoly we'd soon have faster, better, cheaper service. We'd get rid of an enormous bureaucracy which soaks up postage increases of any size like a blotter.

Competition helps keep businesses lean. One of the benefits of the recent recession has been the dumping of millions of unnecessary management layers from larger businesses. It took a downturn in revenues to force them to cut their accumulated layers of fat.

Modern communications and computer technologies have made it possible to eliminate those old bureaucratic layers. Businesses can react faster without all that. The most recent Tom Peters video programs have to do with the amazing success stories of businesses which have learned to react quickly to changing market demands. Well, his observations apply to government as well as business. We should think of government as a business — with us as the board of directors.

As members of the board, we should be getting reports on revenues, expenses, and operations. We should get in-depth reports on how our business is being run so we'll be better able to elect officers.

Jay Leno made an insightful comment when he was discussing the proposed term limitations. He pointed out that, after all, it's we who have been endlessly re-electing these guys. Any time we want to limit their terms, all we have to do is vote for someone else. Novel concept.

I suspect that the framers of our constitution never considered that the voters would be as uneducated as ours are now. And mis-educated. With 20% of our work force functionally illiterate and 50% of the population not reading any magazines or books, whoever best manipulates TV and the newspapers is in firm control.

So here we are with faster and cheaper means for getting information and most people don't want to be involved. The Hill-Thomas show was such a great success it'll probably sell well in syndication and then as a videotape series. It got better ratings than *Roseanne*.

There's too much going on in the government to reduce it to easy-to-understand reports. We'd undoubtedly end up with two-inch piles of gobbledegook and get fed up even trying. Bureaucrats are well acquainted with the concept of obfuscation. And they love cranking out voluminous, unreadable reports.

Perhaps, in our efforts to simplify government, we can try to decide in what areas we feel we really need to have our government operate. Then we can start trying to get it out of areas better served by private (profit-making) businesses.

Let's just take a very small New Hampshire government responsibility and look at it. For instance, how about the issuing of hunting licenses? Could this be run by private companies? We want to adjust the hunting so as to keep the game under control. If private companies issue too many licenses, the game'll be killed off and they'll go out of business. So there's a limiting factor. If they control it too tightly they won't make any money. They want to make the most money they can, while not putting themselves out of business. And that's just what we need to control the number of deer so they don't starve.

Private companies, being in competition, would keep their prices down. They'd help manage the deer population. They'd register the killed deer and have their agents checking to make sure hunters have licenses. And it wouldn't cost New Hampshire a nickel. Indeed, we'd want to get maybe a 5% cut on revenues.

Could we do the same with fishing licenses? The fishing companies would be stocking our rivers and lakes far better than our bureaucracy ever could. Further, like the hunting companies, they'd be advertising far and wide to bring in vacationers to fish. That would boost our tourism and vacation revenues for hotels, camps, restaurants and so on.

The road infrastructure is more complicated. Everyone in New Hampshire benefits from our road system. We can levy some taxes on road use via fuel taxes. We can charge tolls. We can set up mini-malls at interstate interchanges and tax their sales. We can continue to tax vehicle ownership. We might even add some taxes to tourist businesses to help pay for the roads which make it easy for their customers to come. That's not unfair, is it?

I'd like to see some cost accounting on our road system and get an idea of what shortfall we have right now.

We think we need some better roads across the state. Will they pay for themselves by bringing in more tourists? By cutting transportation costs for business? By attracting more business to areas which could be developed?

When I was born in Littleton in 1922, it was an isolated small town. The nearest paved highway ended at White River Junction. I remember the one-lane, twisting, bumpy, dirt road down through Franconia Notch. An approaching car had to pull off the road to let the other by. When I drive up 93 through the Notch and on to Littleton, I'm awestruck at the changes just in my lifetime.

Today it's easy for people from Boston to drive up 93 and go skiing on Cannon Mountain or at Loon. They come up by the thousands from Massachusetts, Rhode Island and Connecticut.

Now there's talk of a high speed railroad from Boston to Portland. If we had an interstate highway going up to North Conway, could we get vacationers to take the train to Portsmouth and then drive to the Mount Washington area? In Europe I'm used to driving my car onto trains to save time driving through the Alps. It doesn't take any longer than a normal train ride and is more fun than driving through mile-long tunnels.

Can we tackle each state expense and see if we can find a way to have those benefiting pay? I like the idea.

087 Say Yes To Drugs

The normal reaction to the suggestion that drugs be legalized is one of horror. Reactive horror. It does sound like a very bad idea until you do more than respond emotionally.

One of the unfortunate aspects of this is that when people are responding emotionally they're not open to even considering the pros and cons and weighing them on their merits. They don't want to hear any pros or cons. They don't want to hear anything about it.

It's probably a genetic defect or else an exececssively poor upbringing, but I haven't been able to find very many subjects I'm closed to thinking about. Heck, I can't even work up heated arguments about most things.

With that proviso, here are some of the factors which I considered in approaching the American drug situation. Not being reactively for or against things, including drugs, I've given some of 'em a try when the opportunity arose.

It was the summer of 1948, when I was the chief cameraman at WPIX(TV) in New York. Three of my friends on the staff invited me to have some pot with them. It turned out to be a fascinating experience and I enjoyed it. It didn't exactly turn me into a pot-head. I smoked a couple more reefers at a party in 1970 when they were offered and made the party far more fun. Sorry, but that's about it.

So I'm neither opposed to nor in favor of people using pot. It's as dangerous when it comes to driving as alcohol. Beyond that, it doesn't seem to be much better or worse than alcohol . . . just different. Tobacco appears to be far more dangerous to health and far more addictive.

In 1960 I tried LSD. It was a tremendously positive experiment. Wow! Incredible! I haven't wanted to do it again, but I'm very glad I didn't miss the experience.

I recognize that many people tend toward addictions . . . to alcohol, tobacco, heroin, cocaine, and so on. In the non-drug addictions we could add gambling, sex, and eating. Mine is eating, so I know how it feels to be an addict. I can stop, but it takes enormous restraint. I finally decided to stop being fat in 1972. I dieted for nine months and took off 85 pounds, going from 250 to 165 pounds. Unlike most addicts, I've been able to control the dragon . . . though it's never far away. I've stayed within a few pounds of 165 for 20 years now.

Look, we tried prohibiting alcohol and it didn't work. All prohibition did was build a permanent criminal infrastructure which we'll never get rid of. The mob, as we call them, loves anything illegal. They provide enterpreneurial opportunities.

When we made lotteries illegal, the criminals ran them and made millions. We made drugs illegal, so they went into that business and it's into the billions. Has making drugs illegal stopped them? Har-de-har. As long as drugs are a way to make huge profits, they'll be a big business.

My folks drank all through prohibition. When I was a kid they had a bar in the cellar of our home and had friends over to drink almost every night. My dad was in aviation, so aviation pioneers such as Frank Hawks, Amelia Earhart, and Ed Connerton (Bell Helicopters) visited us regularly.

If we made drugs legal, it's argued, anyone could buy them. Well, anyone can right now. I'm sure I could score pot, cocaine, and probably even crack right in Peterborough within 30 minutes. One chap who used to work for me grew a generous supply of pot in his back yard for years. May still. It's all around, even here in New Hampshire.

By having it sold for such a low price that it isn't worth smuggling, we'd get criminals out of the business, just as we did with alcohol. That would quickly cut our crime problem. That, in turn, would allow our courts to catch up and would eliminate the need to build more prisons. We'd save billions that are being wasted by the whole mess.

Of course this would have a terribly negative impact on the police, lawyers, judges, prisons and so on. It would create enormous problems for organized crime, street gangs, and inner city lifestyles. Maybe we don't want to mess with those things.

Even worse, it could virtually gut our prime-time cop shows. They'd have to go back to plain old murder, jewel robberies and counterfeit money cases, which aren't generally as gory and violent as drug-related crime and might tend to lose audience shares. The gun industry might not ever recover . . . and the beeper business would be seriously hurt.

Considering all those powerful vested interests, legalizing drugs is probably a pipe dream.

I'm reminded of Tom Lehrer's wonderful song, "The Old Dope Peddler."

Every evening just at twilight
Comes a fellow everyone knows
It's the old dope peddler
Spreading joy wherever he goes

He gives the kids free samples
Because he knows full well
That today's young innocent faces
Are tomorrow's clientele

Here's a cure to all your worries
Here's an end to all distress
It's the old dope peddler
With his powdered happiness

Without enormous profits fueling the engine, the whole multi-level drug marketing organization would collapse. Addicts wouldn't have to recruit more and more addicts to pay for their habits.

088 The Amsterdam Example

When they legalized porno in the Netherlands and Denmark, the first reaction was whee! . . . and porno stores opened all over the place. Thousands of porno entrepreneurs went into business supplying films, videos, books, magazines, photos and so on.

It didn't take long before the excitement was over and 95% of these firms went out of business. The industry ended up being far smaller than it was when it was illegal.

You can get drugs in Holland almost anywhere, but drug use has dropped way off and seems to be of more interest to foreign visitors than the Dutch. Anything illegal tends to be attractive and lucrative.

New Hampshire seems like a reasonable place to test legalizing drugs. Of course, as we found when we provided alcohol and cigarettes at bargain prices, we'd risk running into smuggling to other states. It wouldn't be difficult to limit individual purchases and keep computer records which would alert us to attempts at volume buying.

In addition to preventing unrestricted sales of drugs, this would further chill the illegal sale of beer to teenagers.

The arguments pro and con on this, as with any such emotional subject, are apparently endless. I won't even try to cover them here. William Buckley and George Will have presented well-considered opinions favoring the legalization of drugs.

Once we've removed the enormous profits from the drug business it seems reasonable to expect that drug smuggling will cease, as will the motives attracting people to drug-connected crimes.

Will people take advantage of low cost drugs and become addicts? Lacking advertising, and in the face of a stepped up anti-drug campaign, financed by drug sales, we have no precedent anywhere in the world which would lead us to expect it.

A stepped-up campaign against cigarettes could extend millions of lives. It would tend to hurt our sickness care and funeral industries. It could also virtually destroy our social security system, which is heavily dependent on people dying early from smoking and not getting the payments they bargained for. I would expect the tobacco, "health care," and other affected organizations to muster strong lobbying resistance to my plan.

So here I am proposing a state-run drug business. This, I admit, is inconsistent with my stance in opposition to states getting into businesses, either non-profit or for-profit. What if we considered some types of businesses as utilities, where they could be run by private companies, but licensed by the state?

If New Hampshire decided to permit privately run drug stores in open competition, would there be a downside? Remember the proscription on any advertising. And the requirement of a computerized data base to limit sales to any one individual.

We have the technology today to keep track of our New Hampshire licensed drivers, complete with a point-of-sale video camera to record buyers' faces and purchases. A data base could send a photo of the person to the store for the check-out person to compare. We could devise a difficult-to-beat system.

Remember, what we're trying to do is make it difficult for people to buy drugs, but not difficult enough so it will enable a criminal market for drugs to prosper.

089 Creative Solutions

When the war in Vietnam got started, I thought our approach to coping with the problem lacked creativity. We made no serious effort to out-think the communists. What we did was turn the problem over to our military leaders and ask them what we should do. It's no surprise that their answer was to fight. That's their business. They aren't trained for any other response.

Our State Department was equally unable to cope with the communist aggression. In fact we had no agency which seemed to be able to try and counter the communist moves.

My approach was to talk with friends who understood the situation. A good friend of mine was sent over to try and update the South Vietnam police force. I visited the country in 1959 and talked with friends. I also talked with my ham friends in neighboring Thailand.

On a later trip I discussed the Vietnam situation with ham friends in India, Nepal, Burma, Singapore, Australia, New Caledonia, etc. As I talked with them I developed a new strategic approach to solving the war. I then tried to interest Congress in this, but was unable to get through their protective layer of assistants.

My approach used a combination of what I'd learned in visiting Yugoslavia, New Caledonia, India, and Singapore. My idea was to be pragmatic about the situation. Might there be a better plan than trying to kill the North Vietnamese soldiers and rack up body counts . . . which was costing us about $600,000 per body, a ridiculously unproductive price to pay for people who wouldn't ever be worth a fraction of that . . . and worse, involved our losing American soldiers in the bargain? We haven't been able to put a price on American lives, but if we did the cost per dead North

Vietnamese soldier would go way over $1 million each.

My basic solution was simple: spend a fraction of that and bribe them to stop fighting. You have to remember that bribery is an honorable institution in many Asian countries. It's a way of life. Even the most fanatic communist soldiers would understand bribery.

Bribe them with what, money? Well, I took my plan a bit beyond that simple solution. After seeing how hard people were willing to work in Yugoslavia to be able to get an automobile, I knew this would be a powerful attraction.

Suppose we set up some factories in Vietnam to make the simplest kind of cars? Something on the order of a go-cart that could be sold for a few hundred dollars? Basic transportation? This was what the French did with their Deux Cheveaux (2CV) which got the French off bicycles and into cars. They sold for $600 and sold by the millions. They were ugly. They were simple. They were cheap.

The Germans responded with the basic Volkswagen, developed by Dr. Porsche. The VW, combined with the autobahns, quickly got the Germans off their bicycles.

So I'd start by giving a booklet of chits to the North Vietnamese soldiers as they sneaked down the Ho Chi Minh Trail. One would be redeemable for a small hut and an acre of land . . . another for basic furniture for the hut and seeds to plant. A third would be a work permit to get work in a factory making the cars, huts, furniture, and some other basics. We wouldn't give them the cars, only make them easily achievable goals.

Step two would be to set up TV stations around the country. Why? Well, I saw what happened in New Caledonia. There the native tribes had been at war with each other for hundreds of years. It was a way of life. The French came and set up TV stations. The natives had to stop fighting and work to earn enough for a TV set. Then they were kept so busy by their families earning money to buy the products advertised on TV that they never got back to fighting again.

So I'd put in TV and make el-cheapo sets available. Heck, it wouldn't have been difficult to set up an assembly plant, for that matter, but TVs are all assembled by robots these days, so even the cheapest of labor is irrelevant. I visited a plant in South Korea where the labor had been reduced to about 15 minutes per TV set, including packing and shipping the finished product.

The Singapore lesson was even more powerful. A UN team put together the resources and markets within easy shipping distance and got Singapore busy making the right products. I've already discussed this miracle. A similar study of the resources and markets for Vietnam would have made it clear what products should be made there. And with that information, getting the financing needed to build and operate the factories wouldn't be difficult.

I was proposing a generous application of capitalism as a solution to the war instead of wasting billions of dollars and tens of thousands of American lives. Few people seemed interested.

So we tried to outfight them instead of outsmarting them. They outsmarted us and nobody really won, but boy, did we lose!

090 Capitalistic Democracy?

Can we let the capitalistic concept go unrestrained in society? The fact is we can't really stop it. Many people love the socialist concept, even if it's never worked in practice.

When our legislators in Washington support lobbyist causes in exchange for re-election contributions, airplane rides, free vacations, PAC donations and so on, isn't that a normal capitalistic reaction? Where we get into trouble is when we try to convince ourselves that our elected officials are going to ignore money and work purely for the social good. We get all upset when we find they actually have been working for their own good instead of ours.

True, our representatives and senators in Washington are aware that they'll be out of work if they are too callous to their employers (us). So they try to keep us from getting too upset, while using every tool available to keep us happy. They use PR, franked mail, speeches, get on the evening news, and run re-election campaigns which start the previous election evening.

If our legislators got paid on a percentage of the money they saved on the budget, we'd soon see our bureaucracy pared down to a bare minimum. I'm put in mind of the critical media coverage of large corporation executives who are being paid millions of dollars while their companies are losing hundreds of millions . . . even billions.

Salesmen often are paid a small salary and make the rest in commissions. Imagine if Iacocca had to try and scrimp by with only a $500,000 salary and the rest of his pay came as a percentage of Chrysler's profits.

Of course, since our legislators set their own pay and have worked out a wide variety of ways for sneaking in pay raises, we're not likely to see any profit motive inducement innovations.

091 Making The FCC Pay Off

There's a move afoot to start charging for the radio spectrum. If you've ever thought about opening a store in a shopping mall you know that malls take a percentage of your revenues right off the top. It's your problem if you make money or lose it; they get theirs.

Well, here we are with thousands of radio and TV stations making billions of dollars using publically-owned radio frequencies. It doesn't seem unreasonable to me to have the agency involved with assigning frequencies get a piece of the action. Indeed, this could be a profit-making agency which could help to reduce our taxes.

In Britain they charge users a tax on TV sets and radios. This is used by the BBC to produce the broadcasts. The result pleases few. Commercial radio and TV, for all its faults, seems able to provide better fare. Yes, we have National Public Radio and our Public Broadcasting System, both with some fine programs. But these are supported in large by restrained advertising masked as subsidies from private companies.

Broadcasting has historically been an interstate matter. Where it tends to change over to a state or even a city matter is when the broadcasts are delivered by cable instead of radio waves. This is important to consider because we're inevitably heading away from radio broadcasting and toward delivery of radio, TV, information services, personal communications, computer networking and so on, all via fiber optic cables.

We'll still need radio, but mainly as a means of interconnecting with this master communications system while walking, driving or flying. Thus we'll be using a relatively small part of the microwave spectrum for these interconnects.

Let me repeat that we have the technology right now, without having to invent anything new, to set up a world communications system which would make it possible for anyone anywhere to write a letter on a pocket portable computer and have it sent at 25,000 words per minute to any place in the world. It would take seconds to do . . . and the messages could be automatically translated accurately into any language in the world. I'll be glad to go into details for anyone with a technical communications background. I started pioneering digital radio communications in 1949 and wrote and published the first books on the subject.

With broadcasting and other services being delivered via fiber optic cables, states and towns will be in a position to regulate these services for the first time. Should states go the route towns have with TV cable, where one company is given a franchise for an area and all the others frozen out?

We've watched the mess this system has caused, with bribery influencing franchises and the lack of potential competition keeping customer service to a minimum. Socialism doesn't even work on this level.

Some state control of cable communications seems necessary, if only in an ombudsman position. Considering the revenues involved, this would seem to be another case where the state could not just referee the service, but could use some of the taxed revenues to further reduce personal taxes.

Considering the cost of installing fiber optic cables in all homes and businesses, I suspect the telephone companies will probably do this first. Once I have an optical cable in my home I'd want to be able to choose between radio and TV services I'd want to buy and not have to deal solely with NYNEX.

Services which would attract me would be a digital music library available on demand . . . a wide variety of TV channels . . . plus any video rental I want on demand. They've been experimenting successfully with this concept in England. I also should be able to see a replay on any TV program I may have missed or failed to tape.

My optical cable service will also have high definition TV programs and current movies available for rent . . . presumably at a price I won't mind paying.

I'll also be able to not just see and hear any public meetings, but be able to participate. Cables are two-way devices, so I'll be able to be both seen and heard at meetings and conferences.

When I want to go skiing, I'll be able to see how the conditions are at Loon Mountain and not wonder how much their PR person has bent reality in hopes of attracting naive skiers. They got mad at me last year when I complained about their dishonest reports. I called to see what the conditions were. I almost went, but business interfered. A good friend did go and found no correlation between their report and reality. He went home in disgust. I found I'd saved a four-hour round-trip drive.

Our state legislators need to be aware of the changes technologies are going to bring and plan to keep our state climate healthy for entrepreneurial businesses, while not letting large businesses get a stranglehold on any one industry.

So, while New Hampshire can't lease out the radio spectrum, it can see that there's an even playing field for cable service suppliers. And it can make a profit doing it. If the state tries to take too big a bite on any services it regulates, the customers (a.k.a. voters) can change the legislature to correct the problem.

092 Capital Gains Taxes

The more we encourage the federal government to keep capital gains taxes low, the more money will tend to be available to help entrepreneurs start new ventures. "A tax on capital gains is a tax on opportunity, not on wealth. If the reward for risk taking is confiscated, two things happen. Bettors stick to front runners, and the long shots never enter the race." (*Forbes* 11/11/91 p206). Entrepreneurs need the venture capital which a capital gains tax prevents.

We're pretending that black and Hispanic entrepreneurs should have an opportunity in America . . . then we kill that opportunity by turning off the venture capital investments they need to get started.

093 The Social Security Millstone

Our marvelous social security system got started in the middle of the New Deal depression in the thirties. In order to make work, the system was set up to force people to retire at 65. This would make more jobs. So here we are 60 years later and people of 65 are not all happy to be put out to pasture. Some have discovered there's more to life than playing golf or watching ball games until the grim reaper finally finds their address.

I faced the possibility of retiring when I sold my business a few years ago. Should I buy a castle in Spain and vegetate? Should I pursue a goal of visiting 200 countries? I could go skiing in the winter and skin diving in the summer, with homes here and there.

That seemed like a waste to me. I'd spent a lifetime finding out how to start and run magazines. Instead of blowing the money on a life of the rich and famous, I preferred to go back into publishing. In this way I'd be able to help new technologies grow. I'd be able to provide work for a hundred or so people. I'd be able to educate and entertain hundreds of thousands of readers and perhaps brighten their lives. I might even be able to convince some of them to become entrepreneurs and thus help create more wealth.

So I started anew with a compact disc magazine. This led to my getting annoyed at the stranglehold six international megacorporations had on the American music industry. And that led to more publications, building my own recording studios, starting several record labels, a mail order music company, a music distribution company and so on.

My music has delighted millions of people. My guerrilla marketing attacks on the monster companies is starting to bear fruit. If I'd retired instead, none of this would have happened . . . and I'd be playing golf somewhere in Costa Rica, drawing little social security checks and clipping bond coupons.

We don't need to take money from the rich and give it to the poor. What we need is to put wealth within the reach of more people. And we should let people work as long as they want. If we give them a chance, they'll provide the jobs which are needed for entrants into the job market. If we kill off our most experienced people with forced retirement, we're not doing anyone any favors.

094 What About Bush?

Since New Hampshire isn't yet interested in seceding from the union (which does have its attractive side), we've still got to keep our eye on Washington . . . and our pockets buttoned up to keep their hands out.

There's been an increasing amount of media discussion about Bush being beatable in the next election. In the last election, I tolerated Bush mainly because Dukakis presented an even worse scenario.

The recent mess with Thomas made me face the fact that George Bush is a liar. I see him as being as dishonest as Nixon. Nominating Quayle for VP was not honest. That was a lie. He wasn't qualified and still isn't, no matter how much media manipulation is accomplished. And nominating Thomas for the Supreme Court was another lie. We all know these were lies. We know we can't trust anything Bush says. I really hate that aspect of politics.

I'm also at odds with Bush on the right to life issue. I've visited enough countries around the world to get a different perspective on the value of life. I've personally seen how cheap it is in Pakistan, India, Afghanistan, Burma, Iraq, Iran, Lebanon, Syria, Lesotho, Swaziland, Uganda, Sudan, Ethiopia, Colombia, Guatemala, Brazil, and the Philippines. It's been erased with little compunction recently in China, Burma, and the Mid-East.

So I approach these things pragmatically, not from religious beliefs. From that view I find life all too easy to start . . . as do many teenagers. People with every advantage have enough problems coping with the world. Do we need to force women to have children who are not wanted and who they are not equipped to support?

We don't need to double or triple the world population. We're already straining the world's resources. We're burning the rain forests to grow cattle. We are beginning to understand the ramifications of this, but the enormous population explosion in the poorer countries calls for temporary expediency to keep these billions of children from starving . . . and never mind what the world will be like in 200 years.

Well, we're insulated from these problems up here in New Hampshire. A change in the climate will either give us hotter summers or snowier winters. We win either way . . . for a while.

095 Cleaning Up Waste

Money waste, that is. If America is going to regain its financial lead in the world, not only do we have to rebuild our high-tech manufacturing industries and improve our marketing, we're also going to have to get rid of as much wasted money in both government and business as we can. When I see what goes on behind the scenes in business, I almost get outraged. Not quite, because I'm saving my outrage for our court system.

I remember the first time I came up against our courts. I'd been done out of what was a tidy sum at the time . . . $500,000 . . . by an unscrupulous chap. I brought suit. My lawyer said I had nothing to worry about, it was a clear case. Now I worry when someone tells me I have nothing to worry about.

A day before the trial my lawyer called. There was a problem. He'd heard from the judge, who agreed the case looked clear . . . but he wanted $10,000 in cash. Being broke, sure of my case, and believing in the honesty of the judge more than that of my lawyer, I refused. I lost the case and didn't have the money to appeal it.

If you've been watching "Reasonable Doubts" and "Law & Order," you know how little weight rightness carries in our courts. It's long lost in our judicial system. Since there's not much an economic development commission can do to implement a paradigm shift in our legal system, I'm sure I'll be maintaining my outrage level for the rest of this lifetime.

One more small item. The next time you are in court and you are sworn to "tell the truth, the whole truth, and nothing but the truth," you're lying if you answer anything but "no." There's no way in the world those lawyers are going to permit you to tell the whole truth, and you know it. Our court system is organized so that one side exaggerates your guilt and the other your innocence. I've never seen an occasion where anyone was permitted to tell the whole truth.

I got terribly frustrated during a murder trial of a youngster who'd worked briefly for me and had gotten fired because he threatened other employees. He stole a rifle from me and deliberately killed a kid with it. His father and uncle were Mafia members and were arrested a week after the kid's trial for robbing a bank. The jury wasn't allowed to hear anything about his background, so he got off with a couple of years in prison. The whole truth? Sure.

And that brings me to some egregious business wastes. Well, I think they are. Your perspective may be different. I remember being annoyed (low-level outrage) when the publisher of a magazine I was editing bought a 57-foot yacht with the magazine's money. It was a business expense, he said. He justified it by taking the staff out for a yearly party on it. He never took any customers or suppliers. The rest of the year it was his private yacht.

This came to mind recently when I was out on a cruise around Manhattan on *Highlander*, the *Forbes* magazine yacht. We're talking major posh here. It's a floating luxury hotel. They served a nice dinner during the two-hour cruise.

I talked with my fellow passengers. None seemed to be much involved with the magazine. They'd been invited on a cruise and didn't pass it up. I went because I hoped to have a relaxed opportunity to talk with Bob Forbes about some magazine inserts I had in mind. We had an advertorial insert in their November 11, 1991, issue which they liked a lot. I think we'll see if we can find a couple of people to hire who will be able to work on inserts for *Forbes*, *Business Week* and perhaps *Fortune*. I need one writer and one advertising space salesman . . . I just don't know how to find them.

We can do inserts covering the latest in audio developments, home theater, new recording technologies and so on. The idea is to put together several articles and sell advertising to fill out the section.

The dinner was nice. The cruise just fine. But I felt I'd wasted my time and was annoyed. The whole yacht seemed like an enormous waste of money. But then I thought it over and realized that, like my old publisher, the yacht was paid for mainly with tax money. As a corporate expense it would reduce their profits. If they're in the 50% bracket, the yacht would cost only 50 cents on the dollar.

A printer I used for my magazines had his own jet plane. Same deal. He had no need for a jet . . . or even a plane. He could have traveled on commercial flights just fine. But by using tax money he was able to indulge himself. And I got a nice jet ride to Georgia out of it. It bothered me that my printing bill would have to pay for even part of the plane. I'm just not comfortable with waste.

An old friend of mine, whose wife worked for me for years, is a jet pilot for an oil company out of Houston. Virtually 100% of his work is flying their customers to Aspen for vacations. Okay, that may help get some business, but isn't that kinda' like bribery? I doubt if getting business has much to do with it. It's more showing off and enjoying the use of pre-tax dollars.

Am I suggesting it's better to send more tax dollars to Washington than to spend them on yachts and jets? No, they are getting several times what they need to do the work we need done already. What I'd like is to make it more difficult to waste money on baloney like that so corporate officers would tend to think more about investing it in research and development of new technologies and new products. The Japanese are running circles around us on R&D investing. We're running circles around them with yachts and incredible executive salaries. And they're winning.

We might even use the extra cash as venture capital to enable new businesses to be started. One problem America has right now is getting investment capital for new businesses.

Can the tax structure be changed to make it more profitable for businesses to invest their profits in R&D, expansion or other ventures, than in indulging in conspicuous consumption perks?

Might it be possible to encourage New Hampshire businesses to help fund entrepreneurial startups by offering a break on business profits taxes? We might be able to set a precedent for other states, showing them that a small, flexible state can provide leadership for the whole country.

097 Town Growth

I hope we can all agree that our cities are already larger than they need to be and that our quality of life will be best enhanced by encouraging further growth in either our rural areas or in the towns surrounding our cities.

This is the pattern our larger cities are experiencing as "Edge Cities" replace the expansion of core cities. Less than 8% of our population now live in cities of over one million.

People don't want to come to New Hampshire just to live in another city with crime, traffic and crowding. They want some space, an easy commute, plenty of cultural events and a good educational system. Low taxes won't hurt.

How can we benefit from this concept? We can keep housing costs, our road infrastructure and the arts in mind as we plan for the New Hampshire of 1995, 2000 and 2020. We can encourage growth where it will provide a better quality of life, instead of letting developers go berserk, as was done along 101A.

Since not every job we can provide is going to pay middle or above income wages, we should pay some attention to providing at least some low income housing. I'd like to see us consider the quality of life of lower income workers too, and encourage the provision of housing which will meet their ability to pay.

Forcing them to live in small apartments in old houses, thus tending to run the places down even more, won't contribute much to their quality of life. If we can plan some trailer parks away from our main roads, this might help them and still not impact our own quality of life.

By encouraging the development of towns near our cities, complete with low income housing, people would be able to take advantage of not only the cultural events in the area, but also the educational facilities. It takes education to move from low income to middle . . . and on up . . . education beyond that offered in K-12. We want to give everyone a fair chance at being upwardly mobile.

097 Getting Feedback

Quality control means not only inspecting the product, in the case of both products and services, it also means getting feedback from the customers. This feedback can take the form of their satisfaction with the product or service, as well as suggestions for improvements or new products wanted.

I'd never think of running my publications without surveying the readers regularly to see how we're doing. I want to know what features they like most and least . . . and what they'd like to see that they don't. It's feedback like this which has kept the renewal rates of my magazines high and at times resulted in our making major changes . . . even to changing the names of the publications.

For instance, my *CD Review/Music & Audio Reviews* started as *Digital Audio*. That was fine for the readership back when compact discs were new and most of the people interested were more technically inclined. Then, as the readership grew and was more interested in the music than the technology, I changed the name to *CD Review*.

Our growth continued and then slowed. The problem, our reader research told us, was that they were now even more interested in the music reviews. We found many potential readers turned off by a fear that they wouldn't be able to understand the magazine. I changed the title again and readership growth resumed. I went through a similar process when I was publishing computer magazines.

So what has this to do with New Hampshire? Plenty! Just as I am able to maintain reader interest by keeping my publications in line with my readers, New Hampshire can maintain a high quality of life if we survey our citizens.

What do we want to know? We want to know what they think of state services. We want to know what they think of our educational system, cultural events, sports, federal services and so on.

Think of the improvements we might be able to make in our educational system if we had a way of knowing what courses our graduates have found most valuable in business and life. And what courses they wish they'd taken or been able to take.

By polling our citizens, we'll gradually be able to help our educational system provide the education people are finding they really need. We'll be able to help provide further education to meet their interests and needs.

By getting feedback on state services, we'll find out which are worth keeping and which aren't really needed . . . from the people who know best: the customers. State departments which review themselves aren't likely to be very critical. The federal government is packed solid with self-reviewing, ever-expanding groups.

So who's going to pay for these surveys? When you consider that the reports resulting will be of enormous value to other states and to many businesses, we have the means for supporting it. The sales of survey reports would pay for the work.

We're not talking about a huge organization here. Surveys can be done on cards which can be read by a card reader, thus eliminating any need for data input people. The whole works could be run by three or four people, and the reports processed by a desktop publishing system.

We could even eliminate most of the postage costs, which could be horrendous, by distributing the surveys via stacks put into supermarkets. That's one place virtually everyone in the state frequents at least once a week.

And how do we make sure the people bother to fill out the surveys? We have prize drawings. Of course we don't need 100% compliance to get accurate information. With surveys, all we need is an adequate sample to let statistical analysis take it from there. Basically, it means that by the time we have around 200 responses on a particular question, we're reasonably sure our information is accurate.

We want to know how much visitors enjoy our activities and what activities they might enjoy that we don't have yet. We want to know how they liked their accommodations, our restaurants and so on. We'll be successful as a state when we give people what they want, when they want it and at the price they want to pay.

Does that "price they want to pay" bother you? They'll prefer it all to be free, right? It doesn't work that way. People are most comfortable paying the price they feel is right. If you charge too much, sales go down. If you charge too little, sales go down. You have to test prices, otherwise you know one thing for sure: You're throwing away both sales and money. It has to do with perceived value.

We'd get the feedback cards to tourists by making them available in motels and rooming houses.

Yes, I'm suggesting running New Hampshire as a great big customer-oriented business.

The governor of Wisconsin, Tommy Thompson, decided to commit his state to quality. He set up a five-member steering committee to promote and oversee the development of quality in state agencies. He also appointed a quality coordinator for state government. Even the legislature pledged bipartisan support (*Industry Week* Nov. 4, 1991, p13).

098 Quality Awards

Hopefully, you're aware of the impact the *Michelin Guide* has had on France. Well, our New Hampshire Total Quality Awards could generate the same spirit of competition.

Using the ratings we get from customers, both our citizens and tourists, we could issue yearly Total Quality Award certificates to restaurants, hotels, and major activities. These would be listed in a yearly published guide, as well as in *New Hampshire ToDo*, if we decide something like that is worthwhile.

Restaurants could be rated on food, service, ambiance, and prices. Hotels/motels on rooms, service, prices, and extras . . . like a newspaper, continental breakfast, providing a guide to local attractions and services, etc.

Like Michelin, we could give star ratings. French restaurants will almost kill to get another star. Such a guide would tend to improve our quality of vacationability.

Even state services might strive for better ratings. Gone might be the long lines for licenses. Gone might be gripes of bureaucratic pig-headedness in dealing with wetlands, water quality, waste disposal, and so on.

Can we set up information services which will help people get the jobs they want? Which will help employers find the best people for their jobs? Which will help our people find further education and training so they can be upwardly mobile? I believe we can, with the main downside being a need to fight off population growth. I've had to import hundreds of people from around the country to help my publishing businesses, and most of 'em are still living happily in New Hampshire.

Too much growth will spiral housing and land prices upward again, clog our roads, and expand our edge cities. We could be too successful for our own good. I don't have a good answer for that one . . . except, let's see what we can do to create that problem.

099 Better Radio

New Hampshire, being a little hilly in spots, has an opportunity to help pioneer a new radio service. This is digital audio broadcasting (DAB). It's being developed in Europe and is expected to quickly replace FM broadcasting.

One of my *73 Amateur Radio Today* readers in South Africa sent me a clipping about DAB tests recently conducted in Birmingham, England. They set up a 1,000-watt FM transmitter and an 11-watt DAB transmitter for the test. Receivers were installed in a van and driven around the city.

As the van toured the city, the FM signals fluttered, popped, and were spoiled by the hiss caused by reflections and interference from nearby computers. The DAB signal remained absolutely clear. The FM signal became useless about five miles from the city. The DAB signal kept working to over 15 miles.

In addition to requiring about 1/100th the power to cover three times as much area, the DAB system allows six times as many stereo programs to be sent in the same band as one FM station.

DAB is ideal for our mountainous New Hampshire terrain. And with six separate program channels available on each frequency, we'd be able to select among various kinds of music, talk radio, and even educational programs as we drive. This can provide the music quality for drivers that fiber optic cable can provide for homes.

Having started publishing *Digital Audio* magazine in 1984, this development isn't exactly a big surprise. I'm disappointed that the technology is being pioneered in Europe by Grundig, Bosch and Telefunken, rather than by American firms. Or do we have any American electronic firms left? I can't think of any. Perhaps we could encourage an entrepreneur to start one in New Hampshire.

The electronics involved will all be on microchips, so the manufacturing of the radios won't be very complicated. We'll probably have to buy foreign chips since we have almost no radio engineers left in America, and most chip making is moving to Asia.

I predict that within 10 years FM will have changed to DAB. We can take advantage of this new technology and help pioneer it... or we can wait for the Japanese and Europeans to do it for us and grab the big money.

Will our car companies have to buy Japanese radios for their cars for DAB reception? They're buying Asian-made CD and cassette players now, so unless we here in New Hampshire decide to try and change history, it's likely we'll miss this new boat just as we have in the past.

Yet here we are, supposedly with a responsibility to guide New Hampshire's economic development. So isn't this part of our responsibility?

When digital audio was developed, I saw immediately what would happen. I knew in 1982 that I'd have to start a magazine to help this new technology develop and grow. I believed digital audio would revolutionize the music business. Well, we're going to see it again with DAB. Will America be riding the wave or paddling hard to catch up again?

100 Tackling Welfare

Not having any information as yet from the appropriate state bureaus, I'm not sure welfare is a serious New Hampshire problem. It seems as if it shouldn't be, since we don't have the drug, inner-city, minority problems besetting many other states. On that basis, I hadn't planned on discussing welfare in my semingly endless "report."

But then I read in *US News* (Nov. 25, 1991, p.31) that New Hampshire "has had a staggering 88% increase in welfare cases since 1989, the largest percentage jump in the nation." Lacking details, this may be a major problem, or it may mean that we had 100 welfare cases in 1989 and now have 188.

Mind you, this report has not been planned, so it tends to jump from one subject to another as they come to mind. I've already briefly mentioned welfare, but I figured my ideas for creatively attacking the problem might not be of interest since we didn't seem to need them. This report figured to be long enough just covering proposed solutions to our obvious problems.

101 A New Paradigm

If you've read much about our welfare system, you know that the costs are going through the roof. You know that none of the approaches tried so far seem to be effective. You also know that one out of seven American children are on relief. Perhaps it's time to consider a paradigm shift . . . time to consider a whole new approach instead of trying to fix the broken or bent parts of the old system.

My way of doing this is to look for ways other countries or states have solved similar problems.

Being a radio amateur, I have good friends in every country in the world. Thus, when I travel, I can learn much more about their countries than I could by reading *National Geographic* or by talking with hotel concierges and bellhops.

The closest analog to our welfare problem, was the mess Israel found itself in when hundreds of thousands of penniless immigrants poured into their country right after it was formed. They needed jobs, places to live, schools for their children, and so forth. Israel came up with a unique and effective answer.

Now, before I go further, let me assure you that I'm no fan of socialism. I've seen it fail in one country after another. Its basic concept is against human nature. Adam Smith had it right in his *Wealth of Nations*.

The model Israel used was the kibbutz. They grouped their immigrants into small communities where they could communally grow food and build entrepreneurial businesses. Their children were given more than just day care; they were put together into age groups and both cared for as children and educated. They joined their parents in the evenings and on weekends.

By separating age groups, the tendency for gangs to form was reduced. The pattern for older kids to take advantage of younger kids was reduced. Schools taught not only academics, but also ethics.

The kibbutz was similar to our hippie communes of the 1960s, but without our sexual openness. They lived in groups, worked together in the fields and in their businesses.

Just as when Singapore was formed and went to the UN for help in determining what products could best be made, taking into consideration raw material resources and markets within easy shipping distance, we'd want to get some expert advice for our versions of the kibbutzes on what businesses would be best started to match their resources, markets and low skill levels.

Newcomers to the kibbutzes are helped to learn how to garden and apprenticed to the businesses. Most kibbutzes set up classes to help their people learn new skills. In our case, if we locate our new communes reasonably near our cities, we'll be able to let the people attend adult courses given by our schools and colleges.

102 Getting Financing

Do we turn to the federal government, hat in hand, looking for the investment funds needed to establish our welfare communities? Or should we tax our New Hampshire citizens? Not being a big fan of using tax money unless there's no other resource, I tend to look for better alternatives. I remember how easy it is for administrative bureaucracies to build up and filter out more and more of the money . . . just as we have with every well-intentioned entitlement program. I love that name— entitlements. This means people have a basic right to get the money . . . they're entitled to it. Hogwash.

So, instead of dipping a big hand into the public till, if we plan our new communities as profit-making entities, we should be able to sell shares in the ownership as a way to finance the projects . . . just like any other enterprise.

Now I'm beginning to get into familiar territory. We're going to need a communications medium to bring New Hampshire businesses together with these new communities, both to help finance them and to take advantage of the resource they can provide. This means not just a computerized dating system, but also a publication. Funny how I tend to think in terms of information exchange and the use of computers to help solve problems.

I look at my own situation as an example. There are a number of services which I'd be delighted to farm out if I could find groups interested in helping. These would be helpful enough for me to consider an up-front investment in a community stock issue to help fund the group.

For instance, I could use drafting help to take rough electronic equipment sketches and get them ready for publication in my magazines. This is a skill that most people can learn in a few weeks as apprentices. While I wouldn't be able to keep such a service going full time, since it's not practical for me to try and do this with a full time staff, there are many other magazines which would love to have such a service available. It could be shared by several publications and thrive.

Eventually I'll have enough business to keep a full-time public relations group busy, but for now I need one just part-time. Where could a new community find people experienced in this rather arcane business? Heck, I'd be delighted to help train them . . . in exchange for a discount on future work.

I need similar help with bulk mailings, inputting data, and for dozens of other related services. Now, if I can use help like that, by the time we've polled a few hundred businesses around the state we'll have needs for enough entrepreneurial new businesses to keep a hundred new communities busy. And that's just the start. Once they're going, these new businesses could start selling their services or products outside of New Hampshire, further adding to our state revenues.

103 How Do We Start?

Do we send out trailer trucks, round up welfare families in the middle of the night and dump them into our new communities? Well, since this isn't China, I expect we'd want to use persuasion instead of force. We'd want to make it look like it would be more fun and more profitable to join a new community than to sit home, cash welfare checks and sell food stamps for the going market price . . . as shown on "60 Minutes."

If we offer welfare families a nice place to live, work to do, training, and good care for their children, I don't think we'll have much of a problem getting them to opt to move to a new community. People prefer to take pride in their lives. They don't generally like being on the dole. And parents will like the idea of getting better education and health care for their children.

A part of the educational process would be getting parents involved with their children — getting them to help their children be motivated. We know that the main reason Asian-born children are doing so much better than American children in our schools is their parental motivational pressures.

By moving families to a completely new community, we'll have an opportunity to make other changes in their lifestyles . . . changes which should help them take advantage of the opportunities our country provides for people to get wealth.

By developing skills in these new communities, people will eventually be able to move from a socialistic environment to an entrepreneurial one, just as they have in Israel. The community would help them get started and eventually graduate them as they move up into middle income brackets and buy their own homes.

If we make this work, we might attract people from other states and cycle them through our economic start-up communities . . . teaching skills and building their self-confidence and aspirations.

Since these communities would be thriving and provide a strong upward force for the state, we might not run into as much local resistance to them as we might in providing prisons or county work farms.

When I consider something like this, I tend to look around for potential sites for such a community. We've quite a number of old mill buildings which could be converted into communal living quarters. One of the old cutlery buildings in Antrim could easily be converted into small apartments. The other buildings would provide space for the entrepreneurial businesses. And there are plenty of nearby fields which could be turned into gardens to help keep food costs down. I've got around 50 acres on my farm, a mile away, which is just being used to grow hay. And I've got a potential catfish pond which could supply horned pout for New Hampshire restaurants. They make superb chowder.

There are several old mill buildings in Greenville, not far from Milford, which could be converted into apartments and small enterprises. And those are just some examples around where I live. However, they're not as near schools as would be handy for adult education. If we want to break the poverty syndrome we've got to get people used to the idea that education is a birth-to-death matter, not K-12.

Kibbutz-style towns would make it easier to provide child care for babies, thus giving them a better start toward their life's education.

Chapter IV

104 It Won't Work!

When I propose a new idea, is your response one of looking for faults? Many people block off their lives by being negative. They also make the world less fun and more difficult for most other people – seriously defective childhood training.

When faced with new ideas, I tend to look not for reasons why they might not work, but for any weaknesses which could use creative cures. I love to help solve problems.

We can solve the poverty problem in America if we can separate the poor from their past environment and build a spirit of adventure for them. We do know one thing for sure . . . that none of the government efforts at eliminating poverty has had much of an effect. We also know that spending money on such programs has just lost us the money. It's really time to try something else.

New Hampshire is an ideal testing ground for this. We have a small problem compared to most other states, so we won't have to think in terms of investing a billion dollars to see results. And I suspect that our New Hampshire poor aren't as hard-core as those in Boston or New York. It may be a lot easier to get them excited about joining a group to live and work . . . and get their kids a good education.

And being a small state, they're not going to have to move beyond being able to visit old friends when they want.

So, do you think we can eventually get rid of the welfare problem . . . and perhaps even the poor?

One more thing: With such a high percentage of the welfare cases in the larger cities made up of black and Hispanic single mothers, we may be able to break this pattern when we move them away from their old neighborhoods and give them a feeling of worth. The new town businesses will provide better role models for the kids than drug dealers and pimps they now look up to.

A pimp in Antrim would soon go out of business. And these new communities, being small, would be able to keep drugs away . . . if we haven't the guts to fix the drug situation another way.

105 We're Turning Brown!

The world is erupting with small wars. But then, it's been doing that for as long as man's been around. Nasty bunch, really.

The Azerbaijanis are fighting the Armenians. They both have hated each other for years. The Serbs are fighting the Croats. There are wars going on in Timor, Southern Sudan, Chad, Mozambique, the Philippines, and so on. And that's not to mention some aggravation in Northern Ireland, the Basque country, Libya, the whole Middle East, Tunisia, Fiji, etc.

We're not completely without interracial strains here in America, though New Hampshire has far fewer of them than most other states. We haven't attracted very many Hispanics, blacks, and other recent immigrants. Yet.

So how's all this going to end? Are we going to have these wars going on forever? Of course not, and although the obvious end result of all this is inevitable, you probably aren't going to like it.

If you think back over even our short history as a country, you can see the way things are eventually going to go for the whole world. We got this whole thing started just a couple of hundred years ago. We started what we now enjoy calling a paradigm shift. It was the concept of the melting pot. It was the availability of a whole new country that made this possible.

The melting pot system has proven to be an outstanding success. We've mixed Germans, French, English, Irish, Italians, and so on. Each new wave tried to hold on to their roots for a while, but after a couple of generations the roots mostly withered and died. Now these immigrant groups are Americans. We all speak a common language. We all go through a common school system. And the result is a remarkably homogeneous country.

Carrying this concept out to its logical conclusion, we can see where eventually the world will be speaking one langauge. The world will be made up of light brown people with Asian-like eyes. It'll take a while. A thousand years? Five thousand? Maybe, but the end result is unavoidable . . . and I see nothing wrong with that.

Where we have problems and we make life miserable for ourselves lies in our trying to fight this inevitability. We frown on interracial marriages. We stress our roots. We have African-Americans now instead of blacks. We have proud Irish-Americans. We have German-Americans. It's those hyphens which are causing our problems.

Any we/they grouping tends to generate tensions and result in wars. From this viewpoint our religions are another we/they division. You only have to look back through history and contemplate the millions of people the major religious faiths have killed to question the value of having many religions.

The Suunis want to kill the Shiites. Both want to kill Christians. And Christians want to kill as many other Christians as they can . . . like in Northern Ireland.

In the long run, we'll be light brown and all have either one common religion . . . or perhaps understand enough about how our universe works so religious beliefs are no longer necessary to help the uneducated cope with things they don't understand.

Science has gone a long way in the last hundred years, but it's got a lot further to go. Scientists haven't been able to come to grips with the ineffable. Scientists, too, are hamstrung in their thoughts by inculcated religious beliefs, making the questioning of these beliefs difficult.

Despite our scientific progress, we've just barely started trying to understand how the mind/body/spirit works . . . how memories are stored . . . and what happens with death. Is there a spirit which is eternal? We still know very little about the ESP phenomenon. Some scientists deny it, daring anyone to prove it exists. But, having experienced it myself, I'm hoping that scientists with open minds will begin to help us understand this potential area to be researched.

If thoughts can be communicated, will we find them limited by the speed of light? We haven't even the vaguest clue as to how they might travel, so we have no way of knowing. Yet.

Is our government experimenting with communicating with the dead and with other worlds in a research lab in Wyoming? I've talked with a recognized scientist who assures me this is happening, but is top-secret. I like the idea, but until I know more I'll stay a skeptic.

With transportation costs coming down and communications technology making the world ever smaller, we seem inevitably headed toward one common civilization. Will this homogenize everything? I doubt it. America is a pretty good melting pot example now and we still have Chinese, Italian, Thai, Japanese, German, and French restaurants. We still play music from these many cultures and enjoy it.

106 Kill The Indians

When I visited the Fiji Islands, the nation was planning on being emancipated from New Zealand. The population was fairly evenly split between Fijians and Indians. The Fijians hated the Indians. I asked my friends who lived there," why."

The Indians owned all the small businesses. When a Fijian tried to start a business, the Indian storekeepers around him would cut their prices and force him out of business. They were supported by all the other Indians, so they had the economic strength to keep out any competition. Oddly, this did not sit well with the Fijians.

Further, the Indians kept to themselves. They had their own religion, did not intermarry, and had as little as possible to do with the Fijians socially. The Fijian response of wanting to get rid of the damned Indians was understandable.

I ran into the same situation in Uganda, where the Indians had originally been brought in to build the railroads. They stayed on, opened businesses and monopolized the retail trade. Eventually Amin kicked them out of the country, but with little business experience, few blacks even tried to open businesses. The result is that Uganda is well on its way back to the bush, with few farms or ranches left.

In countries where the Chinese were imported as laborers, they've stayed on and been as clannish as the Indians and engendered as much racial bias.

How different from our melting pot concept, which has homogenized most of the people who've come here. Those groups that have resisted the melting pot have been met with continued suspicion and bias.

You've read about the problems the Koreans have been having. They've been networking to help new Korean immigrants open grocery stores in black neighborhoods. The Chinese have long done this in America... and very successfully. But it's not helped them be assimilated.

When I meet people I don't care or even want to know if they're Irish, English, Jewish, Arab, or anything else. I want to know what they're interested in . . . what they enjoy doing . . . what they can tell me that I'd like to know about.

A few minutes ago I turned on my little amateur radio transceiver ... not much bigger than a VCR remote control unit... and asked if anyone was listening. A chap in his car about 40 miles away said hello. He was on his way to pick up a hard disk drive for a computer system. Next thing, he was explaining about nanometer wavelength lasers used to make the new chips with conductors only eight to 10 molecules wide. I have no idea what race or religion he was. I enjoyed talking with him and I learned a lot.

Getting to the bottom line of all this, I'm hoping that New Hampshire will resist all efforts to encourage and preserve ethnic differences. I'd suggest that if New Hampshire hasn't yet made English our state language, that we do it and provide some leadership for the other states.

I keep reading about how Americans are such duds because we can't speak other languages. Horse feathers. Learning anything which requires a lot of memorization is a waste unless it's used often enough to keep it alive. The practical fact is that 99% or more of us in America won't ever really need another language.

There are a lot of things our kids are going to need to know, so the more we can concentrate on those and the less we can waste their time and frustrate them with things which have little practical value, the better off we'll be.

107 Feedback

And how can we decide what kids should be learning? Well, I know what I've found useful and what I've missed. Presumably, you can make a similar list. This isn't a bad starting point. But my concept of setting up a feedback system to poll graduates and get their perspective will give us continuous correction information.

They taught me to read music in the second grade. That was a big plus, making it easy for me to sing in choirs and choruses. Now that I'm in the music business it's most helpful.

They taught me the elements of picture composition in the third grade. This art background helped me when I became a TV cameraman and was even more important when I was a TV director. I use that training in magazine publishing and in advertising.

In the fourth grade they taught us about poetry and its different forms. As a publisher this has been most helpful . . . plus it's helped me enjoy reading poetry. Now I'm planning on releasing poems on CDs.

One result of the America 2000 project will be an attempt to outline what American kids should be taught . . . and to what kind of standards our schools should be held. If we make learning fun . . . if we make it relevant . . . I don't think we're going to need tests or standards. Youngsters will learn because they want to . . . and we'll be able to weed out the useless memorization and concentrate on concepts and skills.

We want our kids to be able to comfortably cope with life . . . with relationships . . . with work. Let's make that our aim.

108 Bilingual Education

A recent book, *Out of the Barrio* by Linda Chavez, makes it clear that this whole controversy is unnecessary. The Hispanic activists are muddying the waters for their own self-interest, not those of the children. Hispanics are learning English, just as did the European immigrants before them. Most second-generation Hispanics are fluent in English and most third-generation Hispanics speak only English. Teaching Hispanic children in Spanish serves to alienate them from the American society, thus helping to preserve the constituency of the Hispanic activists (*Forbes* 11/25/91, p.112).

S.I. Hayakawa, the former California senator, comes out strongly for the melting pot concept (*The Executive Educator* 1/87, p. 36). One only has to look at the Canadian disaster which bilingualism has created: bi-nationalism. It's splitting their country. Professor Hayakawa comes out for officially designating English as our national language. He's opposed to bilingual education.

109 Reform Resistance

My call for educational reform isn't new. Let me quote from an article in the 11/25/91 *Forbes* (p.180), "Big, cumbersome and unresponsive, the public school monopoly is strangling education in America and thwarting the efforts of the majority of sincere teachers and administrators." And that's just the headline for the article!

The article goes on to tell how Anthony Alverado, a Harlem school administrator, "launched an assault on the most egregious near-monopoly in America: the public education trust." He let the teachers create new curriculums and then let the students, with their parents' permission, choose among the teachers and the curriculums. If kids didn't sign up for a program, it closed down. The results were spectacular, with reading scores zooming.

Governor Thompson of Wisconsin has championed school choice, saying, "Every education reform we've ever had has just put more money in the school administrators' pockets. Alas, the current bureaucratic system does everything it can to take autonomy away from individual schools . . . so cumbersome has the bureaucracy become that only about 30 cents of every dollar spent on kindergarten through 12th grade public schooling in New York and Milwaukee actually makes it into the classroom, to pay for teachers, textbooks, computers."

New York City spends $7,000 per student. Chicago spends $5,500 per student. Compare that with Chicago's Catholic schools which spend $1,500 per student for elementary schools and $3,200 for secondary students. 46% of the public school students drop out, as compared to 22% of the parochial students.

110 Our Educational Failure

In a recent state-by-state comparison of eighth-graders' math skills, only one in seven is computing at the expected proficiency level. (*Industry Week* 9/2/91, p.13).

"A comparative study of education in Japan, Taiwan and America found that though American youngsters were learning substantially less in school, American parents were the most satisfied with the performance of their local schools."

It's interesting that our annual public school spending is not quite $200 billion. $12 billion of that comes from the feds. Compare that with the $210 billion business and industry is spending on training!

So here we have a bloated educational bureaucracy soaking up around 70% of our educational funds and forcing industry to spend money to do the remedial work. This added cost of doing business inevitably makes our industries less competitive with other countries. We can't afford to continue to squander our educational funds on administrative bureaucracies.

Our schools have not kept pace with the changes in our world. Tom Sobol says, "We don't have large railroads to build by hand or forests to clear or whatever. We don't have that demand for relatively unskilled labor anymore." (*Time* 11/11/91, p.24). Sobol is pro-choice for schools. He's tried to get pilot programs started, but in the end, the opposition — from the teachers' union, school-board associations, school administrative groups — was so forceful we withdrew the proposal.

111 Factoids and Notes

The Society for Applied Learning Technology: "The most recent international mathematics study reported that average Japanese students exhibited higher levels of achievement than the top 5 percent of American students enrolled in college preparatory mathematics courses.

"One out of three major corporations already provides new workers with basic reading, writing, and mathematics courses. If current demographic and economic trends continue, American business will hire a million new people a year who can't read, write, or count.

"Looking forward to the year 2000, the fastest-growing occupations require employees to have much higher math, language, and reasoning capabilities than do current occupations."

All that, as I've mentioned, is almost enough to make a person think.

Business Week (4/20/87, p.69): 70% of American students complete high school as compared with 98% in Japan. "Our universities are not turning out enough scientists and engineers to meet new demand in the leading-edge areas of high technology."

Re: "rote learning," which is a contradiction of terms, Ben Bloom, a professor of education at Northwestern, said in *Psychology Today* (4/87, p.43), " . . . there is too much drill, too much rote learning, too little active participation by students . . . and most of all, too much failure in today's schools." Bloom found that "successful problem-solvers attacked problems in a systematic and analytical way, while poor problem-solvers simply tried to recall a memorized answer." He characterized the two approaches as active and passive.

Bloom believes that most of the differences we see in student performance are the result of our educational system, not innate learning ability differences. "What one student can learn, nearly all students can learn."

Bloom compared tutored students with those taught in conventional group instruction. He found that the average tutored student learns more than do 98% of the students taught in regular classes. He also found that

90% of the tutored students attained levels reached by only 20% of those in regular classes.

Since student/teacher ratios of 1:1 or even 3:1 are unaffordable, Bloom has developed a peer-teaching "mastery learning" system which approximates tutoring in efficiency. With his system, he's found "the average mastery learning student does better than 85% of students taught in the traditional way. And 70% of mastery students attain levels reached only by 20% of students in regular classrooms."

112 Encouraging Reading

The Holmes School in Darien (CT) has gotten its students hooked on reading (*The Executive Educator* 1/87, p.23). Elementary school students read an average of 13 books from an independent reading list per semester. During one six-month period one student read 160 books.

"Project Read" is entirely voluntary, with the book selections monitored by the teachers. The awards program (hats, T-shirts) costs about $1,000 a year, but could be done for less.

113 Fewer Colleges

Robert Samuelson (*Newsweek* 10/5/87, p.79) suggested that about 20% of our colleges be closed. He pointed out that about 50% of our freshmen don't graduate, so we need better high school preparation. State colleges could raise their tuitions, thus making more money available for scholarships for hardship students.

He also recommends that teachers be certified by states on the basis of the knowledge of the subjects they're teaching rather than on their teaching methods. This would mean a complete change in teaching college curriculums.

114 More Factoids

Fortune 2/1/88, p.86: 38% of 21-to-25-year-olds in a government-sponsored test couldn't figure the right change if they had $3 and bought a 60-cent cup of soup and a $1.95 sandwich. Maybe you've noticed that fast-food cash registers have pictures of the food instead of numbered keys.

The book, *What Do Our 17-Year-Olds Know?*, showed that they sure don't know much about history, geography, math, literature or science.

115 Cooperative Learning

If you're interested in an innovative educational approach you should read *Control Theory in the Classroom* by William Glasser (Harper &

Row 1986). This is such a simple and obvious change it's astounding that the educational bureaucracy has been so resistant.

Glasser points out that people in general, and kids in particular, don't do as well as individuals as they do in groups . . . in teams. Teamwork is fun. It's challenging. And it benefits everyone involved.

Instead of having teachers trying to deal with a classroom full of individuals, Glasser has the teachers break up the class into teams. He tries to put a top-notch student, a slow-learner and a couple of average students together in each team. The result is that all of them learn faster and enjoy it more. The teacher's job is to facilitate.

This approach is very similar to peer teaching, where the students work in teams and teach each other . . . the system I've been promoting as the best approach I've found yet for youngsters to learn the basics of electronics, communications and computers.

This type of educational environment meets youngsters' basic needs for love, power, freedom and fun. It pits their teams against the others, not every lone student against the teacher . . . with no love, power, freedom or fun involved.

The better one team does, the harder the others will try to beat them. They're not out after grades, they're interested in learning and having fun doing it. It's exciting. And the better they can do with their team, the more power they feel.

Kids will want to learn, not for some remote benefit so far in the future that it's almost meaningless . . . like a better job . . . but to help their team right now. Kids don't tend to have long-range goals, else they wouldn't get involved with beer, drugs, or drop out of school. So instead of trying to shovel coal up the chute trying to convince kids to learn for the future, why not make it fun right now and get a better result?

Of course, if one team wins too often, the teacher should reshuffle the members and give the other teams a better chance. They should be shuffled now and then anyway, just to give them the experience of working with different teams.

The team approach to teaching means making some major changes in how teachers teach. It might be worthwhile to read the book before you make your list of reasons why this won't work.

Remember, kids seldom prefer to play alone. They naturally form teams to play . . . so why not go this normal, natural route with teaching?

Our present teaching system where students are embarrassed or humiliated into performing, is completely alien to human nature. The child who does well in class is ridiculed by classmates. The child who does poorly is likewise ridiculed. This tends to alienate children who are slow or fast learners and force everyone into one common mold. It pits the children against each other.

Knowing that only ridicule lies in wait, children become terrified of being called on to perform. Nobody likes a show-off, right? And nobody likes a dummy, either. So if you do it right, you lose. If you do it wrong, you lose. I like the team approach concept.

116 Teaching Entrepreneurship

"Entrepreneurship is like psychiatry was 100 years ago. People thought it was foolishness or quackery," says Emery Turner, a dean at St. Louis University. Entrepreneurship as an academic discipline is still in limbo.

Professor Sahlman of Harvard says, "It's like an intellectual onion. The deeper you go the more you cry, and you don't ever find anything substantive."

There are few endowed chairs, and fewer qualified candidates to fill them. Many are going unfilled . . . and that's probably just as well. As a certified entrepreneur, complete with a doctorate in Entrepreneurial Science from Central New England College, I'd like to let some gas out of the bag. We don't need professors of entrepreneurialism; what we need are more courses in the nitty-gritty that entrepreneurs need to know.

Entrepreneurialism is a frame of mind. But it can't do much for you unless you have a wide variety of backgrounds. There's no such thing as a course in entrepreneurialism. That's like trying to teach an artist with a course on the color red.

Yes, of course I've made up a list of some of the more important things an entrepreneur should know. My goal is to get schools to offer courses in these . . . not to just entrepreneurial and business students, but also as adult classes to help local business people do better . . . and perhaps (why not?) to engineering students as well.

I've listed the courses I recommend in depth elsewhere in this report, so I won't repeat that. They include things like public speaking, writing, speed reading, personnel selection and management, quality control, advertising, public relations, finance, accounting, selling, marketing, direct mail, business law, packaging, collecting, desktop publishing, and so on (052).

Any of us on the Commission who've been entrepreneurs for very long should be able to teach all of those subjects.

117 Reinventing the University

An article in *The Education Digest* (4/88, p.56) by NYU Dean London points out that colleges have been lowering their standards to cope with students who wouldn't have attended college at all before 1960.

Secretary Bennett argued that "success in school work is not related to success outside school," and academic subjects tend to be "of limited consequence in the real world." London says, "What we are left with is college as an adolescent rite of passage which provides a remote chance youngsters will discover an area of vocational interest that may have a lasting effect on their lives. That is a slim reed on which to rest the university's legitimacy."

This was my experience 50 years ago, back when universities were supposedly doing a better job. If they were poor then and have gotten substantially worse, isn't it time for a paradigm shift? Isn't it time to completely reinvent the university, not just to try and fix the more egregious problems? This would seem to provide an opportunity for New Hampshire. A unique opportunity.

If we go ahead with my plan to have our grade 5-12 students teach each other electronics and other science fundamentals, we'll be doing them a terrible disservice if we don't have the university they're going to need ready for them. And really, there isn't any other place to go.

118 Making Math Easier

Perhaps you've been reading about Kumon, a Japanese-developed math teaching system which has been tested with remarkable success in some American schools (*Time* 6/4/90, p.83). It pits the kids against themselves in learning and makes it fun.

There are dozens . . . perhaps even hundreds . . . of experimental new teaching systems which should be investigated, tested and reported on so we'll be able to use the best to help New Hampshire's educational system be not just the best in America, but the best in the world. It's something we can do . . . so what's stopping us?

As far as I know there's no coordinated research group checking into educational developments and publishing its findings. As I've said, I've tried to get RPI to do this, but failed. Now I hope that New Hampshire will set up a research/publishing group. This would put New Hampshire out in front in the nation in education. And the nice part is that the research group should not just be able to pay for itself by selling reports, but should be able to turn a profit. As an entrepreneur I know I could make it profitable.

Am I into the conflict of interest area again? Not far, because I don't have the time to tackle managing such a project. I'll be glad to consult and advise, since what's needed are things with which I'm quite familiar. But I don't have a lot of idle time.

119 Small World Concomitants

The other day I was sorting through my grandfather's pictures from his trip to Europe in 1929. Europe was a big deal in those days . . . something wealthy people did. And he was wealthy . . . at least most of that year. He'd made his money as an inventor and marketer of his inventions. The company that he helped found lives on as Citgo. Like everyone else, he lost almost everything in the market crash.

My father got to travel even more as an aviation pioneer. He started the first trans-Atlantic airline, which took him to Europe many times. But even in his time, travel through most of the world was limited to a few adventurers. He got to most of the European and Mediterranean countries, but that was all.

When I compare the traveling my grandfather and my father did with what I've been able to do, it's indicative of how much the world has shrunk . . . and how much more we can expect it to shrink in another generation or two.

We're building bigger and faster planes. We're not that far from inexpensive supersonic flights. I've had a taste of that on the Concorde, where I beat the clock across the Atlantic. And that was held down to mach 2. Now we're talking mach 5 and better to bring Asia and Australia closer to America and Europe.

I'd visit Australia more often if it didn't take 24 hours to get there . . . and another 24 back. The 12 hours to Asia isn't as bad, so I've done that a dozen times or so. I know my way around most major Asian cities and have many friends there. If I'd just stop starting new entrepreneurial businesses I'd have some time to visit the places I've missed. Friends in Kota Kinabalu have been asking me to come back and see the fabulous new scuba diving area that's been making news in the diving magazines.

Now, outside of bragging about my travels, what does all this mean to New Hampshire and its economic development? Lower cost travel will have a profound impact on New Hampshire. It's obviously going to impact our tourism . . . both positively and negatively. It's going to put our New Hampshire tourist business more in competition with other states . . . and with other countries. It'll also make it practical for vacationers to come here from almost anywhere.

This means that we're going to have to be more vigorous in selling New Hampshire tourism. Ooops. I've got that wrong . . . and so do most of you. It is no longer "tourism" that we're selling. The day when "Scenic New Hampshire" was a big selling point is fading. Now we've got to sell vacations. We've got to sell not just our beauty, but also the things we offer visitors to do. They're not driving all this way just to take pictures any more. They're not "touring."

This means that we've got to (a) have plenty of interesting things for visitors to do and (b) make sure we get the word to them about how much fun they'll have. And (c) we've got to make it easier and not more expensive than vacationing elsewhere.

Should I spend Thanksgiving week visiting London? Or should I head for the Connecticut Lakes for some fishing? The price isn't much different, so which will be more fun?

I've gone to London for Thanksgiving several times, spending about $600 (each) for the round trip, including a first class hotel and two London shows. For two of us, including everything, that comes to around $1,800 . . . including a walk in Sherwood Forest.

For about the same money last year, my wife and I visited Munich, rented a car, drove to Vienna, Krakow and Prague, visiting and making friends in these cities . . . all in a week. This is the kind of mini-vacation New Hampshire is going to be increasingly up against.

One only has to see the success of *Condé Nast Traveler* magazine to know that people are thinking vacations. *Skin Diving* magazine is fat with articles on exotic places to dive . . . 210 pages in the current issue! Not long ago I went on a diving cruise ship where within a week I was able to dive in Belize, Honduras and Mexico. You should see the video I've got of that trip!

My wife Sherry and I zipped down to Orlando for my birthday, spending a day each at Walt Disney World, Epcot Center, MGM Studios and Universal Studios. The whole works . . . and we didn't stint much . . . came in under $1,000. That's what we're up against when we want to sell New Hampshire right now. It's going to get tougher as travel costs drop and travel time gets tighter.

This is why I'm proposing we promote four-day extended weekend packages for New Hampshire vacationers. Let's try to get visitors to come up here Thursday evening . . . keep them busy for four days . . . and drive home Monday night. And, with air travel prices dropping, we can put together fly/drive packages.

A ragtime music festival got Sherry and me to fly to San Francisco, rent a car, drive to Fresno for the three-day festival (which was more than worth the trip), spend an extra day visiting Yosemite Park, and one more visiting Travis AFB, where I got to fly a C-5B (a plane the size of a 747) simulator. It's an incredibly realistic experience which allowed me to do takeoffs and landings at Travis and Hickam airports in daylight, at night and even in the fog. After three dual-instruction landings I was ready to solo. My landing was fine, thank you. I also had an opportunity to lead the Golden Gate Air Force Band . . . another wonderful experience. Hey, I grab my coups where I can . . . don't you? Now I can Walter Mitty about being asked to land a 747 in an emergency . . . and know I can do it.

In my spare time during the trip I worked on this report on my little laptop computer. That's better than doing the crossword puzzle in the flight magazine, right? Yes, I'm ahead of my time . . . but what I've been doing is what will be common in a few years.

I'm hoping to be able to put together a ragtime festival for New Hampshire next spring. I've got the performers . . . superb performers . . . all set. Now all I need to do is find someone who can organize the festival, arrange the venues, the promotion, advertising and so on. I can tell 'em how to do it, but I need to find the person who will follow through. What do I ask for when I call our unemployment service to find this person? They only go by job titles.

In addition to providing entertainment for New Hampshire people, I believe we can attract several hundred ragtime music buffs, bringing business to New Hampshire. Hundreds of people came to Fresno from all around the country.

With the USAF out of Pease, their flight simulator is probably gone. Pity. They could charge several hundred dollars an hour, 24 hours a day, for that experience.

A recent article on whitewater rafting in West Virginia got me to send for information and think seriously about a long weekend trip. We probably have some good rafting here in New Hampshire. I just don't know where to find it. It sure would be easier to do it here, and I'd love it.

But if West Virginia almost got me to come down and visit to do some rafting, New Hampshire can do the same for our more exciting activities. It wouldn't take much to get me to sky dive, to try ultra-lights, gliders, go ballooning, or even hang glide. Tell me how much fun I'll have . . . and where to go . . . and I'll be off. Well, it's the same for millions of other people. We need to help our entrepreneurs develop more activities and then get the word out.

You've probably read about how much fun orienteering is. I'd love to try it. I know I enjoy car rallies . . . so when and where are those?

We have a WWII submarine open to the public up in Portsmouth, right? Well, how about investing some money and making it into an experience for visitors? I've tried to get the Battleship Commission in Mobile to set up my old submarine, the *USS Drum* (a Portsmouth boat, by the way), with a simulation which would allow visitors to relive a realistic depth-charge attack. It wouldn't be all that difficult or expensive to do.

Visitors would hear a taped story as they visit each submarine compartment, telling what went on there when the boat was on war patrol. Then the lights would dim, the diving alarm would sound, and the captain would warn that the boat should stand by for a possible depth charge attack and for everyone to be absolutely silent, that even a whisper might be heard by the attacker. The speaker system would let the visitors hear the screws of a destroyer passing overhead . . . then barrage after barrage of depth charges would shake the boat. No movie has ever reproduced depth charges the way they really sound. We'd be able to do that. We could arrange to have some light bulbs go out and water to pour in through some "leaks" in the hull for realism. We'd end it by announcing that we'd evaded the destroyer, sounding the surface alarm, followed by the screaming whine of the low pressure blowers. It would be an experience which no one would ever forget . . . and which would bring thousands of visitors.

I remembered my idea for the *Drum* as I enjoyed the simulated earthquake disasters at the Universal Studios in Hollywood and Orlando not long ago.

Alas, I didn't have any success in getting the Navy to do this for the *Drum*, but we might be able to do it in Portsmouth. By the way, the skipper of the *Alabama*, which is anchored right next to the *Drum* in Battleship Park, got so frustrated about this that he took early retirement and is now working for me as a sales rep.

120 Travel and Education

With travel costs dropping and travel times shortening, it's going to be more practical to send our kids on visits to Europe, South America, Africa, Asia and the Pacific. I'm talking about class trips, not vacationing with parents.

It wasn't long ago that a class trip to Washington, D.C., was a big deal. My daughter was offered a class trip to Singapore. With lower-cost travel and communications, kids will be able to visit the Ogaden personally and see what's really happening there. They'll even be able to talk/see their parents every day by satellite and keep up with their regular schoolwork. I'm not talking 100 years in the future, just another generation.

Our kids will not only know how to pronounce the capital of Burkina Faso, they'll have been there. Ditto Mbabane, the capital of what country? How about Bandar Seri Begawan, the capital of what other country? How's your geography? I haven't visited Burkina Faso yet, but I will. I've visited the other two and have good friends in those capitals.

So, if it's been practical for me to get to these places, it's going to be easy for kids in another 10 or 20 years. And, as our schools shift from long summer vacations to all-year sessions, with short vacations between semesters, our kids are going to be spreading out all over the world.

This is the environment in which New Hampshire is going to have to be competitive in a few years. We'd better understand that and start making our plans now so we'll be able to take advantage of what's coming when it gets here and not have to set up another commission to try and bail us out again.

We're not only going to be in competition with Singapore and the Philippines in manufacturing, but for vacationers, too. If we don't want to be left with anything but the dregs, we've got to plan ahead.

I saw what happened to Coney Island when the 1939 World's Fair drew away its middle-income customers for two years. Coney had to adapt itself to low-income people. The middle-incomers never came back, so today all the old entertainments are long gone . . . Luna Park, Steeplechase Park. Coney turned into a dirty, sleazy place and never recovered.

If we're able to provide fun things to do which will attract a middle-income clientele, we'll do fine. If we decide to go the Atlantic City route of bars and gambling, we'll lose out. I'd prefer us to go after skiers, mountain climbers, canoers, kayakers, music lovers, and so on. We'll make far more money per vacationer that way. It's like the difference between commodity and high-tech manufacturing.

So let's think (and plan) in terms of offering middle-income-oriented vacation entertainment, an attractive business climate for high-tech and mail order businesses, and the most advanced educational system in the world. That ought to do it.

121 Dying Cities

Perhaps you've noticed how different modern cities are from those which flourished a hundred years ago. Older cities, with manufacturing centers, mass housing and downtown shopping, were fine for the transportation systems of that era. Then came the automobile . . . and everything changed.

Cities changed. Now shopping and entertainment have moved into shopping plazas and strips. Neighborhood theaters are largely gone, replaced by cinema complexes. Downtowns, like Coney Island, have been deserted by the middle class and left to lower and lower income groups.

Downtown Fresno, which I visited recently, was a ghost town . . . even though they'd obviously spent millions trying to redeem it. They'd built several blocks of walking plaza, but half of the stores were empty and the other half had thrift shops and stores catering to a very low income clientele. I doubt if the store owners were getting 20% of the normal rents. The city's largest department store was closed, with the main floor now filled with flea market booths.

A few years ago I looked over the old mill buildings in downtown Manchester with an eye to refurbishing some of them and opening them for small shops and office space. I found that it would cost me almost double what it would to build a brand new building in a neighboring community. With the middle income people mostly moving away from the city, it would be more and more difficult to get them to patronize these shops. Parking was limited. Access streets were crowded and beset with traffic lights.

The fact is that cities which meet our needs have been developing . . . and they've been developing in suburban areas. The current increase in mail order shopping will tend, even more, to reduce business in downtown areas . . . and eventually, even in malls. It's faster and more convenient to shop with catalogs. It's often more economical.

With mail order I can shop anywhere in the country and get my purchases in a few days. As communications drop in cost, we'll be able to mail order shop anywhere in the world. Indeed, I sell CDs by mail order and about 5% of my sales already are to foreign countries.

As catalogs move to on-line services, complete with video advertising, as our homes are connected to fiber optics and we're interconnected with satellite two-way systems, we'll be shopping electronically. How far in the future is this? Well, since we already have every bit of the technology needed, I'd guess we'll have maybe 10% of our homes connected within 10 years, and 50% in 20.

Is this the best time to invest in building more shopping plazas? Or is it maybe a better time to concentrate on mail order sales? Mail order is the wave of the present and the tsunami of the future. Mail order firms will be all set to go with home-selling via interactive fiber optic and satellite systems.

You only have to consider the incredible success of PC/Mac Connection in Marlow to see how New Hampshire can benefit from encouraging mail order business growth. They're selling nationwide, shipping by overnight air.

There are opportunities for similar mail order centers to be developed for other electronic fields such as home entertainment, communications equipment, and so on. As more and more entrepreneurs start new firms, the proliferation of makes and models of equipment makes it impractical for small neighborhood stores to stock more than a few lines. It also increases their costs of doing business. Mail order firms can keep costs low and provide a wider selection because they're selling to the whole country instead of an area a few miles in diameter.

As communications improve, it's easier to talk with a salesman in Marlow and get straight answers than with a local computer store salesman. This has already signaled doom for computer store chains. I'm sure glad I sold out my chain of 58 Softwaire Centers a few years ago, while the selling was good.

Chapter V

122 Seek Ye a Path

New Hampshire is in a serious economic fix today because there hasn't been any attempt at guiding its growth. When the Massachusetts-based minicomputer firms looked for nearby growth areas with good tax benefits, they expanded into New Hampshire. That was fine while they were prospering, but now that they're in a terminal decline, perhaps it's getting time for New Hampshire to take on a little more responsibility for its future. Can we learn from this bad experience?

If we leave our growth to chance, as we have in the past, this will give those states which do develop pro-business policies an advantage over us. I suggest we propose a long-range development plan which cites specific kinds of businesses we should encourage and nurture. Further, I suggest we plan on having a continuing Commission which will keep tabs on our progress and provide steering corrections as needed.

From this viewpoint, the exercise at our second meeting — where we reviewed our strengths and weaknesses as a state — was not as much of a useless exercise and waste of our time as some critics grumbled.

Of course, with my background, I tend to urge us to concentrate on publishing, mail order sales, high-tech . . . particularly in electronics . . . and education, since these fields are in tune with the future and should continue to grow and provide high profits. Being entrepreneurial more than big-business oriented, they'll be much more resistant to recessions and technical obsolescence.

Publishing is nice in that it'll be quite a long time before shipping costs make it practical for foreigners to compete. With modern communications systems, a publishing headquarters can be anywhere in the country. It's still more practical to have national magazines printed near transportation hubs to keep mailing costs down, which is why my largest magazine is printed in Nebraska.

But for smaller publications this is not a significant matter, so I'm mailing them from New Hampshire. One of them is my *Radio Fun*, which explains to 40,000 amateur radio newcomers how to build simple circuits, how to pass the license exams, and how to get in on the fun we're having talking to each other via our network of about 10,000 automatic relay stations, several of our own satellites, via our computers, via television and so on.

Education holds great future promise for entrepreneurs. Eventually there's going to be an enormous market for interactive video education . . . programs which make learning real fun. I see the day when video education will start prenatally and continue to death . . . and will greatly increase the effectiveness of our school system. Schools will eventually be more for team projects and skill building.

This is going to provide an enormous opportunity for entrepreneurs, just as the microcomputer industry made it possible for thousands of small companies to get into the software business. We'll be seeing interactive video programs teaching thousands of subjects . . . in business, the arts, helping develop skills, and so on.

It would be nice if New Hampshire could have the work force these entrepreneurial firms are going to need so we'll be able to attract them. These firms will need mostly upscale workers and very few unskilled or semi-skilled workers. Will our educational system provide the needed work force in 20 years? That's mostly up to you.

123 Those Weaknesses

While I tend to think in terms of problems and problem-solving instead of listing strengths and weaknesses, it's obvious that many of the items which made the weakness list from the second meeting would qualify as problems with my approach. So I'll tackle 'em.

(1) Parochial, inflated self-image.

We must, as a group, recognize that New Hampshire is in business competition with the other 49 states and with a couple of hundred other countries to boot. We and our state will prosper only when we're able to sell our goods and services outside of the state. Out-of-state sales are the key domino in the chain.

(2) High and rising energy costs.

Oh, piffle. How many businesses do we have where energy costs are a major element . . . where they will tend to make our products less competitive? We're not refining aluminum here.

(3) Rising property taxes.

If you want your property taxes to go down, perhaps it's time to look into cutting our educational administration overhead. We'll be able to cut down many other state expenses if we follow some of my recommendations. I believe we can lower all taxes substantially.

(4) Dearth of new business incorporations.

In the short run, we can create jobs and more businesses by quickly building our vacation industry. In the longer run, we'll do best if we change our educational system, so we can provide a high-tech work force.

I've also suggested we organize a statewide employment system which can match business needs to available skills. Plus, we can establish a computerized system to match businesses with available buildings.

(5) Excessive dependence on large companies.

This was due to a lack of state planning. The weakening of the minicomputer firms which expanded from Massachusetts was well known in the computer industry and should have triggered a NH response to attract smaller firms long ago. I warned the High-Tech Council and Governor Sununu eight years ago that this would have to happen.

(6) Entrepreneurial stagnation.

Oh yeah? Not around Hancock. My suggested remedy is to encourage local schools to offer night courses which will help entrepreneurs succeed. See my recommended list.

(7) Unfavorable mix of jobs.

Manufacturing jobs and marketing jobs . . . such as mail order . . . bring revenues into New Hampshire that spur our economy. Service jobs, which merely recirculate money within the state, do not help much. Thus the Commission should work toward building out-of-state sales. How many mail order oriented adult courses are available in the state? Any?

Mail order people need to know list management, list rentals, list generation, product selection, product pricing, post office regulations, shipping alternatives and costs, packaging, advertising, promotion, catalog design, desktop publishing, inventory control, accounting, printing, and so on.

(8) Widespread credit crunch, dearth of capital.

Of course there's a credit crunch. When business slowed down and unemployment went up, that meant housing prices dropped and rents had to go down. With most income properties mortgaged to the hilt, thousands of mortgage payments got behind. The banks were in trouble. They just don't have any money to lend, with so much being tied up in home loans.

Many people with income property are having a very difficult time. A good friend of mine who owns several rental properties has had to declare personal bankruptcy to try and hold on to his properties, hoping the recession will turn around before the courts can act. I don't see any reason why we should expect a fast upturn in business . . . unless the Commission gets into gear a lot faster than seems possible.

With larger firms reducing their middle management, there's little money to buy homes, cars or other big ticket items. The worry over job security is keeping thousands more from spending much. Surveys show that Christmas buying is expected to be far below even last year. Consumer confidence has been shaken and it's going to take a lot of good news to turn that around.

What can we *do* about it? If we act quickly to get New Hampshire's vacation industry beefed up, and follow that with a heavy barrage of good news in the New Hampshire media, things can turn around fairly quickly. Since we're dealing with perception, a little good news can be made to go a long way.

That dearth of capital . . . for what? The banks are in bad shape, so they're not very interested in lending money right now. But there are growing pressures for venture capital business investments. When the stock market is in question there's a lot of cash looking for places to be invested.

I've proposed a publication which could bring entrepreneurs together with venture capitalists. This is a very good time for such a medium.

(10) Tax structure.

When we recognize that business taxes are regressive, that they make our businesses less able to compete with those in other states and countries, we'll make our biggest step toward helping New Hampshire over the long run.

We can cut taxes if we are merciless about revamping our state government and our government-run educational system. Perhaps we can even get started on ousting some of the federal government employees working in New Hampshire and set an example for other states.

(11) Credit and assets controlled by the FDIC.

If we get business moving in New Hampshire our banking problems will fade away.

(12) Lack of state investment in infrastructure.

I'd like to see some data on this one. I doubt if our infrastructure is much worse than other states. I'd like to be assured that we're getting our money's worth when we buy . . . with honest bidding and fair contracts. I'd also like to see the cost of the infrastructure apportioned in a fair way to those who are using it.

(13) Two states with one government, north and south.

The North Country, being less populated and having less

infrastructure, seems to be getting its share. If we want, for some reason, to start developing the North Country we're going to have to borrow a lot of money and make a long term investment. Are there enough benefits to warrant such an investment?

The North Country lacks the roads, airports, power, work force and communications it takes to attract businesses. Sorry about that, but I come from the North Country and I'm living in the southern end of the state where I do have the infrastructure my businesses need.

I don't see any shortage of business development potential in the southern end of the state. Perhaps we should consider plans to increase vacation business in the North Country since these businesses are not generally employee heavy and do not require as trained a work force as high-tech and mail order businesses.

(14) Conflicts of interest between municipalities.

I proposed a newsletter information resource which should substantially ease this weakness. We do need to have good communications between the towns and the state and this can be accomplished with a profit-making publication.

(15) Vulnerable to external pressures, especially federal intervention.

Let's really take a close look at every potential here and see what moves we can make which will tend to get the feds out of New Hampshire and give us back our freedom. Live free or die, isn't it? Let's tackle this weakness and eliminate it as much as possible.

(16) Weak telecommunications network.

Well, it could be better, but I doubt it's much worse than some neighboring states are living with. Again, let's be specific about our problems with this and tackle every problem vigorously. Let's handle this as a quality problem.

(17) Cumbersome and slow regulatory process.

Aha! If we set up a quality of state government action committee, we'll be able to sort out the complaints and find out why things aren't working smoothly. If it's people, we need to know who and why. If it's a bum system, we need to fix it. It's probably both.

(18) No identifiable technological or manufacturing base.

With technologies changing so rapidly, this may be more of a strength than a weakness. One of the reasons we're in such serious trouble now was our allowing such a large part of our business to be concentrated in the minicomputer industry. Microcomputers are doing fine, thank you.

The day when large manufacturing companies employing minimally skilled workers can prosper in America is fading. We're much safer betting on a thousand small companies with 50 employees each than one big one.

(19) Weak effort by state government to understand business.

Government has a terrible time understanding business. If we can convert our state government to run more like a business, we'll get far more cooperation between the state and business.

Government is a socialist entity and business is capitalist. Government doesn't aim to make a profit. The concept of quality of performance is alien. The concept of higher pay for higher productivity is alien. What counts in government is politics and longevity. I believe we can change this whole concept and perhaps re-invent our state government. Watch out Washington . . . you're next.

(20) Inadequate economic development policy and planning process.

I hope we can cure this weakness. That's up to you. I've provided my thinking and ideas. If the Commissioners react by doing little or nothing, we're lost. If you take up my challenge, we have the opportunity to change New Hampshire, America . . . and even the world. It's up to you.

(21) Lack of support and coordination for regional planning.

My proposed town/state newsletter should help with this. But again, if we have a quality control system set up to help solve problems, even regional difficulties should succumb.

(22) Remote, distant, peripheral location.

What remote? How could we be much better located as a state? We're right at the end of the Eastern Megalopolis. We're well located to deal with Europe. If we develop our port at Portsmouth, we can handle more ships. If we develop Pease as an international airport, we'll have to depend less on Logan.

We are going to need a far better east-west highway system to tie Portsmouth to Concord and down to Keene.

I don't have any problem traveling anywhere in the world via Logan. It's only two hours from my office, which is reasonable. Nor do I have any problems shipping mail order items anywhere in the world from Hancock. I don't find any serious trade-offs in doing business in New Hampshire.

(23) Provincial perspective of business community.

I haven't run into this.

(24) Lack of technical support and education for international trade.

Yep, I agree. But this is something which can be rectified in short order. All it takes are a few well-organized adult evening courses in our schools and we'll be in good shape.

(25) Lack of investment in economic development.

Seems like this is redundant with other weakesses. If we turn around the business climate we'll have investment funds available. First things first.

(26) State government averse to innovation and fearful of change.

Then they're going to have a terrible time reading my report. Of *course* the government is averse to change. Most civil servants or teachers hate change. For that matter, most people hate change and resist it. I'm used to that. It's normal.

In order to bring about change, you have to show people how they are going to benefit from the change. You have to overcome their fears. Okay, this takes some strong management skills and a lot of selling.

The plans I've outlined will tend to keep the state government to a minimum and will eliminate most of the cushy jobs. On the positive side, it'll give those really doing their jobs an opportunity to make more money . . . possibly a lot more money. It'll provide job satisfaction and a whole state full of happy customers.

During the war my submarine crew was top-notch and we knew it. We were damned good and were proud of it. As far as I know, we're the only submarine crew from WWII that has well-attended yearly reunions. We're the only one with a newsletter which has been going for years.

I'd like to see the same esprit de corps with our state government. The potential is there and our Commission has the power to make it flower . . . if we don't drop the ball.

And that concerns me.

(27) Poor coordination between state and local government.

I've already covered this problem with a good proposed solution . . . a communications system.

(28) Absentee ownership of significant portion of commercial and industrial assets.

If we aim to attract smaller businesses, this won't be a problem. This was one concern I had over the Airbus Industry situation at Pease. Of course the upside, if Airbus does come in, would be the opportunity for hundreds of small supplier firms to spring up in the area to provide manufacturing support.

(29) High business taxes.

I've already covered this in depth.

(30) High workers' compensation.

Let's find out why this is high so we can get it down. I'll be surprised if we don't find a huge built-up bureaucracy and endless administration. We should be able, if we really have the support of the legislature and the executive, to cut this way down.

(31) High, not competitive, operating costs.

How come? More details are needed to explain this one. I haven't found this to be true for any of my businesses.

(32) Questionable quality of education.

It's not questionable at all, it's terrible. It's awful. The only saving aspect is that our quality of education in New Hampshire isn't any worse than the other states. It's just worse than the education provided by all of our competitor countries.

(33) No major airport.

I'm not familiar with what the options are for Pease. But we do have an airport there which is presumably large enough to handle international traffic. It just isn't near anything much . . . yet. If there were a decent highway, it would only be about 25 miles from Concord and Manchester, and perhaps 40 from Nashua.

If a high-speed railroad is run from Boston to Portland, it would have to pass right by Pease. Between the two, this might help open the southern half of the state for small high-tech manufacturing and marketing businesses.

(34) The government reacts slowly to change.

As do all governments and large corporations. Bureaucracies are that way. If we want to change we'll have to reinvent the government . . . which is a very good idea.

(35) Inadequate public revenues.

Oh baloney! What we have is overadequate public expenses, just as Governor Gregg mentioned in his address at the Chamber of Commerce. We need to get some of Ed Deming's quality concepts applied to the state government.

(36) Intolerance to progressive thought and open debate.

Shades of weakness #26. Any bureaucracy hates progressive thoughts . . . they lead to possible changes. Civil servants want things to be comfortable until they retire with a good pension.

(37) Entrenched political establishment sustains status quo.

This is not a new concept, either. The question is, how effective can our Commission be? Are we too infiltrated or controlled by the political establishment to be able to make changes? The lack of any response to my first suggested approaches leads me to wonder how real the Commission is.

How many legislators are there whose first priority is the health of our state? For how many is this beside the point? And ditto for the executive, the judicial and the state employees? Oh, I hope for the best, but I haven't lived this long without having my hopes occasionally disillusioned.

(38) Want of political consensus.

This requires better communications. I've made some proposals which should help considerably with this.

(39) Lack of public financing programs.

Good, let's keep it that way . . . unless we're going to ask the state to put up venture capital which will be repaid.

(40) Excessive amount of property in current use.

Hmmm, maybe.

(41) Aging population.

Every state has an aging population. Is ours worse? It sure can't be worse than Florida. I suggest we make the best use we can of our seniors . . . encouraging some to help with child care and thus cut those costs, getting more retired executives to help small businesses with their expertise. Get them to help teach in our business-oriented courses.

Also mentioned was our poor record in dealing with the federal government. Here is another opportunity for us to use the quality approach. We should be sensitive to problems and find out why we're slow to react to federal regulators so we can fix them.

Mostly we need to establish systems for communicating . . . between towns, the state, and business. Without good communications we have suspicion and paranoia. I've recommended several ways to help build the communications we need to make this state work.

124 The Competition

Since New Hampshire's in competition with the other states . . . plus more and more exporting countries . . . we should at least look into what our neighboring states are using to sweeten the pot to attract businesses.

Business/NH did an article on this in their October 1991 issue. They pointed out that "Connecticut offers an 80% property tax break for companies that move into targeted urban enterprise zones." And "Rhode Island bills itself as providing 'One of the most attractive tax incentive packages in the United States: no local property tax on the manufacturer's machinery and equipment; no manufacturer's inventory tax; no sales tax on manufacturer's machinery, equipment and replacement parts.'"

Massachusetts is trying to woo foreign investments and Maine offers "the most comprehensive training, retraining and education program . . . and the lowest start-up and operating costs in the nation."

We're up against North Carolina, which has been very aggressive. In 1990 new and expanding businesses in North Carolina created more than 42,000 jobs . . . and more than half of the expansions were in towns of less than 10,000 people. They've been running about 100 new plant announcements a year. *Site Selection* magazine gave New Hampshire credit for seven new manufacturing plants or expansions in 1990 . . . a matter of about 570 jobs.

Well, at least we managed to be first in the nation in one thing: personal and business bankruptcies. And we made the other end of the list as 50th in growth of personal income. Dead last! We also came in last in amount spent per student on higher education. We've got our work cut out for us. The only bright side is that it probably can't get worse.

125 How To Attract Business

There's no big mystery to attracting new businesses to New Hampshire. If we think in terms of selling a product . . . if we think in terms of the capitalistic approach . . . we'll be on the right track. We need to market New Hampshire.

So let's look at all the normal marketing elements . . . such as advertising, promotion, quality control, customer service, product development, customer targeting, and so on.

If you agree with my basic concept of aiming to sell New Hampshire primarily to small businesses rather than big ones, this will tend to give us a safer customer base . . . and will simplify our sales efforts. Instead of having to make up inch-thick proposals and send sales teams to visit major manufacturers, we'll be able to sell more by mail and telephone, keeping our sales costs down.

By appealing to smaller businesses, we'll also not have to make tax deals we may regret. Let's let the other states push for the big industries while we go for thousands of new small businesses. Besides, small businesses will fit into a small state much better . . . and they'll match our small town work forces. We know that large cities are a remnant of the 19th Century, so let's keep our eyes on the future . . . and that means edge cities and small rural and suburban towns.

126 Advertising?

I'm not thinking so much of big ads in site selection magazines as I am in generating all the visibility we can for New Hampshire in publications which reach the types of small businesses we're targeting.

Remember, we're primarily after small businesses which sell out-of-state or export, and not so much those which provide local services. We want to bring revenues into the state . . . from there on they'll feed our local businesses.

So let's say we decide to target the computer software industry . . . just for example. There are thousands of small software firms, so this isn't a bad high-tech industry to tackle. We can discuss the best industries to go for later.

The first thing I'd do if I were going to sell New Hampshire to new businesses would be to put together a booklet which would explain all the benefits involved. It would also list all the possible negatives people might come up with and turn them into positives.

Like what's there to do in New Hampshire? We have so many interesting things to do I've proposed a magazine just devoted to that subject. We have all sorts of activities and cultural events. We have music from one end of the state to the other. We have little theaters. We have county fairs.

Businessmen want to know how our tax situation compares with other states. This is where our no state income or sales taxes are a big plus. If we follow my suggestions, reduce our state expenses, and start some profit-making enterprises, we'll even be able to cut our property taxes.

Mostly we'd promote our quality of life. Now that housing prices have dropped to a more reasonable level, newcomers to the state will be able to afford homes. Of course, if we do trigger a big influx, that'll push housing costs back up again.

Perhaps Hancock is an unusual area, but just on my road there are two new houses being built . . . two people have added garages and one has expanded his home. That's the upside. The downside is that one third of the homes on the road have for-sale signs on them.

Now, to attract software firms, I'd put small ads for the booklet in the computer magazines . . . classifieds will do. I'd search the computer publications for any firms already in New Hampshire and get testimonials from them, which I'd use in PR releases to the computer trade press. It takes visibility to make sales . . . and it doesn't have to cost a bundle to achieve.

127 Quality Control

If we're going to attract more businesses, we're going to have to coddle them. This means doing what we can to help them find space for their business. We should help them find workers. We might even help their workers get any training they need. And we want to have them let us know when they run into problems.

Yes, all this could cost millions, if we're going to go down the old path of providing everything free. Well, we don't have to do that. Entrepreneurs want help, and will be willing to pay for it. But they want quality help that is reasonably priced. We want to get away from the all-too-familiar civil service employee mind-set which equates free service with poor service.

If we're able to attract 30 new firms a month, that's about 360 a year. If they have an average of 20 employees, that's an additional 7,200 jobs a year. That would generate around $330 million more in revenues for the state . . . an extra billion in three years.

Once we get our act together you can bet we'll be seeing articles in *Inc.* and other business magazines citing New Hampshire as a great place for entrepreneurs. Will we have to worry about attracting too many new businesses? Not for a while. We've still got an enormous amount of room for business expansion in our state . . . room for lots more people without degrading our quality of life.

128 Targeting Our Customers

We're aiming in general for high-tech businesses . . . since they tend to have higher revenues per sale. If we build a high-tech career work force in New Hampshire, we'll have our pick of high-tech firms wanting to come here. We should keep an eye on new technologies such as digital audio broadcasting, fiber optics, and medical electronics.

We'll do better to look for new industries which will be developing . . . industries which will tend to favor smaller companies. There's no use getting involved with microchips, which take a billion or so investment just to get started.

In addition to manufacturing, I mentioned the growing opportunities in marketing. We're well-suited geographically to market imports from Europe. We'll have to start planning for a better port at Portsmouth and a major international airport at Pease if we want to make this happen. It has to be easy to ship things to and from Europe . . . and easy to move them to the other states.

I've set up a warehouse in Peterborough to help record companies handle their eastern sales. We're handling CDs from about 150 companies so far. We're starting to solicit warehousing and distributing business from European record companies. This has the potential to grow substantially.

129 What About the Environment?

Good grief, what should the Commission do about our disappearing ozone layer, acid rain and the greenhouse effect? Isn't New Hampshire an ideal place to set an example?

Alas, our popular media, though deeply in love with catastrophe (good news doesn't sell papers) comes up sadly short when it comes to doing their homework. The media can always find scientists to support almost anything . . . such as doctors who'll swear that they haven't seen any positive proof that cigarettes really cause cancer. The power companies have some well-paid scientists who say the same thing about power lines.

So here we are, poisoning our rivers, our air, our oceans . . . all in the name of greed. Of course, when you get down to brass tacks, it's more a question of jobs than greed, but we're not used to our media being really honest with us.

Having taken a long walk in a sequoia forest recently, I can understand why we have tree-huggers anxious to protect these huge old trees. Having flown over mountains in Oregon where every tree has been cut down for miles, I can understand why many people hate to see such devastation.

I had an uncle who was in the logging business . . . chap named Henry, up in Lincoln. But he never left the mountains as flat as those I saw in Oregon. They looked like our mountains after the 1938 hurricane roared through Franconia Notch.

We're harvesting trees from my farm in Hancock, but we're leaving most of 'em standing. The farm is in the middle of a forest . . . so I tend to practice moderation over greed.

I also tend to be very wary of activists. I've tried talking with some, but I've found them both ill-informed and uninformed, acting more on religious beliefs than facts. Like religious fanatics, they're also almost totally impervious to facts.

I'm sure you remember Sununu's vilification when he challenged the rhetoric on the greenhouse effect. What a hate campaign that stirred up in the media. Now that we have a lot more data on the subject, I'll bet you won't hear one word of apology from those strident vilifiers. The latest word, in case you've missed the news, is that there is no sign of any change in the earth's temperature attributable to changes in the atmosphere.

Things have warmed up slightly in places, but that happens with every sun spot maximum . . . and we had a corker in 1991. Of course, there are scientists claiming that we are headed toward another ice age . . . while a second group is saying we're all going to fry. I have a good deal of faith that Gaia will keep things in balance.

Gaia? You've missed the books and articles by Lovelock on Gaia? Tsk! Check 'em out from your local library and see what a fantastic balancing act our planet has been doing to maintain comfortable living conditions for us. They even did a wonderful PBS program on the subject a while back.

If we can make our New Hampshire state government more responsive to its people, then perhaps we can start trying to get Washington responsive. And next, why not the rest of the world? So I'm not opposed to people blowing the whistle when they see things going wrong. I am just not in favor of us acting on too little data. I'd like our whistle-blowing investigation teams to make damned sure they look into all sides of problems before swinging into action.

Yes, there are some egregious things going on. In the Philippines they are catching fish by poisoning their reefs, doing lasting damage. They're also using dynamite to kill fish. Then there are the baby seal bludgeoners, the drift netters who are killing porpoises wholesale, and so on.

I'm not sure how long it's going to be before the anti-fur activists are going to try to stop us from eating any more meat. Talk about cruelty to animals! Perhaps we'll all become vegetarians . . . at least until some group discovers that broccoli, too, has feelings.

Of course, we have the evil World Bank paying ranchers in Brazil to burn down the rain forest so they can grow beef to help keep our cholesterol levels high. And the Japanese are wiping out the Indonesian rain forests for wood to build their homes.

Perhaps we could get started with a small New Hampshire state group which would could check out environmental and other activist complaints in our state. Their reports alone might put enough pressure on transgressors to bring about needed changes. Lacking that, I suspect the New Hampshire legislature will sense the political correctness of going with the flow.

How could such an office possibly pay for itself? Is this a service which is so important to us that we'll gladly pay taxes to fund it? Perhaps. But being an entrepreneur, I prefer making it self-funding, if possible. In this case, I naturally fall back on my usual solution: a publication. Investigate possible problems and then sell the information about them.

Since ecological and animal rights matters contribute to our New Hampshire quality of life, and since so many of us are interested in preserving and improving our quality of life, we might be able to fund the team needed to follow up on complaints via a *New Hampshire Preservation* publication.

Of course, until we get Washington cleaned up, there are undoubtedly millions available to help fund this project. Since the basic approach in Washington is for legislators to get every buck possible for the home state . . . because anything they don't get will be taken by others . . . we should play the game until the rules are changed — and play it to kill. Thus speaks a pragmatic idealist.

If my callousness toward our environment irritates you, how about splurging for the book "Galileo's Revenge: Junk Science in the Courtroom" by Peter Huber? You might just enjoy reading it and finding out, for example, that the worst damage done in Prince William Sound was by the cleanup crews, not the oil spill. This was also covered by the *Scientific American*. Environmentalists forced the waste of billions of dollars and did incredible harm in the process. You might also check out the article in *Forbes* (12/23/91, p.160).

Acid rain alarmists are not going to be happy to find that this is only a nuisance, not a catastrophe. *Scientific American* published a nice article on that a couple years ago . . . or you can read *Reason* (1/92, p.20). This is just another example of how activists blow things out of proportion . . . crying "wolf."

130 War, Jobs and Quality of Life

We're very fortunate way up here in New Hampshire. We're isolated from many of the ethnic problems besetting other states. We're relatively free of ghettos and the worst urban miseries . . . except in Manchester.

But we are having a few problems, and they're likely to get worse. We'll be better able to cope if we understand them, so let's get down to some basics . . . not just of human nature, but of life itself. And that's where most (all?) of our problems start.

It has to do with the food chain and our position on it. And that brings us to pecking order. Big fish eat smaller fish. Bigger hens peck smaller hens. Being at the top of the food chain, we don't have many enemies . . . except ourselves.

One result of the pecking order syndrome is that everbody is, to some degree, aware of it most of the time. This starts out from the first days of childhood, with boys tending to fight with each other for dominance and for girls to compromise.

All of us operate to some degree with a sense that others are better than we are . . . which gives us feelings of inferiority. We may feel inferior due to looks, intelligence, strength, and so on. We tend to overcome these inferiority feelings by both bragging and exaggerating our accomplishments. We also try to boost our own morale by putting others down.

Kids can be particularly cruel, but almost all of us are guilty of seizing upon any pretext to boost our self-image. We put people down for any differences we perceive. We make people miserable if they have big ears, a big nose, a lisp, an accent, are tall, ugly, short, fat, skinny, have any kind of deformity, a different color skin, a different religion, are poorer, dress in any way not totally accepted by peers, and so on. Boys put down girls. Girls put down boys. Both put down homosexuals . . . and so it goes.

One way to lessen the fighting and pain is to make everyone exactly the same. Well, even that might not do it . . . but it does help. The need to dominate . . . the need to overcome those basic inferiority feelings . . . can't be stopped; it can just be reduced. It's all part of a genetic drive in every living thing to survive.

So we see it coming out in ethnic hate. We see it in cruelty to the disadvantaged. We see it in biases in life and in the workplace. Many of us have been taught not to express these feelings, but they're never far below the surface. Even politicians, who have to be much more careful of everything they say than the rest of us, can't help but let loose a joke now and then . . . about blondes, women, Poles, Jews, North Dakotans, homosexuals, etc.

Naturally a member of the media jumps on the joke, finding groups of sensitive people who are outraged and see no humor whatever in it. The politician then has to apologize . . . and stop telling jokes.

So what's this got to do with New Hampshire? Well, as I said, we have an advantage over most other states in that we are already so homogeneous. The American melting pot system has worked well here. We do have a few small ethnic enclaves . . . such as some Finns in the New Ipswich area and French-Canadians in the Berlin area. There may be more, but those are the ones I'm familiar with. Oh yes, Bethlehem summers Hasidic Jews, but they're vacationers, not residents.

Bethlehem, which is built high up on the side of Mount Agassiz, provided a hay fever refuge. In its heyday in the 1920s and 1930s, it had 30 hotels and 100 rooming houses . . . and they were packed all summer every summer with Jews, mostly from New York and Boston.

The more we start getting kids to work together in school as teams . . . and shuffle them around onto different teams, the less stress we should have from the pecking order syndrome. Our present educational system, where each child is isolated as an individual and forced to perform under threat of humiliation, makes the situation worse, pitting each youngster against the whole class, forcing kids to seek outlets for their frustrations.

They can't take it out on their teachers or parents, so they take it out on each other. And this builds a lifetime response pattern that is almost impossible to change.

Perhaps you've noticed that federal legislation has not been very successful in eliminating racial prejudices. In my experience it has tended to polarize blacks and whites. It's made us so aware of color that there's no way to forget it, even for a moment.

Blacks are making the situation worse by refusing to integrate. They refuse by flaunting their own hair styles, calling themselves Afro-Americans, insisting on schools having black studies, speaking their own dialect, and so on.

Most foreign groups that have come here have melted together within two generations. The first generation speaks the mother language. The second generation speaks both the old language and English. The third generation speaks only English.

Even in Boston there are pressures to provide education in Spanish for Hispanic children. That does them a disservice and slows down the melting pot system.

If we can emphasize teamwork, right from the earliest pre-school years, I believe we'll be able to have happier people with less friction. We may even be able to enjoy dumb jokes that exaggerate stereotypes and not be hurt by them. And we can do this by understanding each other, not by becoming numb to insults.

By gradually eliminating our larger cities and moving our businesses to edge cities and suburban towns, we'll further this melting pot system. If we provide low income housing in our towns we'll be able to gradually clean up our cities . . . and improve the quality of life for everyone.

131 Tariff Protection

Can we keep out foreign products by erecting tariff barriers? I don't think history has many cases where such barriers haven't caused more problems than benefits. It's difficult to build walls against imports without having walls built against our exports. And when the walls get high and price levels out of kilter, smuggling takes over and builds criminal empires.

Unless we build a wall around our country we can't preserve many tariff restrictions. We know our border patrol, even when helped by our military, has been unable to keep drugs from being smuggled in by the ton.

With this in mind, how can we lay a foundation for a future for New Hampshire that will give us an advantage over other states and countries and give us a good crack at a better than average quality of life?

As transportation and communication costs go down, we'll still have two potential advantages over other states: 1. Our educational system will be continuing to attract high-tech businesses by providing an outstanding work force; 2. We'll be able to take even more advantage of our vacation potential by providing an endless list of activities and experiences.

As our large cities continue to decay, our system of edge cities and small towns will be increasingly attractive for businesses. And as more people seek short, interesting vacations, we'll have more to offer than any other easily reachable state.

Every attempt at protectionism and isolationism has hurt our exports far more than it has protected us against imports. New Zealand tried for years to protect their industries . . . and set their country back decades. It's a natural response to competition, but it's never worked.

132 Can We Fix The Government?

One thing we know for sure: our state government isn't working well. This is not to throw any stones at our legislature, executive, judiciary or civil servants involved. It's just that we know that no state government works very well, including ours.

The same problems which have corrupted our federal government are at work in our state governments, just on a smaller scale. Thus, I believe we can learn a good deal about the fundamental problems state governments have by looking at what's happened in Washington.

I hope you've all read C. Northcote Parkinson's book, *Parkinson's Law*. While the book is hilarious, it's also soundly founded on facts. It's just that the facts are so ridiculous, even though true.

Another gem is *Augustine's Laws*, by Norman Augustine. Like Parkinson, Augustine's credentials are impeccable. His laws, like those of Parkinson, are totally absurd . . . and completely verifiable.

Now, to be specific, let's take Augustine's Law #1: "The thickness of the proposal to win a multimillion dollar contract is about one millimeter per million. If all the proposals conforming to this standard were piled one on top of the other at the bottom of the Grand Canyon, it would probably be a good idea."

Ridiculous, right? Sure. But Augustine shows a chart of almost 100 such proposals, plotted by thickness in feet vs. millions of dollars. It's a remarkably straight line. As the Chairman of the Defense Science Board, Augustine was in a good position to get this data.

His second law: "The source selection process is based on a system of rewards and penalties, distributed randomly." If we start looking into New Hampshire contracts, will we find the same random pattern?

I have personally verified Law #3: "Ninety percent of the time things will turn out worse than you expect. The other ten percent of the time you had no right to expect so much." He bases this conclusion on the actual vs. estimated costs of 81 major programs.

He shows that the cost of tactical aircraft has grown in a remarkably straight line on a logarithmic chart from 1910 to 1990. This chart shows that by 2054 the entire defense budget will purchase just one aircraft, which the Air Force and the Navy will have to share. By 2120 it'll take our entire gross national product to buy one aircraft . . . but I'm sure it'll be a corker.

Before you smile condescendingly and shrug this off as just another weird result of our military purchasing system, you'll want to check out his chart for commercial airliners. It follows the same straight line as military planes.

Having worked as an engineer for Airborne Instrument Laboratories, an Air Force R&D lab, I'm familiar with the reasons why costs increase logarithmically as complexity increases and why reliability goes down on the same curve.

This is another reason why the prospect of Airbus setting up shop at Pease AFB worries me. Technology has this inexorable tendency to increase in complexity, particularly when it gets into corporate hands where it's being managed by accountants or lawyers instead of entrepreneurs.

It's also interesting that as the cost of the aircraft goes up, its reliability goes down. The same holds for all weapons systems. Law #12: "Aircraft flight in the 21st Century will always be in a westerly direction, preferably supersonic, to provide the additional hours needed each day to maintain all the broken parts."

Augustine also charts CEO wages against company profits. Law #13: "There are many highly successful organizations in the United States. There are also many highly paid executives. The policy is not to intermingle the two." And indeed his chart shows there is no correlation.

133 And Our Commission?

Augustine writes, "It has long been recognized that the formation of a committee is a powerful technique for avoiding responsibility, deferring difficult decisions, and averting blame . . . while at the same time maintaining a semblance of action." He continues, "Perhaps it is not simply happenstance that it seems to defy human imagination to identify instances wherein committees have been formed under circumstances which lead to *measurable* contributions."

Will this be the fate of our Commission? Are we for real, or are we a facade cooked up to tide over the state until other events, over which we have no control, eventually ease the recessionary pressures and our

Commission is no longer considered necessary?

Part of the answer lies in the productivity of the Commission . . . in our ability to (a) come up with some proposals which we agree are worth implementing and (b) the actual interest the legislature and executive have in making changes that will inevitably be deemed controversial. I say that because, in my experience, *any* change will be considered controversial by some group. And when we're considering changes in education and our state government, both of which areas are protected by well-funded militant lobby groups, the liklelihood of our success would seem remote.

The lack of response to my initial reports could easily be interpreted as a recognition of the futility of pursuing any but the most modest of Commission goals on the part of wiser Commission members. On the other hand, we all know that in any group there tends to be a much smaller group of activists who do a large part of the work. In most clubs that I've joined I've found the active members to be approximately one or two. Perhaps this is why I seem to find myself being elected president of the clubs I join. Have I learned anything from this? Obviously not.

Augustine puts it this way in his productivity law. Law #20: "One-tenth of the participants produce at least one-third of the output, and increasing the number of participants merely reduces the average output." He points out that the top 1% produce nearly 50 times the per capita output of the bottom half.

There are many small changes we can make in areas where there are no organized groups to oppose change. But if we're unable to bring about changes in either education or in state government, we will be unable to perform our role and will fail in our goals.

The work force needed in the 21st Century can, I'm convinced, only be achieved if we can make some major changes in our educational system. I've proposed some changes for starters, but beyond that I've proposed a system for bringing about a continuing series of changes. Will these proposals die in committee?

Likewise, I've proposed a few changes for starters in the state government. And beyond that I've proposed a system which will continue the process of reducing the cost of our government and at the same time increase its productivity.

My proposals, if implemented, will help us avoid the usual big business and big government traps, which Augustine has shown are dead ends.

134 Entrepreneurs Über Alles

The future for both the military and commercial applications of complex technology, where systems costs continue to escalate by powers of ten as system reliability plummets at the same time, bodes well for entrepreneurs and small business. Big business and big government will keep bloating until they collapse. Meanwhile, smaller businesses designing and building simpler systems will win in the long run. So let's gear New Hampshire to take advantage of this inevitability by aiming to encourage small- and medium-sized businesses . . . and by educating our people to provide the work force this business base will need.

If you've been keeping your ear to the ground and your eye to the keyhole you know that customers are demanding service even more than low prices. They want what they want, when they want it, and in the color of their choice. Meeting this demand is increasingly difficult for large corporations, where efficiencies are based on economies of scale in production and sales.

Smaller companies can gear up to make quick changes. Customers who don't want to wait for a custom-made product to be made in Hong Kong will be looking for firms able to make delivery next week, not next month.

Just as clothing manufacturers are starting to bring their factories back to America so they can react faster to market demands, some styles come and go very quickly. Even in electronics there is a building need for fast turnaround that Asian production can't satisfy.

There's also a general trend for retailers to carry thinner inventories and depend on faster response from their suppliers. Stateside manufacturers can adapt to this better than international megacorporations with overseas factories. This is another reason why New Hampshire will benefit in the future from attracting small entrepreneurial businesses.

135 Activism In New Hampshire?

We made *Business Week* (12/16/91 p.43): "Voters are mad as hell in New Hampshire." I admit I'm at a disadvantage in this since I'm not a Democrat. But then I sure don't feel much like a Republican either. I guess I've moved over into the Undecided. That's a euphemism for a plague on both your houses.

I don't think I qualify as a right winger, since I'm not an isolationist. And I sure am out of the mainstream of current Republicanism as a pro-choicer. I'm not a liberal, since I don't believe we should throw money at problems. Nor do I believe that socking it to the rich does anything but hurt business and lose jobs. Without venture capital we'll grind to a halt.

As Lord White, the CEO of Hanson Industries, put it, "The worst thing (that would happen in the U.S.) would be more creeping socialism. This legislative attitude . . . soak the rich . . . was what wrecked Britain. I'd hate to see it happen here." (*Fortune* 12/30/91 p.35).

As Jack Kemp said, "The capital gains tax is not a tax on rich people. It's a tax on poor people who want to get rich . . . I am convinced that all too many members of the U.S. Congress are worried that somewhere someone is going to get rich. They are not worried about how many people are getting poorer as we snuff out and tax capital, the source of seed corn for the next generation of entrepreneurship" (ibid).

I admired the job Governor Sununu did for New Hampshire. I was disappointed that he, like Governor Sherman Adams, wasn't more politic while advising the President. But I had a lot more confidence in his decisions than Bush's.

The *BW* article closes by saying New Hampshire seems ready for a dose of old-fashioned government activism. Well, that's what our Commission could have to offer, if we can get it into motion and agree on some initiatives.

It doesn't do us much good to have the lowest tax rate of all states (*Reason* 1/92 p.14) if we're going bankrupt. We don't need tax cuts for the rich, the middle-class or the poor. We need more business.

Yes, capital gains tax cuts will tend to make more money available for investment in business . . . despite populist cries that this is a tax cut for the rich. Hey, the rich have the money, so why shouldn't we work on ways to get them to invest it where it's going to help everyone, including the poor? When you need money it makes sense to me to go where it is and try to borrow some.

Bush's extraordinarily poor performance as President has opened the political gates. That's nice for us in New Hampshire, since the candidates will be up here entertaining us and spending money. We've got a nice little business going with this first-in-the-nation primary dodge.

I don't think I'm alone in being upset over Bush's history of vacillation. I hoped that Sununu would be able to counter that. Bush's decisions on Quayle and Thomas, as I've mentioned, did not help build my confidence in him. His collapse on his no-tax stand made him look like a wimp. His stand on pro-life is so out of touch with the world population problem that it angers me. His weaseling on the human rights bill lost even more confidence in him for me. The only person who's made any sense at all on dealing with the deficit is P.J. O'Rourke, (the *Rolling Stone* writer who lives in Sharon, NH), and he's not running.

I'll be interested in what Pat Buchanan has to offer . . . and Governor Clinton. Pat nicely fielded the usual nasties from Sam Donaldson on the Brinkley show and didn't come off as isolationist as he'd been painted. Clinton has done wonders with education in Arkansas, so I'll be looking at his proposals.

"Protectionism, in essence, represents still another attempt to live beyond our means, by barring foreign competition rather than undertaking the belt-tightening and hard work necessary for beleaguered U.S. industries to become more competitive. Protectionist measures would doubtless be still more widespread were it not for the fact that protectionism is so clearly inflationary." (*Beyond Our Means* by Malabre, p.61.).

Malabre goes on to point out the ramifications of the car quota. "The average price of a new car between the introduction of the quota arrangement and 1984 rose to nearly $2,000, benefiting Japanese producers and their dealers by at least $2 billion a year. As for American consumers, the average per-car sales price was some $800 higher than if the restraint program had not been launched. The cost to American consumers works out to about $160,000 annually per auto-worker job saved . . . there is no evidence that the quota system advanced the competitiveness of the U.S. auto industry." It's interesting to note that the hourly employment costs for the U.S. auto industry are some 60% higher than the average for all U.S. manufacturing.

We are in bad trouble in New Hampshire, but I think we can help ourselves just fine without protectionism. I've proposed some inexpensive ways to turn things around quickly . . . but what actually happens depends on the Commission and how much clout we actually have with the legislature and executive.

Considering the urgency of our problems, we don't have the luxury of months for debate. Moving our meetings to every three weeks instead of monthly is a step in the right direction, but still the only communications we seem to have, other than my "reports," are when we meet. With 32 of us on the Commission and a meeting aimed at lasting an hour or so, this nets us about two to three minutes each before we're usurping someone else's time. And that presupposes no time at all for the chairman.

I've set about writing my ideas and recommendations, and the background for them, on the conviction that no meeting schedule of which I could conceive would allow them to verbally be presented, discussed, considered, and acted upon. I must admit to some disappointment at the lack, so far, of response from my fellow Commissioners either to my ideas or with their own recommendations and the rationale behind them.

I'm used to a "I don't agree with all your ideas" response. That to me means that (a) I'm up against a belief which transcends reason, (b) there could be data which I didn't take into consideration, but should, or (c) I need to provide more information. I tend to write minimally, giving just enough background to make my points. In most cases I've done considerably more homework than I present and am prepared to provide much more substantiation for my positions. I don't enjoy reading literary overkill, so I avoid writing it. Many people, comfortable and quite used to points being made repeatedly, require this approach to be convinced of new ideas.

Others are infinitely resistant to new ideas and often react by getting mad. It's easier than thinking.

In view of the makeup of our Commission and its impressive vita, I expect my ideas to at least be considered before being rejected.

136 International Competition

Ready for a couple factoids? *Fortune* 12/30/91 p.107: "According to the Bureau of Labor Statistics, Germany's wages have leaped from 74% of America's in 1985 to 144% in 1990, and Japan's have moved from 50% to 87%."

This narrows the lower wage excuse for manufacturing overseas. There are still many countries with dirt-cheap labor, but most of these present political problems that make doing business more difficult.

The bottom line is that America in general and New Hampshire in particular can take advantage of this changing wage differential to bring more manufacturing business here. We offer faster turnaround, lower shipping and communications costs, plus we speak the same language.

What we're not bringing to the table so far are modern production facilities. "*American Machinist* ranked America 21st among industrial countries in the purchase of metalworking machine tools per capita last year . . . behind Romania" (ibid). To the extent that this lack of investment in modern machinery is attributable to our tax system, we need to press for change. This is not one of my fields of expertise, so I bow to any Commissioners who understand this problem and can propose some remedies. I wonder if there are some ways New Hampshire can lead the way in this?

This dependence on old technologies obviously hurts our productivity. You've probably read about the Honda Civic requiring only 10.9 hours of direct labor per car vs. GM's over 30 hours per car . . . both made in America (*Fortune* 12/30/91 p.117). Malabre (*Beyond Our Means*, 1987, p.64) says the Japanese auto industry is two-and-a-half times as productive as ours.

He points out that it's our tax system that is largely to blame. We discourage saving by taxing it twice . . . once when we earn it and again when it produces an investment return. "In 1985, capital outlays in the U.S. amounted to 18% of our GNP. The comparable investment rates in Japan were 30% and 22% in West Germany."

Is there anything New Hampshire can do to encourage the capital investment we need to modernize our plants?

137 The Freeloaders

Back in 1987, Malabre said, "The number of Americans living largely or entirely off a government check for which they perform no labor is roughly 100 million. That constitutes nearly one government-dependent individual for each working citizen . . . .the federal government now pays over $4,000 each year . . . it exceeds $7,000 if state and local government payments are added . . . over twenty years the entitlement payments have risen from 24% of federal spending to 41%."

Undoubtedly, some of these millions are bona fide needy, "but the bulk of these huge payments clearly have been delivered to Americans who are relatively well off."

Perhaps we can find out what New Hampshire is doing in this arena. How much are we paying in entitlements and to whom? Is this an area where we might be able to observe some economies or do we think the money is being wonderfully apportioned? It would be a first.

Chapter VI

138 Warming the Incubator

If you're in agreement with me that in the long run New Hampshire will do best to nurture small entrepreneurial businesses (see 015), aiming generally for those in high-tech fields with the prospect of selling outside of New Hampshire, then let's consider what we can do to attract them.

Rensselaer Polytechnic Institute (Troy, NY) has a very successful small business incubator system. I've had the privilege of working with and advising this group . . . which gives me a small head start in this field as far as understanding the problems facing a wide variety of high-tech startups is concerned.

In order to provide a nurturing support system for new businesses, we have to understand their weaknesses and help solve their problems in these areas.

Entrepreneurs in high-tech fields tend to be scientifically oriented more than business oriented, so we're going to have to help them with business support services. As a good general rule, I think we'll find a high percentage of these entrepreneurs will be combining youth with their inexperience . . . a not unusual pairing.

New businesses are going to need help in a wide variety of ways . . . most of which we'll be able to provide. For instance, they're going to need help in finding employees. I've already recommended a statewide computerized job/work matching system approach which would solve this need for them (see 052).

Of course, if we re-orient our schools so New Hampshire can offer a high-tech educated work force, this in itself will be a powerful attraction for new businesses.

One of the most serious entrepreneurial weaknesses lies in planning. This is an area where we might be able to provide the most help with the least investment. This is where retired executives or groups such as the New Hampshire High-Tech Council could be organized to assist.

There is a need for a manual on planning for entrepreneurs . . . a book I've yet to find in print. When I've done workshops on entrepreneuring at colleges, I've found a great interest in this subject. Indeed, planning is critical for new businesses.

Well, I know what I want to do," isn't a plan. I have file boxes full of business plans sent to me by entrepreneurs in search of venture capital and they all have one thing in common: They're useless. Some entrepreneurs even go to the expense of having professional plan-writing companies do their plans. They aren't any good either.

You successful entrepreneurs know what I'm talking about. You've learned the hard way the importance of planning and know what kind of plans are important. You can tell at a glance whether a business plan is just a show exercise or will actually be a working instrument.

When I explain to budding entrepreneurs that they're going to have to do a whole lot of homework if they're going to have a good chance at succeeding, they think I'm exaggerating. By the time they've got Plan 1 (the action plan) down on paper, they're beginning to see what's ahead.

An action plan, for anyone who hasn't been through this process, lists every action which needs to be taken, showing the date it's to be initiated and the date to be completed.

Plan 2 is the cash flow plan. Here the actions taken are assessed, with the planned expenses and revenues put into calendar form. This plan should give an indication of the maximum total cash expected to be needed for the project.

Plan 3 is the profit and loss plan. This is aimed at accountants and is of little value to the entrepreneur. This is the plan that unsophisticated venture capitalists and banks like to see.

There's one other figure which will help steer an entrepreneur: The net worth of the project. This is the sum of all assets, minus the liabilities. I prefer this figure be added to the cash flow plan. After all, buying a computer for the project may cause an immediate expense of several thousand dollars, but it still has an asset value and this should be shown as a separate function. It's not an exaggeration to think of the net worth estimates as Plan 4.

Once the planning is done there's the little matter of matching, at least month by month, the actual expenses, progress and so on against the plans. This will result in a continual updating of all four plans on a monthly basis, taking into account unexpected delays. Let's not worry about anything getting done ahead of schedule since that's not a problem that's likely to occur.

Since planning is so critical to a startup success, and since the process doesn't seem to be either covered by any books or offered by any colleges, this is an area where New Hampshire might be able to provide some leadership.

I'm suggesting the formation of a planning group made up of successful entrepreneurs . . . perhaps as a special interest group within the New Hampshire High-Tech Council. This could also draw upon SCORE and other advisory groups.

Further, I recommend that this aspect of business startups be covered by night courses offered in our colleges near areas where we want to encourage entrepreneurs to form their companies.

I also recommend that these groups start work on a planning manual that would act both as a workbook for entrepreneurial classes and as reference for new businesses. There's no reason this publication, which can be updated periodically, can't be a profit-making enterprise in itself.

139 Getting Venture Capital

I've briefly mentioned a possible venture capital and entrepreneur mating service. Several years ago, when I was more active in the venture capital business, I got an idea for providing a service which would help to bring venture capitalists together with deserving entrepreneurs.

I got an idea of how disorganized this field was when I sold my publishing company for a few million dollars and suddenly found myself the target of hundreds of business plans. They were piling up all over the place . . . and most of them did not inspire much confidence. Some were based on ideas with a good potential for growth, but most of the plans had serious weaknesses.

I tried to help some of these entrepreneurs. It took a lot of time, but I found that I was getting heaps of heartfelt thanks and not much more. So, after thinking about the situation from both the venture capital viewpoint and from that of the entrepreneurs, I came up with a solution to both their problems.

I then looked around for someone with the background and the entrepreneurial spirit to get my project started. I tried a couple people, but they didn't have the drive it takes to get something new like this going, so I iced it.

My approach is still a valid one . . . and could be organized by New Hampshire as a profit-making business. Here's how it works . . . and yes, of course there's a publication involved.

We want to make it possible for venture capitalists to find the kind of entrepreneurial businesses they're most comfortable with. Further, we want to make it as simple for them as possible to get the information they need to make their decisions. The venture capitalists are the ones with the money . . . the customers, as it were . . . so we want to make investing as simple as we can for them.

What I have in mind is a publication that would outline the investment opportunities available. Each entrepreneur would have one page in the publication in which to explain what the company would be making or doing, what the experience of the officers has been, and what level of investment and participation is being sought. It would be a one page ad seeking an investor.

Venture capitalists would thus be able to look over dozens to hundreds of investment possibilities and pick out those that interested them the most. They'd send a fee ($50 or so) to cover the cost of the full business plan. This would cover the expense of printing the plan for the entrepreneur, it would help pay for the matching service, and it would weed out only casually interested investors.

The entrepreneur would be out the cost of the ad, but wouldn't lose on the business plans. That's a far cry from the cost of sending out hundreds of them blind.

The publication would have a consulting service to help entrepreneurs with their business plans. Indeed, only okayed plans would be allowed to be advertised.

The publication would then work with the entrepreneur to help with the match. If capital is invested in the company, the publication would then get a small share of this, plus it would reserve a small share of equity in the company and want to have a seat on the board of directors as a way to keep in touch with the progress of the company . . . and possibly help protect the investors.

140 Other Incubator Services

Even small companies need a wide variety of services to prosper. If they try to do all of these in house the overhead soon tends to sink the company.

For instance, most businesses need help with accounting, legal problems, advertising, promotion, public relations, publishing, printing, graphics art, photography, list handling, dealing with the post office, and purchasing. They need help with data and information handling, computer networking, telephone switches, and so on.

By setting up supporting services that can be shared by several small companies, we'll enormously simplify startups. These services will be able to help entrepreneurs with cost estimates for their business plans too.

If these services and the entrepreneurial companies are located in nearby communities, not only will it be easier for everyone to meet regularly, but it'll make it practical for college students to work for all of these firms on a part time basis, helping to pay for their tuition and probably getting them more practical business experience than they'd be able to get any other way. This would, in turn, provide an enthusiastic, motivated, intelligent, low-cost work force for these firms.

One desktop publishing firm could handle the catalogs and mailing pieces for dozens of small businesses. Each business could have a Macintosh system which would be networked to a host system to provide finished printing, color separations, and so on.

This supporting firm concept has worked very well for the RPI incubator program.

141 Where To Incubate

The best area to get started with the program would be on the periphery of Manchester or Nashua. Since we know that large cities are a remnant of the past and are not in tune with the quality-of-life concept, I suggest we not consider setting up any small business incubators and supporting services in cities. They do want to be within easy commuting distance of reasonably-priced homes. They also should be close to an educational center that would provide both the special educational courses entrepreneurs need and also a source of students to help as part-time workers.

Once a primary incubator system has been established, we might consider setting up a second group in the vicinity of Dartmouth, in the Hanover-Lebanon area. A third could work well in the Keene area . . . and perhaps a fourth in the Portsmouth-Durham area.

It'll take an initial investment to establish the incubator systems, but this should be easily repaid and continue to pay dividends to the investor, whether it be the state or a venture capital group.

One thing I am not suggesting is that state-run organizations be established to handle any aspect of this. This whole operation should be entrepreneurial . . . and that means it is basically capitalistic. Government, by its very nature, is socialistic. This is why virtually no government-run entity is ever run efficiently.

Have we learned from the debacles in the USSR, in China, in Eastern Europe, in Sweden, and all the other socialist disasters? Have we learned from our own socialist catastrophes such as our educational system? No, of course we haven't, otherwise we'd have long ago replaced Social Security with a better, cheaper system. And we wouldn't be paying 29c for postage stamps. Capitalism seems to work, so let's give it a better chance.

142 The Net Effect

Let's say we're able to attract a hundred new businesses with each of five incubator areas . . . including the supporting companies. That would give us 500 new companies. If each does at least $5 million in sales, this would bring us $2.5 billion in additional state revenues.

If we figure they have an average of about 30 employees per company, we'll have created 15,000 jobs . . . making the project seem almost worthwhile to tackle.

But beyond that we'll see some incubated firms graduating and growing into mid-sized businesses with hundreds of employees. If only one in 10 make the grade to $50 million, that's still 50 firms . . . and another

$2.5 billion in revenues . . . and another 15,000 jobs.

Some startups will fail, despite our nurturing environment and help. But these will be replaced by new startups as the word spreads. Our incubator system will tend to keep on growing as long as we can provide the work force and growth environment they need.

But unless we make a major change in our educational system, we won't be able to provide the high-tech trained work force these firms will need.

I would suggest that we learn from the past and aim toward a diversification of high-tech industries. Further, in view of the problems caused when big businesses fail, I suggest we gear our growth policies to encourage small businesses.

Unless we're able to change how government works more than I think possible, we'll find that big companies will be able to spend enough in the right places to assure their comfort in dealing with government.

The strength of capitalism lies in its competitive nature. Even democracy works when the competition between parties is allowed a free hand. Perhaps, as our information systems improve, we'll be able to have better educated voter groups.

We're well aware of the weaknesses of our present "democratic" system. I wonder if the Commission might tackle this situation and aim at setting New Hampshire up as a test site for a new, improved democracy?

Can we come up with creative solutions to incumbent advantages, to PACs, to well-financed lobbying pressures, to bribery? It's one heck of a challenge, but I think we might be able to clean up much of the mess changing times have made of the original government concept.

Just as a good business plan has to be updated regularly by feeding back the information on actual performance as compared to the plan, our government needs to be able to be updated so it can cope with new circumstances. The framers of our Constitution did a great job, but the world we're living in is enormously different than it was 200 years ago . . . so we're bickering over right to life vs. freedom of choice. These are clearly religious matters, matters of belief, not matters of fact. So we're seeing the government messing with our religious beliefs, despite the Constitutional mandate to keep religion and government separate.

As our communications systems improve, we'll find it easier to get the exact information we want. Our systems are making it easier to access information. We're gradually building data bases and decreasingly expensive ways to tap them. As information storage costs go down, we'll be seeing hyper-information services . . . something like a Library of Congress, almost infinitely cross-indexed, and instantly available anywhere. Just books? No, we'll eventually have more and more available in full color 3D video format.

France took a major leap ahead by setting up a national information and communication system . . . which has paid off nicely. I went to London and checked out the British version. Is something like this practical for New Hampshire? It's worth thinking about. If we want to live better than the rest of the country . . . and the rest of the world, for that matter . . . then we've got to work smarter than they do. So let's gear our schools to provide the educated, enthusiastic work force we need to set an example.

We're starting off way ahead of the other states in some ways as it is. We have the most beautiful state of all. We have a great four-season climate. We have clean air. We have a low crime rate. We have the lowest taxes. We have a good infrastructure. We have a great location . . . midway between Europe and California . . . with a seaport and a potential international airport.

Our North Country is ideally suited for development to attract vacationers. The southern part of the state has plenty of room for the rural and suburban development of entrepreneurial businesses.

Now all we have to do is pull like hell on our bootstraps and get out of this funk we're in. As soon as we get busy doing things, instead of sitting around and talking and griping, we'll see New Hampshire taking off like a rocket.

143 No, Not Another Publication!

Hey, I'm a writer and a publisher, so you're expecting me to propose drilling oil wells? We're getting well into the information age now, so let's think in terms of information to help solve our problems. And, until I see some leaps in technology that aren't yet detectable, I'm going to think in terms of publishing.

Having had careers as a radio engineer and announcer and a TV engineer, producer and director, I'm not discounting these media. I'm watching them and have some gradiose plans for using them as they mature. But for now, good old-fashioned printing has a solid niche.

The advent of desktop publishing has brought publishing within the reach of even the smallest of businesses. My wife, who produces and markets how-to-dance videos, has her own Macintosh publishing system. She produces her advertising, catalogs, business forms and a newsletter with it.

The cost of these systems is now about 10% of what similar systems cost just a few years ago. Just as microcomputers have brought the cost of computing down by a factor of 10, so we see most computer applications going down.

The lowered cost of publishing makes it practical to put out newsletters and small magazines that would have been economically impractical not long ago. It brings user and customer newsletters within the grasp of even small companies.

A year ago, when I started *Music Retailing* as a medium to reach the approximately 9,000 record stores around America and encourage them to sell more independently produced music, I also had to start a newsletter promoting advertising in *MR*. This is written and mailed to about 500 potential advertisers.

Then there's my *IMPS Journal*, which goes to about 5,000 independent music producers. This is supported by a monthly sales newsletter which goes to about 500 potential advertisers such as CD plants, cassette duplicators, recording equipment manufacturers, label makers and so on. Our desktop publishing system gets a good solid workout.

144 State Legislature Newsletter

Being one of the smallest states and having the largest legislature is an interesting combination. It has both advantages and disadvantages.

One problem legislators have is in getting the information they need to make intelligent decisions. The size of the body makes it impractical for the state to provide the supporting staff it would take to adequately brief everyone on every subject that comes up for a decision.

Where there is a weakness, there's an opportunity. In this case this information shortage is often taken advantage of by lobbyists who are funded by special interests. They may be able to present some information for legislators with an even hand. But when it comes to matters involving their sponsors, there is reason to suspect some bias may be involved.

Suppose we had a legislative newsletter that discussed all aspects of proposed legislation? This would tend to nullify the pressures lobbyists can put on measures they're interested in furthering or defeating.

Yes, we'd give lobbyists an opportunity to present their side... in paid ads that would help fund the newsletter.

145 Recession Benefits

Benefits from the recession? You bet! The process is painful and we hate it, but it's doing us a world of good. It's forcing business to face realities and make changes that are long overdue. It's forcing politicians to do the same. Just look at what the recession has done to cut through the baloney and force us to see President Bush in a clearer light!

Any business executives who have been keeping in touch with the reality of the 1990s know they have to cut the overhead, shorten new product development cycles, pay more attention to the customers, increase productivity, invest more on R&D, start planning in longer periods than the next quarter, do something about our educational system, and so on.

Executives who aren't totally asleep are at least dimly aware of the preachings of Tom Peters and know they have to make changes if they're going to cope with the world of 2000. The recession has forced many executives to recognize that they can't put off making changes any longer.

The recession is forcing reluctant executives, and even more reluctant politicians, to accept changes that will help America be more competitive. It's taken a double-dip recession like this to hold corporate hands in the fire long enough to bring about the changes that will, in the long run, greatly benefit our country.

Computers and communications are making it possible to reduce management overhead. Our educational system doesn't need to spend 80% of its money on administration and then cry for more. A recession can help bring about the painful changes which are needed. When we were making lots of money we didn't have to do anything about waste . . . we could live with it.

So we're finally seeing those needed white-collar staff reductions. We're seeing an increased interest in automation as a way to cut costs and save American blue-collar jobs from going overseas. After all, if we're able to cut the labor costs of making products down to a small percentage of the total costs, the edge foreign countries have in lower labor wages will be blown away by the shipping charges. Then we won't have to listen to politicians and uneducated executives frantically recommending destructive fixes such as tariff barriers.

As I've mentioned, it takes General Motors 30 man-hours to make a car vs. 10.9 for Honda . . . both using American workers. We've been fighting this obvious evidence of excessively poor management with import quotas . . . and paying dearly.

So GM is finally recognizing the problem and actually starting to do something about it. Ross Perot told them this several years ago and got so annoying when they ignored him that they had to spend $700 million to shut him up. The "they" in this case is "us." We paid for this massive blunder through higher car prices for all cars, through a loss of stock value, and the effect this has had on the whole stock market.

Will GM start planning ahead for a change? Will they plan for 2002 instead of the first quarter of 1992? Will they start investing in R&D that will bear fruit in 2002? Will they be able to fight the unions and implement work-saving machinery that will cut the labor component of their cars down even below Honda? Will they be able to get the union wages down to 110% of the average American wage for comparable work instead of 160%? Will they be permitted by the unions to modernize the factories? It could be a long, hard, bitter fight.

And how about their layers-upon-layers of administration? Will they be able to bring GM into the 1990s, even if it means firing about 75% of their white collar workers?

And how will the GM board respond to the tens of thousands of blue and white collar workers screaming at them via video sound bites? Screaming, pleading for jobs! How will politicians respond to this? How much will their hearts go out to these angry, frustrated, terrified voters? How deep in our collective pockets will they reach?

But GM is just one very large example of what's gone wrong. As the recession forces executives to face reality, what's happening to GM is happening or will happen all over the country. The fact is that American industry must become more efficient . . . more productive . . . faster-reacting . . . and more concerned with quality in both products and service . . . and this is going to make major changes in jobs.

So how are we going to generate millions of new jobs? What are we going to do with the administrators who haven't been needed for some time, but have been taking a ride on the borrowed money that we see as the deficit? Are we going to eliminate a big part of the middle class and downgrade them to lower incomes? That's the way things have been going for the last ten years, and now it looks as if this trend could escalate . . . unless we come up with a way to change it . . . which I think we can.

We're heading into the old rich-get-richer and the poor-get-poorer system if we don't come to grips with what's going on and make some major changes. And these changes have to make sense in terms of capitalism. This is no time to grab at socialistic straws.

This is also a terrible time for us to have weak, indecisive leadership. The recession has forced many people to re-evaluate our leaders. There is an increasing frustration and anger with the President for letting all this happen. The President looks nervous and whines that it's really Congress that's doing all this. Darn, he's proposed some really big changes and they have refused to do anything.

At the risk of being put on a union hit list, I'm going to include the educational unions in the list of culprits that are hurting America. Should I mention the postal workers union? And did you read the article in the January *Reader's Digest* about the way the city unions are destroying New York? And the total inability of Mayor Dinkins to cope with the situation?

Unions are supposed to be working for the benefit of their members, but not to the extent that they take unfair advantage of their power to corrupt our whole system of government. A hundred years ago unions were needed to protect workers against unfair employers . . . and they've done well in that role. But power corrupts, as we know all too well, and I watched unions destroy one New York newspaper after the other. I've worked in union shops and have seen at first-hand the power of the printing unions, the stagehands union, and so on. These unions were corrupt beyond belief . . . and arrogant about it.

We've seen the mineworkers union at work . . . the automotive unions . . . the teamsters. How can we possibly explain the teamsters union in terms of benefits to our country?

New York City has gone deeper and deeper in debt under one disastrous union contract after another. The mayor has lost all control. For instance, school custodians now have to sweep only every other day and mop three times a *year*. Cafeteria floors are mopped once a week. For this work the custodians get an average of $57,000 a year, with some going to $80,000, and even more! The unions have a stranglehold on New York.

Tax the rich? They're leaving, as are businesses, which are moving to the suburbs and to rural areas. New York is dangerous, dirty, and expensive. I lived there off and on for 30 years, so I know it well. In 1962, I got fed up and moved to New Hampshire. Perhaps I should say "back to New Hampshire," since I was born in Littleton.

146 Even More Unemployed?

It sure looks as if we're just seeing the beginning of a major readjustment in America, with large companies downsizing to be competitive. Loyalty and length of service are out the window. Productivity is in. We're in the time of voice mail, telephone bulletin boards, cellular phones, fax machines and networked computers. We're into the time when magazines such as *Home Office* and *Mobile Office* (did you see their nice article on me?) are prospering.

Two years ago, I eliminated my layer of managers. Out went my general manager, my circulation manager, my advertising manager, and so on. We didn't need managers, we needed to get work done. This eliminated an enormous overhead and made it possible for my company to grow faster.

So what can America do about this flood of unemployed? Are we going to dither and go deeper in the hole voting further unemployment "benefits" for them? They need help getting jobs, not handouts.

I see this as an opportunity for New Hampshire to do something positive and show the rest of the country how to cope with the problem. Well, we are fortunate in this respect in that we were hit early and hard. The minicomputer industry was already on thin ice, so it was one of the first to have to bite the bullet, bringing us long lines for unemployment checks.

We need more jobs. So where do we turn? Do we try and prop up dying businesses? Do we try to force businesses to keep workers, whether they need them or not? This seems to be the liberal approach. I love the idea of forcing businesses to let workers know months ahead if they're going to have to close a plant. Talk about harebrained!

Where do we turn? We turn to the same place we've been turning for the last ten years as big business has been gradually cutting their work forces. We turn to small business, which has not just picked up the slack, but has been providing about 80% of all new jobs.

Instead of wringing our hands about GM dumping 74,000 workers and IBM dumping another 20,000 workers, let's start making it easier for small businesses to get started. Let's start making it easier for people to learn the skills they need to work in and start small businesses. Let's make it easier for small businesses to find the workers they need.

147 Worker Retraining

Few workers in large businesses have the skills needed by small businesses . . . even when they are in the same general industry. Take publishing, for instance. As *Yankee* magazine downsized I hoped that I would be able to tap a good resource and hire people to help me in my publishing company.

What I found was a group of people who were highly specialized, each in one small area, but who knew little else. One woman was just great at customer service, but had no experience with newsstand, direct or subscription sales. I'd have to bring her in as a trainee, at far below the salary she'd had as a customer service specialist. Since this didn't appeal to her, I knew it wouldn't work.

People are going to have to be retrained in order to be of value to smaller businesses. This calls for classes in computer literacy to help them deal with data bases, spread sheets, disk drives, data backup, windows, desktop publishing systems, and so on. It means developing typing, selling, telemarketing, and customer service skills. It means learning about postal rules, inventory management and packing.

Where New Hampshire can get a jump on the other states is by developing these classes, and then packaging them as video courses that can be sold to people in other states who suddenly discover that they're unemployed and haven't the skills small business employers need today.

Once good video courses are available, they'll benefit the whole country . . . and many other countries too. Those will be an internationally needed resource. My wife produces educational videos (how to dance), so I know they can be made very reasonably. She even does the video editing herself in what was our dining room.

To be good, the courses must be not just interesting, but exciting. This means we'll need outstanding performers to do the teaching . . . first-rate writers to make it fun to learn . . . and whatever it takes in props. Obviously, these courses aren't going to start out being as good as they can be, any more than the early television programs match up to the level we're able to achieve these days. If you watch many old movies you know what I mean. Some of our famous old stars weren't all that great as actors. And look where we've come with special effects!

This is the sort of business where entrepreneurs will get the ball rolling. Then, as one company does better than the others, it'll grow and gradually take over the competition. Eventually, we'll likely have still another international megacorporation able to spend what it takes to keep governments from cramping its style. Let's aim to have it based in New Hampshire.

148 Dropping The Ball

Okay, I hope we agree that there's a need for retraining millions of people. Further, I hope we agree that New Hampshire has a clear and present need to get started on this as a way to reduce the pain we're suffering from our present unemployment situation. Again, we seem to be leading the country . . . I just hope that we'll use this lead to our advantage and not dither it away in committees.

By being there first with the best, we'll be able to build a New Hampshire industry . . . a new educational industry . . . which will first give us a head start on the rest of the country in coping with the recession . . . and then will start bringing us revenues from other states . . . and international revenues.

The universal need for adult education to help people cope with the changes technology is forcing on business . . . and particularly on large businesses . . . will inevitably result in these resources being developed. Will this Commission grab the bull by the horns and run with it before still more water goes over the bridge? Will some other state take the steam out of our sails? (That's for you cliche lovers.)

149 What To Teach

Outside of a few of the more obvious skills, such as I've mentioned, how will we know what educational courses to set up? That's easy. All we have to do is go back to the teachings of Tom Peters for clues. Tom says smart businesses are developing the products their customers ask for. So all we have to do is ask small businesses what skills they're looking for. This ties in with the suggestion I made earlier (052) about our expanding our unemployment data base to include both the skills available and the skills sought. If we see a buildup of needed, but unavailable, skills we have our answer.

Teaching old dogs new tricks isn't easy, so retraining middle managers and administrative employees is going to present some serious obstacles. Fortunately, the most important obstacle, their agreement that changes are really needed, will be forced on them as their unemployment benefits expire and their cash reserves dry up.

We're going to have some emotional problems to deal with. Like any other trauma, the first reaction is to deny there's a problem. The end of benefits will help get this concept accross. Then we can start trying to convince them to acquire new skills. We also need to get many of them to accept a new work philosophy.

Among the skills developed in large corporations are the abilities to do as little actual work as possible, to spend more time on office politics than work, and to avoid accountability. These are not helpful skills to bring to entrepreneurial companies.

We need to teach some of the basic concepts that contribute to personal success. Napoleon Hill did a beautiful job of researching this field back in the 1920s and his teachings (*Think And Grow Rich*) are as valid today as they were 60 years ago. We should try to convince people that working for smaller companies is quite different . . . that the company's success is uniquely dependent on every employee's dedication and work quality.

It'll probably be easier to teach children the basics of success than Middle-Aged Former Administrators (MAFAs), who have a lifetime of self-destructive skills accumulated. It'll be a challenge.

150 Let's Get Cracking!

The sooner we can get going with adult classes aimed at re-educating our unemployed with the work ethic and skills needed by small businesses, the sooner New Hampshire will be out of the hole.

We need to enlist the help of successful entrepreneurs to provide the enthusiasm and counseling many of the unemployed are going to need. Middle-and upper-middle income people are going to need help in coping with the change. For many it's going to mean a considerable downsizing of living standard as they get used to working with smaller businesses.

We're fortunate that the top executives of the larger corporations are insulated from all this and will be able to continue their generous salaries and benefits. It's one thing to retrain a $50,000 manager to accept a $35,000 small-business job. Imagine trying to help a $500,000 a year executive come to grips with small-business salary levels! The indications are that the recession isn't going to be tough enough to shake these birds loose.

Perhaps you noticed that the GM board of directors forced only administrative and worker firings. The top management . . . the men whose bad decisions and poor planning caused the trouble . . . are still there, complete with their astronomical salaries.

I expect more *Fortune-500* boards will note the GM and IBM actions and push their executives to reduce unneeded management and workers. I also predict they won't trim many executive salaries, no matter how egregious they are.

Once we are able to develop a working system for retreading our unemployed, we should package the process and sell it to or in other states.

151 Cleaning Out Government

This is going to be much more difficult than recycling corporate management into small businesses. While the continuing recession is forcing corporations to downsize and become more productive, there is far less pressure for city and state governments to follow suit . . . even despite bankruptcies.

Let's take New York as a marvelous example of how bad things can get . . . with no forseeable hope for any improvement. But we may be able to tackle these problems on a much smaller scale here in New Hampshire and develop some solutions that could eventually be applied to The Big Apple.

Between the fire, police, education, and sanitation department, city civil servant and the Transit Authority unions, New York is a terrible mess. It has 40% more employees per capita than other large cities . . . and they're all doing their level best to bleed the city dry.

One solution is to privatize as many services as possible. In those cities that have done this, 100% have saved money . . . an average of 25% . . . and the work done by the contractors was far better (*Reader's Digest,* Jan. 92, p.39).

Even if we're able to unload city employees, we're still going to have to re-educate them to work in the private sector. This is going to be a much more difficult challenge than retreading managers forced out of large corporations. I had an aunt who worked in the New York City Unemployment Service, so I have an idea of the mind-set we'll be up against.

Then there's a little matter of accrued civil service time and retirement obligations. How do we counter the job-for-life socialist mind-set? Private enterprise has little need for people who've been trained for years never to make waves, to go by the rule book and never to think.

I'm sure some will exclaim that not all city employees are like that! And I agree there are exceptions. But if we don't face up to the worst possible scenario we're asking for failure.

And what can be done about work rules agreed to by a city that calls for employees to work five hours a day, 180 days a year, with 12 sick days and 12 paid holidays? How do we get school janitors (known as custodians) to sweep the floors daily? Of course, my solution would be to get the students to clean their rooms . . . just as they do in Japan . . . and fire a few janitors.

There are very few school maintenance jobs students couldn't do if they were given the responsibility. They could do carpentry, replace broken window panes, mop floors, shovel snow, empty trash, and so on. They might even take more pride in their schools as a result.

We know the post office could cut costs enormously if Congress would allow private firms to deliver the mail. I'd like to see bidding for city sanitation work. Could motor vehicle departments be privatized? Why not?

Private prisons are proliferating. How about private fire departments? Could we put that service up for bidding? Why not? Police? That's a really tough one. Any ideas?

The more we can eliminate unneeded state and city employees, the lower our taxes can be . . . and that will contribute considerably to our quality of life.

I've looked down the long list of New Hampshire state departments and administrations with awe. I've been trying to find out what all these people are doing . . . wondering how many are really needed and how much overlap there is.

In a private business we want to see a plan showing the costs and benefits of a new project before we fund it. Is this a poor concept to apply to government projects? How many state departments are cost effective? How many could be eliminated without leaving a trace? How many could be consolidated? How many really should be expanded? How many are efficiently run and are providing the promised benefits to the public? I hope this is something our Commission can tackle and answer . . . or is this an untouchable for us?

We have several Commissioners with conflicts of interest . . . not even considering me. We have at least one union man. We have educators. We have legislators. We have members of the executive. Thus we have several Commissioners with oxen which may be gored. Do we turn our heads? Do we avoid their oxen? Do we expect them to be impartial . . . perhaps even helpful when it comes to their oxen?

If we are going to shoot for the long run, we've got to pare down all state, city and town government expenses as much as we can. The more we have to pay for government, the less competitive our businesses will be with those in other states and countries. We've got to run our governments just as we would businesses, looking at the bottom line. We've got to make them cost effective, yet provide the product we want.

Can we set an example here in New Hamsphire of how town, city and state governments can be run? Can we apply business methods to government, changing it from basically a socialistic organization to a capitalistic one . . . run for the benefit of the people?

152 Why Magazines Are Dying

Our continuing recession has been providing quite an array of benefits. Sure, it's a pain, but in the longer run it's a good pain. It's forcing executives to look over their operations and eliminate waste (144).

Alas, for the media, one egregious waste area is in advertising. For years I've been preaching the gospel of economy in advertising . . . an odd lecture series from a publisher. But as a publisher I'm right in the middle of the mess, so I see it stretching in every direction around me. I've been trying to educate advertisers to help them save some of the money I see them squandering.

Our advertising industry is largely a product of an era when large corporations were making so much money they could afford to be careless. They didn't have to worry about advertising productivity any more than they did worker or management productivity. So we had featherbedding, office politics and huge advertising agencies all sapping American business vitality.

Our megacorporations have so tightly controlled their industries that they could afford to waste millions. As I've mentioned, just six companies have the American music industry in such tight control that they share 96% of all music sales . . . leaving only 4% for several thousand small independent record companies. And we see this megacorporate domination in one industry after another.

These corporations are so large and profitable that they've been able to weather brief recessions. So they rack up a few quarters of losses. Big deal. But between Bush and Congress, the 1991 recession has managed to hang in there long enough to force GM, IBM and other giants to actually start looking for ways to cut costs.

They're closing plants and laying off tens of thousands of blue and white collar workers. They're also, at long last, starting to take a closer look at their advertising costs. It's about time.

153 Reflexive Destruction

When businesses find their cash running short, they first look for any easily controllable expenses. Instead of cutting staff, which is painful and means paying severance, they turn to advertising, which is a mystery to most executives anyway. This is almost always one of the first areas for cuts. Since advertising really does sell products, cutting back advertising usually turns out to be a disastrous decision. This hastens the downward sales spiral.

Let's look at the basic idea behind advertising. If you're making a product or providing a service, your prospective customers have to at least be aware of your product, otherwise they're not going to buy it. Does that make sense?

In order to make your prospective customers aware of your product, in some way it has to be visible to them. This is where the battle starts. This is why we're barraged by advertising via radio, television, newspapers, magazines, billboards, matchbook covers, taxi roofs, subway, bus and trolley cards, posters, junk mail (by the ton), mail order catalogs, telemarketing calls, junk faxes, skywriting, pens, calendars, t-shirts, baseball caps, backscratchers, and so on. It's visibility they're all trying to buy . . . so you'll at least be aware of their products. It's a huge industry.

Obviously some media provide more visibility than others. But which? And then we come to the second step in making the sale, convincing the prospective customer to buy your widget instead of that crappy piece of junk Brand X is foisting off on unsuspecting, gullible people. Should you go for image advertising or the hard sell?

Well, when you want an answer to an advertising question, where better to turn than a professional, right? That's when you need an advertising agency. That's when you need people who've been making their living understanding how advertising works. Sure, and we turn to politicians to get government working right too?

Alas, when we turn to advertising agencies we face two major problems. The first is one heck of a conflict of interest. What agency is going to suggest that you cut your advertising? You'll come across that right after you've had a talk with an assistant who recommends a reduction in his own salary.

The second problem is that, with few exceptions, advertising agencies don't have anyone on their staff who has ever studied the art. One of the best moves I ever made was in 1953 when I took a course in advertising put on by the Advertising Club of New York.

Having dealt with some of our largest companies such as Texas Instruments, Radio Shack, Apple, IBM, Commodore, and Atari, I can tell you that I seldom saw the slightest sign of advertising intelligence from their agencies.

These days my magazines have to deal with the largest consumer electronic companies in the world . . . and again, the agencies that show any sign of understanding how advertising works can be counted on one hand, with fingers left over. I see hundreds of millions wasted.

It's interesting to note that in a time when dozens of magazines are folding every week and even the large magazines are hurting, the advertising in my publications has held up well. It's even better than it was in 1990.

154 The Remedy

There are some fairly good books on advertising . . . books that few advertising professionals have read. There seems to be a strange belief that when people graduate from college their education is done. They've spent 16 miserable years getting educated and, whew, it's over.

It's over only if they're going to be a clog in the wheel. It took me a while to figure this out, but then my youth was blown apart by WWII, which came right in the middle of my college years and stole four years from me. I finally got out of college at 25, not knowing what I wanted to do. I tried radio and TV broadcasting. They weren't it. At 27, I became a professional psychologist, which included a good deal of self-introspection, and got my life into focus. I started on reading and learning binges that have never let up, even after 42 years. Now it takes two rooms of my home for my library . . . 60 bookcases packed solid. I bought two more books this week . . . and ordered another six.

Obviously, I've gone off the deep end on reading . . . there are just too many things I want to know about. But on the other hand, half of all Americans don't read books at all . . . no continuing education. All they've got to go on is what little they haven't forgotten from school. That's not nearly enough. And in the case of advertising, that is one way to waste enough money to ruin a company.

This isn't the medium for even a short course in advertising fundamentals. If anyone wants some help, I'm available, but I'm not cheap. I've been planning to make more videos on practical advertising and promotion.

New Hampshire should include courses in advertising fundamentals to help small businesses keep from wasting money on ill-advised ad agency programs. Remember, every dollar wasted on ineffective advertising means a company is going to have to make at least ten more dollars in sales just to break even.

I'd estimate that at least 75% of the money being spent on advertising these days is wasted. And the more money we waste through such inefficiencies, the less competitive we're going to be globally.

155 Test And Measure

One of my more eye-opening experiences came in college when I got part-time work doing Daniel Starch readership surveys for magazines and newspapers. That's when I found out how few ads are actually read . . . and even fewer remembered. Unless you're in the public sector, you're probably involved with advertising . . . or at least should be. How much have you read about readership studies? How long do the average magazine or newspaper readers remember the message from an ad which they've read? How about at least remembering the company name?

Any firm interested in increasing advertising efficiency is going to test the effectiveness of every ad they run. In that way they can eliminate the ads that aren't resulting in sales and invest more where they are.

Mail order houses key every ad they run and mercilessly measure the results. They don't waste money long on media that don't produce sales. They even go to the extent of measuring the sales they get for each square inch of ads, eliminating slow-selling products and adding new ones.

They test every direct-mail effort and know the sales results in percentages of response. With magazine subscriptions we track the response to every list we rent, including how many renewals each list brings two and three years down the line.

You can tell when a magazine is in trouble because you'll see them listed in the sweepstakes mailings. Magazines only get about 10% of the money from firms such as Publisher's Clearing House and American Family Publishers. They do get an immediate response that builds up their circulation figures temporarily. But these subs are famous for not bringing renewals . . . and not selling many products either.

My magazines have renewal rates in the 70-80% range. Those bargain subs pull more like 10-20% . . . a bum deal all the way around. They're for the desperate. When I saw my competitor *High Fidelity* on these lists, I knew they wouldn't last long. They didn't. Inexperienced circulation management killed a perfectly good magazine.

If we can get some good advertising courses going in New Hampshire, we'll at least provide a way for our firms to have a substantial advantage over those in other states. And we may be able to prevent the knee-jerk reaction of cutting ads when the cash flow slows down . . . thus cutting sales even further.

156 Who's Going To Pay?

Just here in New Hampshire, where we have 44,000 unemployed, we're going to have a massive re-educational need . . . so what's it going to cost? Even if only half (the half that read) of the people go for the classes, there's a need to accommodate 22,000 adult students. Plus, I think we'll have to plan for some businessmen who are still working being interested in the classes. Let's say we're going to want to handle 40,000 students.

If we have 40 students per class, we'll need 1,000 classes. I suspect we'll probably want to have the classes only about half that size, so that'll call for 2,000 classes. That's going to take some high-power organizing. We're going to need classrooms, teachers, course materials, books, and teaching aids.

In the case of computer literacy, we're going to need a few trailer loads of computers. We're going to need some fax machines, telephones and so on. How on earth can we pay for all this? Who's going to foot the bill?

We know that a good part of the 22,000 unemployed students probably aren't going to be able to pay for classes . . . at least not until they get work. Can we set up an adult student loan system for them? I don't see any rationalization for training them at government (taxpayer) cost just because they weren't provident enough to continue their education on their own, before their paychecks hit the fan.

Their past lack of continuing education indicates a lack of planning for their personal and family futures. Why should I have to pay for their laziness by being taxed more? I'm doing well because I've invested my time to build my skills, and I resent being penalized for that.

So yes, let's organize a student loan program for adult students. And let's make it so there are some good reasons for repaying the loans . . . like fairly stiff interest charges. I want to see these classes making a profit. We already know how good a free education is . . . it's not worth the price.

If we organize these classes in twenty cities and major towns around the state, that'll be an average of 2,000 students per area. I think we can handle that. We've plenty of empty classrooms available evenings.

Between our retired executives and volunteer entrepreneurs, I don't think we'll have any big problem in getting volunteer teachers. We can also bring in outside experts to help teach and pay them with a governor's award of merit for their help. I'll bet we can get the regular high school students to come in and video tape the expert talks; so we'll be able to continue using them . . . with a small royalty for each use.

The government tried using television to centralize teaching on American Samoa, but they ran into insurmountable problems when it came to residuals for the teachers. The result was that each video was used only once and then erased. What an enormous waste!

We might want to consider a similar television approach. The course material could be taped and then shown all around the state. If we go with my plan for students working in teams and not as individuals, we'll be far less dependent on teacher expertise.

Now, about those computers. If we figure that everyone is going to need some computer time . . . say 30 hours . . . we'll need to be able to provide about 1,000,000 hours of computer time. They're not going to have to all do this at once, so we'll have the luxury of spreading this million hours over several months.

If we invest in 1,000 computers and use them seven hours a day, six days a week, that's 42,000 hours a week of computer time. We'd reach our million computer hours in less than 24 weeks . . . under six months.

These additional computers could also be used by the daytime students, getting double use from them. If we invest $500 each for the computers . . . and I think we can do better than that . . . we're still only talking about an up-front investment of $500,000 . . . plus installation and software. If we aim at $750,000 for the works, that comes out to about $75,000 (10%) in interest for a year, plus $125,000 toward retiring the investment . . . $200,000 a year. Split 40,000 ways, it'll cost us about $5 per student. I think we can afford that. Let's make it $20 and have some left over for expansion and growth. We might want to buy a few Mac desktop publishing, and some 486 whiz-bang systems.

How much will it cost to set 'em up and get 'em working? Not much if we let students do it. This would be good training . . . and fun.

If we charge students an average of $50 per course, we ought to be able to make a profit. If they take an average of ten courses each, they'll run up a $500 tab, which shouldn't be too onerous to repay over the next year. That comes to around $10 a week for a year . . . little enough for getting trained for a whole new career. Yet we've a $20 million business.

157 Can Bush Really Lose?

New Hampshire people aren't the only ones around the country who are being hurt by the recession . . . and hurt badly. Despite some signs of relief, the inertia of corporate job cutbacks will probably continue, further depressing both high- and low-ticket sales. This is going to slow car and housing sales . . . and that'll have a domino effect right on down.

So if Bush is weak, who might have a better chance at winning? I suspect that the frustration I've seen around New Hampshire with our choices is a national phenomenon, not just local. We don't trust Bush. We've seen him dither, lie and try to shift the blame for his weak leadership.

We watched him botch the war in Iraq we almost won by stopping it a few days too early. We've watched the Noriega trail baloney and reflected on the wisdom of his Panama invasion.

If either Colin Powell or Norman Schwartzkopf ran, it would generate a lot of excitement. What a team they'd make! We trust them, and we don't trust Bush.

We're looking for a leader, not a bureaucrat who wants to avoid criticism. We're looking for someone with a positive program to turn around the recession . . . someone who will then go out and convince the people to back him in making it happen. What we're seeing so far is a political gridlock.

All this tension and indecision has to be weighing heavily on Bush, who is not exactly a youngster . . . and is looking haggard these days. What would you say the odds are that if we vote 'em in again that we won't have Quayle as our President within a year? I remember how Roosevelt looked during his last election campaign.

We need someone with a positive program and the vigor to sell it so thoroughly that even the Democratic majority in Congress, dedicated to fighting anything the President offers, no matter what happens to the country, will have to give in. We have to fight our way out of the hole Bush and Congress have gotten us in, not go for more debt through government giveaways and trade barriers. It's time to fight back, and we need a leader to get our juices up.

That $300-per-person bonus plan couldn't have been given any serious thought. That was a play to unthinking, reactive voters. If they do send us all a check, I suspect that most of the money will just go to pay bills. And the tab will add still more to this year's $350 billion national debt . . . which means that we'll have to get more foreigners to buy American companies to balance the books . . . or pay them interest for a few years if we just borrow the money from them.

Chapter VII

158 Recapping: What Went Wrong

How come New Hampshire, which was way out ahead of the other states until just recently, went into such a disastrous nose dive, right down to last place? As I mentioned in the beginning, we have to understand what broke before we can fix it.

If what broke is permanently broken, then we need to recognize that and work out some new approaches which will help us stop leaning on a broken crutch. If what's broken can be fixed, we'd better recognize and admit the problem and get going on repairs.

With the Commission members' extensive and varied backgrounds, I'm sure many of you understand what's gone wrong better than I do. From my perspective I've watched our three largest industries get gutted . . . and that spells disaster to any state . . . or even country.

Is it within our power to patch up the three gutted industries? One of 'em, yes. One maybe. The other, probably not.

The three affected industries, in case your memory is short or you skimmed too fast through my report, are (1) tourism, (2) minicomputers, and (3) defense.

With the collapse of our major enemy, the USSR, it's unlikely the defense industry is going to have the control over our economy it used to. There are some glimmers of hope for New Hampshire, even so . . . if we play our cards right.

As the military budget is mercilessly pruned back, the major contractors will be most seriously affected. This will cut purchases from subcontractors, thus hurting many New Hampshire medium-sized businesses. But even more, the cutbacks in military spending will tend to put hundreds of thousands of more people out of work around the country, making an even larger market for educational retraining materials. If we start early to develop these retraining aids, we'll have a fast-growing market opening for us. That's the "making an omelet out of broken eggs" entrepreneurial system.

Minicomputers are a lost industry, as I've explained, so let's write them off. It'll take a while for them to die. It'll be a slow, painful, expensive death. We can exult that one of the largest microcomputer mail order businesses is right here in New hampshire, so we're in the right business at the right time in that respect.

So what happened to our vacation industry? The big crusher was, I suspect, the 1986 Tax Reform Act which discouraged (almost stopped) people from building vacation homes. Vermont got hurt even worse than we did, for what little consolation that is. But we got hurt badly enough. Then, when you add the loss of jobs in the defense and minicomputer industries, with the concomitant drop in home building and prices, our banks collapsed. That, in turn, stopped cash being available to start new businesses. Quite a domino effect.

Can anything be done to help encourage vacation homes being bought or built? How difficult is it to get that miserable Tax Reform law reformed?

The collapse of the minicomputer and defense industries hit Massachusetts hard, too. This has tended to put a chill on Massachusetts drivers from endangering us while vacationing in New Hampshire. It's understandable that families unsure about jobs would tend to start saving money, just in case. This has deprived us of the few hundred dollars they'd normally spend while littering our highways and contributing to our room and meals tax collections.

Of the three collapsing industries, the one we can do the most about is vacationing. Please stop calling it tourism. Don't even think that outdated concept. I've proposed several ways we can quickly rebuild this potentially gigantic industry.

Let's let people go to Paris or London as tourists . . . and bring them to New Hampshire to *do* exciting things in a beautiful environment.

As our major defense industries either collapse or shift to non-military production, our small businesses will have a better crack at what few military contracts there are . . . so this may eventually benefit New Hampshire.

The upward spiral of military expenditures on planes, guns and ships may finally end. It won't take huge industries to provide things such as radios for our smaller military force.

We're not going to need much of a nuclear submarine fleet either. I can see the long faces in the Pentagon now . . . and at The Electric Boat Company in New London.

War seems to be being replaced by business. Japan tried war . . . and lost. Then they tried business and won big! It makes sense, when you think about it. When we fight a war we spend billions on armaments which we then throw away. When we do business we spend billions making products . . . and get paid for them. Hmmm, not a bad system, really.

Business has replaced war. If we want to win we've got to start fighting with our brains for a change. We've got to outsmart our competitors . . . and we're sure not going to do it with our present educational system.

My message is to think of education as a product like any other. If you don't do R&D, you're going to get beat in the marketplace. You've got to keep improving the product.

My message is the same when it comes to government. We have to keep improving the product. That means quality control and feedback from the customers. We, the public, are the customers, right?

If we want to cure our ills we've got to think creatively. If we want to solve our welfare problems we've got to figure out how to convince the welfare addicts to want to change.

There's a war going on out there and we're losing. I say it's time to fight back.

159 Selling New Hampshire

To vacationers, that is. In addition to getting 'em to come here in droves to do fun things in a beautiful, clean environment, we can apply some subliminal pressures that should favorably dispose people to visit.

For instance, if we want vacationers to send New Hampshire-oriented gifts to friends to brag on visiting us, we're going to need more for them to buy in our gift shops than praying hands and miniature back houses.

A few years ago I got the idea to produce a cassette on how to speak "N'hamsha." It would have to be both authentic and humorous. Coming from Littleton, I love a strong New Hampshire accent . . . and I love good old New Hampshire Yankee jokes. It was time to put 'em together.

I got Fritz Wetherbee, a long-time friend, to write the material and do the narration. The tape has been selling just fine in New Hampshire gift shops. It's a perfect gift.

Fritz, by the way, can be seen regularly on Channel 11 on "New Hampshire Crossroads." I think my tape may have helped him get the job.

I've another New Hampshire-oriented project which should help make people feel good about our state. A long-time friend of my father's (and mine), Amos Blandin, who was a judge in the New Hampshire Supreme Court, also was a marvelous poet. Once you read or hear some of his poetry I think you'll join me in trying to get him appointed posthumously as New Hampshire's Poet Laureate.

I'd like to get Fritz to record Amos' poems in my studio. Then I'd put 'em on cassettes and CDs to sell in New Hampshire gift shops. I'd record 'em myself, but I choke up when I read some of them. Makes a mess of the reading.

I tried to get Amos to let me publish his poems 30 years ago, but he felt it wasn't right for a judge to write such sentimental things. After Amos died I kept pestering his wife about them. She finally relented.

Just to give you an idea, here's one of Amos' poems.

Sidney Day

The hill belongs to Sidney Day
Though he's left it now and moved away
In September's blue and November's gray
It will always belong to Sidney Day

The little red house, the big red barn
The three hundred acres of upland farm
The curve of the river far below
Where the current winds so still and slow

The view to the north through October's haze
When early frosts set the hill ablaze
The sweep to the south on a day in spring
When the warm clouds blow and the first birds sing

The pasture swamp on an April night
When the frogs sing loud and the stars shine bright
The splash of the brook, the wet earth's musk
The snowdrift agleam, a ghost in the dusk
The kitchen lamp that shines at night
To the hunter lost a beacon light
I'd be wandering yet, men used to say
Except for that light of Sidney Day

There are other things that are Sidney's too
Through seventy years a course so true
A way of life that was never small
A smile and a kindly word for all

And they still belong to Sidney Day
Though he left last fall and moved away
I hate to go; I want to stay
But I'm too old to farm, said Sidney Day

Yet the rocks and even the winds that blow
Mayflowers in bloom at the edge of snow
The very earth has become in some strange way
No longer a hill, but Sidney Day

I wonder when we move away
Will we leave as much as Sidney Day?

160 Fighting Change

Most of you, being successful in business, are not just friendly to change, but enthusiastically enjoy it. You recognize that it's a key to being successful in this age when changes are happening so rapidly.

Electronic engineers who didn't start over new when the transistor and solid state integrated circuits arrived were cast aside. Then, no sooner had they accepted this new electronic era than it all changed again as microelectronics made digital circuits practical. It was back to school . . . or else.

Just in my lifetime I've seen enormous changes all around me. When I was young, New Hampshire was still a farm state. A hundred years ago all of Southern New Hampshire was farmland. Now it's mostly forest . . and strip shopping centers.

Just look at what's happened to our country! Today 1.5% of our population are farming, yet we're producing 25% of the world's food supply. Change. Compare that with the USSR where 33% of the people are farmers and their countries are starving.

With changes happening that fast, to be successful you have to not just grudgingly change when there is no other alternative, you must keep a weather eye out for changes. They're coming. Will you take advantage of them or will you lose out to a competitor who has?

There are still a few writers using typewriters. I have to admit that my comfort with the familiar kept me using my old Royal far longer than I should have. And I had some slick portables I took with me on trips. Then one day I reluctantly tried out an IBM electric . . . and that was the end of the old Royal. I never went back.

When the first microcomputer-based word processors came along, being an inveterate techie, I jumped aboard. But I still had to lug my old portable typewriters on trips. The video displays were inherently too big to be used for a portable word processor.

Then one day a Japanese friend brought me a sample of a new Sharp pocket calculator with a liquid crystal display (LCD) screen. Until then, hand calculators used light emitting diodes (LED) for readouts. Wham, I saw the future, and described the inevitably coming laptop word processor.

My friend was K. Nishi, a Japanese radio amateur who was fascinated by these new microcomputers. I'd started an I/O (input-output) section in my *73* amateur radio magazine to explain microcomputer technology to my readers. Nishi saw the future and started *I/O* magazine in Japan.

When he came to the U.S., where the microcomputer revolution started, he first came to visit me. I was the publisher of the first microcomputer magazine, *Byte*, and was starting more magazines to help this new industry grow.

When I saw the Sharp calculator with the LCD screen I described a laptop computer with a word processing program built in. Nishi went to Kiocera in Japan with the idea and the Radio Shack Model 100 portable computer was born. I bought the first one to appear in a local Radio Shack store (in 1983) and that's what I'm still using for all my writing. It's gone with me everywhere in the world.

There have been hundreds more laptop computers designed since then, but none have been as easy to use . . . and I've tried dozens. Many are in my closet.

The change from family farming to corporate mass production punished those who were slow to see the change and rewarded those who adapted. IBM, DEC and other old computer companies are suffering from their resistance to change.

My call to the Commission is my call to New Hampshire: the world is changing, so let's understand the change and go with it as winners instead of fighting a losing battle to try and stop it.

The wars we're seeing around the world have to do with fighting change. Real fighting. We can see that transportation is getting faster and cheaper. That means that products can be easily shipped anywhere in the world . . . and that means that these days we're in competition with the world, not just the next town or state.

Communications are getting faster and cheaper . . . though you might not know it if you buy TV advertising time. Many of the proposals I've made for change in this report are based on changes in transportation and communications. We can write and distribute newsletters quickly and inexpensively, making them practical as aids in implementing change.

I mentioned the TV program "The Wrong Stuff," showing new teaching ideas (WBZ, Dec.19). I liked the closing lines, "The rote memory and passive learning of the past century needs to be replaced by creative thinking and teamwork. Until we fundamentally reform education, America's survival is at stake."

Look at the miseries we see around the world where people have been resisting change. We see the Arabs being left behind as they cling to a religion which urges them to fight change. We see their fundamentalists impoverishing their whole culture. We see our own fundamentalists doing all they can to resist change and impoverish us.

We see the church vs. state battles going on around us everywhere . . . even in the Supreme Court, where Roe vs. Wade could be overturned. This isn't politics, it's a religious battle against change. The religion with the most people will tend to win in a democracy . . . at least for a while. If you build a big enough wall on your sand castle, it'll hold back the tide . . . for a while.

Change doesn't come easy to any of us. Change means you have to face new situations. It means you have to think. It goes against a basic human motivation to get by with as little effort as possible . . . which definitely includes thinking. What percentage of your daily conversation involves much serious thought?

We tend to fall into patterns of living. I eat the same breakfast every day. My lunches don't vary much either. The waitress at the Rynborn restaurant knows exactly what I'm going to order when I turn up for lunch.

So we get used to doing things a certain way, even when it puts us at a disadvantage in our work and in our lives. I held back my writing productivity for several years by holding onto my old typewriter. When the laptop computer came along I embraced it immediately and never went back to my old electric . . . too slow.

My little laptop computer enabled me to handle all my own correspondence, have the files and data with me that I need to write and make decisions, and write articles which don't have to be retyped again to be printed.

Just take a look at the size of the report I turned out with it! It's a book, yet I wrote this wherever I happened to be . . . at home, in my office, on planes, lounges, in my van while being driven. And all that while writing editorials (some at considerable length) for eight publications.

My publishing business takes less than half the staff I'd have needed just a few years ago. Between computers for almost everyone in the company, networked together and the low cost and speed of desktop publishing systems, we don't need secretaries, stenos, a typing pool, typesetters, and paste-up people. Copy comes in from our authors on disks or via our telephone bulletin board, is run through spelling and grammar checking programs, is checked by an editor, and is fed into a Macintosh-based publishing system. It comes out in pages, ready to be turned into film. By the end of this year it'll come out in film, complete with color separations.

With a fraction of the staff, we're turning out eleven publications a month . . . plus brochures, liner notes for CDs, catalogs, and an endless bunch of mailing pieces. With just a few more people we could turn out twice as much.

My competitors, with their larger staffs and managers, are failing. Most of the publications I sold eight years ago failed to keep up with changes in technology and the marketplace. They died, wasting tens of millions of dollars, seriously depressing the Peterborough economy. This helped reduce area housing prices and contributed to all the car dealers going out of business.

In our Commission work we'll be challenged to bring about changes in education and state government, despite every effort to prevent change from well-healed educational and government employee unions.

When you run into opposition to change, try to remember the millions of Russians who are so upset by the changes taking place around them that they are wishing for the old days of Stalin and communism.

We know that we have to change if we're going to be competitive with the world. We've got to change our vacation business to make it more friendly and better promoted. We're in competition with Europe and the Caribbean for those vacation dollars. We're in competition with Colorado, Utah, Vermont and even the Alps for skiers.

I can fight the lift mobs in Zermatt, skiing the face of the Matterhorn, as easily and for about the same price as Aspen . . . so which is going to get my money? Or will I ski Loon, Cannon or Sunapee instead, saving a few hundred dollars and two days travel time? That's where marketing comes in. And marketing is changing as technology changes.

Have we the guts to bring changes to New Hampshire which will give us an edge? If we don't change our educational system we're going to continue to lose out. So let's start fresh and build a new educational system. Let's build a whole new state government . . . one that's efficient and responsive to the customers.

161 Heeding the Environmentalists

The cry goes up from some "concerned scientists" that if we don't change our profligate ways we're going to run out of food, oil, water, air, forests, various minerals. We're using up our natural resources! The cry is echoed by mobs of sincere protesters — and amplified by our newscasters with endless interviews.

Voices pleading reason are part of the coverup — apologists for the greedy corporations wasting our precious resources.

So what's running out? Not much, when you look at how the prices of these rapidly vanishing resources have been going over the last 10 years. Food prices have gone down more than 30%. Mineral prices have declined about 20%. Forest products by 15% (*The Public Interest* #106, p.98).

How about oil? Twenty years ago we were being told that by the year 2000 all of the world's oil reserves would be used up. Gas prices in real terms are lower today than before the OPEC price increases.

"On average, natural resources are roughly 20% less expensive today than in 1980, half as costly as in 1950, and five times less costly than in 1900, relative to the amount of time a person needs to work to purchase them" (ibid).

The global warming scare turned out to be a dud, as have the acid rain and snail darter furors which swept through the evening news, talk shows, and Congress, leaving an expensive swath.

But how about the world food supply? We're used to seeing starving Africans on our TV screens. World hunger is a serious problem, right? Check out "Global Food Progress 1991" by Dennis Avery of the Hudson Institute. "More people enjoyed adequate nutrition in 1990 than ever before in the world's history. Per capita crop production continued to increase, with important gains in such countries as India and China. Given the increase in food production and the breadth of the gains in a wide variety of countries and basic food staples, there is little doubt that a higher proportion of the world's population had adequate food than ever before."

Despite the evidence that we're not running out of anything, we see Bush and Congress considering energy proposals such as price controls, mandatory conservation measures, energy taxes, and subsidies for alternative-fuels programs. Sigh.

It's easy to get swept up by activists and the enthusiasm of the crowds they attract. Mob psychology. Let's be wary of strident voices, bumper-sticker credos and evening news sound bites. There's an awful lot of empty-headed conviction luring the unsophisticated. We've enough real problems to solve without going off on expensive tangents chasing phantoms.

162 Modern Construction

For several years I've felt that there's been a need for a publication devoted to modern construction technology. I've talked with people in the industry and they've agreed. The current New Hampshire situation provides a unique opportunity for New Hampshire to develop a new kind of construction industry, one which could grow enormously over the next few years.

First we have to generate jobs for people so they'll be thinking in terms of building new business buildings and homes. If my suggestions are implemented, that'll be taken care of fairly soon.

Next we need to make some tax changes which will encourage home building. The 1986 Tax Reform Act not only stopped our building new homes, it in turn led to the downfall of our banks.

Thirdly, we need to overhaul and modernize our building codes so they will encourage the use of new technologies, new materials and new ideas. If we throw out most of our building codes, we'll encourage new construction ideas and that'll get entrepreneurs started with new businesses.

There are an endless number of new technologies which can be developed. New building materials such as foam concrete, plastic concrete, wonderful insulating materials, new kinds of windows, and new heating systems.

There is a need for a publication devoted to reporting on new developments in materials, modular techniques, computerized designs, various heating systems, waste disposal, computerized communications, control and entertainment systems, and so on. This would help bring people needing buildings, architects, construction firms, and other suppliers together.

It would cover what's new in kitchen sinks, toilets, showers, waste recycling, passive solar heating, and so on.

By getting rid of age-old building codes New Hampshire would encourage the starting of new building technology entrepreneurs. Once their ideas have been proven here, other states would start removing their code restrictions and our entrepreneurs would have a head start selling elsewhere.

As building gets more and more involved with technology, the industry will be getting away from stick buildings and move toward modular construction. Economies of scale can then make mass-produced building sections lower in cost and more competitive.

This will be particularly important to us as we strive to develop housing areas to provide a better quality of life for lower income families. As much as we try to develop small businesses which provide higher incomes, we're still going to need the support of lower income workers to do lesser skilled work.

Businesses all need people to handle the mail, drive trucks, and maintain buildings. There's no reason we can't plan to have nice places for them to live.

We can counter our New Hampshire winters with more underground buildings, and better insulated walls and windows. We can turn New Hampshire into a center for modern building technology development. We have a unique opportunity right now to lay the groundwork for such an industry. We know it'll be developed somewhere else if we don't — it *has* to. Will we let this opportunity slip away from us through inaction?

This new industry will need a publication to bring it together — to focus its energy. A publication would allow entrepreneurs with new ideas to reach people wanting buildings, architects, and construction firms. It would help new ideas be accepted and be improved. It would provide an inexpensive way for firms with new products to reach their potential customers with their message.

How much would starting such a publication cost? If you start with a publisher experienced in startups, one which already has the production facilities and a trained core staff, the costs would be minimal.

A large publisher would budget $10 million or so for such a start-up.

An entrepreneurial publisher with experience could do it for less than $500,000. How long would it take to recover the initial investment? Probably two to three years, at the most. If the New Hampshire economy gets going the publication could be in the black within a year and cost considerably less to start.

Circulation? Thousands of architects and construction firms would have to subscribe. Firms and people considering new buildings or homes would also need it. Several thousand suppliers of home products would also subscribe — home entertainment, kitchen, communications, security, bathroom, furniture, heating, waste removal, windows, doors, module builders, roofing, and garages.

Again the Japanese are way ahead of us. We'll be lucky if they don't come over here and take over our construction industry . . . too. They're well along with modularized home construction — as you've no doubt seen on some PBS programs.

When the Japanese are interested in buying a home they can look over several blocks of model homes which are set up opposite Shinjuku Central Park in Tokyo . . . where I do my early morning jogging, when I'm visiting. Then they go to a home builder, outline what they're looking for, and see it come up on a computer screen. They can see any room from any view, or look at the whole house and rotate it. If they want the dining room a little longer and this door moved over there, the computer does it and lets them see how it'll look.

When they're all done the computer will print out the views and then produce the complete building plans. The modules are built in factories, complete with plumbing, heating, ac power, lighting, light switches, telephone wires, TV cables and any desired computer connections. The modules are then trucked to the home site and assembled in a few hours.

It's much faster and cheaper to mass-produce the modules than to build stick homes. So what do you think? Is this an industry we should try to get started in New Hampshire? We don't have entrenched construction, carpentry, plumbing, and electrical unions to fight, so perhaps we'll be able to modify our building codes so we can get going with this.

Without a publication it'll be difficult to tackle the welter of building codes which are restricting technological progress in home and business construction. New plumbing materials and techniques, new electric systems, new insulating materials, new approaches to radon and magnetic field avoidance, information on the toxicity of paints and furniture materials, ways to use waste products to heat buildings, solar heating and power generation, the best plants for indoor air cleaning, lighting advances, vitamin D lamps, bringing sunlight into buildings, designing home theater rooms, designing audiophile listening rooms, new air conditioning technologies, using waste heat to de-ice driveways and roofs, new hydroponic and hot-house technologies . . . it's almost endless.

The publication would also provide data on progress in getting building and other restrictive codes changed in various states and cities.

It's possible that New Hampshire could develop a strong new building industry without the support of a dedicated publication . . . but not likely. But how can the Commission help bring about a new industry? Just agreeing that such a move is a good idea isn't enough. The Commission will have to take action to implement its good intentions. What action?

We already have the seeds at hand. We already have some small modular home construction firms in New Hampshire. We already have a few small companies making products which are in line with new building technologies, so we're not starting completely cold.

163 Yes, Another Publication!

The first step might be for the Commission to form a group dedicated to the development of this new industry. The publication . . . I suggest the title be *New Habitat* . . . would require about $500,000 in funding. This could be made up of investments from the seed companies in the field, plus the backing of the state. These investments would be made on the basis of their being repaid from the publication profits, with some residual equity remaining.

There's a general pattern I've found after having launched some 25 successful publications. I've found that it's safer to start new publications modestly and then build them in circulation as you fit the editorial material to the readership. This approach prevents the expensive catastrophies we've seen in some recent magazine launching attempts.

Just in the Peterborough area we've seen millions wasted on *PC Resources*, *In Computing*, *PC Junior*, and other turkeys. Big starts can be big flops.

New Habitat, with an advisory committee from firms already in the business, plus a Commission group, would have a good chance to succeed. The Commission's legislature liaison would also be helpful in getting needed code changes made.

In general, a publication with 100,000 paid readers will have revenues of about $5 million and should be making at least a 10% net profit. I favor offering about 40% of the stock in the project to the seed investors, 20% to the staff in exchange for modest salaries, leaving 40% of the stock for a later IPO, which would establish the value of the previously issued stock.

A publishing business generating $5 million in revenues is generally worth about $25 million or so. This would give the original investors a return of about $10 million for their $500,000 investment. A 20:1 return isn't a bad gamble. Even if the normal 90% attrition rate for new publishing ventures was operative this would still be a good gamble. But you can lower those odds substantially by betting with someone with a history of successful launches. My legendary modesty prevents me from citing examples here.

It's the extraordinary return on investment that is possible in publishing that has made me such a fan of using publications to help solve so many problems. You may have noticed that I've proposed publications as ways to provide support for new industries, and to provide the information exchange we need to make present industries . . . such as government, education and health care . . . work better.

I've been trying for several years to get RPI (Rensselaer) to set up a publications department as part of their School of Management as a way to help the new technologies being developed in the RPI engineering labs to grow. These publications would also tend to help RPI become a center for the growth of new industries around these technologies. They would also help attract better students and faculty to the university, plus they would attract funding for innovative new technologies.

Well, what RPI won't do, perhaps New Hampshire, with the leadership of the Commission, can. There are many nascent industries that new technologies are making practical . . . such as my proposed support of new building technologies. We know the world is going digital. I saw this as inevitable back in 1949 when I first discovered the concept and started writing books on its applications. Now we see digital computers, digital audio, digital telephones, and digital TV all coming together, piped into homes and businesses via fiber optics and to our cars and trucks via satellites and repeater systems. Will we in New Hampshire be just reading all this or will we be out front, leading the parade?

We already have a wealth of experienced publications people in New Hampshire as a result of the magaziness I've started and which have been subsequently lost through poor management by later owners. They can be used to form a core group. Beyond that my system is to enroll rookies and train them . . . jobs with great potential for youngsters just out of school. No, not just jobs . . . these are careers.

I'll be watching with interest to see if the Commission is able to take advantage of the unique opportunities which it has right now. As the recession abates, the pressures will be off and action by the Commission will be more difficult to implement.

As I'm writing this one more Peterborough publication has been trashed and the staff fired. This was *Portable Office* magazine. The basic concept was good, but there already were two other strong magazines in the field when it was started, so there wasn't a real need for it. The magazine then made up for this weakness by serving up pap for articles. Further, it was managed by people of known inadequacies in publishing. Nice people who've worked for me in the past, so I know them well. Some are good friends. They have their strengths, but not in management.

What the project lacked primarily was the strength of a dedicated entrepreneur to give it the guts and drive it needed. But then I'm not at all a fan of starting a second or third magazine in a field. Why bother going up against a well-established front-runner when there are so many fields which need publications and don't have them?

Front-runners have tremendous advantages. While an industry is growing it can be forgiving and secondary publications can prosper. But when the inevitable downturn comes and advertisers find sales slowing, they have to be more selective. That's when the secondary publications fold up and blow away.

Of course, if the secondary publication is more attentive to changes in the industry than the front-runner, their positions can change. In the computer field we've watched *Computerworld* fall into a weak second place because the management refused to recognize the impact of the microcomputer. *PC Week* stepped into this vacuum and is now the unchallenged winner in the computer industry.

We saw a similar scenario when *A+* came in as a second publication and ran rings around *InCider*, both dedicated to the Apple II computer. Then, when Apple decided to stop making the II, *A+* wisely sold out to *InCider*, leaving them to eke out a few more years in a doomed market.

Perhaps you can see from all this that starting new publications successfully is not as mysterious as imagined. I've found there are four basic requirements which tell me whether a new publication has a good potential for success or not. All four requirements must be met, not just three out of four.

One: There must be a sizable group of people who are interested enough to be willing to pay to read about the particular subject . . . the subscribers.

Two: There must be a continuing source of articles that this group wants to read.

Three: There must be a number of potential advertisers who have no other economical way of reaching this particular group of people.

Four: You must have an editor who lives and breathes the subject and can make it exciting to read about.

If you have those four elements, plus some money to get started, you've got a nice little gold mine. Better, if you start a publication to help a new technology grow, you may be able to help generate a whole new industry . . . and that's addictive!

164 A Guerrilla Opportunity

While in Las Vegas attending the Consumer Electronics Show, it occurred to me that we have a marketing opportunity which hasn't been considered. I was keeping up with the new technologies we'll be seeing coming from Japan later this year. I might point out that few Americans handling the importing and marketing of these products have any say in the marketing strategy of the products they handle. That's all done from Japan.

My *Music & Sound Review* magazine deals with the major electronics firms and I know of none where the advertising or any other significant marketing decisions are made in America. The positive side of this is that if an American company ever did want to get into the consumer electronics field it would have a golden opportunity to run marketing circles around its Asian competition.

Indeed, I've watched many outstanding new Japanese products be introduced here, only to die from a lack of promotion and advertising support. This is an awesome strength American firms have, if they use it. This is an ideal chance to use some guerrilla marketing where we hit the competition in their weakest spot.

We know that our consumer electronics has to be recovered from Japan. We're not going to be in a good position to do this until we can field a better educated high-tech work force, which could take three to five years. Once we have the work force and start attracting high-tech businesses, we'll be ready to start rebuilding our consumer electronics industry . . . right here in New Hampshire

While we're building our educated work force, we must turn to some faster responses to the current recession. I've suggested 29 Initiatives (so far), so let's see which have the best chance at getting us going and turning the recession around . . . until our revamped education system can kick in and get us into consumer electronics in a big way.

164 Getting Specific

Take my Initiative #7, a *New Hampshire ToDo* publication (see 032, 055), as a way to build our vacation industry revenues. With an agreement to go ahead on the project, the first issue could be in Massachusetts, Connecticut and New York vacationers' hands by September!

How would we get the needed circulation so quickly? We'd build a list of known New Hampshire visitors by getting their names from our hotels and motels. We'd send direct mail subscription offers to these people, offering as a premium my "How To Speak N'hamsha" tape (value $10). If you haven't heard it yet, shame on you, it's hilarious.

We'd also see that the publication was on greater Boston, Hartford and Springfield newsstands, using our own sales force to get thorough coverage.

How much could a publication get people excited about the things to do in New Hampshire and increase the vacation traffic? Well, since the publication should quickly be not just making money, but able to repay the start-up costs, the increase in the vacation business for New Hampshire would be a bonus.

It would be nice to get a publication started earlier, but it does take some time to hire editors and an advertising sales crew. But you know, it only took me six weeks from the day I decided to start *Byte* magazine until the first issue went on the presses, so we just might be able to get something going even faster. Lordy, on that schedule we might even start with a May issue! It would take a lot of scurrying, but it would be fun.

Yep, it was June 15th, 1975, when I decided to start *Byte* and hired an editor. The first issue went to press the first of August, complete with articles and advertising, and was in the mail to several thousand paid subscribers by August 24th!

The Peterborough area is knee-deep in unemployed publishing people, what with the recent layoffs and magazine deaths, so it wouldn't be difficult to staff a new publication. Indeed, it would be a great gift to this presently depressed area and could help the town psychologically.

If *New Hampshire ToDo* turns out to be as successful as the *Byte* start-up, it could be in the black as soon as a month after the inaugural issue is published.

What kind of publication do I have in mind? Well, since this is going to be an action publication, not one trying to sell the scenic beauty of the state, we might want to opt for the economy of a good quality newsprint tabloid. I've had a good deal of success with this format recently, using it for *Radio Fun*, *Music Retailing*, and *IMPS Journal*.

This is much less expensive and much faster to have printed (here in New Hampshire) than a regular glossy magazine, yet it'll still handle full-color photographs just fine. With only a little encouragement I can get my staff to work up a cash flow plan for the project and see what the maximum expected cash needs would be for the project.

I've several potential funders for the publication, but I'd like to see New Hampshire participate in some way.

This Initiative is so obviously a conflict of interest with my position on the Commission that I recommend I be fired . . . thrown out . . . excommunicated. It's even more than a normal conflict of interest because (a) it's probably the best quick approach to turning around the New Hampshire recession you're going to get . . . yet it has long-term benefits; (b) I'm the only one in the state with the experience, the facilities and the people to make it happen.

But then, if I get drummed out, as I should be, how will I be able to help the Commission and the state with all my other Initiatives? As an entrepreneur who is primarily interested in making things happen and not in making bundles of money . . . and as a publisher with 25 successful startups, New Hampshire needs me not only for *New Hampshire ToDo*, but to get several more publications started.

As I've mentioned, my plan would be to issue stock in each new publication, with part going to me for my experience and help, part to the investors, part to New Hampshire, part to the staff involved, and the rest kept as treasury stock for an IPO once the project is safely in the black. Look at the bright side, if you bounce me from the Commission, you'll be rid of a pusher and prodder who aggravates the heck out of people by saying exactly what he thinks. Of course, you might just blow an opportunity to put New Hampshire back into the number one spot in the country on a permanent basis. We can do that.

By the way, I suggested that we bring any interested media into our deliberations as a way of both tapping their resources and of defusing distorted reporting. In that spirit I'll be sending copies of this *Report* to any interested media. I have zero interest in hiding what could appear as a conflict of interest. If my position on the Commission gives me an advantage over someone equally or even better qualified to do the job, I'd agree that there is a conflict. But where I have no advantage over anyone else, I don't really see a conflict. Of course I could be blinding myself.

166 The Other Priority Initiative

There's one other initiative I've recommended that should be put on the front burner immediately. This is Initiative #18, the setting up of entrepreneurial courses to help our unemployed retrain for work in small businesses (see 016, 053, 148, 157). It isn't going to take a monster bureaucracy to get this into gear.

We'll need to set up a for-profit company to handle the organizing and accounting. It'll take a writer, a PR person, a bookkeeper, a Macintosh desktop publishing system, and a Mac operator. I think it can be done with four people plus a part-time advisor to help them learn the ropes.

Step One would be to get a group of small-business people together to advise on what training these unemployed need to be of value to them. Either that or use the list of subjects in 053 and save some time.

Next, I'd suggest a letter be sent to all New Hampshire schools asking what classrooms they have available for evening adult classes. There should be more than we can use.

Step Three would be to contact SCORE and any other retired executive resources to find teachers for the courses. I'd also send letters to every known small-business in the state, listing the courses we want to offer and asking for any help they might be able to offer in either teachers or getting students. I know I'd be delighted to spend one or two nights a week teaching, answering questions about entrepreneuring and helping people solve their problems. I believe we have an almost inexhaustible teaching resource, right here in New Hampshire.

Then we'd need to get word out through the newspapers, radio and TV stations about the classes so our unemployed would know about them.

But what about funding all this, you ask? If you haven't asked, you're part of the problem, not part of the solution. One of the last things we need is to run up another need for taxes. We want to be able to cut our present taxes in half within two years, not add even more pressure for a broad-based tax.

It'll take an up-front investment to get this going, but the payoff shouldn't take long. If we charge $50 per course, giving $20 to the teacher, $10 to the school for their trouble, and $10 to our Small-business Education Program, we'd have the money to pay the staff, to mail newsletters, and even to make low-budget videos for showing on Channel 11 to drum up more students.

But what about the other $10, ask you sharp-eyed Yankees? I'd suggest putting that into a development fund, to help get later initiatives going.

If you're worried that the unemployed won't have $50 for each of the courses, that just shows you didn't bother to read my *Report* — or you have a terrible memory. Tsk!

Now, I've walked you through a couple of initiatives which should be immediately implemented so we can get New Hampshire perking up. Isn't that better than gathering every few weeks to make lists of strengths and weaknesses? I've started Lord knows how many businesses and I've never taken weeks to do SWOT analyses — I just go ahead and get them started — and they almost always succeed.

167 Waking People Up

We're all so involved with our own lives that we haven't the time to become activists. And when we do see activists at work they often look like kooks. Many of the activists I've seen are sincere, but acting without really knowing much about their subject. It's a case of conviction and ignorance. Not only that, they don't want to know any more — perhaps knowing on some level that this might destroy their conviction. And being convinced that one is right feels very good — ask any religious fanatic.

The world is a little battered by man, but not on the ropes by any means. Most of the alarms have turned out to be highly exaggerated, with passions ruling the day. The problem with this is that when someone comes along with a valid message, the cries of "wolf" drown it out. So while I hope that people will buy and read my book, and will decide to personally do something to change our country, I haven't any illusions. Surprise me.

Chapter VIII

168 Indicting American Education

As a previous inmate and now outside observer of our educational system, I've been interested to read the articles in the educational magazines — written by educators, naturally — and to understand their perspective. Not all educators are prisoners of the system. Indeed, some have a remarkably good perspective on what's gone wrong. Alas, most educators are firmly caught up in dealing with the trees and seem unaware of the forest. Oddly enough one of the most perceptive I've run across is John Gatto, a teacher from New York City.

The fundamental problems we're facing in New Hampshire are the same as those in every other state, so John's comments are as valid for us as they are for New York. I taped a short talk by John on WGBH. It was aired at 8pm on April 15, 1992. In case you have not been doing your homework and missed this program, here's what he said.

"My name is John Taylor Gatto. Twenty-six years ago I came from Pittsburgh to New York to be a school teacher and I've taught for 26 years. Rich kids, poor kids, and all shades in between.

"In 1989 the National Association of Secondary School Principals named me the New York City Teacher of the Year. In 1990 a state senate resolution named me New York City Teacher of the Year. In 1991 the New York Alliance for Public Schools named me New York City Teacher of the Year, and the New York Senate and the New York Department of Education named me the New York State Teacher of the Year.

"And now I've quit. I just can't do it any more.

"There is no one right way to be educated, there are hundreds or thousands. Literacy was higher in the United States as a percentage of the population twenty years before we made compulsory schooling. But if you want to cripple a child population where words are concerned, put them all in rooms, ring bells in their ears, put work books in front of them and I guarantee most of them will hate reading and will not do it very well — and that's the secret behind short answer tests, standardization, uniform time blocks, age grading — this, and all the rest of the school religion that's punishing our country. There isn't one right way to become educated; there are many. There are as many ways as there are fingerprints.

"We don't need state certified teachers to make education happen. That probably guarantees that it won't. How much more evidence is necessary? Good schools don't need more money or a longer school year, they need real free market choices — variety that speaks to every need and runs risks. We don't need a national curriculum or national testing either. That's the way to make somebody very, very rich and to guard and protect jobs and privileged contracts, but it has nothing to do with education.

"I taught for 26 years, but I just couldn't do it any more. It you hear of a job where I don't have to hurt kids to make a living, let me know — I'm looking for work."

Perhaps, if you haven't been convinced by my arguments, you'll at least pay attention to what one of the top teachers in the country has to say. As you read through the recommendations I've made for changing our educational system, I think you'll see that I've answered all of John's concerns.

So let's let kids learn the things they and their parents agree they want to learn. Let's get rid of certified teachers and replace then with coaches. Let's get rid of rows of desks and the time clock ringing the bells. Let's let kids progress in any direction and at any speed that's comfortable for them. Let's stop measuring them and ranking them against each other. Let's let kids have private time when they feel the need. Let's stop treating them like slaves — where they need permission to go to the toilet or for a drink of water — or perhaps even to think or read.

Our present system punishes individuality, yet emphasizing individuality is the key to bringing out the best in each child. We've been trying to force everyone to be the same and it hasn't succeeded. We're all different and we should prize this difference. "Good kids" do what the teacher asks without any argument, even showing some enthusiasm. "Bad kids" try to decide what they want to learn. Teachers know how to break the will of those who resist. Good kids wait for the teacher to tell them what to do, learning that they must always depend on their superiors to make decisions for them. As an employer, one of my most difficult jobs is to try and re-educate my employees to think and make decisions for themselves. Many never are able to cope with this concept.

Then there's the matter of self respect. In school we're taught that this is determined by others — by our tests, grades and teachers. We're taught not to trust ourselves or even our parents, but to depend on the evaluations of teachers.

As a champion of different kinds of music I've been very disappointed at how unadventurous most people are. They like rock and don't even want to try listening to anything else. People are afraid of the unknown, be it music, foreign countries, or even foreign foods. Have you flown a plane? Been up in a balloon? Been to Borneo? Gone skin diving? Driven a race car on a race track? Been in a submarine? Eaten sea slugs? How difficult would it be for you to jump out of a plane with a parachute?

It takes surprisingly few hours to teach kids to read and the fundamentals of math — enough for them to be self-educating from then on — if we provide the right support and encouragement. Yet we've been able to keep kids in school for twelve years and turn them out unable to read a book or make change. Do you suppose we've been doing something fundamentally wrong? Do you suppose there may be some connection between our educational system and the increase in violence, divorce, drug use, racial hatred, suicide, and child abuse?

Our compulsory education system means compulsory subordination — the state control of our lives. John Gatto and I agree that a national curriculum and national testing is baloney. This produces moral and intellectual paralysis. If we turn kids loose — if we free them — we'll have the scientists, engineers, technicians, artists, composers, astronauts, and shoe salesmen we need. But instead of living lives of "quiet desperation," they'll all be doing what they enjoy — and doing it infinitely better than the present crew. America won't just get back to number one, it'll be so far ahead of second place that we'll have to erect electric fences to keep people from coming here by the millions. We've been preaching freedom for a couple hundred years, yet we've maintained a slave state, denying freedom to a big part of our people — our kids.

Are those interested in preserving this slave state in such solid control that nothing can be done? Are our legislatures so intimidated or controlled that changes are impossible? Can we eliminate all of the federal laws which are helping to perpetuate this system? Can we eliminate state laws? Can we get local towns out of the school business? Can we turn our kid's education over to our kids and their parents?

You only have to look at our educational system from the perspective of John Gatto (or me) and see why we're continuing to have a poor underclass. Our system guarantees we'll continue to have the poor.

In an article in *Whole Earth Review* (Fall 1991), John says, "School is like starting life with a twelve-year jail sentence in which bad habits are the only curriculum truly learned. I teach school and win awards doing it. I should know."

169 Can Education Be Changed?

There doesn't seem to be much controversy over the concept that New Hampshire must somehow provide a high-tech educated work force if it's going to attract high-tech businesses in the future. There's also not much argument that at present there's nothing in place which would do this.

New Hampshire doesn't have many natural resources upon which to draw. Granite doesn't show any signs of developing into a marketable resource, so that leaves us with the natural beauty of the state . . . and our people. I've proposed some initiatives to help us take much more advantage of our vacation potential, now I'd like to suggest some initiatives which should result in our developing a high-tech educated and skilled work force. This is going to call for a major change in our educational system . . . a paradigm shift.

170 How It Started

Education in America was started by the churches mainly as a way of preserving their religious power. Then, when an American government was formed, the concept of using education to preserve and strengthen government power evolved.

These motives are still powerful forces in American education . . . as we can see from the many parochial and "Christian" schools. I recall just a few years ago when many church groups, angry over the spread of sex education in public schools, started their own schools so as to prevent their children from being exposed to this sinful information.

Before the industrial revolution our schools were aimed at providing a farm work force. This is where our long summer vacations started. Schools were small, often one room, with all ages mixed together. There may have been some advantages to the kids from this system which we've lost . . . and which I'm going to propose we try to regain with a whole new approach to classes.

The industrial age demanded factory workers, forcing schools to change. It was necessary to industrialize education, making it mandatory to go to school, and assembly-lining the educational system. Children were divided into age groups and regimented. Do you think it will ever be possible to break this assembly-line pattern? I've an idea for a new approach which I think almost everyone in the educational system is going to hate.

Just as the industrial revolution forced changes in our educational system so that America could cope with the realities of the day, so we've got to come to grips with the third major revolution, the information age. New Hampshire is in a unique position to provide leadership . . . not just for the other states, but for other countries. And leadership is desperately needed right now . . . first in New Hampshire, and then in America. The nice part about it is that New Hampshire can provide this leadership at a minimum cost to make the needed changes, and will benefit the most from having made the changes.

If you're interested in an in-depth history of how our educational system has changed since colonial America, I recommend "The American School 1642-1985" by Joel Spring. Fascinating book.

Our school system has been through considerable turbulence since

WWII, with the result having been a drop in the value of the end product. I hope those readers with strong socialist indoctrination will bear with me in considering services as products. Indeed, one of my proposals for cutting state (and federal) government costs and improving its value to our citizens is to treat it as a service organization with their product having to satisfy our needs. The same holds for education.

As an entrepreneur I tend to think in terms of capitalism and apply this approach wherever possible. As I've pointed out before, I haven't seen the socialist system work well anywhere in the world . . . and I've visited many socialist countries.

We're finding that capitalism seems to be even more powerful than democracy. Look how it's shouldered out our democratic system in Washington! Money and special interests are running our government far more than the voters. And that's not just me being cynical. The 1992 election process has made it clear that the whole country is concerned about this.

171 Pre-School

Despite some pressures within the Commission to ignore the importance of having our children ready to go to school, there's convincing evidence that it's best that our educational system does not start cold at five or six years old.

If we go about this by agreeing upon some goals I think things will fall into place. We know that one goal is to provide a well-educated work force.

Does that mean we have to cram high-tech and the other educational stuff we think is important down kids' throats? That's what we've done for the last hundred and fifty years, so it may be difficult to even consider a change. To me that's the socialist approach . . . the worker bee concept. Don't disturb the hive.

The capitalistic approach would be to get people . . . including kids, who may not qualify in everyone's mind as people . . . to do what we think best by getting them to want to do it. I realize that I'm suggesting a revolutionary concept that kids have minds, can think, and even can be reasoned with. It'll probably never fly. It's easier to pick up the hair brush or a belt to get action. This approach does not, by the way, make for particularly happy children.

Look, with so many two-working-parent families, and with most of the rest one-parent families, we have to get serious about organizing day care. But instead of making day care a system just for baby sitting, why not turn it into an ongoing kindergarten experience? The earlier and more kids are encouraged to play with each other in a series of learning experiences, the happier, more confident, and well-adjusted kids we'll have.

Some great strides have been made in early learning systems. We here in New Hampshire should be sifting through these new ideas and using the best to help our own kids. The profit-making educational research publication I recommended (I-09) will not only help us improve grades 1-12 and college, but also our pre-school education systems.

Once the concept of education being fun is accepted, we won't have to force kids to learn. When kids enjoy learning there'll be no stopping them. This is why I've suggested starting right from the beginning with educational videos . . . first for pre-natal care . . . and then to help mothers through the first few months after birth . . . then the next few months . . . and right on in parallel with what's happening in pre-school . . . grade school . . . and why not college and even adult education?

TV can be a powerful educational tool if the programs are done well and are fun. With a wide range of videos available, both kids and adults can be opened up to the fun of learning about thousands of things. I proposed that New Hampshire get into this video education business (I-19) because I believe it's going to be a multi-billion dollar industry. Inevitably. So why not get there early and start building visibility and market share?

There's a growing agreement that our educational system should prepare our kids to be comfortable in a high-tech world. We also believe that we should include history, environment, arts, languages, ethics, math, science, and so on. Religious groups believe that religious beliefs should be inculcated . . . and as early as possible. No free or creative thinking is advocated on this matter.

There seems to be an acceptance by religious groups that no person with a full access to information would pick their religion. They are quite convinced that only through early mind-control will they continue in business. Our country is supposed to separate religion from government, but we see religious groups continually demanding the government force their particular beliefs on everyone. Worse, they're so convinced of their righteousness that they are blind to what they're doing.

So we have groups killing each other over abortion rights . . . which is a matter of religious freedom that several religious groups want to deprive from others. We have the prayer in the schools battles. I suspect it'll be a long time before we're able to separate religion from government, no matter the lip service we give the concept or the Constitution.

Where do I stand on abortion? I stand firmly on both sides, willing to argue passionately either way, depending on what someone else believes.

172 The Factory Approach

One serious problem with applying the factory concept to education is that the raw materials we start with are by no means uniform. We aren't all created equal . . . not by a long shot. So we're putting all kinds of different kids in one end of the educational factory and are rather upset when they don't all come out the same. Our system sure tries hard to make them as much the same as possible.

That's not only lousy for the kids, it bollixes up the factory, which is not geared for all different sized raw materials. So we turn out a few good products, but the quality assurance is dismal.

I suppose the variance in IQ and other factors among kids is such a hot potato that I shouldn't bring it up. It makes a lot of people mad. So are we going to continue to screw up our educational output by refusing to let our factory machines adapt to the different materials with which it has to work?

Are we going to go on jamming 85-IQ students together with 150-IQ? Which group will it help? Neither, obviously. Can we even look at the facts about IQ? Several scientists have researched IQ levels for different groups and they've been made pariahs. The media and even other scientists have refused to even look at their research.

The January 13, 1992 issue of *Insight* bravely published the information. I wonder how many hate groups are picketing their offices? As one of the founders of American Mensa, the high IQ society, I've had an interest in IQ . . . in how much of it is genetic, how much the result of education . . . the old nature vs nurture argument.

Having worked as a professional psychologist I can tell you that there are ways to increase IQ by ten or more points, but as far as I know no one in the world is using this technique today. I keep promising to write a book on how to do this. But other than with a special technique such as this, most people are stuck with fairly unchanging IQs.

Is it reasonable . . . is it fair . . . to expect an 85-IQ youngster to be put through an educational system geared for 100-IQ students? We've begun to recognize that we do have some special students, so there are schools for "gifted" children. And we have schools for "special needs" children. That's fine for the 70-IQ and the 130-IQ, but that doesn't help the 85-IQ cope with 100-IQ level work. So we've got a probable dropout. We also are likely to have a disruptive kid.

Where the research scientists stepped into it was by discovering that American blacks have a bell-shaped IQ curve centered on 85. Hispanics are centered on 90. Whites are centered on 100. I suppose just mentioning this makes me a racist and probably a bigot too. And if I say anything which might be controversial about Jews that automatically makes me anti-Semitic. Oh, hogwash!

Can we adapt our educational system to cope with a wide range of intelligences? If we're going to be fair to our kids we damned well better. Right now we kinda pretend that every student is going to college. This makes it so the non-college bound kids come out of high school ill-equipped to go to work.

Even in today's job market we don't have many spots for unskilled high school graduates. The job market in ten years is going to be even more punishing. Yet, most jobs don't require four years of college and two of graduate study. Hardly any do.

Most of the people working for me have skills. They don't need a degree in English literature to be a darned good proofreader, to lay out magazine pages on a Macintosh desktop publishing system, to research and write articles, to call potential advertisers and convince them to run some ads which will sell their products. I have artists, photographers, customer service, order takers, telemarketers, and so on.

I need people who enjoy what they're doing and use their heads. I need people who never fail to make deadlines . . . a key element in publishing. As far as I know, virtually none of what I need in employees is taught in school. So what are we teaching kids that is taking them twelve years just to be a high school graduate?

Oh, I agree, work isn't everything. I agree we should be teaching history, politics, religions, all the arts, and a bunch of skills. We want to at least give kids an introduction to what life has to offer. From there it's up to them to follow up.

In the 6th grade they taught me to recognize a whole bunch of classical music. I didn't pick up on that until college, when the government turned off my amateur radio hobby for the duration. So I started buying and listening to classical music. I'd liked it ever since I was introduced to it in the second grade by a friend of the family.

The art basics I learned in the third grade stood me in good stead when I got interested in photography in high school . . . and even more when I became a TV cameraman at WPIX in New York and director in Dallas.

But why aim all students at a college track when only a percentage of them have the IQ it takes to cope with college? That's unfair to them. Japan is much more practical about this. Oh, by the way, Japanese IQs center around 110. Yep, they're smarter than whites.

My wife has video tapes teaching ballroom dancing. She has one-hour videos for just about any kind of dance you can imagine . . . even the Lambada. But she doesn't have one video for each. She has a Tango video. She has a Tango II and a Tango III. The first is for beginners. The second is for advanced dancers. The third is for experts.

Well, why not do the same for our school courses? History-I would provide an overview. History-II would go into more detail on science, politics, cultures, and wars. History-III might include biographies of the people, more about the geography, geology, and the languages.

I'd like to see history divided into different parts of the world. I had almost no history in school, which was a shame because so much of it is fascinating. I can't believe any kid wouldn't get excited about history by reading the books of James Lamb. Hmmm, perhaps I should get permission and read those books onto tapes for kids (of all ages) to listen to. Marvelous books, and all have been published in inexpensive pocket book form.

Books on tape are getting more and more popular with adults too. They're often much more interesting than talk radio while one is driving to and from work. Since I have a recording studio and I know how to read, I plan to enter this market with books for both children and adults.

173 More School Days

Much has been made of the longer hours and more days spent in school by students in other countries. Now that America (and New Hampshire) is in a global competition, I agree that we can no longer continue to turn out poorly educated graduates. And I agree that part of the problem is the small number of hours our kids spend in school.

Just a little over a hundred years ago the school year was 75-100 days long and they only went to school eight or nine years . . . and that was enough. Kids didn't need much more education to cope successfully with the world of 1870.

Today kids go to school 180 days a year for a minimum of 12 years. We just don't have many jobs available for people with less than a high school education. We're gradually replacing unskilled workers with machines . . . dishwashers, microwave ovens, fast food, frozen food. When I was young many families still had cooks, maids and chauffeurs; farmers had hired men and women; elevators had operators.

With science growing exponentially and with an understanding of the world necessary for most jobs, there's a lot more that needs to be learned in school now than a hundred years ago. We didn't have nuclear physics, quantum and chaos theories to contend with. What was going on in Africa wasn't of much significance, though I did enjoy the Osa and Martin Johnson films. And it didn't hurt that my mother knew Osa personally.

Today we expect kids to know about plate tectonics, the big bang, Mandelbrot's fractals, fast Fourier transforms, digital logic and to be able to find the U.S. on a world globe. Heavy.

We also expect them to get along with the other kids, no matter their race, religion or sexual preference, though I'm afraid many families don't provide good examples at home.

I realize I'm out of step with almost everyone in my idealistic vision of an America where everyone is proud to be an American . . . where we no longer have Irish-Americans, German-Americans, African-Americans, Jewish-Americans, Polish-Americans, Hispanic-Americans, and so on. How long will it be before everyone thinks of themselves as Americans and not just transplants from another country? I often wonder if I should start calling myself a Euro-American . . . and start trying to think that way.

All my ancestors came here over 350 years ago, so there haven't been many stories of the "old country" handed down in the family. A Greene published the first Bible in America. Another founded Rhode Island. But somehow I've never thought of myself as a British-American.

Sure, we have some terrible problems in America, but after having visited 120 other countries, I don't know of one I'd prefer to live in, as nice as some are. No, I prefer America, so I'm going to put up the best fight I can against the bad aspects of our country . . . and that includes much of our government system, including education.

Jerry Brown got my attention recently with his call for a flat income tax of 13% for everyone. That would allow us to get rid of about 35 feet of tax code shelf space. It would put the IRS out of business. It would put hundreds of thousands of lawyers and accountants out of work. I'll be delighted to come up with a practical retraining plan to turn these people into useful, productive members of society . . . for a change.

Yes, I know, the socialist belief is that the poor should get all the benefits of society, but not have to help pay for them. They should get the police protection, full medical services, and all the other infrastructure benefits for free as a gift from America's hard-working middle class.

You know as well as I that people do not appreciate things they get for free. These things have little value. This is why low income housing gets destroyed so quickly.

So yes, our kids have a lot to learn in order to cope with today's information age. That means that once we get our schools more productive and wasting less of our money with useless bureaucratic administrative overhead, we can start extending our school hours and days.

Until we clean up our educational act, adding hours and days will just be that much more wasted time. Our educational productivity is a fraction of what I believe is possible. Indeed, if we start considering education more like a product and improve it, I believe we'll be able to triple or better our productivity.

In my proposed college initiative (I-20) I estimated that it will be possible for college students to cut back to three years and still end up with double to triple the education currently provided. Maybe quadruple.

174 Ten Sessions A Year?

Once we have our educational system working better I believe we should go to a 50-week a year schedule. That'll leave two weeks off . . . perhaps one in summer and one for Christmas.

Hey, where does that leave time for summer camp? Or for trips to Europe? I think kids will be better educated in the ways of the world if they don't have to try and learn everything from videos. There's nothing like bicycling across Europe, trekking the Himalayas or taking a train across Russia to learn more about the world. No videos can match real life experiences.

So I suggest we come up with a scheme where kids can, if they want, and can afford it, take time off from school. We're approaching the day when it'll be possible for whole classes to go on trips almost anywhere in the world and still, via satellite communications, be in everyday contact with family and school. We have the technology to do it right now, so I'll give it 50 years to happen.

175 More Terms?

If we're going to go for 50 weeks a year of school, we'll need to break that down into more manageable units . . . like terms. We could run ten five week terms or five ten week terms. The five-week split gives us greater flexibility. Some courses could, of course, run for ten weeks or two terms. But once we start making our courses more effectively taught, I suspect we'll find five weeks just fine.

This system isn't all that different from the current one . . . just longer. But suppose we stopped running students through on a production-line schedule? Suppose we let them take any courses they want, when they want? This would make it possible for students to take off for five weeks (a term) now and then. It would allow students to follow their interests.

Yes, I know, there are some basics which have to be taken by everyone. But there is nothing written in stone that says they can't take an extra few terms if they want. Or pass the required subjects early and spend more time with electives. Nor do I see any reason why courses couldn't be given for more than a six hour day. If we have enough club activities to interest everyone, any unscheduled periods during the day could be spent at the club instead of an (ugh) study hall.

As we get more into the information age we'll have enough computer terminals available to allow students to work on many courses whenever they have extra time. The University of Windsor (Canada) has huge rooms full of microcomputer/terminals, so they're already offering this option. Plus they have dozens upon dozens of modems, allowing the students to work on their projects from home.

The University of Windsor had one other outstanding innovation. Well, it was new to me. Their students rate their teachers on about 30 different items. And who better to rate teachers than their students. I think the time when we can blame students for not passing is fading away, replaced by the concept that it's the teacher's responsibility to teach. I am convinced that teachers will be better thought of if they are good at teaching.

There's a lot of griping about how low teachers are held in esteem by the public. Judging from the teachers I suffered during my 16 years in school, the word "esteem" is ill-used. During all that time I remember two outstanding teachers. Just two who made their classes exciting. Those two certainly had my esteem . . . and the rest of their students felt the same way.

I hope I don't have to beat the concept of flexible terms to death . . . you get the idea, I hope. Yes, it's a paradigm shift to consider letting kids pick their own courses and take off from school when they have a good reason.

Outside of the core required education the kids might opt for more music education, art, software development, geology, archeology and so on.

Remembering the world in the next century I'd require a good deal of math . . . practical math, thank you. In my experience that would include algebra, but not trig. I have yet to meet a simultaneous equation since leaving school, so let's leave handling those for kids who are interested and take it off the basic menu. Ditto calculus and spherical trig. Lordy!

English is basic, complete with grammar and spelling. I must have been asleep the day they taught grammar. I didn't run into the past imperative until I hit it with a dull thud while trying to learn French. Or the future indicative. What a baloney way to teach language . . . any language.

I consider the fundamentals of electronics, computers and communications as absolutely basic for anyone looking for work in the next century. We already have computers almost everywhere . . . now we need to have kids who are comfortable with them, inside and out.

Our telephones, faxes and personal communicators will be part of both business and personal life, so kids will have to understand how they work and not be daunted by them. We don't want our kids to be afraid of technology. We want them to be comfortable with it.

I'd put History-I on the basic list. An overview. Also Science-I. I think that once we introduce these subjects to kids we'll have a hard time holding 'em back. At least we will if we make learning fun.

176 A Letter From Alaska

As I was writing my initial report to the Commission I was also dumping it onto a BBS connected to my *73 Amateur Radio Today* magazine. A ham operator in Alaska accessed my report and passed it on to the mayors of three cities, two city councils, one borough assembly and two school districts. I'll let you know as I hear of progress.

A recent fax from this chap, the publisher of *The Local Paper* in Ketchikan, was interesting and apropos of my proposal to introduce Control Theory into New Hampshire classrooms. This is the concept of putting students into teams of four to learn instead of having each working individually.

Bob Kern writes, "Back in 1955, when I was a freshman in high school, I was part of an experiment where we worked in small groups and did peer teaching. I called Dr. Margie Nier, the Director of Instruction at my old school in Chicago, and found that the entire school is now using cooperative learning. Further, in addition to the usual college prep stuff they have some great vocational classes in subjects such as Radio-TV Broadcasting, Electronics, Hospitality Industry, Starting and Running a Small Business, Graphics and Communications, Transportation, Fashion Merchandising, etc.

Fashion Merchandising? It makes sense, with Sears and many other major clothing manufacturers in the area. They've looked 10-15 years down the road and are training students for the coming 'hot' businesses.

Cooperative learning promotes student-to-student contact, helping kids develop a respect for each other's rights and abilities. They feel this has helped the kids appreciate the rights, feelings, and property of others.

Good luck. As much as I hate to say it, I think that if anything is going to get done in New Hampshire it is going to be done by individuals rather than by a committee that meets every few weeks."

I hope he's wrong about the futility of committees, though I've seen little so far happening with the Commission where I could argue with him.

177 Involving Parents

It doesn't take much looking into our problems with education in America . . . and by extension, in New Hampshire . . . before you see hand-wringing over the lack of parental interest in their children's education. (whatever *they* are) point out how much better students do when their parents take an interest. But you know, one thing I haven't seen in any educational magazines or books is ideas on how to get parents involved.

Educators whine that parents are too busy. Both work, so they come home tired and cranky. The TV is on constantly, making it impossible to either think or talk. It's unlikely that anything that's gone on in school that day is of the slightest interest to either parent, so there's virtually no communication with the kids . . . until one gets into trouble . . . "Oh darn, my kid's gone bad."

Television. Yes, there's oceans of crap on it. But there's also some excellent educational stuff which doesn't deserve to be missed. And there's some great comedy and even a few programs that are better than most movies. It's a marvelous resource, but like other drugs, you have to be careful and not get addicted.

My approach is to time shift everything with a VCR. This eliminates the welter of commercials. It also allows you to fast-forward when a program gets boring. For instance, "60-Minutes" often has segments which are of value to me. But they almost always drag them out far beyond what I need to understand the subject. Fast-forward. And they tend to lean toward subjects with more emotion than educational content. Fast-forward. I can usually get everything I want from the program in fifteen minutes. But those fifteen are valuable.

I know far too many people who surround themselves with TV. One in the bedroom. Another in the bathroom, the kitchen, a really big one in the living room, and even one in the home-office room. None in the dining room? Nope, because nobody eats there . . . eating is done in the kitchen or the living room, watching TV.

Kids will swear that they can study just fine with the TV on. Kids also swear that they can study with the radio or record player on. All of which goes to tell you something about the value of kid's swearing. This is all utter baloney.

And the same holds for the workplace. About the only time music helps people work is when they are doing routine mechanical work which requires no thought. When you hear music your brain puts some of your attention on it. And this gives you that much less to work with. And that holds for kids too.

Kids need all the attention they can muster when they are reading or writing. They don't need the conflict of music or TV.

If you have a shipping department in your company you'll find a direct correlation between shipping errors and the level of the music their radio is playing.

With parents and kids living together but not communicating, how are we going to go about getting parents interested in helping their kids with their education? Yes, I have a sneaky plan to help get parents involved with the school.

A parent-teachers day won't do it. Parents, who know almost nothing about what's going on in school, won't learn much or get involved just from a one-day show and tell. Well, how about the PTA? Sure. Tell me how many parents get involved with the PTA. Also, kids are generally embarrassed by their parents, so they don't encourage parental involvement in the school.

Keeping all this in mind, how can we go about getting parents involved with the school and with their children? How can we break through the daily parental routine of work, Monday Night Football, and more work? And how can we do it without asking teachers to spend their time or further tapping sparse school resources?

I know you're not going to believe this, but I'm recommending a school newspaper! A community oriented newspaper, written and published by the students, paid for by local advertising and a small subscription charge. No, no teachers, no administration.

Well, I must be talking about high school, right? I am. I'm also talking about the 5th through 8th grades. The papers should be relevant to the students . . . and to the parents. What kind of reporting might we see in a 5th grade newspaper? Certainly there would be news of sports, Cub Scouts, school field trips, talks by visiting business people, activities of the radio, computer, science fair, electronic experimenter, astronomy, camera, and other clubs.

How about columns describing what's being taught in the various classes? Kids normally don't want to talk about this "boring stuff." But parents do want to know what their kids are learning. Students in each of the classes could report on what's being covered and how the class is responding to it.

Both the kids and the parents will be interested in knowing which student teams in each of the classes are doing the best work. They'll want to know about innovative team projects. Just reporting on these activities will tend to encourage the other class teams to take more interest and be more excited about what they're doing.

The idea of the newspapers would be to involve the students in more activities and to let parents know what's going on . . . encouraging their participation where it might help.

I doubt there is a single school where at least one student doesn't have access to a Macintosh or PC desktop publishing system at home. That, plus some student writers, is all it takes for the editorial end of the newspaper. That leaves the ad sales, circulation management and accounting.

You get kids started with a newspaper project in the 5th grade and they'll find it so much fun they'll still be doing it in high school and even college.

Shouldn't the paper be given away free? After all, schools are non-profit, so isn't everything supposed to be free? That concept is part of the problem schools have been having. It is very difficult to get educators used to the idea that there is no free lunch. They have been living in a socialist environment so long it feels like home. The very concept of "administrators" is socialistic . . . and we know how poorly that system has worked everywhere it's been tried.

We don't need administrators. we do need teachers, but perhaps we need a new name for the role . . . like a facilitator. We want to move from chalk and talk lectures to peer teaching, with facilitators there to answer questions, not as tyrants. Facilitators should be able to ask questions too . . . questions which might help open new ideas and challenges to the student teams.

I'd like to see the youngsters taking over most of the old teacher responsibilities . . . particularly the non-teaching ones which have been wasting so much teacher time.

With the elimination of most tests and grades, much of the old teacher role has been obsoleted anyway. No tests? No grades? What's all this? Well, I've been sneaking up on that. It has to do with student responsibility. It has to do with getting away from the slavery concept.

178 Compulsory Education

When an adult is forced into "involuntary servitude," it's called slavery. When a child is forced into ten years of compulsory school attendance, it's called "in the public interest." We seem to feel that the end justifies the means.

Is it getting time to admit that compulsory education is a social engineering idea which has failed? We are a Nation At Risk. Can it be that statism as an educational model is flawed?

It's almost enough to make a person think when we see private schools turning out better graduates at half the cost of public schools. Almost, but perhaps not enough to make most people think.

Am I proposing private education? Am I suggesting non-compulsory education? You bet I am. And yes, I don't think you can come up with an argument against the idea that I haven't considered . . . but, hey, give it a try. Remember, I take points off for emotionalism. The more impassioned the cry, the less validity is likely.

Am I suggesting that kids be responsible for their own success or failure in life? Am I also suggesting that the rest of us don't have a responsibility to take care of those who haven't the foresight to educate themselves? Not quite, but almost.

Part of the pre-school education process should teach youngsters that education is available to them, but it'll be up to them to take advantage of it. They are growing up in a country based on freedom. And that means the freedom to live marginally on the city dumps or to live the life of the rich and famous. It's entirely their choice.

I'd like to see our government get the hell out of the education business in other than an advisory capacity. That's right, no national standardized tests. No minimums and no maximums. I'd like to see our student teams rate each other and their members — part of the peer teaching idea. You pass if your peers say you do. This will help encourage individual participation.

A couple hundred years ago when the New Hampshire General Court passed its first law, Article 83 of the Constitution, it merely "encouraged" education. No state department of education or compulsory attendance laws. Literacy levels were far higher than they are today (see *NH Pure Forum* 9/90).

All kids learn to talk and walk at their own speed. They do this when they are good and ready. Some kids are mentally developed enough to tackle abstract concepts by the 3rd grade . . . others don't get there until the 5th or even 6th. We don't all develop identically. So why force conceptual education on kids unready to handle it? And why hold back on the early bloomers?

I've proposed an 8-year course in electronics, computers and communications. I've suggested that the 5th grade is the best time to start this, since there is a lot of conceptualization required. Some kids may not be ready by that time. Some may start late and then zoom ahead. If we have a flexible class format we can adapt to this.

Having to repeat a five-week course isn't as traumatic as having to repeat a half-year long course. Plus, slower learners will have an opportunity to shine the second time around, having the benefit of having been through it all before. They'll have the chance to be more of a teacher than a student and to contribute much more to their team.

179 Club Activities

One of the things I enjoyed about Erasmus Hall High School (Brooklyn, NY) was the enormous variety of after school clubs. They had over 130 different clubs.

After school clubs blew away as teacher unions insisted that teachers must be paid extra for their time spent with clubs . . . and schools refused to bend on their insistence that clubs must have a teacher present, but then they had no budgets for them.

I can't think of any club I belonged to which had a need for a teacher. Like other classes, student clubs should be able to work on the peer-teaching concept. For instance, in our amateur radio club we taught each other radio theory and the Morse Code. The teacher in charge of the Choral Club was also our conductor, so we needed her . . . but we met daily during class hours, so it wasn't a problem.

Even smaller schools can organize clubs for special interests such as a band, small orchestra, choir, drama, photography, music appreciation, dance, hiking, mountain climbing, canoeing, skiing, French, Russian, geology, archeology, astronomy, cosmology, magic, bicycling, reading, amateur radio, computers, science fairs, electronic experimenting, speaking, painting, environmental studies, . . . it's endless. All you need is a half dozen kids with a similar interest and you have a potential club. In most cases the clubs will be able to attract parents with similar interests to help them learn more.

News of the activities of these clubs should be included in the school newspaper so it can act as a catalyst to attract more members, and to keep parents in touch with what their kids are doing after school and even on weekends.

180 Accountability

Should we establish certain minimal educational norms and make sure our kids meet them? There's quite a push on for accountability . . . for schools to be held accountable for how well their students do on SATs and other standardized tests . . . and by certain ages.

There's a demand that all kids have reading, writing, math and so on skills by the time they're 16. To me this is just the old compulsory baloney again. It's a continuing of the factory approach to education.

I've recommended an initiative where we would survey our graduates and drop-outs on a regular basis to find out which courses they've found the most valuable in their work and personal life, which courses they wish they'd had, which courses they may have taken since graduation, and what books they've read. The aim is to provide feedback to our educational system so as to keep it relevant. We should also survey employers to find out what they feel is missing in their employee's education.

I put it to you that how our kids compare with the Japanese on math SATs is nowhere near as important as how successful they are in meeting the needs of American businesses as workers as well as their own career needs. I'm wary of the tendency to teach to the tests rather than to the needs of business and toward a better quality of life for our people.

Since our per capita income has been dropping for the last few years we believe that we are not measuring up to workers in other countries. We have to improve our educational system if we're going to successfully compete in the world market. We know that we're into the information age now . . . a high-tech age. We also know our kids are not able to cope with that with our present educational system. So we do have to help our kids to be technically literate . . . though not to the exclusion of everything else.

I discovered science when I was young and I've enjoyed it all my life. I think we'll be able to interest almost all youngsters in science . . . in technology. But I believe we should let them, with the encouragement and support of their parents, guide their education . . . not the government. So

I vote no on accountability. Student assessment is a hangover from the old factory quality control concept. Bad news, as John Gatto pointed out.

181 College?

As I pointed out, not one job I have to offer requires a college education . . . though most of my people are college graduates. The sorry fact is that as far as their work is concerned they've wasted four years of their lives and who knows how many thousands of their parent's dollars.

Outside of an Air Force electronics research lab, I can't think of any place I've ever worked or any company I've owned where a college degree was of any value. Yet I see high schools setting the goal of getting all of their graduates into colleges. Worse, I have to hire college graduates to do high school graduate work . . . just because most kids with the intelligence to go to college do so.

I didn't know any better when I got out of high school. I don't recall anyone even suggesting such a radical idea as not going on to college. No, high school graduates were considered doomed to a life of menial work.

When I look back on my college courses I don't remember any which have been of any significant help to me in any of the work I've done. Not even in my electronics research job! There my schooling while in the Navy was invaluable, not anything I got from college.

Kids ought to have more information on this so they'll be able to make better educated decisions about their lives. I wish my father had leveled with me about this. Instead he urged me to go to college, even though he hadn't. Well, I suppose there's a stigma involved with not going to college, no matter how useless the experience is.

My father never mentioned any problem with this . . . and he had a successful career in aviation. He designed, built and managed Central Airport (Philadelphia), was passenger manager for Luddington Airlines (became Eastern), and started the first transatlantic airline (became PAA). Didn't seem to hurt him much.

182 Magazine/Texts

I've proposed an eight-year course in electronics, computers and communications which would be taught by a weekly magazine/text. Once this has proven successful I'd suggest a similar approach for several other subjects.

A mag/text makes it possible for the course to be changed easily from one term to the next as a result of feedback from the students. It makes it possible for the students to participate via a letters-to-the-editor column. It also allows students to organize state-wide events tied in with the subject being studied.

Mag/texts might be of value in fast-changing fields such as cosmology, environmental sciences, and biotech. Some might be weekly, others bi-weekly, and some just monthly.

As a magazine publisher for over 40 years I'm not sure why some educators are so bent out of shape over school texts containing advertising. I'm in favor of taking advantage of the money and thus cutting our educational expenses. Have you seen what text books cost these day? And remember, books are at least three to five years out of date by the time we get them. They may be okay for ancient history, but they aren't much use for teaching modern technologies.

Most computer books today have a half life of months. I've thrown out hundreds upon hundreds of computer books because they were no longer of any value to anyone. And I don't throw things out easily. If there ever might be the slightest possibility of a use I put it in the barn . . . just in case. I've got to sort all that stuff one of these days.

183 The Crystal Ball

Let's look ten years into the future. Actually, we should be where I describe in five years, but I'm not used to the world sticking to my timetable. What will schools be like in ten years? That depends, of course, on whether a massive change is made this year or whether we refuse to bite the bullet and try to make do with Band-Aids.

Let's assume the improbable. Let's see what things could look like if we made the leap this year . . . indeed, this fall . . . without spending two or three years planning.

I see schools with kids busy both during school and after school with club work. The Amateur Radio Club will have its own station, complete with a tower and beam antennas. It'll have its own automatic relay station (repeater) to extend the range of tiny hand transceivers and mobile stations. It'll be set up with links via packet radio to school club stations all over the world.

The Publishing Club will have a Macintosh desktop publishing system and will be publishing the school weekly paper, team reports for student teams in many classes, and probably a school magazine of art, poetry, stories, and photography.

The equipment this requires isn't very expensive and should be easily acquired through the profits from the newspaper. It's inexpensive enough right now so that my wife has a complete system in our dining room which she uses to turn out catalogs for her how to dance video business.

The Video Club will have video editing facilities capable of providing professional videos. The equipment for this is within the grasp of a school club too. My wife has a complete video editing system set up next to her desktop publishing system.

The club might lend small video cameras to students in foreign countries so they can do show and tells about their lives. Once cameras are universal only the tapes would need to be swapped.

The club could also do special productions on student activities, special town events, visiting performers, etc.

Videos of student visits to local businesses will make interesting reference material, making it possible to build a video library of such visits.

The Music Club will have a digital synthesizer and midi-connected computer. With this students will be able to write music and perform. Again, we're not talking a huge expense. My wife also has one of these systems which she uses to provide the dance music for her how-to-dance videos. In this way she avoids having to pay royalties for copyright music which could easily add several dollars to the cost of each one-hour video.

The club might also include a rock band, a marching band, and other performers.

The Choral Club would put on concerts around the state and on TV. It might also do some operettas . . . as I did in high school.

The Computer Club would be on line with similar clubs all around the state. It would also allow students to be on line with Compuserve, Prodigy and other such information and communications services. A link with the Amateur Radio Club station would allow the students to communicate with people anywhere in the world. This could be used to help learn more about geography and foreign cultures.

The club would be networked with several other clubs, complete with a bulletin board system (BBS). There are already thousands of BBSs in operation . . . indeed we have one in conjunction with *73 Amateur Radio Today* to access over the telephone. I get mail via BBS, fax, the post office and Fedex every day.

The Chess Club would keep a library of chess books and videos. It would organize interschool tournaments and award programs.

The Camera Club would have its own darkroom and studio. It would have contests and awards. It would work with the Publishing Club to publish the award-winning photos.

There might be a Shop Club, complete with woodworking machines and tools, metalworking machines, and so on. How will all this equipment get paid for? Are we going to need millions of dollars from the state for all this? No way! I believe every club should be able to think up for-profit enterprises to fund their needs.

The Shop Club could, for instance, make furniture and sell it in the community. It could provide home services to people needing carpentry, shelves, doors fixed and so on. Pay for things by earning the money.

There might be a Dog Club where students would help train dogs for people around town. Most people don't have the time or interest to learn how to train their dogs. This is bad for the families and even worse for the dogs.

I think you begin to see where I believe education should be going. It's up to the Commission whether we keep turning out poorly educated, unmotivated youngsters or whether New Hampshire takes the lead and shows the country what can be done . . . and done in a very few years! None of this is likely to happen if you read this, nod and then wait to see. It can happen if you decide to start helping me push. We've got to push this into and through the legislature. One or two Commissioners aren't going to get anywhere with an uphill job like that. It's going to take at least 30 very determined Commissioners using every bit of guile and clout they have. We're talking about cramming an elephant through a keyhole here.

Are you game . . . or are you tired . . . and besides you know it's impossible?

184 Overeducation?

As I look around my own company I can see the pattern. The fact is our educational system is terribly out of touch with the reality of business today. The educators don't seem aware of this. If there is any direction in the field, whoever is doing the direction seems unaware of the reality. Not even our kids or their parents understand what's gone wrong.

The sorry fact is that most of the people working for me are college graduates. So what's sorry about that? It's that the kind of work they're doing for me doesn't call for anything more than a high school education . . . plus an ability and interest in learning.

All I really need in a new employee is the ability to read, write, and learn. Since we use computers for almost everything it's a plus to be able to type. I do expect them to use working for me as an opportunity to learn and to keep on learning. I encourage them, once they're good at one job, to move on to something else and build their skills. I don't want people who learn one job and then settle down to do just that for the rest of their lives.

I want them to learn how to use the Macintosh publishing system. I want them to learn about magazine circulation, about telemarketing, about accounting, editing, public relations, and so on. And when they've learned what they can working for me, I want them to move on to a larger company and continue to learn.

There is little in the work my employees are doing which is helped by a college education. The things they learn working for me are practical, real world skills. My business is like most others in this respect. We publish magazines, newsletters and books, we are a recording company, complete with ultra-modern studios; we are a mail order company selling music from over a thousand record companies; we are a music distributor for several hundred record companies; we have several of our own labels; we are lobbyists for the music and amateur radio industries; we import and export music; we do music premiums.

Some of my most successful "graduates" have been high school educated. Their perceived lack of a college education seemed to drive them to make better use of the opportunities I made available. Many of them quickly outshone most of my college-educated people.

This is why I've recommended combining a college education with half of every day spent working for a nearby high-tech business . . . rotating around the companies every few months into differnt jobs. This would provide a low-cost, highly motivated work force for the participating companies . . . plus an invaluable real life work experience for the students. Many will learn more at work than they will in their classes. And their paychecks should at least pay their tuition. College for free!

If the goal of college is to make youngsters better educated for their own enjoyment rather than gearing them for their life's work, perhaps we should just encourage them to go to fun schools and have a good time during those four years. But I have this weird idea that college should aim to be the bridge between the general education they get in high school and the skills they're going to need for their life's work.

We do expect that of lawyers, doctors, and other professional people. So why shouldn't all college graduates be expected to be professional at something? If they follow my work-study plan they'll be able to walk into almost any business and be ready to tackle almost anything needed.

185 Getting Kids To Read

When I was in high school (Erasmus) one thing they did was very helpful to me. It's confusing for a kid to walk into a library and be faced with thousands of books. I knew that some were packed with things I wanted to know. I also knew that most weren't. So I needed some help in finding my way through this maze.

I've been helping people newly interested in classical music to build a basic classical CD library which will include most of the best music. I am continuously looking for CDs which I think people will particularly enjoy. When I find them I write a short review encouraging the readers to try them. My mail indicates that thousands of readers really are helped by this approach.

So how does this tie into a library full of books? Well, when I started in high school at Erasmus they handed me a recommended reading list. I tried it out and found it was an excellent guide. I got interested enough in reading to join the Book Club, where we had our own private room where we could spend "study hall" periods reading in quiet. We had about twenty in the club, so it was never crowded.

Since not many kids are reading for their own entertainment these days, is there anything we can do which might encourage them to do it? You bet! I suggest the school paper or literary magazine get the students to look for interesting books, write short reviews. The students might even give the books a rating from one to ten on how much they enjoyed them.

These reviews would eventually make it possible to publish a list of the books that most students agree were fun to read. As I've mentioned before, high on my all-time list of fun books were those on history by Harold Lamb. He did a fabulous job with Alexander of Macedon, Genghis Khan, Hannibal, the Crusades, Babur The Tiger, Cyrus The Great, Tamerlane, Omar Khayyam, and others. What a marvelous way to learn history!

Of course, another way to get kids interested in reading is to have their folks read to them when they're young. My mother and grandfather read to me and that worked just fine. For parents that are too busy watching Monday night football, there are wonderful tapes of other people reading . . . and there'll be more, as I get the time to do some recording myself.

186 The Ability To Pay

The present system in New Hampshire is to ask that property owners and the buyers of state lottery tickets help pay for our kids' education. That reflects to renters in higher rents, so they're paying too. So it's the parents who are being asked to pay, which doesn't seem unreasonable . . . if they can afford it.

The problem arises when school costs rise enough to start chasing parents out of the state because the property taxes are perceived to be too high. Yes, I know that our New Hampshire tax rate overall is the lowest in the country. And I also know that we Americans are among the lowest taxed people of the developed countries. Alas, we're talking perceptions, not reality . . . and people vote on their perceptions, so we can't ignore them.

With this in mind, I started thinking about solutions to the problem. We seem to have far more people dwelling on the problems than proposing solutions.

There are two approaches to consider. One is to see what can be done about lowering costs. Another is to consider alternative ways of paying.

If you've done any reading about our educational system you know that we have a list of problems which will fill several books. Many of our school buildings are falling apart. Some teachers are poorly trained and motivated. Worse, they're expected to do too much non-teaching work. And then there's the incredibly bloated administrative bureaucracy which eats up half to two thirds (and more) of the educational budget in many states.

We need to tackle all of the problems creatively, but even so we're still going to need money. And, considering the high-tech direction the world is heading, we're going to need far more computers and other expensive equipment in our schools than we have in the past.

There's a big difference in cost between an overhead projector for film and one for a computer screen. We know that video and computers are on a collision course and we know nothing about the collision is going to be cheap . . . at least not at first. And first is when we need to get kids learning about these things.

One way to help cover school costs might be to charge our kids. We can set up a charge account for them which they can work to pay off as they go, or run up a bill to be paid after they graduate.

Years ago I used to have a bunch of high school students work for me after school and on weekends. They collated, addressed and mailed newsletters. They answered the phone and took subscription orders. They had a ball, they learned about business and they made some spending money. They also learned about coming to work on time and keeping busy . . . and that working could be fun.

Then the minimum wage law was imposed on my little company, forcing me to fire them all and replace them with folding, collating, addressing and postage machines. Who benefitted from that? The kids didn't. I didn't.

When I first moved to New Hampshire in 1962 I hired a bunch of college dropout amateur radio operators to work for me. They worked for $20 a week plus room and board. I did all the cooking and we lived together in a huge old house. It was a tremendous learning experience for them as we published a monthly amateur radio magazine. We set up a fantastic ham station high on Mt. Monadnock where my employees could go and operate. It was a fun time for everyone and we turned out a great little magazine.

One of them has gone on to own a top PR firm in the computer field. Another got into the satellite dish business and made millions. One is high up in Xerox today.

When the employment officials got wind of what I was doing I had to fire my whole crew and replace them with three local people working regular hours . . . none of them radio amateurs.

I'd like to see high school students encouraged to work for local businesses, even if they work for less than the minimum wage. I could teach a kid to prune apple trees in a couple of hours . . . just think how many hundreds of apple trees in your area need regular pruning and don't get it. Kids can be taught to do odd jobs around homes in town, organized by other kids.

187 The Loan System

Just as college students are expected to repay the costs of their education when their parents can't afford it and they have to get loans, we might do the same for high school students. There's this concept that things we get for nothing are little appreciated or prized.

Student loans for high school would be charged interest, thereby putting on some pressure to keep the loans as low as possible. The loans could be repaid from their salaries after they graduate, perhaps taking 20% until the loan is retired. Thus at $5,000 per year the student would owe $20,000 upon graduation . . . providing the student contributed no money to reduce the loan while in school.

If students and parents were paying directly for high school I suspect there would be a whole lot more interest in eliminating administrative waste and in getting better teachers. Parents and students wouldn't put up with the way things are now if they had to pay.

With the loan system any student would be able to get a high school education, whether the parents could afford it or not. And with their own money at stake, students might take more advantage of the educational opportunity.

I can't keep from remembering my own school experience. I did poorly in school. I just barely eked by. I hated and resented school. But you know, when I came across a really good teacher I enjoyed the experience. Unfortunately that only happened twice in 16 years.

188 Teacher Merit Pay

The educational magazines are full of discussions of the pros and cons of merit pay. Most educators seem for it, while the teacher unions are dead set against the whole idea. Thus it was interesting to find that, in general, tests of the concept have not been particularly successful. Yes, I have an idea on how to help teachers focus on improving their skills. It's a sort of merit pay system.

I was very impressed when I visited Windsor University (Canada) and found that they've a system whereby their teachers are rated by the students on a wide range of things. That makes a lot of sense. It's like business, where the customers rate the service they're getting. The teachers know their jobs depend on good ratings from the students, which establishes a different relationship than normal. I suggest that high school students rate their teachers at least twice a year, perhaps on a simple one to ten rating on how good they consider the teacher has been at teaching them. I'd also ask for a peer evaluation by other teachers, plus an evaluation by the school principal.

I'd propose weighting the ratings, giving 50% of the weight to the students, 30% to the teachers, and 20% to the principal. A 1-10 rating by the students, a 1-6 by the teachers and a 1-4 by the principal would give a total of a possible 20.

Those with the top 20% ratings would get a merit pay bonus. Those in the bottom 20% might be urged to improve their teaching skills pronto or seek work elsewhere.

If we implement high school loans and teacher evaluation, I believe we'll find parents getting more involved with their children's education. And that, in turn, will help children focus their attention on learning.

We should consider the education we provide our children . . . note I did not say "give" our children . . . as important a part of our infrastructure in New Hampshire as providing telephones, power, roads, and bridges. Without a well-educated work force we're not going to be able to provide a quality of life in the next century which will keep New Hampshire healthy.

Our work force in the year 2000 will depend on what we do in 1992 . . . on what the legislature does . . . the administration . . . the strength of the support or the resistance of teacher unions . . . the support of school boards and teachers. But all of these factors will be enormously influenced by the dedication of our New Hampshire people. If very few care enough to push for changes, we're not going to just stay in trouble, but it'll get worse as other states and countries take away our small businesses.

So what's it to be . . . Monday night football and a few brews . . . or action? What is your local school board thinking? What are they doing? How about your state representatives? Your state senators? How about the governor? We have a small state and you not only can get to know your legislators personally, you can help them restructure our New Hampshire school system and make it the finest in the world . . . an example that will have other educators coming here to see how we did it.

Of course if you're comfortable with our kids hanging around the malls, smoking cigarettes, cruising in their cars, throwing beer cans and used condoms on our back roads, fine. You'll get what you're comfortable with. But let's not hear any complaints about your kid "going bad." They don't go bad, they're allowed to spoil.

189 The Good Old Three Rs

Well, our educational system may be in bad shape, but at least they're still teaching the three Rs, right?. Sure they are. Readin', 'ritin', and 'rithmetic.

Now what was that percentage of functionally illiterate high school graduates? How do we explain half our people never buying a single book . . . and half the books bought not being read? And what was that stuff about high school graduates not being able to make change? If you think we're teaching writing in school you should see the thousands of letters I get from my readers. 90% of 'em are pathetic. So much for the three Rs.

So we start kids off by forcing on them by law a second-rate education. We make it almost impossible for kids to be taught at home. With this lousy start most kids are unequipped to continue their education on their own after leaving school. Perhaps this helps explain why such a small percentage of our people become really successful. I assure you it doesn't take an awful lot of extra education and determination to get ahead of 99% of the people.

We're getting well into the information age, which means that people with the ability to communicate are going to have a decided edge. Verbal communication skills are well worthwhile building, but we should remember those dismal retention figures for verbal vs written communications. Writing wins hands down on retention, so we should be concentrating on building writing skills all through school . . . and on through life.

The work of this Commission is a case in point. We've heard endless talk, but how much of it do you remember? What did we talk about at the October, November and December meetings? In retrospect, how profitably was our time spent at those meetings? How much have those meetings contributed to the output of our Commission? Here we are, coming into six months in operation, and as far as I can see, the only signs of any progress are my reports . . . which have yet to be acknowledged in any way by one single member of the executive committee. I can see why no one other than Dick Noyes has bothered to contribute. His excellent contribution also seems to have been totally ignored, by the way.

It isn't that I've had any letters, faxes or phone calls disagreeing with what I've been writing. Indeed, I've had a few cheering me on, for which I really thank those who took the time. Is it that everyone else is too busy to pitch in and help? Is it that I'm the only one with creative solutions to the New Hampshire recession problems? Is it that it's only the prestige of being on the Commission which has attracted many to the group?

While I've proposed several short term fixes for the New Hampshire recession, in the long run everyone agrees that we need to provide a high-tech educated and motivated work force. And that means making major changes in education. Will these happen without the intervention of the Commission? It doesn't seem likely. There are some changes in the works in our educational system, but I know of no group other than the Commission in a position to bring about the radical changes needed.

I've been attending the Commission's Educational Subcommittee meetings, so I'm getting a pretty good idea of where the New Hampshire educational establishment is right now, as well as where it's heading. I've had the pleasure of meeting several educators who recognize the critical nature of the problem and who seem open to even quite radical ideas for solutions. I'm encouraged. But these educators need all the weight the Commission can bring to help them overcome bureaucratic inertia and hidden political agendas.

If we're failing to teach the basic three Rs, we've got to fix that situation as well as come up with a way to introduce science and math courses. A high-tech work force that can't read well, can't write and can't make change of a dollar isn't going to attract many new businesses or help our present high-tech businesses to grow.

190 Implementing The Initiatives

As if getting the Economic Development Commission to (a) come up with proposed initiatives and (b) agree on some of them as worthy of implementation isn't enough, that's just the beginning of the Long March.

There's a formidable array of firepower aligned against educational change. The Commission is going to have to run the gauntlet of (a) school administrators, (b) local school boards, (c) educational unions, (d) the legislature, (e) the administration, (f) various educationally responsible state bureaus, (g) citizen apathy, (h) parent disinterest, (i) political opportunism, (j) media emphasis on the negative, (k) normal media distortion, (l) state employee union lobbying power, (m) self-interest anywhere down the line, (n) Commission indecisiveness and sensitivity to pressures, (o) teacher inertia, and at least ten other factors I haven't even considered.

Can the light of reason cut through 25 layers of self-interest and apathy? It seems unlikely, even considering the alternative of New Hampshire continuing to produce a poorly educated and unmotivated work force and thus suffer a lowering in our quality of life.

By the way, for those who've been sold a bill of goods on how well New Hampshire students have been doing on their SATs, let me rain on that parade. When the SATs are normed for our small percentage of blacks and Hispanics, our SATs are no higher than any other state. Our white student SATs are just average, and that average is terrible when compared to most other countries.

Given the the urgency for our success vs the depths of our problems, what's our best bet for tackling the 25 insurmountable obstacles? It's going to take some fast footwork to get around, in between and over the endless objections. It can't be done. Freedom for kids? That's crazy! It'll never work. We don't have the money. We can't retrain our teachers. Parents don't care anyway.

Question: if we start with the legislature and educate them, will we be in a better position from which to tackle the other 24 obstacles? Right now all we have as a Commission is the power to advise, and I'm not even sure how clear that power is. There are constant hints of hidden agendas and these, combined with otherwise seemingly unexplainable events, maintain their credibility. I'm used to things in politics seldom being what they seem, so I'm not particularly surprised at some of the rumored agendas.

These secret agendas will only be sustainable if the Commission members are so inertia-bound they allow the Commission to avoid pursuing its goals. Those who sit there silently, allowing nothing to happen, aren't contributing any more than those who've given up in disgust and stopped attending meetings. I hope enough members of the Commission have the persistence it's going to take to see this through.

191 The Campaign

If we're going to have any influence on New Hampshire's educational system, I suggest we plan our campaign just as we would the selling of a new product. We need to plan what we're going to do, step by step. To get the legislature behind us we're going to have to educate them, answer their questions and overcome their objections . . . just as we would in selling any other product.

This means our initiatives need visibility. The legislature needs first to be made aware of the initiatives. We can build this awareness through a newsletter, through the press, magazine articles, and radio and television interviews. Yes, this takes time and effort, but on the other hand none of it costs much to do.

If all 32 of us pitch in and use our contacts and influence to get media coverage, our initiatives will be one of the most talked about things in the state. Promotion like that will make it difficult for the educational union to block action . . . presuming that this is going to be an obstacle.

If my initiatives are implemented, the role of our teachers is going to change substantially. We're going to ask them to become performers, entertainers, facilitators, and team leaders. Their authority will be reduced, but at the same time their prestige will be greatly enhanced. We may be able to make it possible for educators to move way up the social scale . . . and we may, as a result, find education attracting our best and brightest for a change.

192 Cutting Expenses

We need to know more about where New Hampshire is spending its education money. How much of it is going for administration? How much for work that may no longer be important and can be eliminated? We know that in most states administration has grown in true Parkinson's Law progression and could be decimated (cut 90%) without significantly affecting the end product.

As with my proposed initiative for reducing our New Hampshire state expenses, I propose the establishment of an educational Quality Control office. This would solicit complaints from teachers . . . ooops, facilitators . . . from students, parents, and any other involved parties. A certain percentage of the complaints will prove to be valid and worthy of solution. In this way we'll gradually reduce our educational problems, get rid of the problem makers, and encourage problem-solving.

Our New Educational Paradigm (NEP) promotion will help enlist parental cooperation and support, giving them a vision of a far better education for their children and lower taxes at the same time.

The legislator-oriented newsletter, explaining the concepts involved in NEP and affording them a medium for airing their arguments or constructive ideas, will also be of interest to the New Hampshire media. This input will help them pinpoint the key players and work with them in bringing this information to the public.

We might also consider making this information available to economic development committees in other states. I've been amazed at what action even my preliminary reports to the Commission has been able to trigger as far away as Alaska. Indeed, there's been far more action there than in New Hampshire so far.

193 Any Help Out There?

While I enjoy writing, our mandate is for a group effort. Presumably all Commission members know how to write, so I don't think I'm off base in suggesting that the members share the responsibility for writing.

There's nothing wrong with New Hampshire that we can't fix if we put our mind to it and refuse to let anyone stop us. The same holds for getting our educational system out of the 19th Century and into the 21st ahead of everyone else. We have to decide not to take "no" as an answer to anything. We know it's going to be difficult . . . but we also know it isn't impossible. So let's do it! Let's declare our own war on the recession and win. Get out your Sun Tzu reference manual on war, let me know if you have the will to win, and the tenacity of purpose it's going to take. Please advise.

194 Adapting Education

We are most fortunate in New Hampshire in that we have relatively few black and Hispanic minorities. As I've mentioned, this is the main reason our New Hampshire SAT scores are higher than in other states, rather than our kids being better educated. No, our educational system is no better than the rest of the country.

If we change to the system I've proposed where we eliminate grades and compulsory attendance . . . where we have ten terms a year and thus less trauma when one has to be repeated . . . where the students have a strong say in who passes and who doesn't . . . and where we have a strong pre-school education to indoctrinate both parents and children with the value of an education and its connection to a better quality of life and pride in one's self . . . our system will be better equipped to deal with a wide range of intelligences.

In many larger cities special schools have been developed to cope with children on the low and the high ends of the IQ bell curves. Youngsters with special needs is our euphemism. This might be a possible route for a combined Nashua-Manchester-Concord area. With the rest of the state being rural, we might want to try some smaller learning centers, perhaps harking back to the one-room schoolhouses of a hundred years or so ago. We certainly don't want to abandon our special needs children, but neither do we want to have to spend so much on them that we are forced to deprive our mainstream students . . . which has happened in some school districts.

We want to give every youngster in New Hampshire the very best education we can manage. We know that being able to read, write, and speak well are critical skills for a successful work force. Blacks in ghettos often discourage other blacks from speaking regular English . . . that's "being white." And they're making life miserable for black kids interested in education, which is also "being white." This is terribly destructive to the blacks, the community involved, the city, and the state. It enforces poverty over yet another generation, leaving few alternatives other than welfare, drugs, and crime.

To the extent that we have these problems in New Hampshire we should consider creative solutions. We've got to step in somehow and change this terrible self-perpetuating pattern. My suggested initiative (I-25) for solving the welfare problem is one potential route out of this disaster.

195 Role Models

Blacks have a serious problem with role models . . . something a good educational system should solve. The present role models for black youngsters tend to be religious leaders, athletes, musicians, and criminals.

Blacks, as a result, have had a difficult time running normal middle-class white businesses. It's enough of a problem so that when a black does open a store in a black neighborhood, many blacks will avoid doing business there and patronize a white or Asian store down the street.

I've a black friend in Baltimore who publishes a black newspaper. I've been trying for several years to get him to address this problem by running articles on successful black businessmen. I've failed so far . . . his articles have mainly been on black clergy. I'll keep trying.

Keeping in mind the black IQ curve, the lack of good black schools and educators, and the polarization of black students attending mixed racial schools, the present situation is understandable . . . and it is not going to be easy to change. The change is going to have to start right from the beginning, with pre-school . . . which few blacks have available yet.

My proposal for parenting videos (I-19) may be the best entry into this arena. We can make such videos available for inexpensive rental. If we start mothers using these videos early in their pregnancy and get them used to being educated about how to raise their children, we may see the results in a few years in black kids with a whole new outlook.

How much would it cost to provide a series of videos to help mothers? My wife, who's made over 120 one-hour how-to-dance videos assures me that it's easy to do them for under $5,000 each, including talent, music, and post-production work. We're not talking about Hollywood extravaganzas here.

If you've watched Channel 11 you've probably seen many excellent programs which do exactly what I've described. These have been shown on most PBS stations around the country. The videos are also available for around $40 each, but this is much too high for welfare families. They'd be used more if they could be rented.

The information is already available . . . now how do we get it into the right hands at the right time? The first step is to recognize the importance of this and not leave it to chance. Again, this is an opportunity for an entrepreneur. Someone will have to make a deal to get rental copies of the best programs and then advertise their availability to mothers and expectant mothers for mail-order rental.

196 Private Schools?

That's my recommendation after reading everything I could find on the subject . . . pro and con. The compulsory government institutions are not democratic or capitalistic, they're still another sorry experiment in socialism. We need competition in the educational industry if we're going to improve the product and cut the costs.

You only have to look at every single socialist-oriented institution we've set up to see that central planning isn't working here in America any better than it did in the USSR and Eastern Europe. Our public schools cost twice as much to run as private schools and the education stinks. Experts are adamant that our post office costs more than twice as much as would privately run mail services.

So let's get New Hampshire out of the education business by empowering private schools. We could save millions in taxes by paying private schools half what it costs to run our public schools.

If we allow schools to bid, as would any other business, costs will plummet. When New Hampshire needs roads built they get bids. When the state needs printing done they get bids. Well, we need educating done, so let's get bids . . . or go with a voucher system.

There's been some impressive suggestions made about changing the property tax system. Perhaps, if we can halve our educational costs, there will be less resistance to making a major change in the property tax system.

Dick Noyes has provided a strong argument for taxing land instead of improvements. This apparently provides a whole raft of benefits to the state and to business. It makes a lot of sense, but I'd want to hear all sides of the argument before jumping.

We are indeed fortunate that we haven't a large minority population and therefore been saddled with busing. This has turned out to be an enormously expensive and largely fruitless exercise which has frustrated almost everyone involved. Another great example of our government at work.

How do we get from our present government institutions to private schools? I'd have to know more about the problems involved before proposing some solutions. If we adopt some of my strategic educational initiatives it'll be a lot easier to make the change. We'd be able to do away with accreditation boards, for instance.

By the way, there is a good deal of evidence that when schools go private that parents suddenly start taking a whole lot more interest in the schools and their children's education. What happened in Milwaukee is a fine example, as reported in the March 1992 issue of *Imprimis*, published by Hillsdale College.

A small group got together in the inner city and pushed for a voucher system so their children could go to local private schools. They knew that 60% of all ninth graders do not complete high school, and of the 40% who do stay only 10% graduate able to read. And for this Milwaukee pays about $6,000 a student, with the administrators pleading for still more money. Some 62% of the teachers and administrators refuse to send their children to the public schools.

The black parents . . . even the single black mothers . . . know that education is the only way out of poverty, so when the small group called a meeting, expecting perhaps a dozen parents, hundreds of enthusiastic parents turned out. It turns out that poor parents care very much. They don't take education for granted, they'd just been locked in a no-win situation by the public school system.

Poor people are not dumb . . . or even uninformed. They do have enough sense to make decisions about educating their children. "But the teachers' unions, the NAACP, the bureaucracy, and the educational establishment didn't agree. In the name of protecting the poor they opposed choice. We didn't try to beat them . . . they were too powerful. Instead we went to the parents, and we organized the community from the grassroots level, from the bottom up. And they kept coming to our meetings by the hundreds . . . even the Joe Six-Packs and the Archie Bunkers. Republicans, Democrats, Jews, Catholics, Protestants and Muslims publicly spoke up in favor of the plan."

When parents found out they might be able to take their children out of the public schools they began sitting in the galleries at the state capitol and watching the legislators. Like the educators, they also believed the poor didn't care. The result was the first voucher bill in the U.S. passed into law. It allowed 1,000 students to claim $2,500 worth of tuition vouchers.

"Now every private school in the inner city has a waiting list. Hundreds of low-income families want out of the public school system. Those who have succeeded are spreading the word. Their children, two or three grade levels behind in the public school, are now working at their grade levels. Once always absent, they are even refusing to stay home sick! There are no gang problems and only a 2% drop out rate." This was written by a black, poor, inner-city, single mother who helped her community beat the system.

Question . . . can we beat the system in New Hampshire? How much clout does the Commission have? How much will we be backed up by the legislature? Can we get a voucher system going in New Hampshire? It's called parental empowerment.

No, our public schools aren't as bad as most inner larger city public schools, but we know beyond a doubt that they aren't much good and cost too much. The voucher system should be able to save the state millions on our education bill. As soon as a voucher system is enacted I believe we'll see private schools opening up all over the state. Good schools. Competitive schools. That's the way capitalism works.

197 And In Indianapolis

Another case cited in *Imprimis* tells of an insurance company that offered to pay half the tuition for grade school children wanting to go to

Indianapolis private schools, but unable to afford it. The full tuition was $1,600, so the company paid $800 per student.

"In the first school term of this year, 705 students were awarded vouchers and there were 199 on the waiting list. The list would have been larger, but many parents knew that the private schools were full."

The company did this because, "according to their own standardized tests, Indiana public schools are failing to teach adequate basic skills and are far behind the private schools in terms of overall student achievement." And "who has ever heard of a private school with metal detectors or with an 80% drop out rate?"

New Hampshire schools aren't that bad, but they aren't good either. My daughter attended the Peterborough Consolidated School for a while and dropped out in disgust. A few years later she got her equivalency diploma in Concord.

198 Organizing Day Care

With today's living costs leaving little choice but for both parents to work, there's a need for good day care services for younger children. So let's consider what "good" day care should entail . . . and what it isn't doing at present that should be done.

We know that children entering school are much better off if they've had good pre-school education . . . educationally directed play. We also know that many day care outfits are little more than baby-sitters, often using Sesame Street and Mr. Rodgers to keep the kids placated and semi-hypnotized.

We want kids to enter the first grade with a minimum of transition from pre-school. We want them to be enthusiastic about learning and to already understand the value and fun of learning. It'll take well-organized and run pre-schools to handle this transition. If we're successful at this our children will be unstoppable in their desire to learn and may even be trusted to handle a non-compulsory educational system.

Much as many people may want to dump this responsibility on the government . . . federal, state, or even local . . . I believe that the marketplace will best provide us with the quality we want for our kids. Government planning has never worked well for anything, so why turn to this proven losing system in something as important as the whole future life of our kids?

We all know that government service tends to weed out people with creative ideas, enthusiasm, and high productivity. Yet these are exactly the things we want most for our children to learn. So let's only consider private day care providers. I must admit I'm tempted to use the same argument in favor of all our schools being privately run, even if all or partly funded by the government.

199 Children Need Their Mother

Mothers who are away at work eight hours a day . . . virtually the entire waking day for younger children . . . are missing out on the close personal contact which is important for both them and their babies. But with the cost of homes, cars, food, and so on, mothers have little real choice . . . they have to work to make ends meet, even if this causes psychological harm to their children.

So I'm proposing a compromise solution. Instead of mothers working eight hours a day, suppose they worked five? In this way two mothers could cover one job on a 7:30 to 5:30 basis, with one taking the first shift and the other the second shift. This would give both of them a half of every day at home with their children . . . or they might spend one or two of their half days helping at the day care center, getting to know the other children and becoming familiar with what their own child is learning at pre-school. They'd only make 5/8ths as much money, but they'd be able to have both a career and quality time with their kids. When the kids get into kindergarten or the first grade mothers could go back to 35 or 40-hour work weeks.

Of course, if the mothers are doing work which can be handled from home, they could take advantage of the home-office environment modern technology is providing. I do 90% of my work at home, with my laptop computer for word processing, a telephone and, most important, a little fax machine at my elbow. About the only "work" I do at my office-office is attend meetings and walk around to see how things are going.

When one of my sales reps had a child we moved her office to her home, providing her with a networked PC and a telephone. She used this during the last stages of her pregnancy and the first few weeks after her child was born. It worked just fine. Eventually she moved back because it made communications easier with the editors, production staff, and other supporting people. But this was her decision, with no pressure from management.

I would have no problem with many of the jobs in my companies being done by half-day workers. Indeed, if they'd work on Saturdays too, extending their work week from 25 to 30 hours, I'd encourage that.

With this system mothers would be able to spend half of their day with their children until they're ready for school at five or six years of age. Remember, it's during the first few years that the patterns of the lifetime are implanted. This is the time when the most basic programming of the child's mind is taking place. If you've seen the movie interviews with children of seven . . . and then the subsequent interviews at 14, 21, 28, and 35, you have seen convincing proof of this concept. Many mothers would prefer to have more influence during these extremely formative years and not leave almost everything to the day care people and Mr. Rodgers.

200 The Pre-School Curriculum

There are several agendas at work with day care and pre-school, so we'll have to satisfy some conflicting goals. For instance, there's the baby-sitting function . . . caring for children while their parents are at work. The kids need to be fed, entertained, kept healthy, kept clean, and kept from harm. They need an outlet for their energies too, so that means facilities for outdoor play . . . and supervision. They should be returned to their parents reasonably tired.

Now we add the educational elements. We can teach them letters, numbers, a basic reading vocabulary, to speak foreign languages, and start helping them understand more about the world. We can help their universe expand from the neighborhood to the town, then the state, the country, the world, and finally the universe.

Pre-school can help answer the unending "why" questions which drive parents to distraction. But let's not re-invent the wheel. Let's see what's been proven the most successful in pre-school education around the U.S. and in foreign countries. Let's not close our eyes and minds to good ideas from anywhere we can get them. We know babies can be taught to swim, so let's teach them. We know some girls can do well at science, so let's get rid of the barriers preventing women from going into scientific careers. We know most of these barriers are erected in the pre-school years.

If my educational technology publication (I-09) is implemented, we'll have the information we need to help our pre-schools develop the best possible students for our schools . . . and more well-adjusted adults later on.

Obviously, pre-school education is going to cost more than ordinary day care. The children are going to need books, videos, and other educational aids. They're going to need teachers too, not just baby-sitters. All this is going to cost.

I've recommended we draw upon grandmothers, non-working mothers, and even retirees to help . . . without increasing our costs substantially. Fully half of the old folks in the nursing home where my mother spent her last four years would have loved having children to care for and teach . . . and they could have done a marvelous job of it.

As with all of our schools, since our kids are an important part of our infrastructure . . . our future work force . . . we should all invest in their education. Yes, taxes. I like the concept of the property tax, just not part on buildings and improvements, which has turned out to be far too regressive. The state would then provide parents with vouchers. I'd recommend the pre-schools be private and go after parents for their business, with the vouchers offsetting much of the cost.

201 What About College?

Yes, I wasted four years going to college. And most of the people I've had work for me down through the years have wasted four years with their college . . . at least as far as their careers were concerned. Does that mean I believe we should get rid of colleges and have everyone go to work when they get out of high school? Of course not!

I'm not sure yet how much education can be provided kids in twelve years of school, but I suspect it's several times what we've been accomplishing so far. I do believe that we'll be able to improve our educational productivity to the point where around 90% of our people will be well-equipped to enter into a high-tech work force right out of high school. Further, I believe we'll be able to also educate them in a wide range of skills and interests, give them a good sense of history, and help them cope successfully with ethical problems.

That leaves around 10% of our youngsters who will be interested enough in some subject to go on and become a specialist . . . scientists, teachers, or perhaps even advanced technicians. Perhaps 10% is high? That'd give us 25,000,000 specialists. Is that too many? No, actually not, because only 10% of those are going to be outstanding, and we really do need 2,500,000 outstanding scientists and teachers. I think we're in the right ball park.

If we go this route we'll need fewer colleges, but we'll need much better ones. Does that mean we're going to sentence the other 90% of our kids to mediocrity? Only if we don't make some major changes in our educational system. Perhaps you're still locked up in the way things are rather than how they should be . . . and how we can make them.

If we reorganize our educational system so that high school graduates are well-equipped to work in high-tech businesses we know they're going to have to continue their education endlessly if they're going to keep up with developing technologies. Further, remember that I've proposed that we change from a compulsory educational system to a voluntary one . . . one based on freedom rather than slavery, which we eliminated a hundred years ago for blacks.

High school graduates will have been essentially self-educating themselves all their lives . . . with the help of their peers, schools, video, and teachers (facilitators). There's nothing to stop them from pursuing any area of interest they have via more books, special classes, videos, online communications services, clubs, field trips, and so on.

The days when a college freshman has to face largely memorization courses in basic physics, literature, chemistry, calculus, psychology, drafting, and so on are gradually dying. Many of these will be covered in far better ways in their earlier years using cognitive learning instead of rote learning (an oxymoron).

Here and there I see some colleges beginning to break through, but 19th Century educational concepts still rule far too often. We need the information resource I proposed (I-09), an educational research reporting publication.

I'm also suggesting a major change in the whole concept of teaching teachers . . . one which will help them to become experts in the field they plan to teach rather than just an expert in teaching itself and never mind what the subject is. It's no wonder so few teachers are excited enough about their subjects to get their students excited too. That takes passion. I've seen it in action twice in my 18 years of formal education, so I know what an incredible difference it can make.

Am I suggesting that college students be completely specialized? When I went to college I hadn't a clue as to what I wanted to do after graduation. Heck, I only went to an engineering college instead of Dartmouth because I was advised by professional advisors in high school that I should do it. They didn't ask me or discuss it, they just gave me a battery of tests and then said what I should do. In retrospect they did me no favor.

At the time I was interested in electronics, radio, and music. My music teacher tried to convince me to go into music, but after mulling over how few successful baritones there were, I decided this wasn't a fruitful career path. In retrospect on this one I was dead on.

What did not come out in the tests was my entrepreneurial bent . . . I'd started my first commercial business at 12. But at that time there were no entrepreneurial colleges, so no wonder they didn't test for that. My interest in electronics won out. I'd already built a portable ham radio transceiver and written about the experience for the high school literary magazine. I still have a copy.

If my college had had optional courses in music, I'd have jumped on them. I was considering becoming a composer. My deep interest in music still brings thoughts of composing. I tried leading a concert band last year and that was incredibly exciting. I'd love to do that more . . . to be able to bring out what I feel is in the music. I'm succeeding with that to some extent with two of my pianist proteges that I'm recording.

What would I have preferred learning in college? I have only to look at my extra-curricular activities to get an idea. I was active in the theater group as a sound man. I sang in the glee club. I became the president of the radio club and started the Campus Broadcasting System, WRPI, which today is the largest student-run activity in the school. I helped pay my way by organizing a business which sold sandwiches at night in the freshman dorms.

I tried two years of electrical engineering . . . went to war for four years as an electronic technician . . . then changed to management engineering when I returned after the war. By that time I knew I was much more interested in the management of technology than in the technology itself. Alas, my college management courses weren't of any more practical use than the engineering courses had been.

My advice to youngsters who would like to run their own businesses is to skip college and go to work for a small business in the field of their interest. This is how they'll learn more quickly. With some ingenuity they'll be able to learn accounting, purchasing, inventory management, data processing, personnel management, marketing, advertising, promotion, telemarketing, office management, contracts, taxes, business law, and so on. I point out that it's dumb to learn all these things at your own expense when there are an unlimited number of people anxious for you to learn on their money.

It would be nice if practical courses in the above were available in colleges . . . particularly colleges where students could be in a work-study program which would pay the tuition (as I've recommended in I-20). This would enable youngsters to learn at a greatly accelerated pace and allow them to put their education into practice as they go along.

When I went to college the goal was for graduates to be hired by Fortune 100 companies. Their interviewers swarmed over our graduating classes, creating a feeding frenzy which caught students up in the excitement. Too bad for them. Even my old college is beginning to recognize that entrepreneurialism is a better route. But those old habits die hard. There are still many tenured professors who aren't about to learn new tricks.

If we get New Hampshire to open a high-tech university such as I've proposed, we should be able to gear it to the needs of the 21st Century, adding needed scientists and skilled technicians to our high-tech oriented workforce.

202 Will Freedom Actually Work?

We are well-aware that education is very important, but how sure are we that we can convince our youngsters? Perhaps it's better to continue our present slavery laws and force kids to go to school, whether they like it or not. After all, all too many of us are living proof that we are unable to live in anything other than the present . . . otherwise we wouldn't be smoking, become alcoholic, take drugs, or get fat. Can we really expect more of our kids than we can manage ourselves?

We know that cigarettes are going to shorten our lives. We know that they are in all probability going to make the last years of our lives a living hell. We know they cause cancer, heart trouble, and emphysema. But that's tomorrow sometime and one needs a cigarette today.

My proposal for making school voluntary was based upon two concepts. My first aim was to make school so much fun that we'd have to fight to keep kids away. Indeed, in schools which have been converted to learning teams and where kids are excited about learning, they won't miss school, even when they're sick.

I think we've all read about kids breaking into schools at night just so they could use the computers.

My second caveat was that we spend a good deal of the pre-school years making sure kids understand that the quality of their life is going to depend primarily on their education.

We can make sure they understand that 95% of the people in prison are high school dropouts. They might also want to know that it's costing society (and that's them, when they become taxpayers) $25,000 a year to keep these losers in prison. Unless we continue our present practice of keeping their little minds virtual blanks by having them sit and watch cartoons on TV for their first five years, I think we can have them not just ready for the first grade, but raring to go.

If we're going to try and avoid continuing to feed uneducated kids into our prison system as a graduate school, do we have to make laws which will guarantee that kids get educated? And how can we square these laws with the freedom which we preach? Or shall we stay the "land of the free," but only if you're 16 or older?

We do have a general agreement that freedom can be limited when it affects others negatively. We have limited freedom. Kids who drop out of school are very likely to affect us all negatively. Indeed, we taxpayers are going to be asked to pick up the tab for them, whether it be as welfare, unemployment, crimes, our criminal system, or prisons. So we do have a vested interest in making sure kids get an education.

I was interested in the talk by Ira Magaziner at Plymouth in which he proposed a system very similar to the one I suggested where slower students would continue to repeat courses until they pass them. My five-week term schedule would be far kinder for this than the usual five-month terms.

Ira proposed that students would have to be accredited in the subjects they've taken . . . like getting Boy Scout merit badges. I like the concept. But I still prefer to have one's peers make all or most of the decision on who is accredited and who isn't.

Until my system proves workable we might insist that youngsters stay in school until they have a minimum number of courses passed.

These courses could include many which teach skills. If we decide to stop wasting college on youngsters who are more interested in developing skills or being apprentices, we'll be doing everyone a favor.

As Ira pointed out, 80% of employers don't even care about a high school diploma, what they want to know is how strong a work ethic a youngster has developed. His study showed that only about 5% of employers asked about a potential employee's education.

We here in New Hampshire are well-aware that we have to make a choice and make it quickly. Are we going to opt for a highly skilled workforce or a low wage quality of life? We agree on the importance of skills . . . and we know this means high-technology skills.

You know, in Germany and Japan 70% of their top management are not college graduates! Their managers work their way into their jobs. Our large corporations are run mostly by lawyers and accountants, and I don't think this trend is helping us be competitive. I suspect it has a lot to do with the erosion of our larger businesses. I know my own experience with accounting-oriented management has been consistently disastrous.

About fifteen years ago America was the highest wage country in the world. Today we rank 12th. Our real wages have dropped 13% in that time! Just in the last ten years we've sold off 20% of our manufacturing base and are now $4 trillion in debt. We seem to be getting close to the limit of foreign bankers' patience with our borrowing to prop up our living standard.

We've got to become competitive with other countries . . . and that means we've got to avoid trying to compete with them with lower and lower wages. New countries are coming on line with 15c an hour wages. If we're going to compete we've got to do it on the basis of higher quality, newer technologies, or customized products.

One thing I haven't seen anywhere is any other fast, simple and inexpensive solution to our generating high-tech educated youngsters starting almost immediately. Make that youngsters with a strong work ethic to boot. I don't think anyone is going to come up with a better solution than my I-22 initiative.

Building a source of high-tech career youngsters will also help us improve productivity. America has been lagging the world in productivity growth, holding at about 1% per year for the last 15 years. We grew at 3% per year for the previous 15 years. Compare that to Europe where they've grown at 3.5% a year since 1975, Japan at 6% per year, and the new Asian tigers at 10% per year!

Is that enough incentive to get our collective Economic Development Commission juices going or are we still in dawdle mode?

203 Now, That Electronics Course

We agree New Hampshire needs a high-tech educated work force if we're going to attract high-tech businesses. We further agree that either we attract high-tech businesses to New Hampshire or we're going to be in trouble. Make that continue to be in trouble.

The logical next question is: how are we going to create this high-tech work force in time for it to be of any use in pulling our chestnuts out of the fire? Sure, we have to teach technology, that's obvious. What isn't as obvious is how to do it.

Having learned everything we want our kids to learn, I have a fair perspective on what's involved. Having published magazines and books on the fundamentals of electronics, communications, and computers for forty years, I'm right at home with this. I know both how difficult it is to teach these mysterious subjects . . . and I know how readily kids take to them, once exposed.

During WWII the Navy was faced with the need to train thousands of electronic technicians in as short a time as possible. Radar was their best weapon, but it required electronic experts to set up, operate, and service. How could they take farm kids and teach them to be expert technicians in just a few months?

They turned to a chap named Cooke who designed just what they needed. Using his curriculum the Navy turned youngsters into top-notch electronic experts in only nine months. They took kids who didn't know an Ohm from a Volt and had them able to service any electronics equipment the Navy had . . . or would have. This was not servicing by the numbers . . . these youngsters knew how every circuit in every piece of equipment worked and serviced by reason, not by rote.

I went through this educational system starting in 1942 and by 1943 I had graduated and was aboard a submarine heading out to sink Japanese ships. I was responsible for the maintenance (and operation in battle) of the radar, radio and sonar equipment . . . the eyes and ears making it possible for us to deliver our torpedoes while sailing right through the middle of Japanese convoys without being detected.

As a sideline, the Navy school teachers had almost all been amateur radio operators before being enlisted to teach. Indeed, over 40,000 of the 50,000 licensed amateurs went into the armed forces during WWII. Plus much of our radio equipment was bought by the government and put into use. My own radio was sent to Brazil and used by the Rubber Development Corporation, a government agency aimed at growing rubber trees in Brazil to replace those lost to the Japanese in Malaysia.

Now, since the Navy was able to teach a bunch of kids all that in just nine months, it shouldn't be difficult to teach our youngsters that and a lot more in eight years. Yes, electronics has progressed enormously in the fifty years since that Navy course, but the fundamentals haven't changed . . . we're just able to pack thousands of relatively simple circuits onto tiny silicon chips and accomplish miracles by assembling them into Rube Goldberg combinations (Rube was a friend of mine, by the way) and using brute force to overcome problems of complexity.

Even our most seemingly complex computers and microchips are basically quite simple and can be understood by youngsters.

Sections 060-067 of this report explain the basics of my proposed teaching course. There doesn't seem to be any other practical approach to New Hampshire generating the needed high-tech work force without delaying the project for years. If we try and go the normal route and first teach teachers what they're going to be teaching, we'll have delayed the whole process by several years . . . which seems like a completely unneccessary delay . . . one which we should not permit the teacher's unions to force upon us.

Indeed, as I've explained, we could have our first courses in electronic fundamentals started by the fall term of 1992 if we act immediately. As an entrepreneur I'm used to doing things quickly. I already know several splendid writers who could start preparing the courses for publication in September.

We'd start out with electrons, batteries, electric current, resistors, volts, amperes, ohms and so on. We'd cover the fundamentals of magnetism and how a current passing through a wire generates a magnetic field. From there it's easy to understand how a transformer works and then diodes.

Within weeks, kids will be able to read schematic electronic circuit diagrams as well as English and will be tackling pentagrid converters in superheterodyne circuits with excitement. They'll adapt to base two arithmetic as well as base ten and be off and running in the digital domain. I watched all this happen when microprocessors suddenly made inexpensive computers available to kids fifteen years ago. They ate 'em up.

And, as I've recommended, if teachers step back and learn right along with the children, the mysteries of computers, radios, fax, television, and the other tools of the 90s will fade away for them too.

I see no other practical solution to our high-tech work force problem . . . and solving problems like this are my specialty. The question I have is how long the Commission members are going to dawdle over this . . . and then, how can we get the legislature to actually implement the plan? Can we get the administration to support the idea? It's a question of how important a high-tech educated work force is for the future.

204 Profit Or Non-Profit?

If we agree on the need for a publication to teach our youngsters about electronics, communications, and computers, there is the question of whether it should be published by a for-profit or a non-profit organization. To me the side you take on this depends on your faith or lack of faith in socialism. A non-profit group would be doing the work for the good of the state, but not for any personal rewards. I applaud the concept and will be happy to endorse it as soon as someone will show me where this concept has worked out well in actual practice.

Having seen socialist experiments up close in Sweden, East Germany, Czechoslovakia, Hungary, Yugoslavia, Russia, Ukraine, China, North Korea, and Burma, I'm afraid I've developed almost terminal skepticism about the basic utopian concept. And having seen the endless futile socialist-inspired experiments in the U.S., all of which have failed dismally, my skepticism has not flagged. Our state-run socialist systems such as our public education, welfare, and post office are monuments to the failure of this whole concept.

So let's set up a for-profit educational publishing group to provide the course material. It probably should start off as a monthly publication, but I believe it'll want to go twice a month and then perhaps even weekly.

Yes, I know that left-wing zealots will be up in arms over letting businesses pick up the tab for the publication via advertising. But how else can we let kids know about the hundreds or even thousands of inexpensive experimenter kits which will become available to help them understand high-tech fundamentals? If we refuse small entrepreneurial firms advertising in our text-book magazine, we'll cut our kids off from a priceless resource.

205 Initial Investment

Having started over two dozen successful publications I have a general idea of what it takes for a startup. These days, with our dollarette badly battered by our trillion-dollar debt and no hint that Congress has any serious interest in slowing down this borrowing, it costs around $500,000 to start from scratch and get a new publication into the black. And I'd estimate it would probably take around three years for the operation to make a profit.

If the New Hampshire economy were in better shape it wouldn't take as long, but the economy is the reason this project is so critically needed. On the plus side there is no shortage of publishing-experienced people . . . particularly in the Peterborough area, a publishing center which has been very hard hit by the recession.

206 Why Start With Grade Five?

If the Commission recommends my proposal for ten five-week terms per year, plus throwing all courses open to any students wanting to take them, we could see some students opting for this electronics, communications, and computers (ECC) course as early as age eight. It would depend on the mental development of the children. In general, most children are capable of understanding the concepts involved by the age of ten or eleven, which is why I suggested starting at the fifth grade. In the heyday of high school amateur radio clubs in the 1950s one half of all newly-licensed radio amateurs were either 14 or 15 years old and came via this infrastructure. My plan is to rebuild this resource.

I already have a new publication aimed at this group, *Radio Fun*, which I started last year. It's for newcomers to amateur radio. As soon as we see computer clubs being formed in every New Hampshire school we'll need a monthly publication to help bring them together. Ditto electronic experimenter clubs, science fair clubs, and so on.

207 The ECC Startup

A publication requires several staffs: writers, editors, production, typesetting, film, photography, art, circulation, ad sales, accounting, legal, advertising, promotion, and so on. It's more efficient to share some of these staffs between several publications, since not all require full time workers. This is why it's much less expensive for existing publications to support new startups.

Our electronics, communications and computers educational publication needs a name, so let's call it Basic Electronic Technology (BET) as a working title. Of course, we'd have to check with the Copyright Office to see if the title has already been taken.

We're going to need some seasoned writers . . . writers who are able to explain things simply and with some humor. We've had enough boring texts, so we want a publication with an "attitude." I'd budget for four writers, with them getting around $25,000 each for starters, plus a share in the profits which might bring them up to around $35-$40,000 a year. We're going to be needing them for a minimum of eight years, so we want them to be able to live comfortably here in New Hampshire.

We need a good editor. Here we're talking about $50,000, tops. The editor's job is to provide overall guidance for the publication, see that the writers get their work done on schedule, make sure the production staff turns out good looking pages, works with the art staff for good layouts, and in general is responsible for everything working smoothly and looking good.

The editor should also be active in helping schools provide feedback to the publication . . . in developing supporting hobby clubs . . . in getting new products of interest to the kids reviewed, etc.

Then there's the advertising sales staff of at least two persons. They'll be selling largely by telephone, backed up by an ad newsletter. These two key people are going to need around $50,000 each, plus $15,000 for an ad coordinator to do the nitty gritty details.

How much will ads cost in BET? The rule of thumb is to charge around $20 to $75 per thousand readers, depending on the type of market. For this one I'd put it on the low end, say at $40 per thousand per ad page. With around 190,000 children in school, that would give us about 125,000 in grades 5-12, so our ads would run about $5,000 a black and white page. Color would cost a bit more. By the time various discounts are in place we're down to more like $4,000 a page. Thirty-five pages of advertising would give us around $140,000 in advertising revenue per issue.

We'd spend about $40,000 of that for printing and paper. Figure about $45,000 for salaries and $35,000 for overhead and we're better than breaking even. All of the work, including the printing, would be done in New Hampshire.

What's the next step?'

208 How To Be Opinionated

There are two basic approaches to achieving the state of being opinionated. One is to do your homework and know enough about things so you understand them. With this platform it's difficult not to have opinions which are fairly difficult to shake.

The other, much more popular approach, is to keep your homework to a minimum and substitute intuition for data. Then you parrot someone else's equally unfounded opinions.

Both approaches qualify you as opinionated, and both will tend to make you frustrating to others. The first type of person is difficult to sway because he knows what he's talking about; the second because his ego is on line.

So how do you deal with opinionated people? The best way is to agree with them, whether you do or not. The chap whose opinions are well-researched isn't going to change unless you've done more homework than he has. You're going to have to come up with new data for him. He's the easiest to change, really, because if you are able to provide him with new information, he'll re-evaluate the data that went into developing his opinions.

The close-minded chap will just get mad, so there's no benefit in trying to change his opinions.

As an officially registered Opinionated Person, I'm amused at the reactions of people who want to change mine. I'm not sure I can recall the last time someone tried to use reason as an argument. The usual approach is to use repetition, often with increasing frustration and passion. When that doesn't work, they shift to heavier duty emotion, working through sincerity, vehemence, on into anger. Boy, am I obstinate! No amount of "reasoning" changes my fixed opinions. "Crusty old SOB."

209 The Entrepreneurial Approach

As an entrepreneur I have to be damned sure I'm right about business decisions. I'm betting the farm when I start a new business. With everything riding on it, I'm not going to last long if I'm depending on intuition instead of heavy duty homework for success. To put it scientifically, luck has been broken down into a set of universally fundamental laws (Murphy's Laws), obviously designed by a malevolent higher intelligence to put you out of business. This is no arena for the intuitively opinionated.

Since successful entrepreneurs are accustomed to doing their homework . . . as part of their basic survival pattern . . . they're going to tend to be very difficult to deal with when it comes to opinions. Avoid them. Almost everyone avoids me. At first I worried that it might be an underarm problem, but not even the application of enough deodorant to keep an elephant half safe prevented clearings opening around me at cocktail parties and receptions. Now I avoid these soirees unless the hors d'oeuvres will offset the shunning.

When you've done your homework, entrepreneuring isn't as much of a gamble as many people believe. And when you consider the rewards vs. the potential losses, entrepreneuring wins hands down.

210 What's So Hot About Entrepreneurs?

I guess it all depends on what you want from life. When you consider that it's not much more difficult to be successful than it is not to, the balance seems to shift toward considering a path through life which has a greater potential for success.

So what's "success?" For nit-pickers, let's define it as being connected with the quality of life. Some of it is making money, but that's incidental for entrepreneurs. Oh, we know we have to make money or else we won't be able to achieve our goals, but you're not going to find any studies which show that entrepreneurs are driven to make money.

Though I've made a bunch down through the years, it's been incidental and never driven me to live the life of the rich and famous. I don't feel driven to show off or prove to others how great I am. I've got my goals and they're what's important.

Goals are the main dividing line. A group once did a survey of the 1953

Yale graduating class, asking them what their goals were and what plans they had for achieving them. In 1973, they checked the same group to see how they'd done. At graduation, only 3% of the class had goals and plans. Twenty years later this 3% accounted for 97% of the entire class' net worth. It's almost enough to make a person think!

211 How To Fail

That's easy! Our educational system aims us at failure. If we'd planned it that way, we couldn't have cooked up a better system for making sure that 99% of the people never make much money.

For instance, there are three virtually sure-fire career paths which will assure you'll never have a healthy positive net worth. One is to work for the government, including the military. The second is to work for a large corporation. The third is to teach. Professors really hate that concept when I'm giving college lectures.

Yes, it's very soul satisfying to teach. But I find it even more soul satisfying to teach and make money, which, as a publisher, is what I do. I beat the system.

So what do our colleges encourage? Golly, you can't do much with a B.S. or B.A. You need to go on and get a master's degree . . . then a doctorate. By then, having missed out on several years of practical business experience, you're virtually unemployable. So you become a teacher.

One of these days, either by dumb luck or by the intervention of a power higher than any of which I can conceive right now, there may develop a college which is worth kids investing four of the best years of their lives. Until then, my advice to youngsters is to stop wasting your life going to school and spend the time educating yourself.

I agree it's well worthwhile to have a broad education. I don't agree that any school or college has yet found a good way to accomplish this. Lectures are garbage. You listen, take notes, memorize them, pass a test and then a year later have virtually no recollection of any details . . . and not much of the concepts involved. Garbage.

Textbooks are baloney too. In your entire life have you ever read a textbook that was fun to read? A textbook that got you excited about learning? More garbage.

A survey of the people listed in *Who's Who* showed that they averaged reading 20 books a year. They've made *Who's Who* because they learned long ago that their education didn't really start until they got out of our abysmal school system.

People keep asking me how come I'm so damned good at this visionary thing? How did I know that microcomputers would become a huge industry? How did I see what the compact disc would do to the music industry right from the day it was introduced? How did I know that laptop computers would grow the way they have?

Believe me, it wasn't anything school did for me. I read a lot. Oh, I read a little fiction . . . love Clancy's books . . . but 95% of my reading is, like the *Who's Who* listees, non-fiction. I read about management, technology, business, psychology, words, selling, and so on. My library fills two whole rooms of my home.

Then there's magazines. I don't see how anyone who hopes to be successful can be ignorant about technology, government, education, and the world in general. I'd say that a minimal magazine subscription list for an entrepreneur (or any other well-educated person) would include *Newsweek, Time, US News, Fortune, Forbes, Business Week, Discover, Omni, Scientific American, Popular Science, Reader's Digest, Success, Inc, Foreign Affairs, The New Yorker,* and *The Public Interest.* Of course, that's only my opinion. I'm entitled to that, right?

Newspapers? Waste of time! If it's of any real importance it'll be covered more concisely in a news magazine. If you're going to get the data you need, you have to avoid wasting your time.

Schools aren't all bad, I have to admit. I took an adult speed reading course many years ago without which I wouldn't be able to read a third of what I do.

In addition to the above magazines I also have to keep up with my special interests such as electronics, communications, computers, music, audio, and publishing.

So why are entrepreneurs so important? Because they've supplied 82% of the new jobs in New Hampshire in the last few years. They're our state's major strength and our bulwark against the recession. And that's my opinion.

212 Stunting Growth

There is mounting evidence that the roots of our American educational crisis may lie much earlier in life than expected. This doesn't by any means reduce the importance of making major changes in our school system, it just means that we have to do even more than that if we're going to end up with the level of education we're hoping to reach.

Our whole culture has gradually been changing. The change has been so slow that, though we're aware of it, we haven't given the implications of these changes much consideration. For instance, we know that family life has changed markedly in the last fifty years. We know that most families today consist of either two working parents or else a single working mother. The pre-nuclear family with a working father and a child-rearing mother is a rarity today.

One ramification of this is that children — small children in particular — are exposed more to television during their first few years. Sesame Street and other children's programs help sedate the kids, making them easier to handle. I saw the day care centers doing this to my children, so I'm familiar with the system. At the time this worried me, but I didn't stop to think through the ramifications. When "everybody's doing it," it's difficult to challenge what's happening.

Now that we're faced with the failure of our educational system on a massive basis, it's important not to indict some aspects of the system and to continue to try and ignore others which may be just as seriously contributing to the disaster.

We're frustrated that our kids aren't learning much — that they not only are lazy about reading and speaking, but don't even want to do anything about it. No amount of preaching, begging, or even threatening seems to be able to motivate them. So naturally we blame the kids, not what we've done to them. Heck, we've just been doing what everyone else has been doing, so where's the problem?

When I felt that something was wrong about the day care use of TV to keep kids quiet and manageable I should have taken the time to follow my nagging concern and thought things through. In retrospect I can see what happened and the thought is chilling. I suspect we've been allowing our children to be permanently crippled in their mental growth. Is this just another imaginary concern to get upset over, or am I onto something? Are we in much deeper trouble than we suspected? Let's consider the situation reasonably and rationally.

We know that when babies are born their brains are in very rapid growth phase. We know their brains quickly build up neuron interconnections to deal with sight, sound and other perceptic inputs. We also know that deprived of the needed stimulation their brains will fail to grow these important circuits. Worse, once the time for the building of these circuits has passed, it's passed.

It's during these early months that children learn to talk. Their brains are open, for a while, to learning language. We've gotten some strong hints on this when we've exposed young children to not just one language, but to many. They seem to have little problem learning almost any number of different languages, and with little confusion. Those of us who've tackled a second language in our teens know how difficult it can be and we marvel that kids of three and four can so quickly learn what we have to struggle so hard for.

The problem is that once the period for establishing the language neuron circuits has passed, learning language is no longer a natural function. The implications of this should be clear and smack of tragedy. At the time when we should be providing the stimulation needed to help kids brains develop the speech and then the reading neuron circuits they'll need for their lifetime, we're feeding them Sesame Street and other TV placating pap. Then we wonder why our children have short attention spans. We wonder why they find reading boring. We wonder why they are so in need of instant gratification. Well, that's just what they've been programmed by TV to expect.

I remember reading about the phenomenon of permanently altering the growth pattern of organisms by interrupting their early development cycles. I believe Alfred Korzybsky discussed this in his book, "General Semantics." He stressed the importance of providing children with the right stimulus at the right time so as not to stunt the growth of their minds.

If we want our children to be able to speak well, to enjoy reading, to think for themselves, and to be creative, we're going to have to change our approach to early learning. Of course if you have no problem with inarticulate, scatterbrained kids who have no interest in reading or their own education, there's no need to worry about making changes.

The movie showing interviews with kids of seven, with further interviews at 14, 21 and 28, which was broadcast on PBS a few years ago, should have convinced even the most resistant persons of the importance of early education. That movie will be around soon with added interviews with the same people at 35 years of age. The film shows clearly that the child of seven is the man or woman of 28 and 35, with astoundingly few real changes. This period before our educational system has a chance to do its damage has set their life patterns for them — and it's done the same for us.

Now, if our brain wires itself with its basic circuits during the first few years, no matter how many changes we make in our school system, we're still going to be fighting a losing educational battle. By the time kids start in the first grade they've already been damaged beyond repair.

So what can we do about this? We're not going to have much success in changing kid TV, the opiate of day care. Sesame Street is comfortable and well protected by its display case full of awards. It's like trying to attack motherhood. Yet perhaps it isn't as impossible as it at first might seem. I know that many mothers have the same worry I had when I saw my children being opiated by TV. We know on some level that this isn't right! But look at all those awards and the praise from child psychologists. Lordy, they must know what they're doing, right? Do you also believe in the Tooth Fairy?

213 So What's The Answer?

The obvious problem is how to see that kids have an opportunity to get the best possible exposure to stimulating experiences during the months when the critical brain growth is in progress. And we need to accomplish this whether the family (or mother) can afford it or not. It's just too expensive for our society not to have this happen.

The usual approach when society has a need is to pass a law making whatever it is mandatory. Further, since this is a societal need, obviously it should be publicly funded. And that means there'll be pressure to have the program run by the government. Well, I happen to be philosophically opposed to compulsory anything. If we want people to do things we should be smart enough to figure out how to get them to cooperate without having to use fines or the threat of prison. Experience has shown us that if it's government-run it's going to be poorly run and overly expensive.

Since most families these days need day care help for their kids, and since a fairly good percentage of them can afford to pay for this service, we have a start. This leaves us with two problems to solve — combining child education with the day care, and a means for providing this for families that can't afford it. Neither of these are particularly difficult problems.

Our schools have long been considered combination baby-sitting and educational institutions, so combining day care and education isn't an altogether new concept. Indeed, let's just think of day care as schools for babies where we can provide them with the mental and physical stimulation they need for optimum mental and physical growth.

Babies are going to need loving care. We've seen some TV reports on what's happened with babies in institutions where they were deprived of such care. Again, as with the deprivation of other stimuli, the babies failed to develop mentally and physically. Between non-working mothers, grandmothers, the elderly, and retired people, we should be able to provide the love, care and teaching environment babies need — and at a reasonable cost.

The concept of combining nursing homes and day care isn't new — and it's good for everyone involved. Elderly people do far better when they have work to do and responsibilities. Even many Alzheimer's patients can be helpful with babies. The idea is to keep costs low and use all available resources.

As the babies develop we'll want to expose them to the stimuli that will help them develop. Since all babies will develop on slightly different schedules, we're not talking about a factory production line operation. The care givers will provide the right environment and help make the experience fun.

This seems like as good an opportunity as any to provide the best possible assortment of stimuli we can manage. Our goal should be to help our children develop the best mind and body growth possible. This is the time when the habits of a lifetime, both good and bad, are established, so let's do all we can to make sure that our educational system isn't responsible for the bad influences.

We know that children who are read to are more likely to enjoy reading later on. My mother read to me during lunch every day, so I was an avid reader from the time I learned to read. I loved the Oz books and read them over and over. I loved the poetry of Eugene Field and Robert Louis Stevenson. By the time I was seven I could recite several Field's poems.

There's much to be said for listening to books being read. It's like the old radio days when we built the pictures in our minds instead of watching them on a TV screen. This tends to help the brain establish circuits which will assist in creativity later on. So I can see a library of audio cassettes of children's books as a pre-school resource.

We'll want video resources too. If we're going to help our kids get exposed to the fundamentals of several languages, we'll need to show them things to help build their vocabularies. But let's not let Big Bird or Oscar get involved. Let's not try to artificially hold our children's attention with flashing colors and squoink sounds. Let's treat them as small people, not imbeciles. Their attention spans are going to be short at first — well they've got an enormous amount of things to learn — so let's let them set the pace and the direction. All we need to do is provide the choices and the best learning systems we can, whether it be via audio tapes, video programs, interactive video, computers, or whatever.

One of my readers was telling me how much fun his four year old son has with his computer. He not only uses it to play some fairly sophisticated games, but is able to go in and change the software to improve them. I don't think there's anything particularly unusual about this. Most kids, given the opportunity, are avid learners. Some kids are ready to read at three or four, others are slower. We haven't done enough experimental work, providing kids with the environment and tools to know what the limitations are.

Okay, I think you have an idea of the pre-school I have in mind, If you are a normal negative thinker you're fairly bursting with objections. How can we afford all that teaching equipment? How are we going to get babies to the pre-school? How can we help poor families afford to have their children in such an environment? What about liability?

Are you in agreement that we can't afford, as a country, to keep stunting our children's minds, permanently reducing their potential for learning and success? Once we agree on that it's just a question of solving the resulting problems — and I don't see any which are insurmountable. If we can bus kids of five to kindergarten, we can bus babies of one to nursery school. That's a lot more cost effective than asking families to chauffeur their babies to and from school.

For parents who prefer teaching their babies at home, let's make educational equipment available for rental. We need an educational resource publication to help parents know what's available where — tapes, video tapes, satellite broadcasts, local TV, computer software, books, magazines, and so on. Teachers will also need this resource guide. I'll go into my plans for such a publication in more detail in another section.

The resource guide should not only help parents and educators know what's available, but should publish evaluations and reviews. Remember, we're just starting to learn how to teach babies, so we have a lot to learn — a publication is going to be needed to help this new educational field develop. We already have some excellent clues on what to do, but we've got an enormous learning world ahead of us as we find out more and more about helping babies to have the best minds and bodies we can organize.

For instance, we know that even the youngest babies can learn to swim. They love it. Well, they don't really have to learn — it comes naturally, if we give them the opportunity. So why bring up children who are afraid of the water? Or, for that matter, afraid of anything else? They need to learn to respect things that can hurt them, but there's no good reason to instill fear. Fear tends to make us more reactive and less able to think — and at a time when thinking is particularly important.

So let's get started in New Hampshire giving our kids the very best start we know how. And let's keep on top of the research going on anywhere in the world on making these early years the most productive. No, I'm not recommending we cram anything into their little minds, trying to generate geniuses. But I'm also not recommending we deprive our kids of every opportunity to build the best brains and bodies we know how to give them — or perhaps I should say, let them develop. If we can do this we'll be quickly followed by the other states, and then by other countries. I believe we should share what we learn and just make every effort to stay ahead of everyone else by being open to new ideas.

As we work with babies to help them develop their minds and bodies, we'll find out more about what characteristics and which time tables are genetic and what can be taught. We're fortunate that bio-medicine is developing so rapidly. I know some people are afraid of genetic experimenting. But if they were able to discover a serious genetic defect in their babies and, through genetic manipulation, spare their children of some dreadful genetic disease, would their religious beliefs be strong enough to do this harm to their kids?

We don't know for sure how much we'll be able to change people with genetic engineering. Will we be able to increase IQs? Are there parents who would prefer a child with a 70 IQ to one with 140? Would some parents prefer fat children? Children with a tendency to early cancer and other diseases? We're not sure about things like timidity, but we do know that homosexuality seems to be genetic.

Perhaps we can use our present predicament as a springboard into the 21st Century in education setting an example for the country. This will not only help cure our present recession, but should prevent something like this happening again. The teaching systems we develop can be turned into an enormous industry.

Once we have children started on the road to a lifetime education, they're going to be in need of the most efficient learning systems we can devise. With their brains open to learning, reading, speaking, and highly creative, they're going to be in good shape to move into a whole new K-12 learning environment.

We can't keep ignoring our children and letting them grow like weeds. We need to cultivate and nourish them as we would our garden. We need to open them to experiences and ideas, watch which way their interests develop and help them explore the world. We need to open them to music, art, poetry, books, and learning. We've got to stop sending growth-stunted children into our grade schools. I'm not talking just about some remedial attempts to help the children of poor families via Head Start to overcome the incredibly bad early programming they've had.

If you think of children's brains as enormously complex computers, you'll understand why the earlier the programming is installed, the more it's going to affect everything that follows. The brain builds its understanding of the environment one step at a time. When it gets bum data early on that will poison everything that comes later to some degree. By making sure we're providing the best early programming we'll end up with the most sane, rational and intelligent kids we can create. By helping them not to feel inferior and afraid, we'll be helping to counter the usual inferiority reactions such as putting other kids down for any differences in color, height, weight, or other physical differences. Who knows, we may be able to start reducing racial, religious and other such conflicts. We could generate a bunch of healthy, creative, enthusiastic, intelligent youngsters. It's a worthy goal, isn't it?

By the time we've found out more about how children's minds and bodies develop, we'll have a better idea of how to continue their education. We'll know more about what kids can handle when they are different ages. I suspect that the whole idea of starting every kid in kindergarten at the age of five will be considered ridiculous. Or grade one at six. Children will, I suspect, all develop differently, with some able to handle different concepts at different ages.

Just as we're getting used to having to custom-make our products to fit the needs of the customer, flexibilizing our manufacturing systems, we're going to have to provide incredibly flexible learning systems for our kids. We've proven endlessly that trying to force all kids into one standard educational system mold doesn't work. When kids are ready, they'll progress. I've always been kind of a slow learner. I remember being about three years old when I learned to walk up stairs. No one pushed me to do it. But when I was ready I knew it. I knew I could do it and I did. And what a sense of accomplishment! My folks never pushed me to do things, but they didn't discourage me either. The educational environment I'm preaching for kids would make things available, but not push them.

This is why I got upset when the first reaction of the Educational Subcommittee of the Economic Development Commission was to push for cookie-cutter standards — to try and establish what kids should know, accreditation for teachers and all those things which have failed us so miserably. This is the factory production mindset for education. Standardized tests measure how well the child fits into the accepted mold.

As Fiske says in *Smart Schools, Smart Kids,* "The reforms on the 1980s were doomed from the outset because they asked American public schools to do something they were never designed to do, never did do, and never could do. We have been asking schools to prepare students — *all* students — for demanding, fast-changing jobs of the future with rigid structures and teaching methods designed for the factories of the early industrial age. We have been asking a 19th Century institution to educate people for life in the 21st Century. Public schools, as currently organized, are as archaic as a turn-of-the-century Model T rattling down a thruway."

Our pre-school system has started our kids toward life-long learning, and started them learning at their own pace, so there's no longer a practical dividing line for when kids should start in grammar school. They should start when they are ready to start, not when they are six years old. I don't even see any dividing line as far as what they're learning is concerned.

Babies one year old require different care than toddlers, so our care providing will be different as the youngsters develop. We'll need different teacher-care-providers and different technologies. The youngest will need cribs to keep them from getting into too much trouble and simple visual toys to help start their eye-brain systems building. The use of community toys will be economical since they'll be usable over and over and not just retire to a box in the attic or closet when finally set aside for more appropriate toys. This could have the beneficial side effect of discouraging the manufacture of instantly self-destructing toys such as we see on the shelves at supermarkets.

While the critical importance of giving our children the best start in life we can via early education is probably worth whatever it costs, and will be returned a thousand times over by the work force we generate as a result, we still don't want to rush off into space project investment numbers. I don't think the whole project is going to be nearly as expensive as negative-thinkers will assume.

We can start off by admitting that early child care and education isn't going to be much more expensive than plain child care. If we have these new nursery schools run by private for-profit companies instead of government institutions we'll cut the costs by about 50% and get a better product to boot. Much of the savings will be in the elimination of administration. Imagine how much money will be saved if teachers don't have to pay union dues, which are passed along to high-living union officials and in huge wads to Congress as PAC money. That will save millions, with little real loss.

Parents are in the best position to evaluate the available schools, so how much do we need the local communities, or even state officials in the mix? Remember, we're trying to get away from standardization and measured accountability. My proposed *Educational Resources* publication could review schools as a way to help parents and their children make choices. I can even see where students might go to one school for one or two five-week terms and then shift to another which has courses which are more attractive. This will tend to make schools very competitive in what they provide, benefiting the youngsters. They'll also have to be competitive pricewise.

The education is going to cost money, obviously—even if we're able to get rid of inefficient public schools and government administration. The costs are an investment for us, granted. But they're mostly an investment for the kids, so why not tote up the cost, add the interest, and present them with the bill once they are part of the work force? And that's just about what we're doing when we collect taxes right now and pay for our educational system with them. So let's continue to tax every adult for the education he or she received and use it to pay for our kids.

Let's round the figures off and look at 'em. Let's say our kids will in general be going to school for about twenty years. Actually, if we get the system working right I believe we'll be able to teach several times as much in far less time. Then let's assume that most people will be working productively for about forty years. If their education costs an average of $3,000 a year, they'll be taxed an average of $1,500 a year for the payback. If we shorten the education and lengthen the payback years it could even be less, but that's a very reasonable cost.

I like the voucher system for transferring the tax receipts to the schools via the parents. Let's not let the parents get their hands on the actual cash, or even make the vouchers cashable in any way, thus tempting a few parents to take the money and run.

I'll get into our tax situation in more depth elsewhere. I'm not a fan of taxes, but I do recognize that there are community services which must be paid for, hence some sort of taxation is necessary. What I don't like about the process is the group of people who have elected to determine how our tax money is spent. There is more than a little validity to Governor Gregg's observation that the only way to control spending is to limit revenues. Almost daily we read of egregious examples of government waste and corruption. These stories do not make paying taxes as welcome. As a businessman I want to see where my expenses are in detail. Should I get any less a detailed report of where my tax money goes? If we knew more about that we taxpayers would throw out the rascals.

Meanwhile, my aim (and I hope yours) is to give our kids every chance to be the best they can—to give them every opportunity for success. And this, as I hope you'll now agree, means starting their education from the earliest moment, making as sure as we can that their brains and bodies develop on nature's schedule, without being crammed into age groups, and forced to be as much alike as possible.

Without this early education we're making our job of generating a good work force extremely difficult. In the past we've been proud of what America has accomplished. Now we're faced with stiff competition from Japan and Germany. Now we've watched our average wages for high school graduates drop almost one percent a year for the last ten years, while the pay for college graduates has increased at about the same rate. This making the poor poorer and the rich richer is the opposite of what we've been aiming to do. Our system hasn't been working and we'd better do something about it. Indeed, now that we know how to greatly improve our educational system, how can we fail to act? Since our politicians are either too afraid to do something different, or have been paid by unions not to, perhaps it's time for we New Hampshire citizens to take over.

One element of the New Hampshire constitution that I always admired was the part where it says that we have not just the right, but the obligation to oppose any laws we don't agree with. It's part of the "Live Free or Die" concept.

215 Irrelevant Education

We are not sending a good message to our kids when we teach them irrelevant stuff. A kid has to be pretty dumb not to realize on some level that the binomial theorem has little relevance in the real world. Ditto the endless memorizing of facts about tin and Bolivia, New Zealand and sheep, and Holland and tulips.

Where in our everyday life at home or even at work will a knowledge of trigonometry, solid geometry, spherical trig, and so on be handy? None of these have come up in my life yet, and I'm well toward the end of it.

Fortunately I've forgotten 99.99% of what I went through in grammar and high school, so I can't go on at length about how badly my time was wasted in those institutions. I've already grumbled about having to take French. I suffered enormously—even had to change high schools because of this cruel and unusual punishment. No, I won't forgive a society that inflicts punishment like that on defenseless kids. But I sure can see why so many kids drop out of school. It not only seems irrelevant to them, for the most part it really is. If we want to keep kids going to school, we'd better figure some way to change our educational system so it will teach things kids need to know. I hope that makes sense.

It's almost getting time for us to take stock and decide what sort of things kids need to know to function comfortably in our society and have a good chance at being successful. I don't think trig, calculus, and the products of Bolivia are going to be high on the list of importances. Nor will a large percentage of the trivia we're inflicting on our kids under penalty of law.

I'm not going to make a list of what I think kids should learn, but I do think we can come up with a list we can agree on if we poll businesses to see what they're looking for in new employees—and then poll parents to see what social skills they deem important.

For instance, one of the most important decisions in life has to do with marriage. How well are kids equipped to deal with their raging hormones and the effect this has on their ability to reason? It's like trying to deal with an alcoholic, where denial makes communication impossible. Would kids drink, smoke and do drugs if they really understood the realities? You aren't going to get through to them with preaching.

Some schools are doing a good job of helping kids come to grips with the complexities of our society. Kids have to learn to live with their peers, with older kids, with parents (of all kinds), with adults and even with old people. They have to be able to cope with religious, race, ethnic and other differences. They have to learn to cope with success and failure. They have to learn to understand and deal with their own feelings.

Several educational texts have pointed out how incredibly important the pre-school years are. It's during this time that kids' brains and bodies grow the fastest, if given the right food and stimulation. It's during these years that they come to an understanding that works for them on how the world works. Later, in school, when they are taught how things really are, for many kids this doesn't really change their early beliefs. They are able to keep both sets viable, even though they may be conflicting. Thus another challenge for pre-school education is to find and revamp these early life beliefs, helping kids build better understandings of how the world works right from the beginning.

The sun sure looks like it's rising in the morning and setting in the evening. And this is confirmed by our language, which says it is. That doesn't make it easy for children to come to grips with the earth turning, giving the impression of the sun moving.

Our educational job is made even more complex by the wide differences in children. We don't know how much these differences are genetic and how much are learned, but we do know that some children learn better through visual input, some via audio, some by tactile and so on. Children also vary widely in their spatial cognition. It may be that by enhancing pre-school learning we'll be able to help kids build better neuron networks in their brains to deal with these various concepts and thus not have as wide variances as we see now. These may be due more to learning than genetic differences.

216 Conflicting Data

On the one hand we tell kids that their success in life depends on how much they know. Then we turn around and load them down with obviously irrelevant information. Worse, much of it we drill into them, insisting on memorization, followed by tests of their memories. It doesn't take long before kids realize on some level that they are actually remembering very little of all this in the long run. When they figure out that cramming for exams is a total waste of their time, with no benefits other than a passing grade which will permit them to move on to even more memorization and tests, all of which will soon be forgotten, it's good-bye school. And good riddance.

The terrible aspect of all this is that with such a bad experience, the likelihood that these kids are going to try and teach themselves anything is remote. To them a lifetime of education means a lifetime of torture. The whole concept of it being fun to read a book is alien. It's no wonder that half of all Americans have never read a book after leaving school. It's a wonder that the other half have.

If we can get rid of our present educational system — get rid of memorization, tests, grades, standardization, compulsion, and so on — if we can make learning and reading fun and exciting, we won't have to worry about dropouts, only about getting the kids to go home after school. We won't have to worry about working the poor darlings fifty weeks a year — they'll be loving it. The problem may be getting them to leave school and go to work. Oh well, we have that problem now with some students, but not so much because they're enjoying it, but more due to a fear of having to work in the commercial world. They continue as long as they can as students and then teach.

Will we be able to bring about the needed changes in our educational system, or are our children going to be held prisoners of the old unworkable system?

217 Start The Changes Here

We have an incredible opportunity to change our New Hampshire educational system — to totally change it, not just try and tweak it here and there. This is going to call for everyone to make sure our legislators know what we want done. We're going to have to make sure the Governor and his administration know that we are adamant on this. They're going to be under enormous pressure from the educational unions, complete with almost unlimited political action funds. School boards are going to be scared stiff to make changes. Many teachers will fight almost to the death to keep from changing. After all, we're asking them to step down from the front of the room and start building teams of kids to vie with each other to learn. Lost will be the teacher as the source of all knowledge.

We're going to have to start providing better educational materials and resources. Kids are going to have to have computers and software available. They're going to be depending on satellite programs, on video and audio tapes. Some may even get the notion of inviting in experts to be pumped for information. I'm going to be promoting the idea of weekly or biweekly magazines instead of out-of-date text books.

Are you game for the battle? How about you — have you ever decided you were going to do something and then done it? It's a wonderful feeling — whether it's stopping smoking, dieting, taking a trip you've wanted, or learning something. If you'll help me change New Hampshire's schools, you'll have done more for your kids, your grandchildren, the state, and eventually the country and then other countries, than anything else you'll ever do — or have done.

I've been going to reunions of my old WWII submarine crew. Our sub was #8 in total tonnage sunk, so we have a lot to be proud of. We did a damned good job. We also had some close calls. We were bombed, strafed, and depth charged dozens of times. But that was fifty years ago. Now those kids of 18 are 68 years old and mostly retired. The enormously depressing thing for me has been to talk with them and find that almost none of them have done anything of any significance since our old Navy days. The most important days of their whole lives were during the year or so they were on the USS Drum, SS-228. The Drum is a Portsmouth boat, by the way, and is now a tourist attraction in Battleship Park in Mobile, right next to the Alabama.

If you haven't made your life really count so far, here's an opportunity to do something which will benefit humanity. All you have to do is make up your mind that no amount of politics is going to stop you from getting these changes made in our schools. No teacher's unions, no Democrats or Republicans playing party politics, no bureaucrats, no school administrators are going to stand between you and success. It's probably going to take letters, phone calls, getting groups together, marching, and drawing on every friend you have. Let's let our Representatives know how we feel — our state Senators — the Governor. Let your local school superintendent and principal know. Let your kids know and get them to help. Hey, they have the most to gain of all! Get your local papers into this — your radio stations — and even our New Hampshire TV stations. Don't let this die — there's too much at stake.

I'll do all I can to back you up. I've been writing articles for the newspapers and hoping we can get them printed. The proceeds from those articles and this book will all go 100% to a fund to get New Hampshire moving again and to support the needed educational changes. I'm not asking for donations — not passing the hat. All I'm asking is for you to be excited about this and help make it happen. You'll feel awfully good about yourself if you pitch in and we're able to pull it off as a result.

One more thing. I am not running for any office. I am not available to run for office even if asked. I'm 70 years old now and I have my work cut out for me. I'm also trying to stop a bill now in Congress in Washington which I believe will cost our country tens to hundreds of billions of dollars. Plus I'm working to change the music industry. Those jobs will keep me plenty busy. I'm always happy to help provide creative solutions to problems if anyone needs 'em. Oh yes, if we can re-invent our state government, then it'll be time to tackle that mess in Washington. Yes, I have some creative ideas on that too, but I'm saving that for another book.

218 Better Teachers?

The present system for recruiting teachers leaves a little bit to be desired in some minds. The inescapable fact is that the average-to-bad and bad learner college graduates have tended to become teachers. Now, imagine, if you will, teachers who've been taught by bad learners who've been taught by bad learners for several generations. Talk about natural selection! Yoiks.

Of course we know why this has come about. A combination of lousy pay, the frustrations of trying to work within a really lousy system of bureaucratic administration, being stuck with a terrible teaching system, plus no respect, is not calculated to attract the best and brightest.

Obviously we're going to have to make some major changes if we're going to hope to attract the kind of educators our children should be having. Anything less is cheating them, just as we've been cheated by our parents when they went along with the system we had to endure when we went to school. The wonder isn't that so many kids hated school, the most amazing thing is that there were some who enjoyed it. I don't think I've left any question about my feelings. I hated the whole process from as far back as I can remember.

Okay, if we're going to develop some good educators for our children we've got to come up with good solutions to the problems which are making teaching so frustrating. I've proposed a way to get rid of administrators — just make schools private and thus turn off the seemingly unlimited public funding. I've proposed some major changes in the whole educational system which should go a long way toward helping educators gain a feeling of accomplishment and success from their work. Once private enterprise is at work we'll see some value being placed on the better educators and salaries will start going up. We'll start seeing a demand for excellence.

We might even want to re-examine the need for teacher's colleges. With educators acting more as team leaders and facilitators than as authoritarian dictators and jailers, there may be more emphasis put on a knowledge of their subjects and the practical experience they bring to their students.

Along with re-inventing education in America, we're going to have to re-invent teaching and the role of teachers. This may be as big a change for them as the talkies were to silent film stars. I suspect it'll be as devastating to many teachers as the invention of the transistor was to engineers almost forty years ago, and then the change to digital processing and the microcomputer seventeen years ago. One either accepts the new technology and learns it or one falls by the wayside. Those engineers who failed to accept that education is a lifetime project were passed by. I just wonder how many teachers will be able to adapt. The prospect is not bright, knowing that teachers, on the average, read just one book a year. Perhaps we'll be better off without them.

219 Teachers 2000

If we can bring off the changes I've recommended we're going to see our American kids the best educated in the world. Further, they're going to still have plenty of time for part-time work and travel. I believe most teachers will be helping kids to find resources, not lecturing them. We'll be seeing the widespread use of video tapes, interactive satellite teaching, and combinations of computers, video and interaction which are just beginning to be developed. I believe we'll be seeing mobile laboratories and workshops which go from school to school, making the latest in technology available to all students.

As I've mentioned, it's my hope that we here in New Hampshire will pioneer these new teaching technologies. In that way not only will we be helping our country (and the world), we'll have some new multi-billion dollar businesses in our hands. That'll help provide our kids and their kids with top-notch qualities of life.

Since change is inevitable, the best way to handle it is to be there first and take maximum advantage of the changes. New Hampshire has long been a leader, so let's keep it that way.

220 Schools As Businesses

Since I'm proposing that all schools be privatized, as a way to provide better and less expensive education, the next obvious step is to run them just as we would any other profit-making businesses. With the removal of laws mandating compulsory education, the school business, like any other, is going to have to attract the customers — in this case the children and their parents.

One aspect of sales that even the largest companies have discovered is the need to provide virtually custom-made products, and provide them quickly. Since I hope we agree that every child is different and that the factory approach to cramming education into them, ignoring their differences, has proven a failure in today's world, the schools best able to custom fit their educational product to their customers will attract the most sales.

As with any other new market, I expect we'll be seeing schools opening up along the lines of McDonalds and Burger King, franchised by chains. Well, we have chain restaurants for people who want cheap, but good eats — and we have 'em for people who want a wider menu and are willing to pay more. I really like McDonalds' sausage biscuit with egg breakfast and I love Wendys' salad bar for a light dinner. Translating that into education, I might want to send my kid to one school for some courses and to another for more specialized studies. Just as no one restaurant can provide everything I want to eat every day, so I suspect we're being unreasonable if we expect any one school to be everything to all kids.

One school may be great for computer integrated education. Another may have great physical training equipment. Another might specialize in electronics. With so many diverse needs will we do better to bring the kids to our schools or our schools to the kids? It'll be interesting to see how this develops. I can visualize busing taking on a new meaning as kids are shuttled from one school to another so they can take advantage of specialized facilities. I can also see the development of mobile workshops and labs which can be moved from school to school — as I've mentioned before.

I'm not sure that every school needs a swimming pool or a gym. As with any business, you farm out work that requires specialized equipment. If a school has enough students to keep a pool busy all day every day, fine. If not, its use can be shared with other nearby schools. Ditto wood and metal working shops, photo darkrooms, electronic test shops, inside running tracks, etc.

Schools, like any other business, should have a customer service department. If we find private schools tending to develop as franchises, we'll expect to see the corporate headquarters doing R&D, aimed at developing better courses and systems. Franchising will also help cut costs by making it possible for one central organization to prepare sales videos showing what is covered by courses and pointing out the benefits of taking them. It'll also help bring costs down by allowing some central purchasing of educational materials, equipment and software.

Yes, this will mean an end to local school boards and even state educational administrative departments. But at the same time we'll be seeing far more participation in the educational process by parents and their children. I suspect that they will be more personally involved and the end results better than we've achieved with school boards. Indeed, school boards are probably more part of the problem than part of the solution.

We're already seeing the start of this movement with Whittle preparing to open a whole bunch of new schools. You remember his controversial Channel 1 project. The main objection to his satellite educational programs seems to be the taking away of the class from the teacher for eight minutes — a loss of teacher authority, even if only for minutes. I can see where changing teachers into coaches could generate fierce opposition, no matter how beneficial to the students.

Have you a problem with schools being run as businesses? To me the difference is the same as that between socialism and capitalism. Despite many honest attempts at creating socialist states, none have ever worked as well to promote progress and quality of life as capitalist systems. Our state-run schools — institutions — have failed miserably, so let's try competition.

221 Educating Our Children

With the day of the pre-nuclear family long gone, with fewer and fewer families being able to get by with only one breadwinner, how can we give our kids a decent break in education? With most jobs these days requiring parents to be away from home for at least eight to nine hours—

most of the waking hours for younger children—even if parents knew what best to teach their children, they're not around to do it. This is a situation parents have to recognize and come to grips with.

As I've pointed out, by far the most critical years for children are the earliest. This is when the patterns of a lifetime are established. No amount of remedial work later on is ever going to completely erase a mind-set that is developed in these first few years. This is when the exposure to mind-expanding experiences help their brains to build the neuron circuits which will allow them to cope with language, reading, and other such critical skills. Once this window of opportunity has passed, it's closed forever.

Thus you can see how millions of children are being permanently hobbled mentally by the lack of good early education. Working parents find a nearby day care center and park their babies for nine or ten hours a day. With few exceptions day care centers tend to be just that and little more. They keep the babies and young children in their care fed and dry and as quiet as they can. How many parents have ever spent a whole day at their children's center to see what goes on? One in a hundred? One in a thousand?

Babies need personal attention. They need love. They need someone to read to them. They need to be held. They need toys to attract their attention and involve them. They need to be encouraged and congratulated when they try something new. They need to feel what success feels like. They need to learn how to be adventurous. They need to understand that failure is all part of eventually winning and not to be feared. They need to understand that they are different and that this is good. They need to find out that they can do almost anything they believe they can.

Yes, this is a lot to expect from a day care center. But no day care should provide any less! This is why I've recommended that we enlist the help of retired people, of the elderly from nursing homes, and that mothers start job-sharing so that one can help with day care mornings and the other afternoons. These families will have one and a half pay checks instead of two, but they'll know that their children are getting the best possible start in their lives.

With day care like this I believe we'll be headed toward a country with fewer poor, much less crime, less of a drug problem, and with highly motivated kids, anxious to get all they can from our educational system.

Have you noticed that whenever we can't pay attention to something it seems to fall apart? Well that certainly holds for educating our babies—and our children. We haven't been paying attention. For some reason we seem to feel that even though our government has failed us in almost every other way, at least as far as education is concerned, we can depend on it. Well, it's doing education as poorly as it's handling our banks, the deficit, and almost everything else we see exposed in the news.

Your children are going to get a good education when you pay some attention to them and start trying to change the system which our collective neglect has allowed to strangle our country. It's our educational system which is at the bottom of virtually all of our problems. It's been making the poor poorer. It's been decimating our cities. It's been allowing more and more jobs to be exported.

If our babies had been properly educated we wouldn't have millions on welfare, millions more on unemployment, all watching sitcoms, ball games, game shows and soaps to pass the time as painlessly as possible until death them do part.

Yes, I know that every day at work is important, but if you had a death in the family, could you take off a day? Well, you do have a death in the family—it's your child's death. So take off a day now and then and spend it with your baby at the child-care center and see what's going on. You may want to take another day off and see what's going on in another center, to see if it's better or worse. Then, after seeing what's going on, you may want to quit your job and open a more intelligently run center yourself.

In many centers you're going to see babies and youngsters sedated with television. Hours and hours of TV. Sesame Street, Mr. Rogers. I've already explained why these programs are so disastrous for kids, despite their shelves of awards. If you want to find out more about all this I suggest you read *Endangered Minds* ($11) and *Your Child's Growing Mind* ($10) both by Dr. Healy. The first is from Simon & Schuster, the second from Doubleday. Get 'em, dammit.

If you got a call from the center saying your child was sick, could you spare the time to go help? Well, your child is sick and needs your help. Your child is being permanently crippled, a little bit at a time. Of course you can wait it out and wonder why your child "went bad." What did you do as parents to rate this lazy, rock-music immersed, pot-smoking, beer-drinking teenager? No, *you* created this monster.

With a high percentage of homes fatherless, working mothers have an even greater problem. Fatherless kids tend to do much more poorly than those with two parents. I'm convinced that when we have a generation of better educated kids we'll have fewer divorces and fewer one-parent homes. I think we can credit the increase in divorces to our lousy educational system.

222 Paying For Pre-School

Day care with education instead of baby-farming is going to cost more. It's going to be out of the question for welfare mothers, lower income families, and many single-parent families. So who's going to pay?

Why should someone with no kids have to pay to educate other people's children? Perhaps we should encourage people who can't afford to pay to bring them up not to have children. While that makes sense from a practical standpoint, the idea isn't going to get much support from the religions which promote having babies, whether their people can afford them or not. So let's not try to deal with reason. Let's come to grips with the religious and emotional realities. We're going to have a lot of children who need education that the parents will be unable to afford. We know that the poorest people are having the most babies, so we know the load for supporting an educational program for them is going to rest more on those with fewer children.

Instead of looking at kids as parental property, let's think of them as part of our infrastucture. These kids are just that. They're the work force of the future. They're the people who will have a fundamental affect on our American quality of life in the next century. If we ignore them we'll have more poor and more crime. Crime may make great movies and TV shows, but it sure hurts when it hits you personally. It's in our own interest to invest in their early education.

So should we get started on a massive federal program to set up day care/pre-school centers? Should we invest billions of dollars we have to borrow from Germany and Japan for this? Or should we set up state-run centers? Well, we know that public schools tend to cost about twice as much to run as private schools, so let's not consider federal or state-run institutions. I'm suggesting the use of state-collected money to pay for private centers. The old voucher system.

But who's going to control these centers? Don't we need state accreditation, complete with state inspectors and administrators? Absolutely not! This is a big part of the problem we have today, and not a part of the solution. I would go along with the state setting up an information service, complete with a newsletter for parents. This would inspect the centers and report on them. From there on it'd be up to the parents to take action.

If I were doing it I'd make the whole operation self-funding by charging for advertising in the newsletter, plus charge nominally for subscriptions. Parents unable to afford say $10 a year for a newsletter could read it in their local libraries. What advertisers? How about the toy makers with educational toys? How about children's books? Children's videos and cassettes? Children's clothes? The revenues from these firms could easily support an investigative team to visit centers and report on them.

Are you critical of me for thinking in terms of publications to help solve problems. Publications happen to be one of the best ways of distributing information. Some day we may get more input from electronic publications we read with our laptop and notebook computers, but that's still a dream for most people.

I tend to think in entrepreneurial terms—of making publications at least not lose money. I believe in the fundamentals of capitalism. I believe in making our state governments as capitalistic as we can instead of trying to run them on the old socialistic system. So I tend to want to privatize as much of our federal, state and local government activities as possible. They'll cost us the least that way and we'll tend to get better service.

I admit that the capitalistic system is not working well with Congress. Gore Vidal isn't completely wrong in his estimation that the international megacorporations and big unions with their lobbies have bought our government. This situation could be improved with a publication which would expose which members of Congress have gotten money from which lobbyists, and what legislation has resulted. If we had a publication which informed the public, the media, and potential candidates on these matters, it might act as a deterrent.

I remember when *US News* did an expose on Senator Bentsen, showing what payoffs he'd gotten in return for tax breaks for large corporations. The formula seemed to be about one dollar in his kitty for every thousand in tax breaks he was able to put through for these special interests. Just the kind of guy we need for vice president, right?

The information is public, if you fight hard enough to get it. So let's throw the light of day on these things. I can't think of any advertisers for such a publication, but I'll bet it could easily make a profit just on subscriptions. A couple thousand newspapers who want it, plus who knows how many potential congressmen interested in upsetting incumbents. It should sell well.

It would be interesting to show how much foolish legislation Waxman (Hollywood) has introduced to support the movie and record industry giant corporations. And also how much Gore (Nashville) has proposed for the record industry. As the Washington insiders keep telling us, it's so much worse than you think, that you can't even imagine how bad it is.

The bottom line is that I propose we plan to pay for pre-school education by having our states collect the money and make it available in voucher form for parents. If we manage to keep the state and federal governments out of running or controlling the schools we'll keep our costs to a minimum. I'd like to see the states organize a profit-making information publication for parents as the controlling system.

How we should collect the money for this is another story. I have some ideas on this, but this isn't the best place to go into the details. That's a whole n'other story in itself. Do we want an income tax, property taxes, sales taxes, or what? Each has plusses and minuses. Most tax approaches have aims other than just plain revenue collecting. That'll be an interesting subject to discuss.

223 Keeping School Costs Down

The Chinese and Japanese help keep their school operating costs down by having the students do virtually all of the normal maintenance. Having the students keep the classrooms, halls and cafeteria clean has eliminated any interest in graffiti. Blackburn College has gone a step further, requiring students to work 15 hours a week without pay at an assigned campus job. This has enabled the college to keep its tuition remarkably low. The students not only handle the routine maintenance, they also run the bookstore and snack bar, and do actual construction work. The indoor swimming pool was built by the students.

Building construction and running businesses provide superb practical experience for students. The resulting lower tuition costs help attract students from lower income families. The next step in logical thinking would be to have students take over more and more of the administrative responsibilities for running schools — at least for high school and college-aged students.

Taking this concept one step further we can envision students helping teachers for lower grades, again more as coaches than as lecturers. In my businesses I stress the concept that people, as much as possible, should do work that they are uniquely qualified to do and to seek lower cost help for work which doesn't really require their skills. If we apply this concept to teachers we'll be able to substitute student help for much of the administrative and overseeing work which reduces their productivity.

One more step in reasoning has students seeking outside part-time work, all as part of their educational experience and as a way to help pay for their education. This is going to call for some serious battles to change minimum wage laws, which undoubtedly will be vigorously fought by the unions. I have many areas where students could earn and learn in my company. This would benefit them as practical learning experiences and would help keep my costs down, allowing my business to grow faster.

If we accept that there are a limited number of jobs to be done and that allowing lower-paid and lower-skilled workers to come in might thus tend to put higher-skilled workers out of work reminds me of the situation I found in my trip to India. Unemployment was so serious that work responsibilities were carefully divided so as to provide little jobs for the most people. One man's responsibility was to collect shoes from outside hotel room doors and polish them. Another brought the morning tea. Another cleaned bathrooms. Another made beds.

I don't believe we need to subscribe to the make-work concept here in America. The more we get across the concept that success in life depends on skills and knowledge, the more competitive America will be with the other countries. By protecting jobs and encouraging people to believe that it's possible to make money without having to develop their skills, we're doing both us and our country harm.

It looks to me that we could eliminate a large part of our unemployment problem in America if the states would set up data bases which would help businesses find needed workers — and workers find the jobs best suited to their skills. Germany long ago went this route. The next obvious step is to provide education to help people build more skills, no matter their age — as I've already proposed earlier. If we inculcate the idea that education is a life-long process when kids are young, we'll have a stronger country and happier people. We also will see the poor moving into middle class. There is no need for a poor class in America. We don't have work for them or even places to live — so let's change the system that has perpetuated this misery.

A few schools have their students work for non-profit organizations such as libraries, nursery homes, hospitals, and day care centers. All excellent experience for them.

224 The Main School Problem

It's interesting to read the almost endless magazine articles discussing our educational problems. For instance, in the Nov. 25, 1991 *Forbes* (p.180), the governor of Wisconsin said, "Every education reform we've ever had has just put more money in the school administrator's pockets." John Chubb of the Brookings Institute said, "..the current bureaucratic system does everything it can to take autonomy away from individual schools."

The article points out that "only about 30 cents of every dollar spent on K-12 public schooling in New York and Milwaukee actually makes it to the classroom, to pay for teachers, textbooks and computers. The number of classroom teachers has grown more than 75% over the last 30 years even though enrollments have grown only 11%. What's more, the number of central administrators has increased more than 140%, and the general support staff has gone up almost 250%. New York City spends, on average, $7,000 a year per student.

Fortune, Oct. 21, 1991, "For all the public optimism and enthusiasm of *Fortune's* educational summit, a number of executives privately expressed a deepening gloom over the willingness of the educational establishment to embrace new ideas." Xerox's ex-boss, David Kearns, now the Deputy Secretary of Education, said, "Think of the Pony Express. To improve it, people tried to make the horses run faster and have stations closer together. Meanwhile other folks were talking about the telegraph. We need to get people to stop looking for a faster horse and start inventing the telegraph."

Jo Ann Seker, head of the Concerned Educators Against Forced Unionism says, "I really believe that the trade union mentality that has come over the teaching profession in the past 25 years is what's gone wrong with education." The bigest trade union in the country is the 1.6-million-member National Education Association. The National Federation of Teachers has 780,000 members. Is it just a coincidence that college board scores began to drop when teachers started unionizing? An article in the Dec. 9, 1991 *Forbes* suggests not, making a compelling case.

225 Taking Back Education

I have an idea that you're going to hate if you are thoroughly inculcated with the idea that the government should be running our educational institutions. I can't help it, there's just very few aspects of socialism that I find attractive, so I tend to look for alternatives.

There's a good deal of pressure to respond to our American educational system turning out poorly educated kids by getting the government to force changes. I feel that it's the government which is the main problem, not our route to salvation. So I have come up with a plan which will allow us, the people, to take back education and run it ourselves, without the usual bureaucrats and administration overhead. You probably are not going to like it.

In addition to our educational system not working at all well, we also have a number of other serious problems. There's the cost, which has escalated beyond reason, all the while giving us a poorer product. But, hey, we're used to that, we've been having the same thing with our health care results — another area where the government is in there up to their neck in wasting our money. But we may get a little irritated when we find out how much more we're paying for a third rate education as compared to what other countries are paying for a far better product.

For instance, with education being financed by school districts instead of by the states or nationally, we see poor areas providing lousy schools and rich areas able to provide far better facilities. We're not sure we really want to see that every child in America gets equal schools — after all, why work harder than others and make more money if you can't provide better education and health care for your family? But still, I think we can agree that the pie could be more evenly split than it is right now.

If we follow through with my suggestions for change we'll see school costs reduced substantially, allowing us to have better facilities, better teachers, more modern equipment and labs, and still have lower taxes.

While I'm not ready to recommend we ask the federal government to tax us and make the money available as vouchers, I do think we would all get a better shake than we're getting now if we moved from a local funding system to state funding. This would give the poorer schools a better chance to upgrade.

This would also tend to encourage state governments to set up more and more laws governing and controlling our schools. I'd like to suggest an alternative. I don't want to encourage the build-up of the usual administrative bureaucracies, so outside of collecting the money and putting it into vouchers for parents and their children to spend, let's keep the states out of this. I prefer turning this whole matter over to the people.

Okay, here's my idea. I'd like to see each local school board field delegates to an annual or bi-annual state conference on education. The changes in rules for the schools would be proposed before conference and the delegates would break into committees to discuss and recommend action on each proposal to the group as a whole (the plenipotentiary), having been instructed via meetings with their local school boards. The group would then vote yea or nay, with the rules thus established being honored by the schools in the state.

These conferences could be followed by national conferences, perhaps every two to four years, with perhaps ten or so delegates per state attending. Their agenda would be set by the proposed rule changes requested by the state conferences. Again committees would be set up to discuss and recommend action by the whole group.

226 Like The UN

Can such a system work without going through the usual political process of making laws? I think it's worth considering. My role model for the concept is the UN, where member countries get together to discuss rules and vote on them. As a delegate representing America at an International Telecommunications Union (ITU) conference in Geneva, I saw this system at work first hand. It works because the countries involved agree to make it work, not because of laws, police, lawyers, courts and prisons.

But can we trust Americans to protect the interests of everyone? Won't we see greed and self-interest run amok as we have with our blessed Congress? I don't think so. Remember, these delegates aren't paid—other than their expenses being covered by local school boards — so there's none of the usual expensive campaigning and running for office. This is what's screwed up Congress so badly. Also, I've watched similar groups at work and they've always leaned over backwards to protect special interest groups which may not even be represented.

For instance, radio amateurs have formed volunteer state repeater coordinating committees to keep repeater groups from getting into wars with each other over frequencies. Repeaters, in case you've forgotten, are automatic relay stations set up on mountain tops, tall buildings and towers to extend very high frequency radio communications. It was the ham radio pioneering of this technology that made cellular telephones possible.

These repeater coordinating committees could easily have ignored the frequency spectrum needs of small groups interested in bouncing their radio signals off the moon, from passing meteors or relayed back from any of the several amateur radio satellites. But they haven't. They've gone out of their way to make sure that even the smallest special interest group gets a share of precious spectrum. I think we'll find the same generosity when it comes to dealing with education and schools. Sure, we have some terrible scoundrels, but we don't tend to let them prevail. And today, with communications cheaper and faster than ever, villainy won't have much of a chance at winning for long.

I'm in favor of getting the federal government out of education as much as we possibly can. We don't need their money or the strings (hawsers, actually) attached. And let's also get our state governments out of education.

Well, golly, we have to have accreditation, don't we? We have to set standards and make sure our schools are meeting them, right? That concept is so thoroughly accepted I may not even be able to get you to consider, even for a moment, any alternative. That's the insidiousness of socialism when it's taught from year one.

227 Choice, Not Mandate!

Look, we buy homes, cars, and food by deciding what we think is best. Most of us check movie and record reviews before we buy. I'd like to see schools rated like any other product or service with something like *Consumer Reports* evaluating them. I read the skin diving publications to find out which diving resorts are best. They tell me how the diving is, what kind of fish I'll find, how clear the water is, how good the guides and boats are, how much it's all going to cost, what kind of food I'll find, rooms, and so on. So why not similar reports on schools to help parents and their kids figure out where best to invest their vouchers?

Of course, my long-range scheme is to make it so kids can take some courses via satellite video either at home or in school, others via video tapes, some in well-equipped labs, some in one school, others in other schools, and so on. With ten five-week terms it wouldn't be a big deal to move from school to school, taking advantage of school specialties. Some kids might even want to start a few college level courses when they are young, because they're interested. After a while we might find all ages in some classes, driven by their interest instead of a standardized curriculum to which all must adhere. And that's all ages, including adults.

I see the day when youngsters and their parents work together to help children follow their interests and build skills and information resources. When that comes we aren't going to need any certificates or graduation exercises. The graduation into working will be gradual, with work needs and interests guiding the building of skills.

How do we get from our 19th Century factory model schools to this utopian dream of the future? Well, it isn't going to just happen. If you like the concepts you're going to have to fight for them. In the past we Americans fought wars for progress. Think of this as another war, with the winners being our kids and the losers being millions of bureaucratic wasters of your tax money. You can organize and slowly defeat the bureaucrats, but it's going to be a tough uphill battle. They won't give up easily and they're fighting you with almost unlimited amounts of your money! Yes, I'm preaching revolution. Are you game to try and get all these people out of the public trough and into working for a living to produce a product or service?

228 Capitalism Vs. Communism

Maybe you noticed that capitalism won out against communism. I see democracy trying to take the credit, but democracy wasn't the winner, it was capitalism. Capitalism gives us all the right to vote for products and services we want — with money. No bureaucrat should be able to tell us what we have to buy or how much to pay. Well, now that capitalism has won in the USSR and Eastern Europe, let's give it a chance in America. Privatizing our schools and letting parents and their children decide what they prefer to learn is the capitalistic approach. The hand of Adam Smith has not lost its touch in the last two hundred years. His "Wealth of Nations" is still a good read.

Many of us check restaurant reviews before we go out to eat. We read travel books to see where we want to vacation. We read brochures, talk with friends and so on. That's capitalism.

Democracy might even work in Washington if we'd try my suggestions and go back to citizen legislators. We might want to cut back — say 90% — on the number of assistants. There are over 80,000 of 'em assisting Congress. Baloney! Without PAC and special interest re-election funds our election process sure would change. And with better information sources we might be able to make better choices when we vote. I think that'll come when we improve our educational system.

Is all this anything worth fighting for? Or is today's baseball game more important? The world you leave to your children is what you're making of it. If you shrug off the responsibility, that'll leave the way open for the rascals to have their way, so don't beef when you see them winning.

229 Where's Everyone Else?

Since this book has been assembled from dozens of short reports there's some redundancy and overlap. There's also been some progression in my ideas as I've heard testimony from experts, and waded through stacks of reports from other commissions, committees, and assorted NH state departments. Plus I've been reading as many pertinent books as I could find.

The main change in my thinking has had to do with freeing youngsters from fixed school curricula, with no state or federal mandated requirements. Yes, kids should learn to read if they're going to work. I now favor this being their option, but without any socialistic safety net paid for by everyone else. I'd like to see the current concept of "entitlements" erased from our bureaucratic dictionary.

I'm not in favor of artificially high wages for unskilled work, such as employee unions in some states have managed. Kids should be made aware in pre-school that their future quality of life is going to depend largely on their education. If they decide not to be educated they are opting for a poor life-style.

I've tried to keep my report as brief as I could . . . getting across my ideas, but not beating them to death with details. I didn't want this to turn into a thousand-page book, as it could have if I'd tried to answer every possible objection up front.

I want to thank the people who've helped me with this project. There's Jim Kendrick, who manages all my businesses. I'm the visionary and conceiver of endless new projects . . . he makes 'em work. Jim, Stu Norwood, Hope Currier and David Cassidy took my lap top-written material and put it in page form on our Macintosh desktop publishing equipment.

Now, with a little time, a few more enthusiastic employees wanting to learn, and some venture capital, I'll start as many of the initiatives I've outlined in this book as I can. I believe that New Hampshire CAN be #1 again and I want to prove it.

230 Proposed Educational Initiatives

(1) Initiate for-profit evening classes in small business subjects for adults and high school graduates entering the work force as a way to help the currently unemployed build the skills needed to work for or start small businesses.

(2) From pre-school onward initiate cooperative learning with stu-

dents working in groups of four and thus vying against other student groups instead of it being each student vs the teacher. This is primarily peer teaching.

(3) Initiate a cost-free peer taught eight-year course in the fundamentals of electronics, communications and computers, starting with grade 5.

(4) Initiate a 50-week school year, divided into ten five-week terms. Lengthen the school day.

(5) Combine day care with pre-school education so as to have all children ready for primary school.

(6) Establish core educational requirements for all students.

(7) Allow secondary school students to opt for career paths to college, junior college, or any of an assortment of vocational choices when it comes to elective courses.

(8) Allow students to progress at their own speed instead of regimenting them by age. This will allow brighter and more motivated students to progress faster, but still enable lower IQ and disadvantaged students to succeed, even if it takes them longer.

(9) Eliminate rote memorization as much as possible and substitute the teaching of concepts. Make education fun and exciting.

(10) Initiate for-profit video courses to help mothers with prenatal, infant education, pre-school, and on through primary and secondary schools.

(11) Initiate a for-profit educational research publication to give New Hampshire an edge in the field.

(12) Plan a year-2000 no-tuition for-profit polytechnical university to accommodate the thousands of high-tech career oriented graduates from our secondary schools. This will help New Hampshire have the best possible high-tech work force.

Chapter IX

231 Recapturing Consumer Electronics

We're so far down the pit in the consumer electronics industries that we can't even see the rainbow at the end of the tunnel. I've been deeply involved with electronics ever since some angel (or was it The Devil) gave me a box of old radio parts one Sunday in church when I was 14. I found a circuit using some of those parts to build a radio in a cigar box in *Popular Mechanics*. That rotten little radio actually worked, changing my life forever.

Today America has lost its consumer electronics industry. At the giant Consumer Electronic Shows held in winter in Las Vegas and in summer in Chicago, we see huge exhibits by hundreds of Japanese companies, showing their new products. These are shown primarily to chain and department store buyers.

Oh, there are a few American firms, but they're mostly small and making niche products. Having published electronics magazines for forty years now, I've sadly watched the gradual loss of the industry.

How bad is it? And what can we do about it? Well, we can get the industry back, but it's going to take some long-range planning and determination. I'm not sure America is up to it.

To build electronics equipment you need technicians, engineers and scientists for starters. Well, we stopped trying to produce them 30 years ago. Then we need parts. I hope that's obvious. Without circuit boards, capacitors, resistors, inductors, relays, and so on you can't design or build much. We stopped making parts when manufacturing moved to Asia about twenty years ago.

To make parts you need machines. specialized machines. You guessed it . . . we stopped making those too, so if we want to make resistors we're going to have to import the machines from Japan. We don't even make the machine tools it takes to make the machines to make parts.

That's a formidable bunch of hurdles. But hurdles are built to be hurdled, so if we decide it's important to regain our consumer electronics industries, we can do it. But we're looking at a twenty-year project. I'm not sure how we're going to sell a twenty-year vision to corporations geared to quarterly reports . . . or to politicians who are running for re-election every minute between elections.

You may remember how quickly the steam went out of the angry Congressional cries over Toshiba selling military secrets to the Russians.

We had a quick TV bite of a Toshiba boombox being axed and threats of boycotting Toshiba products in retaliation.

The phones were ringing in the Senate and House Office Buildings the next morning. Without Toshiba parts construction would stop on cars, planes, rockets, and so on. Military plants would have to shut down. Detroit would too. As would all our aircraft plants.

We do have a few electronic parts still being made in America, but they're mostly used in military equipment, where paying ten to a thousand times as much when an identical part is part of the procurement contract process.

232 What's Our First Step?

We're graduating fewer electronic engineers today than we did 30 years ago, so we need to do whatever it takes to start rebuilding our engineering and scientific strengths. Indeed, what few engineers we have been graduating have tended to go into military R&D, where the big money has been. This has left almost no talented engineers for consumer R&D.

As a member of the RPI Council I can tell you that Rensselaer is hurting badly for new engineering students. Our engineering colleges have been graduating higher and higher percentages of foreign students because they've had so few American students applying. We've been educating our competition.

With about 7% of today's high school graduates even marginally equipped to cope with an engineering college, we've got to start from the beginning. We've got to get kids interested in high-tech careers early on and keep their interest high so they'll want to be engineers and scientists because they enjoy that kind of work more than anything else.

I know what that feels like. Once I got hooked with that little cigar box radio, I was a gonner. I joined my high school radio club and started on a lifetime of self-education, electronic circuit building and experimenting.

When WWII came along, I first learned of the Pearl Harbor attack from a chap I was talking with on my ham radio set. Within a year I'd joined the Navy as a Radio Technician 3/c, just by virtue of my amateur radio license. Nine months later I graduated as an Electronic Technician's Mate 2/c from the Radio Materiel School on Treasure Island in San Francisco. A few weeks later I reported aboard the USS Drum SS-228, where I was in charge of all of the submarine's radio, radar, and sonar electronics. I saw plenty of action during my five war patrols and we ended up being one of the top ten submarines in tonnage sunk.

Now what can we do to get youngsters interested in electronics? I suggest we start with fifth graders, since by then their minds are well enough developed to understand the technology. It's probably a bummer for older people, who are daunted by the clock on their VCR, to know that kids of ten and eleven can easily understand what's going on in digital computers and radios.

Heck, we've got seven-year-old amateurs who'd gotten our highest grade license! And yes, we even have girls that age with Extra Class licenses.

Since America is so pathetically far behind in generating electronic engineers, technicians and scientists, we've got to play catch-up. We don't need just a few more engineers, we need tons of 'em. If we're going to provide enough engineers to rebuild our consumer electronics industry, we're going to need hundreds of thousands.

Once we're able to get small electronics firms going they're going to need to invest heavily in R&D. One thing we know about electronics, it's an incredibly fast moving field. You either bring out a new, improved product at least once a year or you're dead.

I think I mentioned visiting an American manufacturer of radios where I found one old-timer sitting there designing their next model. I compared that in my mind with my visits to Japanese radio manufacturers where I met dozens of young engineers, all equipped with the latest test equipment available.

To get our kids excited about electronics I've proposed an eight year course, starting in the fifth grade. We want to make this so much fun they get personally involved. We need to get every kid excited . . . boys and girls. I believe we can do this. I believe we can do this almost immediately, without having to take ten years to train teachers.

I've already described my approach to this (060), complete with the need for a new kind of college which will take the kids the next step . . . and will give us an enormous advantage over the Japanese (and European) schools (068).

Okay, let's say that by some miracle we're able to overcome the well-funded and limitless objections of the educational establishment and their unions and start graduating the engineers we need (109). What then?

Well, we need to start small, building our strength through niche marketing. We need to select a few new electronic technologies and specialize. Two new fields which we know are coming are high definition television and digital audio broadcasting. Both of these are going to grow into multi-billion dollar industries.

We have a good chance at HDTV because the Japanese, who are years ahead of us in this, have concentrated their developments on an old technology . . . analog. The FCC has made it clear that they're going to hold out for digital HDTV standards. If we get started soon, we'll be able to use this edge to build a niche.

Digital audio broadcasting, as I've mentioned, is being developed in Europe. It's still in its early stages, so we have another golden opportunity.

Since we don't seem to be able to get any significant support from the federal government for an industrial policy which would encourage American firms to develop HDTV or DAB, perhaps we could do something in New Hampshire. Should we try to set some goals or will we do better to just leave everything to chance and hope for the best? That's like trying to start or run a business with no plans. Somehow I find that the more I plan, the luckier I get.

As more and more of our electronics are being printed onto little chips, the need for parts is gradually dropping. A whole room full of six-foot racks of equipment with thousands of tubes has been compressed onto a quarter-inch square chip and is sitting in my laptop computer. I have an all-band synthesized radio that's half the size of a double-CD jewel box.

We still have some integrated circuit manufacturers in America, so we're not without strong resources. We could, if we planned, recover our radio and television manufacturing industries via these two new technologies.

What's next? Shirt pocket digital personal two-way radios (also known as cellular telephones) . . . probably including a pager and even a tiny message readout in lieu of fax. Can you imagine a world without telephone tag and answering machines?

I've given the Commission everything it needs in this report to implement the future, both for New Hampshire and America. It's up to the Commissioners whether anything gets done about it. It's there. It's possible. Everything I've described is going to happen . . . but will it be here in New Hampshire or somewhere else?

233 Black, White And Gray

We've always had racial problems in America. In the early days we solved our problems by wiping out most of the Indians. That was the Darwinian approach. Today we're a softer, gentler nation, to recoin a phrase.

Well, some of us are kinder and gentler. If you watch TV, go to the movies or read the papers you know that distressingly large segments of our population don't really qualify in the K and G departments. I'm not only writing about our criminals and the police, but also the religious groups that are willing to kill for their beliefs . . . such as those closing down abortion clinics. And let's not forget the union groups willing to do almost anything to protect their interests, and that includes beating people and burning homes and cars. Kinder and gentler?

I suppose you didn't bother to watch the movie "Skokie" on TV. This was about what happened when the American Nazi party announced they would march in Skokie (IL), a city with a large Jewish population. For the ACLU it was a test of the First Ammendment. For the Jews it was an incitement to kill.

No, I'm not condoning mass murder, even though from a philosophical view it would come under the heading of a Darwinian survival of the fittest heading. I do get annoyed at selective anger over mass murders. I can understand the anger at the Chinese leaders for the massacre of all those students. I get a bit put out when I see our liberal media making a big deal out of this, but then ignoring the student massacre in Burma. How angry have we gotten over Stalin killing tens of millions? And Mao killing millions of Chinese? We managed to ignore those massive exterminations pretty well.

We're also rather sanguine about the mass murders in Portuguese Timor, in Sri Lanka, Liberia, Nigeria, Cambodia, Laos, and so on. Yes, we did manage to get partially upset over the Russian decimation of the Afghans. And we've almost gotten upset over the death squads in several Central American countries . . . in Argentina and Chile. We're not sure how angry we are over the murder of Haitians and Cubans.

Hitler wiped out about six million Jews, a fact of which we are reminded fairly regularly. He also wiped out about seven million non-Jews, which I don't recall as much complaining about. You know, Gypsies and other undesirables.

Now we're watching the Croats and the Serbs kill each other. Then there are the Armenians at the throats of the Azerbaijanis.

Meanwhile, here in America we have our own race problems between blacks, whites and Hispanics. Of course, as I've mentioned, in the long run . . . it may take hundreds of years, but eventually we'll all be intermarried and all be a tan color. That seems inevitable.

Since we have our racial problems right now, the fact that they'll smooth out in a few hundred years doesn't make things any better. We need to honestly face our present problems and come up with some practical solutions to them.

234 The Real Racial Problem

When *Insight* was started several years ago it was a first class magazine. It was unbiased and covered a number of subjects of current interest in depth. It was unlike *Newsweek, Time,* and *U.S. News* in that it didn't try to cover all the news.

Then, recently it changed. It became more like *People* and aimed at a lower income reader. No, let me be blunt and not use the euphemism . . . it went for a lower intelligence audience as a way to increase readership.

Instead of reading it I found myself just having to skim through quickly, my highlighter seldom needed.

That was until the January 13, 1992 issue. Suddenly my highlighter was busy on page after page. The main topic in this issue was the difference in IQ between blacks and whites. This isn't by any means a new subject, it's just that the emotional backlash to it has been so hysterical that the facts have been fairly well obscured.

Researchers in the IQ vs. race field have been so vilified that few people have dared to continue this work. Why is this so emotional, particularly with blacks? If we're going to get our country back into shape to fight a global business battle, we've got to stop blinding ourselves to facts we don't like and come to grips with reality.

The fact is that there is a serious difference in the IQs of blacks, Hispanics and whites. In each group the IQs form a bell-shaped curve. We've established an IQ of 100 as the average for whites. On that basis blacks are centered on 85 and Hispanics on 90. Yes, I know all about the tests being claimed to be culturally biased. Well, that's been completely refuted. Using the same tests we find that the Japanese IQ centers on 110. Yep, as a group they're smarter than our whites.

When I started visiting Africa 25 years ago, I quickly saw for myself the difference. In Kenya I saw blacks who had been waiting on tables in the top restaurants for years still unable to understand any English. I found I had to learn Swahili if I wanted to ask for bread, a knife or a spoon.

When I talked with white teachers at the University of Nairobi I discovered that they were forced to graduate black students who were unable to read and write. When I went to the main post office in Nairobi and bought five seven shilling stamps a group of four black postal clerks were unable to decide for sure how much the total should be. They had to ask an Indian clerk.

I have run into some highly intelligent blacks from Ghana and Nigeria, so if it ever becomes possible to do more IQ research in Africa, I believe they'll find that IQs vary considerably from tribe to tribe.

These differences in IQ explain a lot of our problems in America. We're trying to put children with IQs from the 60s on up to around 200 all through the same mill. This means that the lower IQ children are going to fail and keep failing . . . but not before dragging down everyone else. Our schools try to match their curriculum to the lowest common denominator, not the middle.

We have this baloney we try to sell about everyone being created equal. Well, we aren't. We're created unequal in many ways . . . in sex, height, weight, beauty, intelligence, and so on. We're all different in many ways, and that includes IQ.

Now let me quote a bit from *Insight.* "The reason such groups as the Association of Black Psychologists, the National Association for the Advancement of Colored People and the National Education Association oppose IQ testing for blacks, and indeed all forms of standardized testing for anyone, is that blacks on average score significantly lower on the tests than whites — so significantly that four times as many blacks as whites qualify as borderline mentally retarded or lower as a proportion of their respective populations. Futhermore, the test scores of fully half of all blacks indicate a mental capacity to perform, at best, skilled blue-collar jobs that require no 'book learning' as part of training, jobs that were plentiful, say, 50 years ago, but are dwindling in a globalized U.S. economy that has exported much of its manufacturing assembly work. By contrast, only 16% of whites score that low."

"The different middle points for the two bell curves explain why few blacks — only 3% — score above 115. This is the figure that IQ experts cite as the minimum level for entering a learned profession, and these are the results they use to explain why many blacks lag in school."

All is not bleak for blacks. "Intelligence does not account for every human talent. Athletic ability, musical talent, creativity, memory and people skills have little to do with intelligence; even borderline retarded people can play in orchestras."

This explains why colleges have been having such a difficult time finding black teachers and students. There was a call for affirmative action for more black philosophy professors when they found that only 1% of them were black. When they checked the IQs of the professors they decided that this was about right. Only 1% as many blacks have the required IQ as whites.

So are the rednecks right, are whites better than blacks? What does "better" mean" We're all different. I have a very high IQ, so does that make me better than anyone with a lower IQ? No, just different. Yes, I'm better at some things, and a whole lot worse at others.

I tend to think of having a high IQ being a lot like having a bigger computer. That's fine, but a computer is no better than its programming or the data it has to draw upon. You need all three elements. The fastest computer made can't do anything without software. And the best computer with superb software is helpless without data.

235 How Mensa Started

Back in early 1960 I read about a high IQ society which had been formed in England. I sent for an application and the next thing I knew I'd passed the test and was a member. A few weeks later I got a call from another member suggesting we get together. Four of us met at his apartment, talked it over, and decided to form an American Mensa Chapter. Being a writer and publisher, I became the secretary and we met at my house for the next few meetings.

We publicized it and the membership grew. A year later I moved to New Hampshire and became the local secretary here. I was a bit dismayed many years later when I mentioned in an editorial that I was a founder of American Mensa to find that the chap who'd called me now claimed to be the founder. Perhaps he forgot there were four of us there that night when we agreed to form an American chapter.

As a member of Mensa I've met and known hundreds of high IQ people. Some of them are brilliant, some are impressively stupid. It's in the programming and data. It's always fascinated me that so few Mensa members are successful in business. Few seem able to make much money, or even to be successful in other accomplishments. Indeed, there seems little correlation between IQ and success in life, at least in the above average IQ ranges.

There are very measurable correlations between educability and IQ. And there are positive correlations between education and earning power. We also know that the college track seems to be a waste of time for those with an IQ much below 115.

236 Nature Vs. Nurture

We've had arguments for decades on how much a person's IQ is determined by genes and how much by later programming. Research with separated identical twins has pretty much quieted the nurture group. Good programming can make a difference . . . probably on the order of 20% plus or minus. That's enough of a difference to make it worthwhile to encourage families to provide the best programming possible.

If we can take a 90 IQ person and boost that to 108, we'll have made a substantial change in the potential for that person. From that aspect I'm very much in favor of developing educational aids for parents to help them give their kids the best possible start right from birth. From well before birth, for that matter.

237 The Peace Dividend

With the collapse of the USSR our country is going to have to reinvent its defense policy. This, in turn, will mean a reinventing of our defense industries.

The current cutback in military procurement has substantially contributed to the current recession in New Hampshire. The normal reaction to this disaster is to avoid getting involved with military contracts in the future. Perhaps the normal reaction is not the best response. Indeed, there may be an opportunity for New Hampshire just because this is the normal response.

Before WWII we called it the War Department. We weren't into euphemisms as much in those days. Then we renamed it the Defense Department. That's much less threatening. I don't think we cut back on our offensive weapons systems, we just wanted to put a better face on our activities. I was kind of surprised when our 1960s flower children movement didn't change the name to the Peace Department.

Between our invasions of Granada, Panama, Kuwait, and Iraq, we seem to be very serious about this peace business. If we're going to take on the role of a world peace-keeper, we're going to need a strong Peace Department, armed with the latest weapons and communications technology.

I'm not being entirely facetious about this. We know now that we came within months . . . perhaps even weeks . . . of having Iraq armed with a nuke which could have been delivered to Manhattan or Tel Aviv. We don't know how close we are to a similar situation with Iran, Libya, Pakistan and points east. We do know that France, Israel, India, and China have nukes, so we should not upset them too much.

So the Cold War is over and our military establishment is going to have to come to grips with the resulting realities. They're going to have to decide what kind of weapons systems and what level of staffing they'll need to cope with the world's potential trouble spots.

It seems unlikely that we're going to be needing battleships any more. And we're unlikely to need many submarines. Those are more for fighting large scale wars. Perhaps, with the resulting downsizing of the Navy it'll finally be possible to integrate the Army and Navy into one unified arm.

238 Cutting The Military Budget

No sooner had the USSR come apart than we started hearing politicians anxious to cut the military budget. Well, without the threat of communism, why not slice the heck out of the budget? We don't need all those military bases. We don't need all those thousands of troops around the world. We don't need to bankrupt ourselves building incredibly expensive bombers.

As I've pointed out, the cost of making planes has been going up by powers of ten, with their reliability going down on about the same curve.

Several times in the past our politicians have celebrated winning wars by hastily dismantling our military supply industry and demobilizing our armed forces. Some of the Congressional voices seem to be singing this same song again. Bad news.

We do need to come to grips with the world as we see it changing over the next few years. We need to decide what role America should best play. Then we need to decide what weapons systems we'll need to fulfill this role. What size military will we need?

The next step is to make sure that we are able to maintain our armed forces at the strength we're going to need. We aren't going to have a year or two to re-establish military supply businesses. We know we're going to have to be able to react quickly to emergencies. This means that our military suppliers will have to be kept in business, even if it costs us extra to do this.

We're well aware that it was smart weapons which kept our losses so low in the Gulf War. That means we will have to keep ahead of the world in R&D in electronics, computers, and communications systems.

But can we hope to do this with our loss of our consumer electronics industry and our dwindling supply of engineers and scientists? Of course, if we can be absolutely sure that Japan will be an ally in any future action, we can depend on them to do our R&D for us on contract. And we can contract out our smart weapons systems to be made in Japan. In return, we can sell them more of our music, movie, hotel, and other industries.

I'm more in favor of putting money into rebuilding our electronic industries. I'm in favor of making what changes it takes to attract youngsters to our high-tech industries as engineers and scientists.

It seems to me that a military planning think tank should be able to come up with a plan to reduce our overseas bases and build up smaller, mobile teams which could be deployed in hours to trouble spots just about anywhere.

So where does New Hampshire fit into all this? Well, one thing we know, if our defense suppliers are going to be ready when needed, they're going to have to be kept in business on a regular basis. I've already explained how New Hampshire could cut educational expenses and come out of it with a well-educated, enthusiastic high-tech work force. The only other thing we need to do is figure out what industries are going to be needed to provide the weapons and communications of the future and see that these are right here in New Hampshire. Yes, it'll take some planning. Is that really beyond us?

I've isolated an industry that is going to be needed and should remain well-funded for decades to come. If we plan and follow through, we'll be there first with the most. And this isn't any small potatoes. We're talking tens of billions a year, which is well-worth a good deal of planning and conniving.

We're also talking spin-off technology which we'd sure like to have centered here in New Hampshire. If this is where the engineers are, this is where the spin-off companies are likely to be too.

Without a high-tech educated work force we'll have little as a state to offer. The defense industries of the next few decades are going to be heavily into R&D and light on production. Are they going to have to bring in Japanese engineers and technicians? If so, they'll probably settle in California in Silicon Valley, which is 3,000 miles closer to home, and never mind our wonderful New Hampshire quality of life. No, we have to grow our own engineers, not import them.

239 Racism

This is a real tough subject to write about. It's emotionally charged. It's an epithet which is used to tar people and for which there is no answer.

There's no way to grow up without being exposed to racist comments, often from parents and other role models. Plus, unless you're particularly isolated, you'll also notice that different groups of people do have some common characteristics. Different groups of people really are different, and thus form stereotypes.

Having lived in Brooklyn (NY) for thirty years, off and on, and having gone to school there from 12 years of age on, I grew up in a predominantly Jewish and Catholic middle-class neighborhood. These were my friends.

My father was a Jew and Catholic hater. If we'd had any blacks around, he'd have hated them too. Well, perhaps "hate" is too strong a word. He did not speak kindly of these groups. But then he didn't have much of an influence over me. He set up fear and hostility barriers early on which prevented us from ever being able to talk or share a pleasant father-son relationship. He was a firm believer in using terror to get respect. So I feared him, but I didn't respect him.

I don't recall any racist antipathies while I was in school. I recall no anti-Jew, anti-Catholic, or even anti-black comments. We did have a couple blacks in school with us, but they were just plain kids to us, like everyone else. We just didn't think negatively in terms of race at all.

Oh, we knew that racial groups were different. But we also knew that just because there were racial characteristics, that didn't mean that everyone fitted the pattern. Being kids together and visiting each other's homes, we could see differences.

For instance, I noticed early on that many of my Jewish friends tended to be abusive. And when I finally got mad and called them names they liked it. I gradually discovered that this was the pattern at home for them. Their mothers in particular tended to insult them, so insults for them were an expression of love. When I got mad and yelled at them, they responded with friendship.

You know, that's not a bad response to inculcate. It sure keeps down the escalation of fights. But it takes some getting used to when your culture has taught you that harsh words mean you should get mad. It's difficult to accept that when someone angrily calls you a dirty, rotten bastard that he is saying he likes you.

Blacks have been crying "racism" so often that it's like the boy yelling "wolf." Yes, there are stereotypes and no, they don't always hold. Not all blacks are . . . shall I make a list? But until the millenium when we're all intermarried and there are no more separate races, we're going to have clashes between cultures.

240 Entrepreneur At Work

One of the reason's I'm an itch about getting classes started to help our unemployed learn more about small business is the endless opportunities there are for starting new businesses. But unless people have some education and start thinking in these terms, we're going to see growing unemployment lines.

When I talk with people about their problems I find there are all sorts of great opportunites which have never occurred to them. Of course, they're bogged down by the shock of what's happened, so it's difficult for them to brainstorm creative ideas out of their fix. The anger, panic, frustration and weight, of trying to cope with the state bureaucrats is enough to put anyone into a mental paralysis.

Perhaps we could get together some groups of entrepreneurs to help come up with creative solutions for people. This was an approach I got the New Hampshire High-Tech Council to implement as a way to help entrepreneurs with problems. These sessions worked very well.

One thing about most entrepreneurs, if you need help, they'll drop everything and come a running. Pay? You're kidding! Now what's the problem?

Just the other day a chap I know mentioned that he'd been laid off by one of our larger New Hampshire companies. What should he do? Hmmm, tell me about the business they're in. Well, they turned out to be a very large photo finishing outfit. Hmmm, wondered I, and who is their major competitor?

Okay, how's your creativity? What would you advise this chap? He had a high-level position, one that's going to be very difficult to match elsewhere . . . particularly in these recession times. He wondered if I might know anyone he could approach. Sure, I could use his skills with my company, but I hesitated to offer him about 25% of what he was probably making . . . which is all I'd have to offer at present.

So I came up with a creative solution. It's one you could think of, just from the information you already have, but I'll bet it never occurred to you.

Okay, here's the idea. You know that vacationing is New

Hampshire's #1 industry, right? Well, you also know that every vacationer brings a camera or two along. So where do they buy their film? And where do they get their pictures processed? We're talking about a multi-million dollar market here.

Are they going into Ames or A&P for their film? Into camera stores? The chances are they're taking their exposed rolls home and getting them processed there. So why not put a small display in every hotel and motel in the state which offers film for sale and has envelopes for the hotel to mail in the exposed films for processing? The hotels will, of course, get a commission on the film and processing sales.

If his old company doesn't want to work with him on the idea, you can bet their competition will. Next I'd have a serious talk with Kodak and Fuji and see how much money I could get up front as a distributor for their products. I'd keep it simple, selling only 100 and 400 speed film for prints.

Once I had New Hampshire covered I'd start on Maine and Vermont. And when it got beyond my ability to get to all of the displays to refill them I'd hire on sales reps . . . probably unemployed or retired people looking for part time work.

Let's see now, if we get the displays into 1,000 New Hampshire motels and bed and breakfast places, and they sold just five rolls of film a week for only three months of the year, golly, that'd be 60,000 rolls of film! If they used a similar number of processing envelopes, that'd be 60,000 orders. Now, if I only make $1 per roll of film and per processing order, I'm still grossing $120,000 a year. But I suspect I'd do several times that, once I got it going.

And that's how an entrepreneur gets ideas.

In addition to the motels getting a piece of the action, I'd put some of the money aside and hold quarterly drawings for larger cash awards.

Next I'd see what cooperation I could get from the motels on the best photo opportunities in their area. Covered bridges? Beautiful streams? What's outstanding? I'd take this information and get it into *New Hampshire ToDo* and other publications as a way to draw even more vacationers to the state.

A quarterly photo contest? Why not? Send in your entries with $1 each to cover our paperwork and we could provide some nice prizes for the best spring, summer, fall and winter photos.

241 What About The Riots?

When the riots erupted in the inner cities following the Rodney King verdict, it was difficult not to notice a lack of constructive ideas on how to keep this sort of thing from happening again. It should be obvious to anyone paying any attention that there's been no progress in eliminating the problems causing inner city riots since the burning of Watts nearly three decades ago. I'm not sure what it's going to take to attract attention, but one might think the burning and looting of parts of our cities might do it. I'm glad to know that President Bush sympathizes with the affected people. I just wish he had some creative advisors within reach to help him come up with some practical solutions.

The silence from candidate Clinton was just as telling. Worse, Perot had a fantastic opportunity to break his silence and propose some ideas. Nothing. I was disappointed, but not surprised.

So I sat down, my trusty Mac PowerBook in my lap, and started writing. First I looked for the fundamental problems which have resulted in the mess. Why do we have hundreds of thousands of uneducated dropouts roving our cities in gangs? Why do we have a huge drug problem which helps support these gangs? Why do we have welfare families going on for two and three generations? Why do we have dropout teenage welfare mothers? Before we can some up with solutions to the problems we have to understand what caused them and then look for solutions to the causes, not just the results of those causes. That's like trying to cure symptoms and not going after the virus or germs causing the disease.

The basic causes of black poverty aren't all that mysterious. Some of them have been touched on in earlier parts of my book. Some will be discussed as they relate to the inner city problems.

At first I was going to present my proposed solutions to the riots as a separate paper. After all, several of my solutions are drawn from ideas I've already covered. But then I got to thinking — this is a good exercise in applying solutions originally considered for New Hampshire to quite different circumstances. Presuming that you won't mind too much a reprise of my earlier ideas in this new setting, I'll include my proposed inner city solutions.

242 Some Inner City Solutions

There's been much hand-wringing about the plight of our ghettos, with the media turning to politicians for proposed solutions. You know, I haven't seen any ideas on what to do about the mess coming from any journalists. Nor I have I seen anything worthwhile being proposed by Bush, Clinton or even Perot. The fact is, no one seems to have a clue about how to get out of the mess our country is in.

Yes, I have some ideas on how to tackle the mess — both a short-range plan to solve the immediate problem, and a longer-range plan to make sure we don't find ourselves back in the same situation again in a few years. And no, I'm not going to present my proposals before I give some of the background that went into their development. I know you, if I just come out with a proposal you'll immediately come up with ten reasons why it'll never fly. I don't need that kind of aggravation, so you're going to have to follow my logic — which I think will leave you with fewer straws to grasp with objections.

We have a number of interconnected problems which have brought our inner cities to the explosive situation we have today. We're all familiar with them. We have fatherless black families. We have welfare mothers. We have black and Hispanic youngsters dropping out of school in droves. We have street gangs. We have crack houses. We have crack mothers. We have black teenage mothers. What we don't have is any plan for breaking the cycle, which has been getting worse and worse. Putting more money into welfare hasn't done any good. Indeed, this is a big part of the problem — even though done with good intentions.

Another big part of the problem is our school system, which really is almost completely irrelevant for these kids. By not solving our drug problem we've made it so kids can make enough money to get by — and some can make very good money. They don't need to study white history, Shakespeare or world geography to sell drugs.

So here we are with a whole array of problems, none of which have we even a hint of how to solve, and the bottom line is thousands of unemployable kids burning and looting our inner cities in frustration. And here we are too, with Wayne Green stepping up to the plate, ready to knock one after another of the problems out of the field. Can I really propose practical solutions to crack houses, our lousy school system, street gangs, overflowing prisons, welfare mothers, school dropouts, a lack of work for uneducated, unmotivated blacks, and the growing schism between blacks and whites? Duck soup.

243 The First Step

Let's tackle the immediate problem first — the street gangs which have been rioting, looting and burning their inner city areas. They are angry. They are frustrated. They blame everyone else for their problems. There's nothing new about that. Alas, the sorry fact is that they are not to blame. These kids are the victims — oh, not of a plot, as they like to think, just of history. The world has been changing and we've let it get way out of kilter. The main ogre in their misfortune is our completely antiquated educational system. We've just recently begun to get concerned about it because it's finally been failing our upscale kids as well as our poor. Well, it's been failing the poor for a long time — and not so much for a lack of money, but mostly because the whole system has been out of date.

Our first priority is not to fix the educational system, it's to figure out how to deal with hundreds of thousands of uneducated black and Hispanic kids who have developed a gang culture and support their lives with drugs and crime. Once we have a way to get out of the immediate mess we're in we can then start re-inventing the educational system so we don't continue to feed more kids into the gangs.

There are so many kids involved — a couple hundred thousand were out there burning and looting — that our police, legal system, courts and prisons are totally unable to cope with them. It's a losing battle. But on the other hand we *have* to be able to cope, so what's the answer? Let's start first with the prisons.

244 Our Prisons

We don't have nearly enough prisons to handle hundreds of thousands of gang kids. We also don't have the $20,000 a year or so it costs to incarcerate them. We also know that prison doesn't rehabilitate people, it's more an educational system, providing advanced degrees in crime. Yes, we've got to solve these problems before we can even get started cleaning up the street gangs.

The French kept their prison costs down by dumping their worst criminals on Devil's Island, thousands of miles from France. England dumped theirs in Australia, even further away. The French prisoners got awful treatment, while the British felons got a pretty good deal. What I have in mind is somewhere in-between.

Spending twenty big ones or so a year to incarcerate prisoners is a lousy buy. We need to shop around for a better deal. I'll bet we could get them taken care of for a tenth that (or less) if we asked for some bids. For instance, take a remote island like Guam — an American protectorate. They really need an industry on Guam, so they might go for this. When I addressed a group of Guamanian businessmen and suggested the idea a few years ago they surprised me by being very enthusiastic. We also might get bids from some African countries looking for ways to make money — like Burkina Faso. China might come in with an attractive bid. So might some of the new Soviet countries.

Areas where it's cheap to live — in a warm climate — where food is easy to grow, would keep costs way down. The prisoners could pretty much feed themselves with their own gardens and farms. But what about guards, walls and so on? Well, with microelectronics it's easy to put a small radio transmitter on prisoners — one which would not be easily removed — so they'd be easy to keep track of. Prisoners kept in a remote area and kept track of by radio, with a computer tracking them, wouldn't get far. And we're talking under $2,000 a year per prisoner instead of $20,000!

There are even more savings possible. Would you be upset if I turned this into a profit-making enterprise? Please forgive me, but as a registered entrepreneur I tend to think in terms of making new projects pay for themselves. So here we have a couple thousand or so gang members removed from our cities for from two to five years, with little to do except plot their escape. Let's put them to work. Let's encourage them to learn some practical skills, to earn some privileges, some money, and also, as a little bonus, have the whole project profitable for the prison.

Okay, here we have a bunch of kids with few useful skills. Many can hardly speak English. Many can't read. If they're going to be able to enter the work force when they get back we're going to have to teach them English instead of black argot or Spanish. And we're going to have to teach them some useful trades. We might be able to encourage them to tackle these goals by convincing them that when they get back they're not going to be able to go back into the drug or crime business. They're not going to find any street gangs when they return. Nor will they be going on welfare. They're going to have to find real work.

Get rid of drugs? Crime? Street gangs? Have I been blinded by reading *Lost Horizons*? Stick with me, all will eventually be explained. But before we can solve these other problems we've got to get as many of our current criminals as possible out of circulation.

Okay, what kind of work can we teach these misfits? I like the solution that Singapore tried when they were thrown out of Malaysia when it was formed a little over 30 years ago. Singapore was a small island of terrible poverty and high unemployment. It was so bad that Malaysia refused to accept it as part of their confederation when they were freed by the British.

Their answer was to turn to the United Nations and ask for help. The UN sent a team which surveyed the raw materials available within easy shipping distance — and the potential markets. They then got funding in Europe and built high-rise apartment complexes to get the people out of rusty tin hovels. They built factories near the apartments. The result, within less than six years, was full employment and one of the most vigorous economies in the world.

So wherever we decide to store our prisoners, let's check out the nearby raw materials and markets and get businesses to invest in factories to use this low-cost labor.

How are we going to convince kids with very little education and a long history of not working that now they want to work? Instead of the whip, how about making privileges the payoff? If they do well and are productive they would be able to earn credits which could be used to rent TVs, boomboxes, tapes, and so on. Let's get them used to working to earn the things they want. Like the idea? If they don't want to work they can sit there in a cell and wait out their time while everyone else has TV, movies and music.

We might even encourage them to do some farming work by paying them for that with credits which are exchangeable for better food. No farm work, no good chow. Provide rewards for good behavior instead of punishment for bad. I know it's a novel idea, but it's worth a try.

With our prisons located in the low-rent areas of the world, we might see less recidivism too. There are many countries that could use the revenues such a business would bring. And remember, we're doing this on contract so we're not talking about a Devil's Island type of incarceration. We want to remove the scum from our cities and do our best to re-educate and re-train them so we can break the poverty/crime pattern.

245 How About The Courts?

Once we've established a system capable of dealing with hundreds of thousands of new prisoners — and doing it on a paying basis so the public isn't socked with more taxes to pay for it — it's logical for our courts to stop the current revolving door "justice" system which releases criminals mainly because there's no place to hold them.

Once we have a better system for dealing with criminals we'll see judges taking advantage and sending offenders to our new criminal vacation spots. This will get them out of the way for a while, and possibly improve their value to themselves and our country. Judges might be inclined to hand out longer sentences in this environment — a boon to all involved.

A prison compound in Southern China, Burkina Faso or Southern Sudan would eliminate much of the need to guard against prisoners escaping — there's nowhere to go. The areas could sure use the increased business activity prison-labor factories would provide. Everyone would benefit.

246 Catching The Criminals

Once we have a better prison system — one which won't cost us anything to maintain — and once we have a justice system geared to handling the load expeditiously — then we have to figure out how to round up thousands of street gang criminals. Our police departments are pretty good at coming up with ways to catch criminals, it's just that they've been frustrated by the old revolving door system. When they find that criminals are not being returned to the streets, I expect they'll enthusiastically go about cleaning up their areas.

Judges, knowing that some prison time could change attitudes, might tend to be more inclined to include a year or two of prison time when faced with petty thieves and even prostitutes.

Look, we know the present prison system doesn't work. We know it's cruel punishment and is not likely to improve their dispositions, but we justify it as "serving them right." We just can't seem to ever get over the idea that if we punish people enough we can force them to be good. Many fathers and bosses seem to believe that. One only has to deal with animals to discover that punishment is a lousy way to teach. The best trained animals are taught with rewards, not punishment. It's the only system that gives consistently positive results. The same concept goes for higher animals — like kids. It even goes for adults.

Yes, I know, we have a few crazies out there too. These loonies do have to be separated from the poorly educated punks, but that's not very difficult to accomplish. Though I haven't seen any real progress in dealing with deranged people in the last few years, I have hopes that we'll start seeing some breakthroughs. We are beginning to isolate genetic-caused problems from nurture errors. Psychiatry is a woefully inexact practice. Note I did not classify it as a science. It isn't!

247 How About Welfare?

We know the welfare system isn't working. It's caused more problems than it's solved. Plus it's a terrible weight on our whole country — wasting billions of dollars. There have been some attempts to curb welfare excesses, complete with liberal hand-wringing. It's encouraging young black mothers to have more illegitimate children. It's feeding these kids into the ghetto street gangs at ever earlier ages.

My proposed solution to the welfare problem is to first organize a combination day care and child education system which starts with babies just a few months old and gives them the mind and body stimulation they need to be ready for our school system. This will free up the mothers to work.

Now, while I recognize that the socialist concept has failed in every country where it's been tried, there are some aspects to the idea which have succeeded and might be used profitably. I have in mind the Israeli kibbutz system. Israel, when faced with hundreds of thousands of impoverished immigrants, set up cooperative villages. The people grew their own food and worked in small cooperative businesses which didn't require difficult-to-learn skills.

If we could establish a few enterprise villages in America and offer welfare families an opportunity to join these cooperatives to provide for themselves and their families, and to learn some marketable skills, I believe we could start emptying our inner cities of the poor. Most of these people want to work, they're just trapped in a no-win situation. I believe these enterprise villages can be made profitable enough so it'll be possible to sell investment shares in them as a way to finance their startup costs.

This is the part you're really going to hate. My proposals for changing our lousy educational system aren't just changes. I'm proposing a completely new system. I already gave you a hint when I mentioned starting at around one year of age instead of five or six. It gets worse. I want to make school non-compulsory. That's right, kids would not have to go if they and their parents didn't want them to.

You see, it's those first few years that make the most difference. By providing day care for working mothers we'd have an opportunity to help babies develop their minds and bodies — unlike so much of day care today where they use TV to sedate the kids. It's in these years that they'll learn languages and build their understanding of the world and how they fit into it. It's during these years that they'll understand that success in life is almost entirely dependent on education — and that education is a lifetime exercise, not one that ends when you get out of school.

In these early years kids are like vacuum cleaners when it comes to learning. They're full of questions and want to understand. Alas, most parents shut them up with TV.

The bridge between day care and school should be simple. Kindergarten isn't much different than day care — and all of school is a kind of day care exercise anyway. The school that I'm proposing would make courses available to kids. They would get together with their parents and look at videos which would explain what they would learn from a given course and what the benefits would be from that learning. Thus kids, working with their parents' guidance, would opt for the courses they want to take. Nothing would be mandatory. No grades, no tests.

Instead of the usual system of a teacher and blackboard, the class would be divided into teams of three to five students, with the teacher as a cheer leader and councilor rather than an authority figure. This process has been tested in hundreds of schools and found to be incredibly effective. It makes learning much more fun and helps make the learning much more permanent than the old system of forcing kids to memorize facts, take tests and then forget 99% or more of what was "learned." Memorization turns out to be one of the worst possible ways to teach.

Will we just pass everyone who turns up for classes? We have to have a system which will work well with student IQs from 70 to 140 or more, plus it'll have to work with unmotivated students too. So I suggest we have the students vote on which of their fellow students have passed each course.

With most courses running half a school year, being left back is a terrible trauma for kids. I'm proposing that schools be run fifty weeks of the year, with ten five-week terms. A kid who fails a course would only have to repeat one course and that for only five weeks, so the depth of the trauma would be far less. In this way slow students would be able to take many courses twice, if they wanted. They'd have a great advantage the second time around and would be helpful in teaching some of their fellow students. Of course, since all of the courses are voluntary, passing or failing isn't a serious matter. There's no credit given for passed courses.

In this educational atmosphere, where learning is fun and exciting, and where students are able to see a direct connection between what they're learning and their lives, I suspect we'd see far fewer dropouts. Of course kids could skip a term or two, if their parents agree, and take trips or work for a few weeks.

In the case of our inner city problems we need to get at the root cause of the mess — and that's a combination of our crummy educational system, welfare, and a decreasing number of high-pay low-skill jobs. There's no one silver bullet to solve the mess. We need to implement both short-and long-range fixes. My short-term proposed fix is to re-educate the current bunch of dropouts who've turned to crime. My long-term fix is to change our educational system so we stop producing these uneducated dropouts.

American kids need to be encouraged to speak our national language, and not get dealt out of most jobs because all they know is black argot or Spanish. They need to be encouraged to learn to read as a means for making a lifetime of education possible.

While we're particularly going to need high-tech workers unless our country is going to go the route of Britain (formerly known as Great Britain), we're also going to need poets, novelists, composers, philosophers, data inputters, programmers, and so on. In the early years we need to convince kids and their families that it's important not to forever cut off any of these potential growth areas.

249 The Drug Problem

The government has been doing everything it can think of to stem the drug industry. Nothing they've tried so far has done diddley. The more they try, the lower street prices have gone for drugs — showing that ever more are getting into the country. We've tried to get the public to stop buying drugs — no deal.

So how do I think I can solve this problem when so many have failed? Well, with about 80% of all crime today involving drugs, I suggest that it's time to stop thinking in terms of interdiction and busting drug marketing groups. If we can stop this whole mess we'll have solved much of the inner city problem, much of the cost of police and courts, and we'll save an awful lot of people from addiction. I ask, is the situation serious enough yet to go for a whole new approach?

No, there's nothing basically new with my proposed solution. It's been seriously proposed by many people. There's a great article in *The Public Interest* on the subject. Bill Buckley has championed the idea. I'm suggesting that we give up with interdiction and legalize drugs. Well, with some restrictions. The idea of pot being packaged and sold by R.J. Reynolds, complete with billboard and magazine advertising, isn't what I have in mind.

Here's my suggested approach. I'd like to see drugs legalized and sold *only* through state authorized drug stores. Further, while we're at it, let's also include all other harmful drugs such as tobacco and alcohol, getting them out of our supermarkets and convenience stores. Further, I would allow no advertising of any of these drugs.

By lowering the price of pot, cocaine, and so on, we'd drive the criminals out of the business. It's the enormous profits which make the business so attractive. We'd have our drugs supplied by contract growers, just as we have our money paper made by special firms. I've got answers for most of the endless reasons you'll come up with as to why this won't work. With the controls I can recommend, we can pretty much keep drugs out of the hands of kids — probably a lot better than we are doing now. And we can discourage the resale of drugs. Without advertising, we should see a gradual drop in drug interest — particularly by kids.

There should be enough room in the price to allot some profits to an advertising campaign aimed at discouraging people — youngsters in particular — from getting involved with drugs. With no positive ads and with what advertising there is negative, the tendency will be to cool sales.

250 Will It Work?

If we can fix our schools, reduce the drug problem, reduce welfare, and turn our prisons into the reform institutions they were meant to be, I think we can clean up not just our inner city problems, but will have made a major step toward eliminating our poor. We don't have to have poor people. We don't have to have *any* poor people at all. But before we're going to move these people into our middle class we've got to have an educational system that works for them — we've got to end the drug mess — we've got to get rid of the whole miserable welfare system. That'll do more to end poverty and street gangs than any amount of law and order and interdiction. And, if my ideas are followed, we can do all this with a minimum of investment. Indeed, we'll be able to save billions of dollars that are now being wasted on welfare, crime fighting, courts, prisons, and so on. We might even be able to see our taxes come down — unless Congress figures out some other wasteful way to screw things up — which I'm convinced they will.

My proposals for solving the inner city mess offer several opportunities for entrepreneurs to start new businesses — some of which could grow enormously. There's a need for a new kind of nursery school, private schools, new prisons, and so on. The public institutions which have so badly failed us all need to be replaced by new private for-profit ones. We know that private enterprise costs far less than anything run by the government, plus it's more flexible and can better keep up with the times.

The health care problem? I'll work on that one once we've gotten going on curing the problems which have been precipitating ghetto riots.

251 Black Pride

There's one more aspect to black education which should not be left undiscussed. This has to do with black role models, and it's a major problem for blacks. It's destructive to black progress when kids look up to black athletes, performers and clergy, but not to black businessmen. I hope this can be changed by better nursery school education. As it is kids look up to successful black drug pushers and pimps, which is terribly destructive to black culture.

Blacks who go into business are not treated with much respect by other blacks. Indeed, blacks will tend to avoid shopping in a black store and patronize a white-run store nearby instead.

For several years I've been trying to get a black friend of mine who publishes *Black Church* in Baltimore to publish articles about successful black businessmen instead of concentrating totally on black clergy. This sends the wrong message to the whole community — and the parents send it to their children. All it would take is a few black publishers to start turning this situation around.

Blacks are frustrated because they're not sharing in the bounty America is offering. They're mad at the whites for denying them success. And yes, there are still monumental barriers for blacks — but that's no reason to accept unnecessarily destructive mind-sets which further frustrate their growth. There are several popular routes to never making much money in our country. But there are also some routes which hold a high promise for success. So why block off the main accesses to money and then rail against the unfairness of it all?

Small business and entrepreneurialism are by far the easiest ways to make more than the average wage in America. Until blacks re-evaluate their role models and encourage their youngsters to start businesses, the blacks are going to be forever behind.

You don't see the Asians making this mistake. They're opening stores everywhere and doing it successfully. The Korean immigrants have been opening stores in black neighborhoods — areas where blacks should have done this, but haven't. Naturally the blacks are mad at the Koreans because they are successful. And the Vietnamese too. They're both entrepreneurial and hard working.

As an entrepreneur I'm hoping that our new educational system will champion small business and get kids fired up to work for or own their own businesses. I'm not a fan of big business. Oh, I know we need 'em, if only to counter foreign-owned big businesses. But big businesses tend to do everything they can to kill off small businesses. Yet the real strength of a country lies in its thousands of small businesses, not in a few hundred big ones. Small businesses employ more people, are more creative, can usually produce products cheaper, can adapt to changing markets faster, and so on.

We need big businesses to make things like integrated circuits where it takes tens to hundreds of millions of dollars in equipment to be competitive. But beyond that we don't need them much and their tendency to form cartels to protect their markets isn't healthy.

If you know any black publishers please see what you can do to get them to give other blacks a break and change this whole role model mess which is helping to screw up their kids.

252 Can Washington Be Fixed?

There isn't much argument that Washington is a mess. We have a Congress and a series of administrations that have brought us one disaster after another. We see monumental corruption in virtually every federal department. We see a continuously growing bureaucracy which seems beyond control. We see a government which admits it's unable to keep itself from generating a growing deficit. And perhaps worst of all, we see no hints of any solutions to the situation being proposed by any of the Presidential candidates or those running for the Senate or House. No one seems to have a clue as to what to do.

Shall I list more of the problems our politicians seem unable to cope with? Crime, drugs, education, environmental concerns, jobs, foreign aid, the loss of technology, import imbalance, foreign loans, increasing American poverty, a ridiculous tax system, IRS and Customs out of control, etc.

So am I suggesting that there may be a simple fix to this mess of worms? Yep. Fairly simple, anyway. Let's take a look at the situation and see how many of the proposals I've proposed as ways to clean up New Hampshire might also work in Washington.

One miserable Washington problem has to do with the whole election process. We're concerned because it costs so much to run an election campaign that most Congressmen have to depend on special interest sources for the money — and that means there's a payback which is unlikely to be beneficial to the country. So we've got to come up with a way to handle that. One proposal which seems to be gathering some power is to make it illegal for candidates to accept any special interest money, either hard or soft. Getting Congress to make such a law is like trying to get an addict off drugs.

Perhaps we should make a stab at re-orienting the priorities of our representatives and explain that they are in Washington primarily to help make our country work and secondarily to see that their state gets a fair shake.

253 A New Election Concept

Candidates for Congress and the Presidency are all under enormous media pressures to state their positions on issues. I hate to be the proposer of a complete paradigm shift here — of proposing a new concept — but I suggest that the last thing we want in a candidate for federal office is a set of preformed beliefs. We need people running our government who's main agenda is to represent us in an even-handed way. I agree that it's a lot easier to fight abortion if you can elect someone who is absolutely opposed to abortion, no matter what. Then you don't have to support your own beliefs with facts or deal with others who think you are wrong. There's no danger of having eventually to go the democratic route and seek a consensus. You're looking for the dictatorial approach to getting your way.

The same thinking can be applied to every "issue" that's being raised. Of course politicians, ever wary for traps, try to dodge being nailed down on issues. As soon as a politician actually commits to being a supporter of an issue (belief), the media rush to give as much exposure as possible to the opponents of that belief. It's a mess.

Instead of trying to dodge and avoid issues, I suggest the best approach for politicians is to admit that there is much to be said on both sides of most issues, but that if they are going to represent us in Washington it's important that they do not go in with either a hidden or stated agenda to support one side over the other.

Yes, we have environmental problems, and they have to be weighed against jobs. Our representatives have the responsibility of getting the facts as best possible and then making decisions on the facts, not on their own emotional beliefs. We don't need Senators who are willing to sacrifice the lives and health of millions of our people because they are getting generously bribed by the tobacco conglomerates.

If the veils of secrecy within which the government and Congress operate can be penetrated, we'll have far fewer nasty surprises. I think we've had adequate evidence that journalists can't be depended upon to uncover corruption. Oh, once one discovers it, the pack is abay, but there seem to be few journalists out there with magnifying glasses doing detective work.

It seems as if in every new exposure of corruption that there have been people blowing the whistle, but no one has paid them any attention. I believe we have more than adequate proof that our government agencies are unable to police themselves. Potential whistle-blowers quickly learn to shut up — or else their jobs will be gone and their careers permanently ruined. Worse, nothing will have been changed anyway.

As I've proposed for New Hampshire, I recommend that a federal commission be formed to encourage, reward and protect whistle blowers. There are few bad things happening where everyone involved is corrupt. There will always be some people who are uncomfortable and willing, if protected, to try and stop what's happening.

The commission should have broad investigative powers and report directly to the people. Their reports should not be able to be squelched or tempered by the administration, by the legislators or even the judiciary. The fact is that we're not sure we can trust anyone we put into power. We've been so deceived and lied to that we don't have any reason to believe anyone. I've complained about the lies by Bush — and we know our legislators can't be trusted. The Thomas hearings certainly didn't encourage our faith in even the Supreme Court.

If we can eliminate the funneling of money from special interests, lobbyists and PACs to legislators we'll be going a long way toward helping them be more honest. Lobbyists will have to depend more on reason than a checkbook to get across their messages. Perhaps we should try this approach and see how special interests are able to get around it.

I'm not sure if anything can be done to make it more difficult for lobbying organizations to flim-flam their constituents by mail or via TV, getting them to pressure Congress to support their own interests. Is such a thing as an informed electorate even possible? We're always going to have people taking advantage of people who don't want to bother to think. Of course, if my educational changes are implemented we'll have far fewer ignorant people and it will be much more difficult for con-men to win.

If we insist on our Congress people not generating outside incomes while they are working for us — presumably doing full time work — we may be able to eliminate much of the graft which has been controlling Congress. This is going to make it difficult for them to mount multi-million dollar campaigns. But then it'll also make it difficult for them to repay the money which buys their elections.

Why should Congress have secrecy when it comes to their finances? If they want secrecy, how come? Let's make their checkbooks open to the people who hired them — us. Let's keep track of their expenses as well as their income. If they don't like the spotlight, they can go into another line of work. We want to know when they get gifts, are given freebie trips, and so on. And if they go on a fact-finding junket somewhere in the world, we want to know which government department has picked up the tab and for how much. We've seen enough Congressional outings to Paris to see nonsense like the new Disney extravaganza.

I do believe that Congress can do a better job of dealing with foreign affairs if they have more than a report from the State Department to work with. But unless they have personal contacts in the countries they visit, they're unlikely to get much help in understanding what's been happening. When I visit countries I get together with the local radio amateurs, computer and music industry people, not their politicians. Thus I'm able to find out what's really happening, not what the leaders want me to think.

Though it's been some time since I've seen any confidential government reports on other countries, I suspect, from the decisions which we've seen made, that our intelligence is lousy. We seem to be seeing endless examples that our leaders have been poorly informed by our intelligence community. Perhaps it's time to stop having a bunch of competing agencies and roll them into one. It would cost millions or even billions less that way.

If we're able to cut Congressional incomes back to what they earn for their work for us, perhaps we'll have fewer lifetime devotees to the job. The original idea was for business people to take off a few years and serve their country, not to become embroiled in endless re-election campaigns.

I also like the idea of getting not only Congress people to sign an agreement that they will not become lobbyists or work for companies they've been involved with legislatively once they leave office, but to also require that their assistants and all White House appointees and employees sign similar agreements. Ditto military officers. We've seen far too many of them retiring and then going to work for the companies they, as officers, steered contracts to. That looks too much like a payoff.

If we make these changes in the way we run our government the deficit will be rolled back in short order. We'll see military expenses dropping. we'll see special interests having to sell their ideas on the strength of the ideas, not via bribery and intimidation. We'll see Congress more attentive to the needs of business and less likely to pass harmful laws. We'll certainly see an enormous drop in the cost of government and a resulting lowering of taxes. We'll see the old pork farms closing down. We'll build dams where they we all agree they are needed, not in the state where a Senator chairs a powerful committee.

The information age is here, so let's start using the potential it offers. Let's use TV, satellites, VCR tapes, audio tapes and so on to help communication between government and people — and between people and people.

255 Cutting Government Budgets

There's one more suggestion I made for New Hampshire which is just as applicable on the federal level, and this has to do with reducing government expenses. We know that each bureau has a budget for the next year. We also know that if the budget isn't spent the bureau will be allocated less the next year. Thus there's a big rush at the end of the fiscal year to spend whatever's left of the budget.

My approach to this, in case you've forgotten or you skipped that part, was to make it so each bureau would split whatever hasn't been spent among the employees. This would encourage them to cut as many expenses as possible and thus share in the savings. Yes, they'd have less money budgeted the next year, but even more cuts in personnel and expenses would again give them a big bonus at the end of the year. This would keep cutting expenses, and perhaps, for the first time, keep government bureaus from validating Parkinson's Laws. This would give government employees a powerful motive to save us money — something they sure don't have now.

256 Can Government Be Honest & Efficient?

If we're able to implement the ideas I've proposed, the answer can be yes. Mind you, many of the concepts I've proposed aren't original. I read all I can. I watch PBS a lot. And I try to look at problems from a different perspective — then I put it all together into new paradigm — a new way of looking at things.

With the deficit out of control and Congress unable to stop spending, we know something radical has to be done. We saw Gramm-Rudman fail. We know full well that even a Constitutional amendment isn't going to stop Congress from spending. They'll just take more off the books. We've watched them steal our Social Security funds and replace them with IOUs. We have no reason to trust them. We've even seen Warren Rudman leave the Senate, saying he could no longer honestly work there.

It's all really up to you. Are you going to continue to be suckered by politicians? Are you going to let your friends and neighbors be suckered? We know, on some level, that we're a bunch of suckers. We elect a

President who promises no more taxes. We've donated hundreds of millions to TV preachers, only to find we were suckered. We let the media flim-flam us — and we buy their baloney. We buy *The National Enquirer*, we waste our lives watching soaps, we neglect our children, we let government agencies run rough shod over us, we allow our educational system to ruin our children's lives and then screw us blind to pay for it. Perhaps we deserve the results of our inattention and almost total involvement with ourselves.

When we discover, as a country, that as soon as we stop paying attention, charlatans will step in and take us for everything they can, we may be able to focus our attention on what this has been doing to our quality of life. There is no question in my mind that we have the power to make sure that we have virtually no poverty in America. No welfare. No homeless. And darned few ditch-diggers. I'd rather see ditches dug by ditch-digging machines.

If you start demanding that candidates for office follow the ideas I've presented we'll see America back as number one in manufacturing, in technology, in finance, and in strength in the world. We'll also be number one in education.

257 Throw The Rascals Out!

I went to a club meeting the other evening to hear a chap talking about our need to vote in a whole new Congress. Throw the current rascals out! I must say he made a convincing case. He cited one huge waste of our money after another. You know, the toilet seats, the $500 bolts, the $20 million mountain road in Utah between two little towns, and so on. I thought about building a long list like his in order to convince any readers of mine that it's time to stop sitting around worrying about who's going to win the pennant and start paying attention to the mess you've allowed to build up in Washington.

The idea of building a new aircraft carrier mainly as a way to keep people in Newport News (VA) in jobs is ludicrous. We could give every worker a generous pension and save billions. The same rationale seems to be keeping us building multi-billion dollar submarines and unimaginably expensive new bombers. Perhaps you've noticed that despite the loss of our only big enemy in the world, we're not cutting our military budget by much.

The Congress we've elected has run amok. They've stolen about $65,000 from every family in America and spent it. Wasted it, is more apt. We've broken the Soviet Union with the arms race — and come close to breaking ourselves. Yet I see that the House Armed Services Committee has earmarked $274 billion for defense in 1993. Worse, the administration expects to request $1.4 trillion more over the next five years. Lordy!

But will bringing in a new batch of politicians change anything? When we look at the gang running for Congress we see few new faces. What we see is a new bunch that will soon be dedicated to their four-year re-election campaigns. There won't be much change from the present mix of 183 lawyers, 50 real estate people, 38 educators, 37 insurance salesmen, 20 news and entertainment people, 14 farmers, 5 funeral home directors and only three people from manufacturing. This was not what our founding fathers had in mind.

Between organized and unorganized crime, plus a lot of foolishness, we manage to waste billions on our own. We eagerly send hundreds of millions to crooked televangelists, we buy worthless diet aids, we are scammed endlessly. I threw away five junk mail letters telling me I'd won up to $5 million just last Monday. A phone call told me I'd won a diamond ring, but they needed my credit card number to verify who I was. Sure. Well, we can clean up that mess if we get angry about it. But are we angry enough about the $65,000 Congress has stolen from every family in America to not just throw out the rascals (thieves), but to insist that they change the way Washington works?

I've proposed some changes which I think would go a long way toward getting the lawyers out of government and attracting businessmen who know about meeting a payroll — who understand marketing, the need for new products, for research, productivity, and the desperate need we have to totally change our whole educational system if we're going to have the quality of workers we need to compete with the rest of the world.

I started out on this project with the goal of helping to get New Hampshire out of the recession. But as my ideas, both original and stolen, evolved, I could see where most of my proposed initiatives applied to not only all the other states, but to the federal government too.

My ideas are intended as a starter. I hope they'll get other people thinking in terms of change — radical change. The old paradigm-shift biz. So much of our future potential lies in changing our educational system that I hope this doesn't get lost in the political fog. A better educated people won't fall for all these direct mail scams. They won't waste millions supporting Jim Bakker and other TV con men. They might not even be spending millions calling 900-number sex hotlines at $4.95 a minute. Well, if they do, perhaps they'll at least be able to have more intelligent conversations.

It'll be nice to stop turning out millions of almost completely unemployable kids who can't read, can't speak English, and have few social or marketable skills — kids with little choice but bitterness and crime — kids we'll have to be taxed to support while they spend their lives out of sight in prison — kids who are another hazardous waste product of our bungled system.

Is helping to make the needed changes more important than watching a ball game on TV with a six-pack and pretzels? Is it more important than an evening at your local edition of Cheers? Is it worth your time to change your state, Washington, and your schools?

The future of your town or city, your state, all of our kids, and our country is up to you.

All I've done is read a bunch of books, read a few thousand magazines, talk with as many people as I could find with interesting ideas, and watch a lot of Nova and other PBS programs. I haven't done anything that anyone able to read and write couldn't do. The only difference is that I've done it. What I don't know how to do is to get you fired up to do something.

Jack Gargan, the chap I heard speak the other evening, did something. He got fed up with the mess in Washington and invested his retirement money ($45,000) in some full page newspaper ads asking people to get mad enough to throw the rascals out. The people responded, sending him enough to run more ads in more papers. Today he's working full time giving talks such as I heard and he's generating enthusiasm for his cause. He claims he's received over a million in donations which he's recycled into more ads.

All you have to do is pick one area where you really want to make a difference and start pushing. I can't change the world alone, no matter how hard I work. But if I can spark just ten of you into action — and you can each spark ten more — we'll change not just America, we can change the world.

Poverty, crime, drugs, prisons, unemployment, can all be rolled back — can be made anomalies. But it's like dieting. It means breaking life-long habits. And habits, by their very nature, are self-protecting. It's tough not to eat that candy, to call or write a letter to your Senator or Congressman instead of watching a soap or sitcom. Will you go to your grave with the satisfaction of knowing that you've never missed an episode of The Simpsons? Or that you've kept up with The World Turns, complete with reading the *Soap Opera Digest*? Or can you get excited enough about helping to change things to force candidates for office to promise the changes we need? And then hold their hands in the fire after they are elected?

My ideas are just starters. We need more ideas for ways to solve our problems. We need to communicate with and support each other. We can wipe out organized crime. We can clean up the messes we've allowed to build. I'd like to see organized crime driven out of the magazine distribution business. That's a very dirty business right now. I'd like to see them driven out of the music business, where they are in firm control on many levels. We have to live with these people stealing our money because we don't care enough to do anything about it.

So we're up to here in car theft, in our homes being broken into, our being mugged on the street, women being raped, stores being robbed, banks being robbed, and all of this is happening to us every day. And if the street criminals aren't robbing the banks, their presidents or tellers are. Retail stores have a major problem with theft, both from customers and their employees — and all of this is being done by the "graduates" of our educational institutions. Do you think we may be doing something wrong?

I had an experience with one of our government agencies about twenty years ago. It was a very bitter experience. But I was warned that if I ever dared write about it they would make sure I went to prison. They assured me that they could do this, whether I'd done anything wrong or not. I've seen far too much proof of their success with this with others to doubt them. Someday, if you'll help clean up our government, I hope I'll be able to tell that whole story. But until that time thousands of other people will be tortured by our government agents as I was. Nothing short of Congress, pressured by angry citizens can stop things like this. Yes, these things can and do happen here, not just in Iraq, Iran or Libya. They happen because you let them happen.

258 Military Preparedness 2000

Both political parties seem to be salivating over carving up the old military budget. There are endless targets for cost-cutting. Do we really need multi-billion dollar stealth bombers, now that the USSR is gone? And what do we need with more submarines? Another aircraft carrier? Lordy!

One of the problems is that we haven't a real foreign policy — one that we've discussed and can agree on enough to implement. We see the war in Yugoslavia and sorta feel we ought to be doing something about stopping it. We're frustrated that the Europeans are so sanguine — why aren't they stopping it? After all, it's obviously a European problem.

Well, who made us the world's police? Just because we were strong enough to outspend the USSR militarily — crushing communism in the process — doesn't automatically mean that we have to settle all the world's wars from now on. We set a bad example in the Gulf when we took the initiative to stop Saddam, brow beating our allies into helping. Actually, we had things going pretty good there until our Commander In Chief decided his generals didn't know as well as he about running the war and suddenly ended it, leaving Saddam in power.

So what should be the role of our military in the next century. We've got to think about that — discuss it — and try to come to some agreement.

Can we come up with a scenario where we'll need stealth bombers, more submarines and carriers? If wars are going to be more like what's going on in Yugoslavia, what kind of military response could we make to that which would stop the war without risking too many of our troops? Are smart bombs and air mastery the right tools to stop civil wars? We see a similar situation developing in Czeckoslovakia, another in Armenia vs. Azerbaijan, and so on. Would these turn out more like Viet Nam and Cambodia for us? We sure didn't figure out how to fight that war with a minimum of casualties.

So let's look ahead and see what role we feel we should play. Let's see if we can figure out what to do about situations such as we faced in Nicaragua and Salvador. Heck, do we even have a Latin American policy?

What kind of weapons are going to be needed for future wars? What size military will we need? I suggest that our past history has taught us that we can't even begin to depend on the Pentagon brains for decisions like these. We haven't yet worked out any incentives for our military leaders to economize.

We see potential dangers from Iraq, where Saddam is re-arming as fast as he can — presumably including nuclear armaments. We know Iran is doing the same. We also know we can't trust Libya and Syria. We know that Israel and India have nuclear arms — and China too. But I suspect that our military leaders have been so wrapped up with the USSR for so many years that they don't have any plans for how to deal with a little war like the one in Yugoslavia. Of course it doesn't help that 99% of Americans haven't a clue as to why they are fighting. If we did rush in there and stomp out the war, what kind of political solutions could we offer to keep 'em from fighting again as soon as we leave? Or would we want to pay for our American soldiers to stay there, as we did in Europe for the last forty-five years or so? I sure hope not. I know I don't want to have to help pay for something like that — and that's who they'll be asking to pay.

If we could re-invent government here along the lines I've proposed, we might be able to sell the idea in other areas of the world that government doesn't have to do any more than serve the people. I know this is an alien concept. It's a world of difference from our present governmental system of taking as much money from the people as possible and having fun spending it. We seem to have lost the concept that government should be minimal. Of course it *is* fun to spend money. It's obviously even more fun to spend billions. It's so much fun we have people spending millions of dollars just so they can have a hand in spending billions. When billions are involved it isn't difficult to have a little rub off here and there.

Every now and then I get so fed up with reading about the corruption in Washington that I wonder if New Hampshire would be better off if it seceded. I don't think we're getting our money's worth. But if we could clean up our political act and have a political system worthy of export, we might be able to nip mini-wars in the bud. The basic idea behind our political system is pretty good, we've just let it get a bit out of date. We need to look creatively at our problems and solve them.

I suspect that it'll be possible for us to organize the forces we think will be needed to handle our defense — plus some world peace keeping. I further suspect that once we retire a bunch of old admirals and generals we'll be able to cut out some carrier task forces and unneeded army bases. Doesn't it seem reasonable that we should be able to get along with no more than half the present military budget and still be geared to handle anything foreseeable? The extra $150 billion could go to reduce the deficit. Of course, if you don't make the changes I proposed in Congress, they'll spend every penny of it on some new programs — and we'll read about ever more corruption. I suggest we get our educational system rebuilt so we won't need to throw gobs of money at the poor.

259 Why No Ideas?

If George Bush, with the enormous brainpower resources at his command, has been unable after some twelve years as Vice President and President to come up with any significant ideas for solving the myriad of problems facing our country, how can an obscure New Hampshire entrepreneur expect to be taken seriously when he offers an armload of proposals for solving America's problems with education, the deficit, poverty, inner city riots, prisons, crime, drugs, competitiveness — and even Congress?

You might be a little more inclined to at least check out what this chap has to say if you knew he had a Ph.D. in Entrepreneurial Science, and contributed significantly to the development of cellular telephones and the microcomputer's explosive growth, was a founder of American Mensa (the high IQ society) and was a founding publisher of two of the biggest magazines in the country.

When New Hampshire was hit the hardest of the 50 states by the recent recession, Governor Judd Gregg asked me to serve on an Economic Development Commission. My report to Governor Gregg, the Legislature and the Commission embodies a wide range of creative solutions to the problems facing the state. Since most of his proposals are applicable to the other states, as well as to the federal government, they may of interest to you.

With the threat of international communism ended and worries about nuclear war reduced, Americans are understandably frustrated by the lack of progress toward a better quality of life. They see the rich getting richer, the poor getting poorer, and the middle class fading away. This was the opposite of what everyone expected. We see endless reports of massive corruption eating up our taxes, with Congress' answer being to levy more taxes. We see almost daily reports of congressional corruption and we know that almost every PAC and special interest payment to Congress is in exchange for special favors, often with a payoff of around a thousand to one,

We see Bush and Clinton as part of the problem, not part of the solution. We don't see any reason to trust either the Democrats or the Republicans. Oh, we know they're not all crooks, but we don't know how to tell them apart, so we're suspicious of 'em all.

So why are none of the politicians able to come up with practical solutions to the messes for which we hold them responsible? They're probably too close to the problems to be able to see them with any perspective. It's well known that virtually every important scientific break-through has been made by an amateur in that field. The professionals know too much that often isn't really so.

260 The Pain Of Change

Bill Moyers has been plucking at the nation's heart strings with endless (seemingly) interviews with Americans who've been laid off because their jobs have been moved to other countries. This is not a failure of our government to protect jobs. It isn't still more cases of corporate greed. It's plain old economics, and still another failure of both our educational system and our media.

How can someone working in a factory for twenty or so years be totally unaware that lower skilled jobs are being moved abroad? How can someone who's been sitting there doing the same semi-skilled job for years not have the slightest inkling that the world is changing? Shouldn't they have developed some interest in learning more and thus having some alternative ready in case things change? This is a government failure in the respect that our whole country should be made more aware that the world is changing. It's also a union failure not to warn members that low-skill, high-pay jobs are blowing away. You either build more skills or you're going to be out of work.

We have a similar situation with our defense contractors. Apparently the end of the cold war came as a total surprise to them. It appears that many have never given a thought to government contractless future. What kind of dumb management doesn't have some plans thought out for what to do when things change. What new products can be made; how can the workers be retrained and so on? Will new products require different marketing approaches?

Yet we have people shocked and angry because competition has forced their company to move their production to Mexico or Asia in order to stay competitive. I gather that though everyone has been buying Japanese and Chinese products it has not occurred to them that the particular product they've been making might be made somewhere else cheaper, and perhaps even better. Then comes the severance check and the shock.

We need to encourage the media to get the word out that jobs aren't forever. The world is shrinking and we here in America have got to be competitive. This means our workers have to work smarter and be more productive. It means more investment in tools per worker and more automation. It means building computer literacy for most of us. It means continuing one's education all through life, not a comfortable life of a job, sleep and play.

We need more and better adult education to be made available and promoted. We need to explain the benefits and the fun of learning to people who believed that once they had graduated from school their education was done. Of course that means that we have to make learning fun — and that means changing our present educational system along the lines I've proposed. I've attended several adult education courses and they were no different than they were fifty years ago — boring.

So let's encourage Bill Moyers to stop airing his TV tear-jerkers and start helping these bewildered people come to grips with the late 20th Century. There's no shortage of work to be done, only a dreadful shortage of people with the skills to do it.

It doesn't take a licensed futurist to see which way things are going. We watched the supermarkets edge out small grocery stores. Then we saw shopping malls, plazas and strips kill off downtown shopping. Now we're seeing mail order about to change our shopping habits again. Mail order, assisted by UPS and video shopping, looks like the future.

261 Viva Mail Order!

I've been selling by mail order since I was twelve, so I enjoy it. A mail order house can be anywhere you want and thus take advantage of the low rent sections of town. When I was young all the orders came in by cash, check or money order. Today most of 'em arrive by 800-number and a credit card number. Small orders go out by mail, bigger by UPS, rush orders by air. you want it tomorrow? No problem. this is one business that isn't going to be moved over seas very soon.

So we're looking for writers, photographers, artists, typesetters, page layout people, designers and so on to put together mail order catalogs. We're looking for people who enjoy talking on the phone to handle orders and problems. We're looking for sharp buyers to find quality new products to sell and see that we get them when we need them. We need computer programmers to get our computers to handle orders and give us the reports we need to make buying decisions. We need people with expertise in advertising to help build our customer base. We need people who understand list buying and rental. We need people who understand promotion to get the most from the media. More and more we need people with TV experience for video promotions. What we don't need is someone with twenty years of experience in soldering parts to boards or ten years of experience in watching an automatic chip inserter put chips in boards.

Can we at least start getting people aware that the world is changing and giving some thought to protecting their futures? The worst part of it is that it's going to be the larger businesses which move jobs to lower wage countries first, thus putting large numbers of people out of work at a time. Smaller businesses tend to be more resilient and able to innovate to protect jobs.

262 More Proposed Initiatives

(1) Set up a for-profit job skills data base to help potential employers find the workers they need. A system based solely on job titles is inadequate in this information age.

(2) Set up a for-profit business site data base to help startup and growing businesses find the buildings and locations best suited to their needs.

(3) Set up a for-profit capital sources data base to help startup and growing businesses with financial needs. This should list venture capital sources, banks interested in small business loans, state and federal government financial and loan guarantee sources.

(4) Set up a for-profit data base of available consultants and their fields of expertise, complete with a list of references.

(5) Establish independent industry councils to help businesses in key industries communicate and help each other.

(6) Establish a for-profit venture capital publication to help bring venture capital together with entrepreneurs and growing small businesses.

(7) Establish *New Hampshire ToDo*, a for-profit publication aimed at increasing New Hampshire vacationing by promoting all the things there are to do when visiting the state.

(8) Establish a for-profit corporation to install kiosks in state liquor stores to advertise and promote New Hampshire activities, hotels, motels, bed & breakfasts, parks, restaurants and camping sites. These would enable reservations to be made and would help visitors find where to pursue their particular interests.

(9) Establish a for-profit health research publication for national distribution to the public by subscription. This would report on medical progress wordwide, thus helping people with specific illnesses keep abreast of developments of special interest to them.

(10) Establish a for-profit sickness care publication which would report on instances of increased productivity in such care. This would help doctors and hospitals provide lower cost care.

(11) Establish a for-profit publication to provide communications between the state and town governments.

(12) Establish a state government customer service department to investigate, resolve and eliminate the potential for further complaints as to state services.

(13) Privatize as many government services as possible — such as the issuing of hunting and fishing licenses, car registration, driver's licenses, state fisheries and so on.

(14) Privatize the prison system, giving out contracts to for-profit prison systems.

(15) Legalize illegal drugs and sell them through state drug stores — including all alcoholic beverages and nicotine products, but with the proscriptions outlined.

(16) Establish a state Planning Referee Committee to help people who have problems with town planning boards.

(17) Establish a polytechnical university to help provide the high-tech work force which will be needed to cope with the technology of the 21st Century.

(18) Establish for-profit mini-malls at key exits to the New Hampshire interstate highways,

(19) Establish Total Quality Awards for restaurants, hotels and activities — much as the Michelin certificates are awarded in France.

(20) Establish a similar award system for state services.

(21) Establish for-profit mutual welfare communities instead of having the state support welfare families.

(22) Publish a for-profit booklet to sell the virtues of establishing businesses in New Hampshire.

(23) Establish a for-profit New Hampshire environmental publication to put environmental concerns into perspective and counter fanatic, uninformed environmentalists who often cause more harm than good.

(24) Establish a for-profit publication covering new technologies in building.

(25) Establish entrepreneurial incubator support communities to attract new firms and help them grow quickly.

(26) Eliminate PAC contributions, special interest and"soft"

re-election funds to Congress.

(27) Establish a federal whistle-blower action committee to act upon information from whistle-blowers and protect them.

(28) Allow civil servants to split any savings in their annual budgets.

(29) Establish a federal customer service bureau to do the same as #12 does for states.

(30) Prohibit government employees from later working for private companies which might benefit from their influence with government decisions.

(31) Privatize as many government functions as possible — such as the postal service.

263 Getting Into Action

This book grew out of a report to the New Hampshire Economic Development Commission. I didn't go to all this trouble and expense to make a buck. I already have a buck. No, I don't have billions. And, no, no power on earth can get me to run for office. I'm too old for that nonsense. The revenues from the sale of this book, along with any donations from supporters of my ideas and dreams, will be used first to help get New Hampshire jump started. The next goal will be to help change our educational system.

I have no plans to leave an inheritance to my children, and my wife is doing fine with a business of her own, making and selling how to dance videos. No, whatever I make will be recycled where I think it'll do the most good. I don't have any interest in a lavish lifestyle. I cook all my own meals, wash my own dishes, and write my own letters. Well, I do have a 25-year old limo, but that was my wife's idea and I don't think it's been driven a hundred miles in the last five years. It was a bargain and it seemed like fun to have it to meet visiting advertisers for my magazines.

And yes, I have a little Miata sports car, but not to impress people as much as to have more fun driving. It's the closest thing I've seen to the old Porsche Speedster. I bought one of those in 1957 and put a couple hundred thousand miles on it before selling it for about what I paid for it sixteen years later. That was the most fun car I've ever had, and the Miata is a close second. Hey, it's okay to have fun! I enjoy skiing and scuba diving too — plus I love traveling and meeting people around the world. I've got to stop starting so many new businesses and see more of the world while I can still walk without a walker. At my age a heart attack, stroke, Alzheimer's, and so on can strike at any moment, so this book is aimed at getting you into gear, not to con you into sending me money so I can do the job for you. But if you do get so excited you can't help yourself, I'll put any donations to good use.

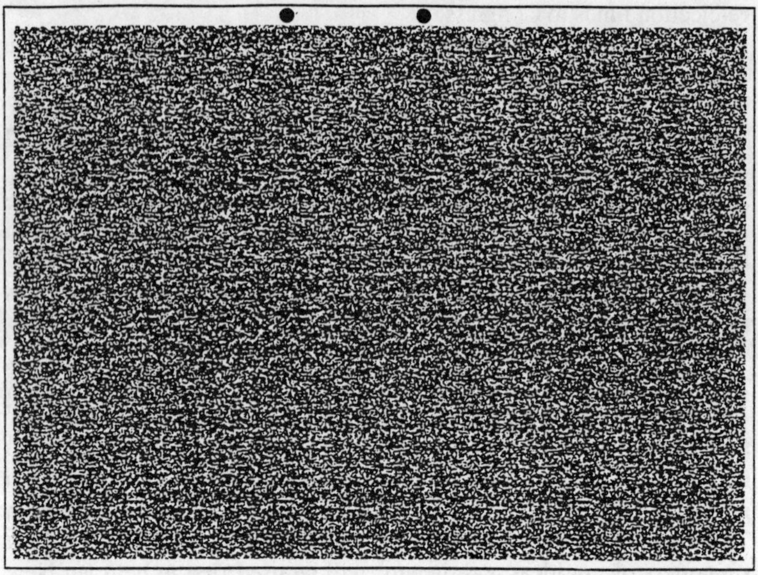

264 What's Going On Here?

Unless you are able to look at the above in a whole new way, it just looks like a mottled mess. But once you learn to focus your eyes beyond the page, you'll see an incredible three-dimensional picture emerge, making order out of chaos. I like the concept, which is much like the approach I'm proposing for solving America's problems. We are so busy focusing on crime, drugs, racial injustices, Congress run amok, poverty, inner city riots, and so on, that we've been unable to step back from the trees and see the forest.

I might warn you that people who are really rigid in their thinking are unable, no matter how hard they look at the above Gaze Toy, to ever see the beautiful order behind the seeming mess. For people with relatively open minds, it takes a few minutes to see the 3-D picture. Alas, this toy, like our complex social problems, is even more challenging. The easy view will show you a group of pyramids. Behind that is a second 3-D image, with truncated pyramids and another set of suspended letters. You can then turn the picture sidewise and see a third 3-D image.

If you get caught up with this toy, you can send for more information from the N.E. Thing, Box 1827, Cambridge MA 02139. If you start convincing yourself that because you can't see them there really aren't any images, I'll give you a hint. Make the two dots at the top look like three, equally spaced. This should get your eyes into focus for the easy pattern. When you see four equally spaced dots, you'll be ready to spot the second image.

I hope that once you understand the quantum leap in education I'm proposing, you'll see how the concept leads to solutions to many of our other seemingly unrelated problems. A better educational system — note, I did not say school system — looks like it could move all but the severely mentally challenged (I like the euphemism) out of poverty and at least into the ranks of the lower middle class.

265 What's All This Retirement Baloney?

Retirement is for wimps. Golf? Cruises to nowhere? Puttering around the house until your heart attack or stroke?

Unless you've been screwed out of a meaningful life by being kept in a play pen or stashed in a day care center for your first five years, you've developed a reasonably useful brain. Then, of course you spent the next 15 years in a government institution run by a couple generations of the bottom fifth of class ranked students who were themselves educated by the bottom fifth of their class. But then nobody learns much during those years, with our sorry educational system, so you started your working years on a par with everyone else.

The next 45 years most people spend their time playing office politics, avoiding work and responsibility, drinking with their buddies, watching ball games, and scoring as often as possible. Or have you been building your skills and information base? If you've followed the safe route through life, working for the government, a large corporation, or teaching, retirement will be mandatory, and the chances are high that you'll have developed few marketable skills, so you'll go for golf and cruises. Or perhaps an RV tour of America.

Of course if you somehow learned to think, perhaps even to write, and developed some useful skills and expertise along the way, you're still going to be in demand, even at 65.

I'm more in favor of arranging one's working life so there are elements of retirement which can be enjoyed as you go. It isn't anywhere near as much fun seeing Nepal when you are 70 as when you are 30 or 40. It's a lot more fun renting a horse and seeing the pyramids in Egypt on horseback than being carted around in a minivan with your walker or cane.

If you enjoy traveling, why not aim for work that gets you around the world? It just takes a little planning. In the computer business I found it important to get to computer shows in Tokyo, Seoul, Taipei, Hong Kong, Singapore, Johannesburg, Rio, Munich, Hannover, Amsterdam, Paris, Birmingham (GB), and all around the US. If you get into the music business you can go almost anywhere in the world. The communications business has gotten me to over 120 countries. Business hasn't stopped me from sight-seeing, taking tons of slides and home movies, going scuba diving, operating my amateur radio station from unusual countries, trying every kind of food I could find, and having a ball.

The golden years of retirement are a bunch of baloney. Once you're no longer working you're nobody. People tend to think of you in terms of the work you're doing now, not what you used to do. When you're retired you're unemployed, and that's several steps down from being a consultant. It's slightly above being homeless.

If you have all that time and nothing to do, why aren't you out there trying to change our 19th Century educational system? Why aren't you organizing pre-school education for kids? It's all too easy to sit around the house and do nothing. It quickly gets to be a habit. But you're as well aware of your worthlessness as everyone else, so you do not get easier to live with. Hey, I've been there and know how it feels.

You know, don't you, that a distressingly high percentage of retirees drop dead within a year of retirement? It's the loss of purpose in life and the loss of importance that destroys. This quickly hits your immune system and from there on that's all she wrote. One thing or another will get you.

I've had several opportunities to go for security over adventure. When WWII was over and the Navy had to release all their reserves, they suddenly discovered that they were about to lose all their electronic technicians. I was teaching at the Submarine School in New London (CT) at the time. I'd worked my way from 3rd class Electronic Technician's Mate to first while in radar school and at sea. I'd turned down a Chief rating in favor of teaching over making more war patrols. The school Commander wanted me to stay and offered a commission if I'd sign up. The offer gradually went from Lieutenant up to Captain. No thanks. And that's how I avoided the wars in Korea and Viet Nam, and became an entrepreneur.

A few years later, when I really got fed up with being a TV director, I considered a Civil Service job. Good pay, great security. Instead I started a loud speaker manufacturing company and had a ball — starting with almost nothing and building a million-dollar business in less than three years!

I tend to get caught up in things which take skill, so I've avoided even trying golf. Not even once. When I tried horseback riding I had to get good at it. I took lessons and lessons, and I got very good. Then I had a wonderful time training my horse in dressage. Like most skills, it's one you never forget.

Winning sports car rallies takes tremendous concentration and skill. I sure put in a lot of time getting good at 'em. That led me to develop my own system, complete with setting up a mail order business to sell rally equipment. I imported special watches from Germany. The special calculators came from Liechtenstein. I wonder if Walter Chronkite remembers coming to my house in Brooklyn to buy a Curta calculator?

When I got involved with scuba diving I got my own air compressor, bought a Chris-Craft boat, and so on. Diving around Long Island can be hairy, so I had some "adventures." Fortunately I managed not to go into the mail order scuba supply business.

My grandmother spent her life shopping and entertaining. My mother did pretty much the same. These days the opportunities for women to contribute far more to our society are much more open.

My mother's father's inventions laid the groundwork for Citgo. Plus he helped rescue Continental Can in the 1930s. My father helped aviation expand across the Atlantic. Perhaps it's some errant gene which drives me to feel a need to contribute toward edging society ahead — and to urge everyone else to think in those terms instead of just about self. Your town needs your skills, experience and enthusiasm. Your state needs 'em too. Our country needs 'em. The world needs 'em — so don't let your abilities go to waste on the compost heap of retirement. Dare to be greater! Don't settle for security and anonymity.

In a few years I'll be gone. There'll be no statues. No Wayne Green Days, no postage stamps. I'll be gone. All memory of me will be gone. But in small ways I'll live on through the little changes I've helped make — in the ways I've influenced others. Would I be able to write on a Macintosh laptop computer today if I hadn't had an influence on the computer industry? On the starting of Apple? On the design of the first laptops? Yes, gadgets like this were inevitable, with or without me. But still, I helped bring it all about.

My intention isn't so much to brag as to use me as an example and give you some encouragement to look for ways you can help improve your town, state and country. Please don't leave it to the politicians. Most of them have failed us at every turn. They're like weeds. I suppose there's a need for a few of them, but the next thing you know we're being smothered by them and their bureaucrat support teams. Please remember that it wasn't democracy that beat communism, it was capitalism that beat the heck out of socialism. Capitalism works. Democracy can work, but it needs a lot of capitalistic help.

I believe we'll see far fewer old people doddering around — far fewer walkers and canes — if people would stop retiring and use the skills and experience to do productive work. This could raise hell with nursing homes and retirement communities, but it would be the best thing in the world for our country.

It would be helpful to us all if we could gradually change our sickness care industry into one actually dedicated to health care. Just because they call it that, perhaps a few people actually believe the name. Most of us can be productive on into our 90s if we take reasonably good care of ourselves and work toward goals. Instead of fighting change, start fighting for change. Fight to make your town, state and country better for the next generation. Change our school system. Change state government. Change Congress. Do your homework so you aren't an uninformed nuisance fighting some imagined environmental catastrophe, and then use your skills to build strength.

We have millions upon millions of older people with valuable skills going to waste. There's plenty for them to do and they'll be the better for doing it. And for those who aren't old yet — if you play it right you will be — but will you have the skills and experience to be of value when you get there? Education isn't over when you get out of school — it's a lifetime pursuit. Once you get the taste of it, you'll have the time of your life and there'll be no limits to where you can go.

It's pathetically easy to make money. Big money. Yet 99.9% of us settle for a pittance, spending our lives worrying about paying bills, getting a raise, working overtime, car payments, rent, and paying for our kids' educations. Once you get involved with doing things and learning, endless opportunities will start opening ahead of you. The traps are all out there, set to get you — traps that will keep you poor for life. These traps are drugs, home entertainment, gambling, ego gratification, and so on. Millions are trapped watching trash TV, listening to trash music, going to trash movies, reading trash magazines and novels, sitting in bars, playing pool, golf — well you get the picture. These are all attractive and addictive.

I'm not a Puritan and against enjoyment. I just caution that enjoyment be in moderation and not keep you from personal growth. I love music — classical, ragtime, country and so on. I love to cook. I love skiing, scuba diving, driving in my Miata or on my little Yamaha scooter. I love to read — mostly non-fiction. I enjoy well-written TV programs. I enjoy the better-made movies. I love to travel and see new places, meet new people, eat new foods, and do new things. But I have never considered for a minute devoting my life to those enjoyments. I manage to work 'em in.

When I find things which I particularly enjoy I have a need to share them, as I've mentioned. This had a lot to do with my starting *73* magazine in 1960. It had a lot to do with my starting computer magazines — and now music magazines. Oh, how much I'd like to get you to enjoy the incredible genius of Scott Joplin's music as played by Scott Kirby. It's so beautiful that I can't help crying. And the incredible haunting beauty of Gliere's Third Symphony! Or the beauty of a coral reef and its fish when you're right there with them. Or the thrill of putting your skis together and zooming down a mountain on perfect snow! The communication you have with a horse when you both know each other. The satisfaction of a letter from a reader telling you that you've touched and changed their life — and thanks.

Until you are able to help me change our whole educational system there will be an endless supply of negative people fighting you every inch of the way. Don't let them win. Don't spend your time on them. Put your efforts where they'll do the most good with the least work — on positive people who are open to ideas and change.

Now, let's get started changing things.

266 The Next Steps

Getting any proposed initiatives acted upon by the Legislature and the Governor may seem like a Sisyphean undertaking. Please so not sell me short. I'm not completely unaware of the problems involved in getting these institutions to act rationally. I have a plan.

Part of the entrepreneuring psyche is making plans, so it comes naturally. It's a whole lot easier to react to the unforeseen if you have a good idea of where you're headed and have planned how to get there.

When you consider the magnitude of changes I'm proposing there is no question that we'll meet some monumental resistance. No matter how important the need for change may be, many people will automatically fight it — some to their last breath. Change means uncertainty. Better the devil you know, and all.

So here's the plan. In order to build up some courage to make changes and bring a healthy New Hampshire into the 21st Century we're going to have to convince the Legislature and administration that they have popular support. That means we have to promote the idea of change. And that means using the media to get across the message. If we talk it up in the newspapers, on the radio, and on New Hampshire TV, we'll start being noticed. We can turn being a member of the Commission from a momentary honor into our being heroes.

There's enough controversy involved with the needed changes to keep New Hampshire journalists busy for months. The media loves controversy — it sells papers. The media is well aware that good news does not sell papers, so we can expect them to look for the downside of every proposed innovation. Fine. We need the exposure, even when it's negative.

Before our plans stand a chance of coming to fruit we need to have the New Hampshire citizens at least aware of us and what we're trying to do. Exposure — repeated exposure — builds awareness. It isn't easy getting through the din of advertising, ball games and block-buster movies and into the minds of our people.

But we have a message for them that they've been waiting for. We can promise them they'll be able to have better children. We can promise them that they will have a better quality of life — that they'll have jobs and make more money — that they'll be able to build the home they want. We can promise them lower taxes without even lying. We can promise them better and less expensive education and health care. We can promise them less crime and less exposure to drugs for their children. And these won't be the usual politically cynical promises — we'll be able to deliver.

The propaganda barrage will be followed up with copies of my report appearing in book stores all over New Hampshire — with reviews of the book on radio and TV stations and in newspapers. It's going to be very difficult for the Legislature to ignore.

We can make it even more difficult for them to ignore by establishing one of my proposals, a newsletter aimed at helping our legislators communicate with each other, with their political leaders, and even with the Governor and his administration. This would provide a medium for them to discuss the initiatives I've proposed.

Of course I hope that the Commission members will endorse my proposals — or at least enter into a dialog with me to come up with a consensus. With only one person on the Commission doing all of the writing, a true consensus isn't practical.

I've been fussing for years about the need for a newsletter to help our humongous Legislature cope with the mountains of bills. When Walt Peterson was Governor I proposed the idea to him. I didn't have much to do with Thompson, but I also approached Sununu with the idea. Perhaps the concept of an informed legislature is scary. I suspect they're easier to manipulate if they're kept uninformed. Or am I being cynical again? The weakness of the present system is that about the only help legislators get, I understand, is from lobbyists who have an ax to grind. Just what we need.

We're now in the Information Age, whether all of us have come to grips with the concept or not. The sooner we all understand the meaning of this, the more successful we'll be. We're communicating by phone, fax, cellular phone, radio, television, newspapers, magazines, newsletters, computer networks, by satellite, billboards and so on. These are the media we need to use to help bring about the changes which will put New Hampshire back into first place. Having been publishing communications and computer magazines for over 40 years and having helped pioneer some of the technologies which are common today, I can help you and New Hampshire cope with this new age. But I can't do it all alone — I need your help.

Bibliography

Control Theory in the Classroom - William Glasser, Harper & Row, 1986. What's wrong with traditional schooling and what can be done about it. Working in small teams, students find that knowledge contributes to power, friendship, and fun.

Job Creation in America - David Birch, A Free Press (Macmillan), 1987. How our smallest companies put the most people to work. Where the new jobs are coming from.

The Growth Experiment - Lawrence B. Lindsey, Basic Books, 1990. How the new tax policy is transforming the U.S. economy.

Parliament of Whores - P.J. O'Rourke, Atlantic Monthly Press, 1991. The best guide book yet on how Washington is screwed up.

The Day America Told the Truth - James Patterson and Peter Kim, Prentice Hall, 1991. What people really believe about everything that really matters.

Thriving On Chaos - Tom Peters, Knopf, 1987. Business is changing. We have to change with it or fail. New Hampshire has failed.

Beyond Our Means - Alfred Malabre, Jr., Random House, 1987. How America's long years of debt, deficits, and reckless borrowing now threaten to overwhelm us.

Golden Goals, Rusted Realities - Richard Mowsesian, New Horizon Press, 1986. Work and aging in America.

Augustine's Laws - Norman Augustine, American Institute of Aeronautics, 1983. Guide to the quandries of the defense business.

Electromagnetic Man - Cyril Smith, St. Martin's Press, 1989. Health and hazard in the electrical environment.

How To Work The Competition Into The Ground & Have Fun Doing It - John Molloy, Warner Books, 1987. Great book by the auhthor of "Dress for Success".

Shooting Straight - John Silber, Harper, 1989. What's wrong with America and how to fix it.

Trading Places - Clyde Prestowitz, Jr., Basic Books, 1988. How we allowed Japan to take the lead.

Honest Graft - Brooks Jackson, Knopf, 1988. Big money and the American political process.

The New Competition - Philip Kotler, Prentice-Hall, 1985. What Theory Z didn't tell you about marketing.

Guerrilla Marketing Attack - Jay Levinson, Houghton Mifflin, 1989. New strategies, tactics and weapons for winning with your small business.

The American School 1642-1985 - Joel Spring, Longman, 1986. The forces that have shaped the evolution of schooling in America.

The Closing of the American Mind - Allan Bloom, Simon & Schuster, 1987. How higher education has failed democracy and impoverished the soul of today's students. In lobbying for tax loopholes, subsidies, and protection from foreign trade, corporations hurt not only the economy but themselves.

More Like Us - James Fallows, Houghton Mifflin, 1990. Putting America's native strengths and traditional values to work to overcome the Asian challenge.

Manufacturing Matters - Stephen Cohen, Basic Books, 1987. This book forces us to see our economy, and plan for its future, in new ways.

Innovation and Entrepreneurship - Peter Drucker, Harper & Row, 1985. The entrepreneurial economy has created 35 million jobs, while big business and government have lost 5 million jobs.

Turnaround - Marvin Davis, 1987. A no-nonsense guide to corporate renewal.

Going For It - Victor Kiam, Morrow, 1986. How to succeed as an entrepreneur.

Space, Time, and Medicine - Larry Dossey, Shambhala, 1982. How modern medicine evolved, why it's in such trouble today, and where it's going.

Microcosm - George Gilder, Touchstone, 1990. How the silicon chip is changing our societies, economics, and technology.

Crisis In The Classroom - Charles Silberman, Random House, 1970. The remaking of American education.

Who Pushed Humpty Dumpty? - Donald Barr, Atheneum, 1971. Dilemmas in American education.

Alternatives To College - Miriam Hecht - Macmillan, 1974. Helping youngsters make an intelligent choice of career paths.

The Open Classroom - Herbert Kohl, Vintage Books, 1969. A non-authoritarian way of teaching.

Suffer, Little Children - Signet, 1962. Why "progressive education" has been such a disaster.

The Case Against College - Caroline Bird, Bantam, 1975. Why college is often a very dumb investment.

Risk, And Other Four Letter Words - Walter Wriston, Harper & Row, 1986. How the world's economy works and why it's in trouble.

Cultural Literacy - E.D. Hirsch, Houghton Mifflin, 1987. What every American needs to know.

Deschooling Society - Ivan Illich, Harper & Row, 1970. How to reform our whole educational system. Illitch was way ahead of his time.

The Economics of Chaos - Eliot Janeway, Dutton, 1989. Revitalizing the American economy.

The Silent War - Ira Magaziner, Vintage, 1990. The global business battles which are shaping America's future.

Straight A's Never Made Anybody Rich - Wess Roberts, Harper Collins, 1991. What are the real measures of success?

Group Memory - Alston Chase, Atlantic-Little Brown, 1980. An indictment of the leaders of education in America.

Who The Hell Is This Wayne Green?

Hmmm, that's another book, not a couple of crummy paragraphs. But, let's see, what do you want to know? Where I was born isn't of much relevance, and had little impact on what I've done so far. For the record, it was Littleton, NH, in 1922, which'll get me free skiing next winter in some ski areas. I find few other benefits to being 70.

My father was an aviator and my mother an artist. One grandfather ran a pharmacy, was the Littleton water and light commissioner, and a state senator. The other, who had the most influence on me, was an inventor. A successful inventor. One great grandfather was the Littleton town doctor and another started Oberlin College in Ohio.

I got interested in amateur radio while in high school and that led to my going to Rensselaer Polytechnic Institute instead of Dartmouth, as I'd planned. After two years WWII came along, so I joined the Navy as an electronic technician. They put me through a fabulous electronics school, after which I decided on submarine duty and served for five war patrols in the Pacific. My submarine, the *USS Drum*, was one of the ten top-scoring subs, and is now on display in Mobile.

After the war I went back to college for two more years. Then I tried radio and TV broadcasting as an engineer and a producer-director. I got interested in psychology, got a certificate as a professional, and did that for a while. I worked as an engineer with an electronics R&D company and then started a successful loudspeaker manufacturing company. Couldn't settle down, I guess.

My amateur radio experimenting with digital communications led me to start a small publication on the subject. This led to my becoming the editor of a ham magazine . . . and that to me starting my own amateur radio magazine in 1960. I'm still publishing it.

When an automatic radio relay system was developed by amateurs in the late 1960s I felt it had a good future, so I started a supporting magazine and published a string of books on the subject. Today, as a result, we have cellular telephones.

In 1975, when the first microcomputer was marketed, I started a series of computer magazines to help the industry grow. I published the first microcomputer magazine and then the first devoted to a specific computer. I enjoy helping new technologies develop by supporting them with dedicated publications.

When the compact disc was introduced in 1982 I saw another new technology that I felt needed help. I sold my computer publications and started a CD magazine. This got me involved with the music industry and starting entrepreneurial businesses aimed at helping independent record companies build a bigger market share.

Central New England College awarded me a PhD in Entrepreneurial Science in 1984 (just call me Doc). I've since lectured on entrepreneuring at several colleges.

One of my major interests has been in improving the American educational system. I've given talks on this to just about every Chamber of Commerce, Lion's, and Rotary Club in New Hampshire. I've been working with RPI for the last few years as a member of the Steering Committee and the RPI Council to implement my educational ideas.

In the amateur radio field I've worked with the FCC as a member of their National Industry Advisory Committee and was a charter Long Range Planning Committee member.

Locally I've served as the Peterborough Chamber of Commerce president, as a member of the board of directors for the Monadnock Health Foundation, as a member of the New Hampshire High-Tech Council and the President's Roundtable.

In 1960 I was in the right place at the right time to help found American Mensa, the high IQ society.

I have a wide variety of personal interests, including amateur radio, singing, cooking, travel, classical and country music, skiing, scuba diving, sports car rallies, reading, psychology, horse training, scientific anomalies, new technologies, flying, photography, cosmology, astronomy, and so on.

My wife, Sherry, has her own video production company. She's made over a hundred how-to-dance videos. We live on a farm not far from my publishing business.

Having visited 120 countries and talked with radio amateurs in over 350 countries, I view our country in a global perspective. Politically I'm a progressive conservative.

Index To Section Headings

Index